MERCHANT COMMUNITIES IN ASIA, 1600–1980

Perspectives in Economic and Social History

Series Editors: Andrew August
Jari Eloranta

Titles in this Series

A History of Drink and the English, 1500–2000
Paul Jennings

Franco Modigliani and Keynesian Economics: Theory, Facts and Policy
Antonella Rancan

Rural–Urban Relationships in the Nineteenth Century: Uneasy Neighbours?
Mary Hammond and Barry Sloan (eds)

MERCHANT COMMUNITIES IN ASIA, 1600–1980

EDITED BY

Lin Yu-ju and Madeleine Zelin

Routledge
Taylor & Francis Group

LONDON AND NEW YORK

First published 2015 by Pickering & Chatto (Publishers) Limited

2 Park Square, Milton Park, Abingdon, Oxfordshire OX14 4RN
52 Vanderbilt Avenue, New York, NY 10017

Routledge is an imprint of the Taylor & Francis Group, an informa business

First issued in paperback 2020

BRITISH LIBRARY CATALOGUING IN PUBLICATION DATA

Merchant communities in Asia, 1600–1980. – (Perspectives in economic and
social history).
1. Merchants – Asia – History. 2. Commerce – Social aspects – Asia – History.
I. Series II. Lin Yu-ju, editor. III. Zelin, Madeleine, editor.
306.3'4'095'0903-dc23

ISBN-13: 978-1-84893-486-3 (hbk)
ISBN-13: 978-0-367-66905-8 (pbk)

Typeset by Pickering & Chatto (Publishers) Limited

CONTENTS

ACKNOWLEDGEMENTS

本書題獻給故曹永和院士
並感謝財團法人曹永和文教基金會贊助本書的出版

This book is dedicated to the late Academician Tsao Yung-ho, with deep gratitude for the support provided for its publication by the Tsao Yung-ho Foundation for Culture and Education.

LIST OF CONTRIBUTORS

Cho Young-Jun is Assistant Professor of Economics at the Faculty of Social Sciences, Graduate School of Korean Studies, Academy of Korean Studies. His major research field is the interaction between commerce and public finance in pre-modern Korea. Dr Cho has published works in Korean including *Ship'ye: The Maladies of Seoul Merchants in Mid-Eighteenth Century Korea* (Seoul: Acanet Press, 2013); 'Stature Data and Measurement Unit in Chosŏn Korea' (*Journal of Korean Historical Manuscripts*, 41 (2012), pp. 125–59); 'A Critical Review on the Statistics of Miscellaneous Taxes in Puyŏk Shilch'ong' (*Han'guk Munhwa: Korean Culture*, 54 (2011), pp. 281–310); and other journal articles. His recent research interests are the organization of merchant communities in pre-modern Korea, royal finance at the end of Chosŏn Korea, and long-term economic trends in Korea.

Choi Chi-cheung is Professor in the History Department at the Chinese University of Hong Kong. He received his doctoral degree from the University of Tokyo. Dr Choi has published on Chinese festivals and popular religion, family and lineage, and business history. His major publications include *Jiao: Festival and Local Communities in Hong Kong* (Hong Kong: Joint Publishing Co., 2000); 'Stepping Out? Women in the Chaoshan Emigrant Communities, 1850–1950', in H. F. Siu (ed.), *Merchants' Daughters: Women, Commerce, and Regional Culture in South China* (Hong Kong: Hong Kong University Press, 2010); and 'Kinship and Business: Paternal and Maternal Kin in the Chaozhou Chinese Family Firms' (*Business History*, 40:1, pp. 26–49).

Stephanie Po-yin Chung received her PhD from Oxford University. She is now Professor in the Department of History, Hong Kong Baptist University. Her research focuses on social and economic history; business history; the history of business law and of customs, migration and enterprises in South China and Southeast Asia. Dr Chung is the author of *Chinese Business Groups in Hong Kong and Political Changes in South China, 1900–1925* (London: Macmillan, 1996) and has published articles in journals such as *Modern Asian Studies, International Journal of Asian Studies* and *Asia Europe Journal*.

Tina S. Clemente is Assistant Professor at the Asian Center, University of the Philippines-Diliman. Her published journal articles explore the institutional and exchange environment in relation to Chinese traders in pre-Hispanic and Hispanic Philippines. Dr Clemente's research interests include Chinese in the Philippines, bilateral economic relations between the Philippines and China, and various issues in Philippine development such as institutional reforms, the economic dimension of national security, and sustainability. Her editorial work includes past senior editorship of *Asian Politics & Policy* and currently, co-editorship for a special issue of the *Asian Studies: Journal of Critical Perspectives on Asia* on emerging Asian communities in the Philippines.

Robert Hellyer is Associate Professor of History at Wake Forest University in North Carolina in the United States. He previously researched foreign relations in early modern Japan; his conclusions were published in a monograph, *Defining Engagement: Japan and Global Contexts, 1640–1868* (Cambridge, MA: Harvard University Asia Center, 2009) and in several journal articles and book chapters. Dr Hellyer has also published on the socio-economic integration of the Pacific Ocean in the eighteenth and nineteenth centuries. He is currently writing a transnational history of Japan's export of green tea to the United States from *c.* 1850 to 1950, a project for which he received Smithsonian, Japan Foundation, and National Endowment for the Humanities fellowships to support research in Japan and the United States.

Ishikawa Ryota is Professor in the College of Business Administration, Ritsumeikan University of Japan. His major research interest is the international trade and market system of Korea after the opening of treaty ports. Dr Ishikawa's published works include 'Chinese Merchants' Trade with Shanghai after the Opening of Korean Ports through the Business Letters of Tong Shun Tai' (*Toyoshi Kenkyu*, 63:4 (2005), pp. 21–56, in Japanese) and 'Commercial Activities of Chinese Merchants in Late-Nineteenth-Century Korea: With a Focus on the Documents of Tong Shun Tai Archived at Seoul National University, South Korea' (*International Journal of Korean History*, 13 (2009), pp. 75–97). His recent research focuses on analysing the trade of Chinese merchants at Korean treaty ports in the late nineteenth century through their business correspondence.

Kwee Hui Kian is Associate Professor of History at the University of Toronto. Her research focuses on Southeast Asia and South China, where she has examined various themes relating to colonialism, political economy and diasporic entrepreneurship, from the seventeenth century to the present. Dr Kwee's publications include *The Political Economy of Java's Northeast Coast, c. 1740–1800: Elite Synergy* (Leiden: Brill, 2006) and 'Chinese Economic Dominance in

Southeast Asia: A *Longue Duree* Perspective' (*Comparative Studies in Society and History*, 55:1 (2013), pp. 5–34), as well as other journal articles and book chapters.

Evan Lampe earned his PhD in international history from the State University of New York, University at Albany. He has taught world history and American history at Endicott College and St Thomas University (Miami Gardens). He is the author of *Work, Class, and Power in the Borderlands of the Early American Pacific: The Labors of Empire* (Lanham: Lexington, 2013). His study of the science fiction author Philip K. Dick, entitled *Philip K. Dick and the World We Live In*, will be released by Wide Books shortly. Dr Lampe is currently working on a 'renegade' history of commercial capitalism in the Pacific from the time of the sixteenth century to the present, which will look at the role of troublesome workers, thieves, sailors, prostitutes, and others who found their own spaces in the margins of merchant colonial cultures. He lives in New Taipei City with his wife and daughter.

Lee Hun-Chang is Professor of Korean Economic History in the Department of Economics, College of Political Science & Economics, Korea University. His major research fields are markets, trade, money, economic thought and economic policy in eighteenth and nineteenth-century Chosŏn Korea. Dr Lee has written and edited many books and papers in Korean, including *Korean Economic History* (6th edn, Seoul: Haenam, 2014). In English, he has co-authored two papers with Peter Temin, 'Trade Policies in China under the Tribute System as Bounded Rationality', in T. Wang, K. Xu and M. Wan (eds), *Zheng He's Voyages and World Civilization* (Beijing: Peking University Press, 2005) and 'The Political Economy of Preindustrial Korean Trade' (*Journal of Institutional and Theoretical Economics*, 166:3 (2010), pp. 548–71), as well as publishing 'How Geography and International Relations Shaped Economic Development in the Republic of Korea', in Yan Jun (ed.), *The Harmony of Civilization and Prosperity for All: Selected Papers of Beijing Forum* (Beijing: Peking University Press, 2006).

Lin Yu-ju is a research fellow in the Institute of Taiwan History, Academia Sinica. Her major research interest is the socio-economic and maritime history of Taiwan and Asia from the seventeenth to twentieth century. She has published five monographs, compiled two volumes of historical materials, and edited three other books, as well as authoring several journal articles and book chapters. Dr Lin's works in Chinese include *The Transformation of the Colonial Frontier by a National Policy Company: Operations of the Taiwan Development Corporation in Eastern Taiwan* (Taipei: Institute of Taiwan History, 2011; Japanese translation, Tokyo: Kyūgo, 2012); *Colonial Frontier: Political and Economic Development in East Taiwan* (Taipei: Yuanliu Press, 2007); *Historiographical Review of Taiwan*

History, 1945–2000 (Taipei: National Science Council, Executive Yuan, 2004); *Local Merchants and their Socio-Economic Networks in the Zhuqian Area of Taiwan during the Qing Dynasty* (Taipei: Lianjing Press, 2000); and *The Spatial Structure of Ports in Qing Taiwan* (Taipei: Zhi Shufang Press, 1996). Her recent research focuses on merchant communities in East Asia from the eighteenth to twentieth century and the social customs of coastal villagers in nineteenth-century Taiwan.

Ogawa Michihiro is a Research Fellow at the National Institutes for the Humanities in Japan. His research focus is on the socio-economic history of western India from the eighteenth to the early nineteenth century. Dr Ogawa's publications include 'The Divided Right to Collect Land Revenue between the English East India Company and Jagirdar: A Case Study of Dutarfa in Ratnagiri Taluka of the Bombay Presidency in the Early Nineteenth Century' (*Socio-Economic History*, 74:3 (2008), pp. 46–64, in Japanese). Currently he is examining the socio-economic transition in colonization in rural areas of Western India, focusing on Indapur Pargana in Pune District under the Marathas and the Bombay Presidency from the 1780s to the 1840s.

Madeleine Zelin is Dean Lung Professor of Chinese Studies and Professor of History, Columbia University. In addition to numerous articles and book chapters, she authored the award-winning *The Merchants of Zigong: Industrial Enterprise in Early Modern China* (New York: Columbia University Press, 2005) and *The Magistrate's Tael* (Berkeley, CA: University of California Press, 1984); co-edited *Contract and Property Rights in Early Modern China* (Stanford, CA: Stanford University Press, 2004) and *Empire, Nation and Beyond: Chinese History in Late Imperial and Modern Times* (Berkeley, CA: Institute of East Asian Studies, 2006); and translated Mao Dun's *Rainbow* (Berkeley, CA: University of California Press, 1992). Dr Zelin's current research focuses on legal history and the role of law in the Chinese economy.

LIST OF FIGURES AND TABLES

PREFACE

John King Fairbank once remarked,

> I think authors ought to look back and give us some record of how their works developed, not because their works are important (they may turn out to be unimportant) but because we need to know more of the process of history-writing.[1]

I could not agree more. Organizing a group of colleagues to produce a book may be far more difficult than writing a book oneself, and so it is even more necessary to share the process through which the work emerged. In this preface, I would like to look back on that process of history-writing and book-editing.

This work came together with the help of many people and through the occasional contingency of fortune. In 2009, I was invited by Prof. Shiroyama Tomoko of Hitotsubashi University to participate in the international seminar 'Merchant Networks in Early Modern East Asia' organized by Prof. Shiroyama and by Prof. Kanda Sayako of Keiō University, in order to organize a panel for the 15th World Economic History Congress (WEHC) to be held in August of that year in Utrecht, Holland. In March of 2011, Prof. Shiroyama and Prof. Kanda convened another workshop, 'Global Trade and Merchant Communities in Eurasia: Transitions from the 18th to 19th Centuries', in the city of Takamatsu in Kagawa Prefecture. The workshop was very successful and I have wonderful memories of it. Afterwards, we decided to try to put together a team to organize a panel for the 16th meeting of the WEHC to be held in Cape Town, South Africa in 2012. Our theme, 'Merchant Communities in Early Modern Asia: Towards a Comparative Institutional Perspective', built upon the important 2006 collection, *The Return of the Guilds*, edited by Jan Lucassen, Tine de Moor and Jan Luiten van Zanden and published by Utrecht University Press. At the same time, we invited Prof. Chiu Peng-sheng of the Chinese University of Hong Kong to work with us.

In June of 2012, just before the 16th WEHC met in Cape Town, Dr Philip Good, an editor with the British press Pickering & Chatto, emailed the organizers of our panel, Prof. Kagotani Naoto of Kyoto University's Institute for Research in Humanities and myself, to inquire about the possibility of publishing the panel papers as part of their Perspectives in Economic and Social History series. After the conference, our group decided over dinner to accept the offer of the press. Ultimately, after further discussion, it was agreed that six papers by seven authors from the panel would go into the collection: Cho Young-Jun (Academy of Korean Studies), Stephanie Po-yin Chung (Hong Kong Baptist University), Kwee Hui Kian (University of Toronto), Lee Hun-Chang (Korea University), Ogawa Michihiro (National Institutes for the Humanities), Chiu Peng-sheng and myself. Thus began a project that was, for me at least, a daunting challenge.

In order to compile a substantive volume, Chiu Peng-sheng and I further invited the following scholars to contribute papers: Choi Chi-cheung (Chinese University of Hong Kong), Tina S. Clemente (University of the Philippines-Diliman), Robert Hellyer (Wake Forest College), Ishikawa Ryota (College of Business Administration, Ritsumeikan University), and Evan Lampe (St Thomas University). At the same time, as I had no past experience editing an English-language work and felt the limitations of my language competence, we decided to ask Prof. Madeleine Zelin, a well-known scholar of economic history from Columbia University's Department of East Asian Languages and Civilizations, to serve as lead editor; besides writing the introduction, she commented on all the essays. The fact that Prof. Zelin, despite being extremely busy, agreed to write the introduction was very encouraging. However, Prof. Zelin also pointed to the issue of language as the first problem to be addressed.

In December of 2012, the Tsao Yung-ho Foundation of Culture and Education agreed to provide funding to pay for two outside reviewers, for professional proofreading, and for other expenses. The generous support of the Tsao Yung-ho Foundation greatly smoothed our path. Prof. He Wenkai of Hong Kong University of Science & Technology introduced us to his wife, Ellen McGill, an experienced proofreader, and she agreed to review all the essays with an eye to improving readability.

In May of 2013, Pickering & Chatto first had the proposal reviewed by two scholars, who confirmed that the work 'represents a nice comparative effort overall, covering various types of economies and geographic spread' and approved the project to go ahead. A contract was signed in June, and the work began in earnest. The two reviewers had provided a number of pertinent comments and stressed the need to ensure the coherence and readability not only of each essay, but of the volume as a whole; they also encouraged all authors to pay attention to the role of institutions and actors. Their suggestions facilitated the compilation of the volume, helping us focus the revisions and speeding up the process.

Thanks to the efforts and cooperation of all the contributors, the draft manuscript was ready in July 2013 to be sent to another two reviewers, each of whom is a well-known figure in the field, for further consideration of the volume as a whole and of each essay individually. Both provided a number of incisive suggestions for the volume and for each author, which helped us avoid errors. They also advised that authors incorporate references to the other essays in the volume wherever possible to improve the volume's coherence. Revisions were completed and the essays sent for proofreading in December, and in February 2014 the revised manuscript was submitted to the press for clearance review and also to Prof. Zelin so she could prepare her introduction. In May, Ms Sophie Rudland, the commissioning assistant for Pickering & Chatto now handling the project, notified me that the series editor had approved the volume and that it might even be possible to publish ahead of schedule. The contributors then made some final revisions based on the comments provided by Prof. Zelin, as well as last corrections, and the essays were given a final proofreading. At last the volume was done!

I would like to take this opportunity to express our deep gratitude to the reviewers invited by Pickering & Chatto and by the Tsao Yung-ho Foundation for their support and guidance, all of which significantly improved the work. Any remaining errors are, of course, our responsibility. I must also thank Prof. Chiu Peng-sheng for his immense help at every stage of the process; although health reasons unfortunately prevented him from contributing his own essay to the volume, he provided invaluable support throughout. Dr Evan Lampe also carefully read each essay and provided the authors with many good suggestions. Ellen McGill's proofreading caught many small errors and infelicities of language, and she also helped with the preparation of the index. At Pickering & Chatto, Philip Good, Sophie Rudland, Frances Lubbe and Stephina Clarke expended much effort on bringing this volume to publication, and their help is greatly appreciated.

As described above, without the whole-hearted support of the Tsao Yung-ho Foundation, this volume could not have overcome the many difficulties in its path to publication. This work is thus dedicated to Academician Tsao Yung-ho, whose outstanding contributions over many decades to the fields of maritime history and the history of Taiwan remain an inspiration to us all.

Lin Yu-ju
Academia Sinica
Taiwan
Summer 2014

INTRODUCTION: ASIAN MERCHANT COMMUNITIES ACROSS TIME AND SPACE

Madeleine Zelin

This is a volume that examines Asian merchant communities engaged in the expanding global trade that saw the circulation of goods between northern and southeast Asia and between this vast region and the Middle East, Europe and the Americas. While some of the studies herein extend that examination to the twentieth century, its main focus is the critical period of the seventeenth to the nineteenth century, when inter-Asian trade was expanding under a logic of its own and the encounter with Europeans was creating new opportunities and new constraints for the diverse merchant communities it attracted. Much has been written about the Europeans, their colonial regimes and the merchants who benefited from monopolistic access to the new Asian market. Less is known about the Asian merchant communities in this quintessential global marketplace.

The authors whose work is gathered here have used the term 'community' not merely as a plural descriptive. In each of the studies in this volume the merchants under consideration were connected in meaningful ways that structured their business, promoted their interests and distinguished them from others, contributing both to their personal and their commercial identities. Ascriptive ties, such as kinship, native place and religion, not surprisingly, played an important part in the creation of trust and commitment to collective problem-solving institutions within all of these communities. However, we are reminded that such mechanisms for the creation of solidarity are common among all sojourning communities and not a characteristic of Asians that explains their success or failure as economic actors. In each case study we have the opportunity to examine how the resources supplied by ascriptive ties interacted with a range of political, social and economic conditions that shaped business practices and business organization in the Asian region. Such data makes possible more nuanced comparisons among Asian merchant communities and other early modern commercial actors, as well as allowing us to gauge the role of these resources as particular merchant communities encountered new conditions in their sojourns across the region as a whole.

Almost all discussions of early modern merchant communities, particularly those engaged in long-distance trade, alight at some point on the 'guild'. The contribution of guilds to the success of merchants themselves and to the overall processes of economic growth have long been a matter of debate among historians of both Asia and Europe. Two of the chapters in this volume focus special attention on the diverse conditions under which guilds arose and the ways in which this shaped their membership, functions and longevity under changing economic conditions. Cho Young-Jun and Lee Hun-Chang provide one of two chapters that examine the impact of changing market conditions in Korea. Their focus on shop merchants in large cities points to the far greater centralization of economic activity in Chosŏn Korea than in either Europe or China. First established by the state to procure goods for the court and for government offices, the *shijŏn* shops tended to be commodity specific, and individual shops participated in a variety of joint activities, including purchase and accounting. Cho and Lee note that as the market, particularly in Seoul, expanded, *shijŏn* shops began to organize in ways that would be familiar to students of merchants in other growing urban centres, providing protection against competition, mutual aid, dispute mediation and so on. The importance of monopoly privileges and continued ties – and often obligations – to the state, however, gave these guilds particular characteristics, including what appears to be far tighter hereditary control by particular families and far less room for innovation than merchant solidarities provided in other parts of Asia.

The guilds described by Lin Yu-ju present a far different organizational dynamic, despite sharing characteristics like mutual aid, dispute mediation and solidarity built in part around worship of particular gods thought to protect those engaged in commerce. While many of the migrants to Taiwan in the early Qing came from Fujian, Lin demonstrates that the special conditions of the cross-straits trade gave rise to organizational forms that drew on but by no means mirrored those found on the mainland. Few limits were placed on the activities of merchants and producers beyond the restriction of trade to the Fujian port of Xiamen and the Taiwan port of Luermen (near present-day Tainan). By the eighteenth century the expansion of that trade led to the proliferation of firms exporting mainland manufactures to Taiwan and Taiwan agricultural goods, especially sugar and rice, through Xiamen to Fujian and beyond. By the nineteenth century – likely around the 1760s – these firms had already formed a number of *jiao*, which, unlike the more familiar *huiguan* formed by merchants throughout China and beyond, did not establish elaborate physical spaces, were not limited to members from one place or one trade, and shared members across associations and across the categories of stationary and import-export merchants. At the same time, they benefited from corporate organizational traditions practised by temple and lineage associations; such traditions allowed them to build social and political capital, solve common problems and satisfy the religious needs of a growing merchant population.

One implication of Lin's research is that the Chinese business model was a flexible one, providing enduring resources for merchants in the changing economic environment of early modern Asia. In Ishikawa Ryota's study of the Chinese-Korean red ginseng trade we see evidence of this flexibility, as well as some of the pitfalls of a changing regional trade regime as Westerners forced open north Asian markets. Prior to the 'opening' of Korea by Japan in 1876, Chinese merchants had no more access to Korean markets than Westerners had to Chinese markets. Much of the trade between China and Korea occurred as a component of Korea's obligations to the Qing dynasty as a tribute state. Ishikawa provides new evidence of the importance of Chinese merchant collaboration in making the tribute system work. Focusing on the export of Korean red ginseng to China, Ishikawa demonstrates the persistence of a Korean bureaucratic trade model, born of Korea's traditional reliance on commerce and grants of commercial privilege as a source of state revenue. Chinese firms, versed in the establishment of branch firms throughout China, had little difficulty moving into Seoul and other Korean treaty ports. But many of the firms that took this step and the parties with whom they transacted were carry-overs from the pre-treaty port regime.

If Chinese merchants in the Korean trade gained experience and entry through the tribute trade and the merchants who dominated the trade across the Taiwan straits benefited from proximity to the sole port open to this trade, how should we understand the success of Chinese merchants who went further afield? Choi Chi-cheung provides an exploration of the Chinese merchant community that came to dominate the Southeast Asian rice trade through the southern Chinese port of Shantou. Chinese demand for imported rice, especially as key rice-producing areas of eastern China turned increasingly to handicraft and specialty production, is well known. Following Qing consolidation of southern China and the lifting of its ban on coastal trade in the 1680s, trade links between Southeast Asia and major ports along the southeast Chinese coast rapidly developed. The Chaozhou traders discussed by Choi entered this trade first as crew on ships owned by earlier entrants, and recruiting of sailors contributed to the native place character of many of the men who entered the Southeast Asian rice market. Many of these men settled in Hong Kong or Southeast Asia, setting in motion a reciprocal relationship between home area and areas of new settlement as Chaozhou firms developed remittance businesses and shipped Chinese goods to Southeast Asia and overseas Chinese returned home with newly developed tastes for rice and other products from the maritime world. As we see in the case of other Chinese long-distance traders in the nineteenth and twentieth century, wholesale marketing often led to the development of what Choi calls 'vertical trading networks'. In the case of the Chen brothers of his study, this meant integrating rice production and distribution from paddy to mill to local distribution to wholesale export to China.

Lest we think that this pattern was uniquely Chinese, Stephanie Po-yin Chung presents the fascinating story of the Alsagoffs and Alkaffs, traders from the Hadhramaut region in Yemen. Like the Gujarati merchants discussed by Ogawa Michihiro, and like many of the most famous domestic long-distance merchants in China, the Alsagoffs and Alkaffs came from a region whose harsh conditions drove them to seek their fortunes away from home. Like the Chaozhou merchants, they maintained a strong sense of native place from their humble beginnings as spice traders in the early to mid-nineteenth century to the height of their business success and eventual decline in the second half of the twentieth century. Kinship played a key role in their success, both as the source of trusted personnel to run an increasingly diversified business network, and as a source of power alliances as sons and nephews married into prominent Malay Muslim families. Beginning from bases in Singapore, at their height the Alsagoffs and Alkaffs were engaged in shipping and retailing as well as land development and their trade ranged from England to Arabia to Southeast Asia. While religion played an important role in their personal faith and identity, their ability to profit from the growing number of Southeast Asian co-religionists eager to make the Haj and to utilize institutions like the *awaqf* to preserve property as a unit added unique elements to the familiar pattern of native place, kinship and religion as sources of business trust, solidarity and profits.

The story of the Alsagoffs and Alkaffs points to another common thread in the histories of the merchant communities presented in this volume. If there is one overriding message to be gleaned from these fine-tuned treatments of merchants in Asia, it is that we have given far too much credit to 'culture' and far too little credit to politics in the evolution of Asian business. Many of the chapters in this volume provide a window into the little-explored role of state policy and merchant–state relations in shaping merchant behaviour and merchant success. The success of the Arab families in Singapore derived not only from their business acumen and their ability to win the trust of indigenous rulers through their common commitment to Islam. Their ability to move into the spice trade relied in great measure on the decline of the Dutch monopoly over the spice trade, for which they themselves could claim no credit. But their greatest good fortune came when the British East India Company took control of the island now known as Singapore and encouraged Arab settlement. British law made possible their investment in landed property contrary to local Muslim practice, and fostered their primacy among non-indigenous residents, including both Indians and Chinese.

Robert Hellyer and Evan Lampe both include Westerners among the communities under consideration. Lampe presents a somewhat different case, not of merchants but of the sailors who made their trade possible and presented frequent challenges to order within the Western community. Hellyer looks at three merchant communities in nineteenth-century Nagasaki, those of the Tokugawa government's own clearing-house that directed the flow of imports and exports, the regional merchants who represented or had loose affiliations with the domains, and Western traders, especially those from Britain. Like many contributors to this volume, Hellyer is concerned with the way in which merchants operated within the limitations and opportunities created by local politics. For merchants in Japan in the 1860s this meant navigating a country in transition, plagued by rural and urban uprisings, efforts to cope with a new foreign presence and increasing inter-domain conflict and competition. Hellyer traces the ways in which the fraught politics of the late Tokugawa weakened shogunal control over trade and encour-aged new roles and interactions among domain-based merchants, illustrating this process with the example of the successful transition from domain merchant to merchant prince of the founder of Mitsubishi, Iwasaki Yatarō.

Both before and during periods of colonial rule, merchants played special roles in sustaining indigenous administrative structures. The Gujarati merchants described by Ogawa extended loans and goods on credit, collected taxes and served in many respects as bankers to the local governments of Indapur, as well as directly participating in funding religious and cultural activities fundamental to local social cohesion. Making themselves indispensable to local government was thus key to their position as both local land developers and commercial inter-mediaries between urban and rural sectors of Indapur. This position continued under British colonial rule. Like their counterparts elsewhere they mitigated their economic dominance by building social and cultural capital, funding local festivals and increasingly becoming accepted into local social life.

The smooth transition experienced by Gujarati merchants under British colonial rule was not always possible as new Western overlords entered an exist-ing market system. The fate of Chinese merchants in the Philippines is evidence of the hazards that could befall even the most flexible and adept merchant community when they could not build such social capital. Tina S. Clemente argues that Spanish administration of the Philippines could not have survived without the fees and income from commerce generated by Chinese merchants. Their ability to act as the conduit for Spanish silver to China was founded on the role that they played in keeping the colonial administration in Luzon afloat. This was particularly so because the colonial rulers of the Philippines could not rely on receipt of their share of subsidies from the Spanish administration in Mexico. Nevertheless, the perception that the Chinese merchant community posed a threat to the Spanish regime persisted. How important their resistance to Christianity was to the Spanish view that they posed a dangerous presence is difficult to gauge. Clemente notes that late Spanish administrators also blamed the Chinese for Spanish failure to develop closer ties to the indigenous population, evidence that here, as in other areas examined in this volume, merchant intermediaries played a critical role in managing the relationship between colonial rulers and local, often agrarian, populations.

Both Hellyer and Chung remind us that colonialism did not simply enact European rule in distant lands. It also, often unintentionally, opened new spaces for non-Europeans, who benefited from new property regimes, new technologies and new opportunities to bridge the gaps between indigenous populations and the imperial regime. Nowhere is this more evident than in the dominant role that Chinese merchants came to play in the territories beyond those studied by these two authors. Kwee Hui Kian argues that we cannot simply attribute this success to unique Chinese forms of merchant organization. As we have already seen, they were neither unique nor always successful in the face of intractable political hostility. Nor were the Chinese alone in their ability to create strong ties to indigenous rulers. Chinese merchants in the seventeenth century were operating within a multinational, multi-ethnic trading universe shared with Europeans, as well as other Asians. Why then, by the eighteenth century, did the Chinese succeed in dominating the Southeast Asian trade? Kwee's answer lies in the complex politics of Dutch colonial dominance and the unique position it allowed the Chinese in the provisioning of the ever-increasing population, not of Asians, but of Europeans engaged in the Southeast Asian trade.

Students of Asian business are often frustrated by the difficulties they face when attempting to reconstruct the activities of merchants in Asian trade, particularly where political turmoil has resulted in the destruction of historical records and where the absence of state involvement in registering and regulating merchants has meant few public records of their activities survive. In addition to their insights into the complex workings of Asian merchant communities, the studies included herein stand as models of historical detective work, teasing out the stories of these often hidden actors through tax records, contracts, legal cases, stone inscriptions, commercial and political correspondence and personal and public memoirs. The rich details these sources provide let us follow merchants from similar backgrounds as they move through differing spaces; merchants from differing backgrounds as they cross each other's paths; and the varied communities of traders as they strove to deal with the rapidly changing business environments of early modern East and Southeast Asia.

1 TRADE, PUBLIC AFFAIRS AND THE FORMATION OF MERCHANT ASSOCIATIONS IN TAIWAN IN THE EIGHTEENTH CENTURY

Lin Yu-ju

Scholarship on the institutional frameworks for Chinese merchant activity in the eighteenth and nineteenth centuries has generally focused on organizations such as *huiguan* (*Landsmannschaften*, assembly house),[1] *gongsuo* (public halls, fellow-regional associations) and *shangbang* (commercial groups).[2] Comparatively little work has been done on the major merchant groupings in Taiwan, known as *jiao* (brokerage cartel).

Fang Hao once noted that *jiao* were the most popular form of merchant organization in southern Fujian and Taiwan in the late Qing era. According to surveys conducted at Chinese ports by Japanese investors in the late nineteenth century, *jiao* were prevalent among merchants operating out of the ports of Taiwan, as well as Xiamen, Quanzhou, Shantou and other port cities associated with the foreign trade networks maintained by merchants based in these locations.[3] *Jiao* could be found as far as Japan, Singapore, Manila, Penang and Siam. The merchant associations known as *jiao*, in contrast to the *huiguan*, *gongsuo* and *shangbang* found in other regions, were made up of sea merchants who spoke Fujianese dialects or other related vernaculars, such as the Chaozhou dialect; one example of such an association outside Taiwan is the Xiang-Le-Xian-Shan *jiao* described in Choi Chi-cheung's chapter in this volume.

In Taiwan, *huiguan* came into being mostly because of the 'rotating military service' system and were distinct from Chinese geographical or industrial *huiguan*. Not many industrial *huiguan* existed in Taiwan. By the mid- to late nineteenth century there is evidence of the associations called Quan Jiao and Xia Jiao in Lugang, Tai-Xia Jiao in Penghu, and several *huiguan* established by natives from the same hometown. In other words, Taiwanese merchant associations were mainly called *jiao* and seldom had their own premises or meeting halls. Most scholars of Taiwan history have not noted the distinct characteristics separating *jiao* from *huiguan* and *gongsuo*.[4]

However, *jiao* almost completely controlled the trade outside of Taiwan and built their own commercial networks around East Asia in the Qing dynasty. It is therefore extremely important to figure out what networks of sea power they created in the eighteenth and nineteenth centuries in order to illuminate the characteristics of *jiao* as institutions, as well as of the regional linkages they structured. As Jan Lucassen suggests, the debate surrounding the 'Great Divergence' helped the literature break away from Eurocentic conversations about development by stimulating global comparative histories.[5] By focusing on *jiao*, which were active in Taiwan and Fujian but have been neglected by historians, this chapter attempts to broaden the comparative historical framework in which we analyse merchant associations in early modern East Asia.

Recent Interpretations of *Jiao*

Although *jiao* have been the subject of considerable study in Taiwan, they have been largely ignored in scholarship outside Taiwan. Until recently only two articles written by mainland Chinese scholars in the general literature on late imperial trade mentioned *jiao*. Fu Yiling noted the existence of ten different types of *jiao* (*shitu jiao*), which he simply described as Chinese firms engaged in foreign trade.[6] Chen Zhiping – using newly discovered private documents – researched the activities of two *jiao* merchant families in Taiwan and in Quanzhou, Fujian.[7]

In 1972, Fang Hao, using ancient inscriptions and local gazetteers, was the first to study and reconstruct the history of *jiao* in Qing-era Taiwan (1684–1895). Although his research was far from comprehensive, he was indeed the pioneer and initiated the study of *jiao* in the post-war era.[8] From 1978 to 1990, Zhuo Kehua, on the basis of Fang Hao's research and newly collected regulations of *jiao*, published several case studies.[9] According to Zhuo's study, *jiao* had five functions; economic, religious, cultural, political and social. However, he often mistook individual actions of *jiao* merchants as the collective activities of *jiao* organizations. Both Zhuo and Fang asserted that *jiao* began to disappear during the late Qing period. In fact, as long as there was ongoing trade between Taiwan and mainland China, *jiao* continued to thrive and prosper in the import and export business, especially in the numerous non-treaty ports in the South China Sea. For instance, the camphor *jiao*, which consisted of camphor traders, first emerged in Zhuqian (today's Hsinchu [Xinzhu]) in the 1890s because the camphor trade was booming.[10] Cai Yuanqie focused on analysing why *jiao* entered local public affairs, and how their participation changed the distribution of local power. He proposed two concepts, 'unofficial structures' and 'unofficial administration', to illustrate the significance of *jiao* involvement in local politics.[11] Compared with the research of Fang and Zhuo, Cai's study presented a new way of thinking about merchant involvement in local affairs, both as individuals and as a group. Cai also demonstrated that the scope of such *jiao* participation rarely extended beyond the prefecture and county levels.

Apart from research on the organizational structure and the functions of *jiao*, studies of the sources of their business capital have also been made. Higashi Yoshio and Tu Zhaoyan both emphasized that the Chinese mainland was the chief source of capital for *jiao* merchants. Nevertheless, Tu also noted the possibility of funds coming from Taiwan. In fact, merchants of local *jiao* who relied on local capital rose to eminence in both trade and social circles through their participation in a flourishing export trade in tea and sugar after the opening of treaty ports during the late Qing dynasty.[12] Lin Man-houng noted that *jiao* merchants in central and south Taiwan were also joined by local merchants who drew on local funding. Over time, the mainland identity and origins of *jiao* merchants became less and less distinct. Lin has further refuted the arguments of Fang Hao and Zhuo Kehua, stating that the influence of *jiao* during the late Qing dynasty had not declined.[13]

Australian scholar Christian Daniels, focusing on the sugar industry in southern Taiwan during the Qing dynasty, noted that *jiao* merchants from mainland China used their capital to invest in the businesses of local brokers in southern Taiwan, and extended credit to local sugar-cane farmers to ensure the stability of the sugar market and secure a portion of the annual yield. By these means, *jiao* merchants were able to place themselves as mediators between local sugar-cane farmers and overseas buyers, and thus monopolize the sugar trade in southern Taiwan. However, with the opening of treaty ports during the late Qing dynasty, Western firms formed new financial relationships with the local brokers and farmers, which altered the previous trade structure and ultimately changed the sugar production system.[14] As to the relationship between *jiao* merchants and the land, Kurihara Jun investigated the 'Eight Jiao' in Lugang, and found that *jiao* merchants not only monopolized the grain trade, but also directly operated water utilities and managed conservancy projects.[15]

In previous work, I have discussed the formation and operations of local merchant associations in regional markets using Zhuqian in Qing Taiwan as an example. The formation of consignment trade systems between *jiao* merchants in Quanzhou and those in Lugang using firms (*shanghao*) of the Quan Jiao in Lugang illustrate these regional connections. I also studied the reasons for *jiao* merchants' high level of involvement in local public affairs as well as land and water management, and their frequent practice of taking root in the places where their business was located instead of returning to their hometowns.[16] Chiu Peng-sheng's recent work is the first to probe into the similarities and differences between merchant associations in mainland China and those in Taiwan. Chiu has thoroughly demonstrated that the former practice of deeming *jiao* analogous to *huiguan* and *gongsuo* is incorrect.[17]

In sum, there has been abundant research on *jiao* in Taiwan. However, no effort has yet been made to elucidate whether *jiao* emerged first in southern Fujian or in Taiwan and how they were formed. The geographical origins of the organization are important to explaining why *jiao* only operated in some places and to describing the role they played in trade and local society.

Cross-Strait Trade and Formation of *Jiao*

In Qing-era Taiwan, there were at least two types of merchant groupings. One type was comprised of informal communities of merchants united by a common location, either the same street or the same town. The '*gongji* of Jiucyonglin [Jiu-qionglin] firms' in Hsinchu is an example of such a location-based organization. These organizations are represented by their eponymous identifier, the *gongji*, which was an official seal used collectively by merchants belonging to each group in order to sign business documents. The other type of merchant association, known as *jiao*, was made up of import and export merchants, or merchants engaged in the same business.[18] *Jiao* were far more common than their informal counterparts without formal organization.

Why were these merchant associations named *jiao*? In 1848, the explanations offered in *Dongying Shilüe* by Ding Shaoyi are as follows:

> Those who do retail in cities are called shops (*dian*). Those who obtain products and then sell them to shops are called *jiao*. Those who trade in Fuzhou, Jiangsu and Zhejiang are called 'Northern Jiao', those in Quanzhou are called 'Quan Jiao', and those in Xiamen are called 'Xia Jiao'. These three combined are called 'the Three *Jiao*'. '*Jiao*' means 'in the outskirts', and also 'transactions'.[19]

From this it is clear that *jiao* were originally made up primarily of import and export merchants. Their emergence was fostered by the port policy of the Qing court and the unique mechanisms utilized by migrants and the farming population of Taiwan to engage in maritime trade as a means to obtain daily necessities from mainland China. It is therefore not surprising that groups called *jiao* appeared first in important port cities along the coast.

In 1684, the Qing defeated the regime established by Zheng Chenggong (also known as Koxinga) and won sovereignty over Taiwan. The island became a prefecture of Fujian province and was administered by a Taotai (*daotai*, circuit intendant) until 1885. In order to facilitate governance, only Luermen, located outside Taiwan's prefectural seat (Fucheng, now Tainan), was open to trade, which was conducted with the port of Xiamen across the strait in Fujian. (See Figure 1.1) In accordance with the principle of comparative advantage, there developed a regional division of labour between Taiwan, a developing region, and coastal areas of China, a developed region. Cross-strait trade subsequently prospered with these two ports of Luermen and Xiamen as their most dynamic hubs.[20]

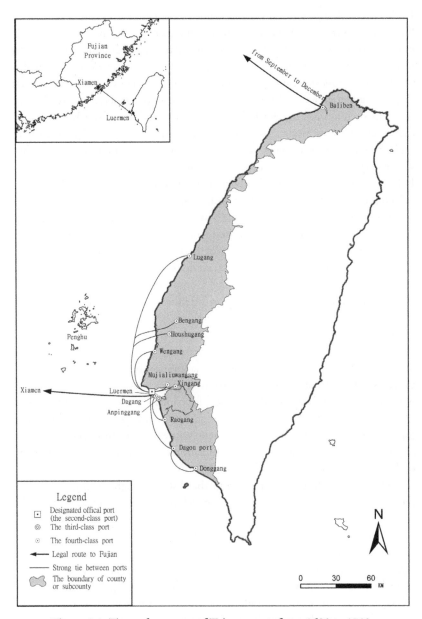

Figure 1.1: The trade pattern of Taiwan ports from 1683 to 1710.

Under the early Qing trade regime, firms (*shanghang*) in Xiamen bought or hired ships to travel to Fucheng,[21] where they exchanged handicrafts and daily essentials from mainland China for agricultural products brought to Fucheng by firms (*hangdian*) or agents from coastal ports along the Taiwan coast. Probably as a result of cross-strait *jiaoguan* (Fujian dialect, business exchange) or regular *duijiao* (trade transactions) among firms, these firms or agents came to be known by terms such as *jiaohang, jiaohu* or *jiaopu*.[22] The authors of the *Yuanli Gazetteer* described these traders as individual *jiao* firms engaged independently in trade. No mention was made of any association yet.[23] Moreover, because they were engaged in maritime trade, they were sometimes called water *jiao* (*shuijiao*). In larger port cities, *jiao* merchants gradually began to form associations based on economic, political and religious affiliations.[24]

When and where did *jiao* in the sense of merchant associations appear? According to Cai Guolin, the most frequently cited scholar on this issue, it was 1725 when the first *jiao*, 'Suwanli' – a Northern Jiao – came into existence. Zhuo Kehua has suggested that *jiao* in Penghu could be traced back to the reign period of the Yongzheng emperor (1722–35).[25] Comparing extant inscriptions on steles in Taiwan and Fujian reveals that *jiao* did indeed first appear in Taiwan, with the Northern Jiao in Fucheng being the earliest.

The emergence of Suwanli was associated with the trade in sugar, Taiwan's chief export during the early Qing. Coastal trade from Taiwan to central China inevitably involved a long sea voyage. Collaboration better enabled merchants to seek solutions to problems related to navigation, sales and business, as well as political issues.[26] In addition, they made joint contributions to the restoration of temples dedicated to deities shared by members of the association, who joined together to pray for smooth trade and safe journeys. From this perspective, *jiao* originally could be viewed as a trade association of merchants navigating to and trading in the same areas.

During early Qing rule, apart from the districts neighbouring the prefectural capital, most of Taiwan was still developing or even undeveloped. The main exports to central China were sugar and oil, which were abundant in Taiwan County (now Tainan). In fact, since the late Ming dynasty (1368–1644), coastal trade between Taiwan and Fujian had already begun, with Taiwanese sugar being exchanged for cotton and cloth goods shipped across the strait from central China.[27] However, under the Qing policy of 'designated official ports' (*zhengkou*), which restricted trade to between Luermen in Fucheng and Xiamen in Fujian, merchants coming to Taiwan were mostly from Zhangzhou and Quanzhou because they were near Xiamen. Their trade routes included both long sea voyages across the strait and along the coast to the north based around Xiamen.[28] Hence, they pooled financial resources to build *huiguan* in important port cities of central China. During the early Kangxi reign (1661–1722), commercial groups from Quanzhou, Zhangzhou and Xinghua, as well as Taiwan merchants, built two Fujian *huiguan* in Ningbo, called the 'old *huiguan*' and the 'large *huiguan*'.[29] In other words, even those traders from Fujian who originally did business in Taiwan and mainland China, who gradually became Taiwanese merchants, and who by the end of seventeenth century joined in the north coastal trade with other traders from Fujian[30] still did not found *jiao*. Second, the transition from *huiguan* to *jiao* indicated the changing characteristics of merchant communities and their trade patterns during the early Qing dynasty. From this view, when and why *jiao* emerged are important issues that must be explored in more detail.

By the early eighteenth century, we have evidence of independent *jiao* firms contributing funds to build local bridges or temples in Fucheng and Danshui in Taiwan.[31] Nevertheless, inscriptions on various donation steles in Taiwan, Xiamen and Quanzhou predominantly contain the names of local officials and individual citizens,[32] but not those of merchant organizations. Let us look at evidence from temple construction. *Jiao* firms engaged in maritime trade, and besides venerating Mazu, a goddess associated with the sea, also worshipped the Water God. Temples devoted to the Water God can be found all over Taiwan and were largely built by *jiao*.[33] Among them, the earliest was located in Fucheng and was built in 1715 by merchants from Zhangzhou and Quanzhou.[34] In 1741, the Sanyitang was constructed.[35] On the 'stele of Sanyitang' was inscribed: 'We fellows repair the main hall, sacrificial pavilion, and the first gate in order to defend the port'; the names of individual benefactors were listed but *jiao* as organizations were not mentioned.[36] It was only in 1764 that the name of the Northern Jiao Suwanli appeared on the stele.[37]

Another example is the Anlan Bridge located at the ferry landing outside the west gate of Fucheng. It was first reconstructed by the Fucheng magistrate, Wang Zhen, in 1720.[38] In 1754, townsman Hou Zongxing called on firms from Nanhao and Nanshi Streets to rebuild the bridge. In 1774, the Northern Jiao erected the 'stele in commemoration of the reconstruction of Anlan Bridge', on which the names of donors in 1754 were mentioned.[39]

It is obvious that even though most of the contributors to these reconstruction projects were probably *jiao* merchants, they had not yet formed a merchant organization prior to the 1750s. The first record of *jiao* involvement in such renovation schemes was that of the Northern Jiao Suwanli as a benefactor of the decoration of the interior of the Water God Temple in 1763. In the following year, the Northern Jiao was appointed the executive director coordinating the restoration of De'an Bridge, an important passageway to Jiayi and Zhanghua counties. In 1770, the Southern Jiao Jinyongshun, together with the Northern Jiao, were recorded as contributing to the repair of the police station in Taiwan County. In 1772, the two once again donated jointly to fund the restoration of the Earth God Temple at Chaitou Port.[40] Thus we can see that before 1760, public works in Taiwan were funded by local officials or citizens and individual firms; while from 1760 onwards, the Northern Jiao and Southern Jiao began to be involved and gradually came to play a leading role in public and religious projects, including the construction of local temples, bridges and police stations. That is to say, *jiao* appeared formally around the 1760s, or at least not earlier than the 1750s.

After the appearance of *jiao* in Taiwan, the first historical records of *jiao* across the strait appear in Xiamen, the 'designated official port' in Fujian province. Even though merchants ferrying between Taiwan and Xiamen for trade contributed resources to build temples in their hometowns to pray for safe sea voyages, the names of *jiao* were not listed among the benefactors. It was in 1791 that the Tai-Xia (Taiwan-Xiamen) Southern Jiao Jinyongshun was first listed among the benefactors contributing to the restoration of the South China Sea Putuo Temple.[41]

This last point is significant. First, the Tai-Xia Southern Jiao was an association made up of merchants from Fucheng and Xiamen who had formed a *jiao* because they conducted bilateral trade between Taiwan and Xiamen. Some of these merchant associations from different areas across the strait even had the same name. For example, the Xiamen Jiao located in Lugang and the Lugang Jiao located in Xiamen were both called Jinzhenshun, indicating that they belonged to the same merchant association.[42] The claims made in the 1840s by Taiwan circuit intendant Yaoying that 'most *jiao* merchants from Taiwan lived in Xiamen' and that 'the majority of *jiao* merchants from Taiwan and Lugang settled down at Xiamen Port'[43] were a bit exaggerated for the period before the mid-nineteenth century and neglected the existence of local *jiao* merchants. However, such perspectives did reflect part of the actual situation at that time.

Second, the term *jiao* appeared originally as a result of cross-strait trade and was first used in Taiwan. This is further confirmed by the fact that business donors funding the construction of the Water God Temple in Xiamen in 1802 were divided into trading firms (*yanghang*), firms and small firms; none of them were listed under the name of *jiao*.[44] Hence, the participation of local merchants in public undertakings in Xiamen in the name of *jiao* most likely began in the nineteenth century.

Differentiation and Activities of *Jiao* during the Late Eighteenth Century

The decade between 1775 and 1784 saw a boom in the rice export trade as a result of the completion of the reclamation of the central and northern plains and full development of paddy fields in Taiwan (see Figure 1.2).

Figure 1.2: The trade pattern of Taiwan ports from 1784 to 1830.

Quanzhou and Zhangzhou in Fujian were the chief export markets for the crops grown in these fields.[45] *Jiao* merchants trading Taiwan's rice in Xiamen and Quanzhou were very active. In Lugang, Xinzhuang and Mengjia, the Quan Jiao and Xia Jiao were both involved in religious and social welfare undertakings, such as building local temples, offering sacrifices to gods, and setting up and managing 'charitable burial grounds' (*yizhong*) and free ferries.[46] In particular, responding to the call for contributions from the Taiwan magistrate Jiang Yuanshu in 1778, *jiao* on both sides of the strait or individual *jiao* firms jointly donated to repair the 'capital wall, temples, altars and graves, bridges, and roads, as well as government buildings'.[47]

On donation steles, the following names of *jiao* were recorded:

> Northern Jiao 'Suwanli'; shipping firms (*chuanhang*) Chenjingshan ... Quan Northern Jiao 'Wangshunxing'; Quan Thread Jiao 'Quanying'; Chenlin Jiao 'Duluanjin'; Zhang Silk Jiao 'Jianan'; Xia Oil Jiao 'Zhengyuansheng'; Xia Cloth Jiao 'Xie Longsheng'; Fur Jiao 'Songruixing' ... Groceries Jiao ... Southern Jiao 'Jinyongshun'; Sugar Jiao 'Lishengxing'; Anhai Jiao 'Gongmaosheng'; Cast Iron Vessel Jiao 'Gaosuixing' and 'Xielianxing'; Silks and Satins Jiao 'Huangzhenyuan' and 'Lizhengmao'; Luzai Jiao 'Zhenhe' and Shengtao'; Deerskin Shops 'Guoyuzhen' and 'Chenlianxing' ... Jia[yi] Lishengxing; Sugar Jiao in Ben'gang; Cloth Jiao in Ben'gang[48]

Obviously, merchants from Taiwan County, Jiayi County, Fengshan County and Zhanghua County cooperated closely with local government and participated in the fundraising. Although the stele was partly destroyed, those names and descriptions that can still be deciphered on the inscription offer evidence for several conclusions.

First, market expansion and growing diversity of trading products had a strong impact on the development of different kinds of *jiao*. Under the influence of these factors, *jiao* in Fucheng evolved into external *jiao* (*waijiao*). One example of this was the Northern Jiao trading to the north of Xiamen and Southern Jiao trading in Xiamen. Moreover, internal *jiao* (*neijiao*), which were formed by merchants engaged in the same trade, such as the Sugar Jiao, Cooking Tripod (*ding*) Jiao, Fur Jiao, Groceries Jiao, and Deerskin Jiao, also emerged. Except for the Sugar Jiao and Groceries Jiao, most other *jiao* were named after individual firms. They were more like independent *jiao* firms. *Jiao* with structured organizations were probably established only around the early nineteenth century as the market grew in size and complexity.

Second, this inscription was the first and the only time that the Deerskin Jiao and Anhai Jiao were mentioned in Taiwan. The Deerskin Jiao and Anhai Jiao were examples of merchant groups engaged in trade in the same merchandise and along the same route, respectively. While there had been many merchants engaged in the export of deerskins in Fucheng in the 1770s, it is likely that the merchant associations associated with the deerskin trade disappeared because of a decrease in deerskin production. The emergence of the Anhai Jiao can be attributed to the prosperous trade between Anhai of Fujian and Fucheng of Taiwan during the late eighteenth century. It was listed also among the benefactors contributing to the restoration of Longshan Temple (*Longshan si*) of Anhai in 1879.[49] However, probably a subsequent decline in business led to the merging of the Anhai Jiao and the Southern Jiao. The rise and fall of *jiao* was closely related to the market situation at that time. Towards the late Qing dynasty, the market situation became more volatile, leading to rapid emergence and decline of *jiao* and more frequent reorganization and mergers.

Third, the presence of the Cloth Jiao and Sugar Jiao in Ben'gang reveal the domestic expansion of *jiao* from Fucheng to the northern ports of Taiwan. It also illustrates the dominant form of exchange at that time, during which cloth was the chief import from mainland China and sugar was the main export from Taiwan. Internal *jiao* appeared before external *jiao* in Ben'gang, indicating that under the policy of 'designated official ports', *jiao* were mainly involved in domestic coastal trade in Fucheng. A Cloth Jiao and Sugar Jiao also appeared in Yanshuigang in 1795. They participated in rebuilding the Mazu Temple in the port city.[50] As Ben'gang and Yanshuigang had close trading relationships with Fucheng, their market spheres almost overlapped during the Qing dynasty.[51] Hence, the Cloth Jiao and Sugar Jiao in Ben'gang and Yanshuigang can be taken as the local counterparts of the two *jiao* in Fucheng.

Fourth, several of the *jiao* mentioned in the inscription also appeared in mainland China, such as the Oil Jiao and Cloth Jiao in Xiamen, the Northern Jiao and Thread Jiao in Quanzhou, and the Silk Jiao in Zhangzhou. They were mainly internal *jiao*, although a few were external *jiao*. However, they were only listed on steles in Taiwan, along with the names of individual firms. Their traces are rarely seen in other contexts. This might be due to the fact that Fucheng merchants traded only with these three places. Whether there were merchant organizations established in these places requires further verification.

The evolution of the two types of *jiao*, which could be divided into those that operated in the local Taiwan market and those that dealt in external trade, merits further explanation. As mentioned above, *jiao* were originally merchant organizations established as a result of maritime trade. Therefore, external *jiao* were formed first, in the 1760s, and included import and export merchants trading along the same route. By the 1770s internal *jiao*, including the Sugar Jiao, Cooking Tripod Jiao, Fur Jiao, Deerskin Jiao, and Silks and Satins Jiao, appeared. Unlike the external *jiao*, these internal *jiao* were comprised solely of merchants from the same industry. Murakami Tamakichi drew a clear demarcation between these two types of communities: internal *jiao* merchants engaged in trade within the island of Taiwan, whereas external *jiao* merchants engaged in import and export across the strait. At the same time, he argued that internal *jiao* traded merchandise imported by external *jiao*.[52] However, the relationship between internal jiao and external *jiao* was not as distinct as Murakami suggests.

As a matter of fact, there were merchants belonging to both internal *jiao* and external *jiao*. Abundant examples can be found in Taiwan and Xiamen. Documents about *jiao* in Puzaijiao (present-day Puchi [Puzi] in Jiayi) during the late Qing dynasty showed that there were Southern-Northern (*nanbei*) Jiao, Penghu Jiao and Sugar Jiao in that area. Among them, the Southern-Northern Jiao was comprised of thirteen firms engaged in trade along the Chinese coast while the Sugar Jiao was made up of fifteen firms in the sugar business. Eleven firms belonged to both *jiao*.[53] Another example is the Grocery Jiao in Fucheng, which also went directly to Fujian for trading and made donations for reconstructing the Anhai Longshan Temple in 1879. In other words, the same firm could belong to different kinds of *jiao*, reflecting different aspects of its business. *Jiao* merchants actually had to attend different *jiao* to protect their interests. Moreover, merchants belonging to internal *jiao* could also import and export products directly, without going through external *jiao*.

Prior to 1740, donations for various activities, such as local infrastructure, charitable work, and temple building and maintenance all over Taiwan came mainly from local officials, members of elites or commoners within certain regions. Occasionally, there were wealthy and influential landlords from central and northern Taiwan like Wang Shijie and Zhang Shixiang who made donations to causes based in Fucheng in the south. Luermen in Fucheng, as the main site of the import and export trade, was at that time the only window to the outside world. Hence, landlords as well as members of wealthy and influential families from the regions outside Fucheng also participated in activities centered on that city. During the early Qing dynasty, the local authorities in Taiwan relied largely on landlords and influential families in their administration.

However, from the 1760s onwards, *jiao* began to take an active role in political, social welfare and religious activities in addition to their economic undertakings. As mentioned above, they were often major benefactors, not only because they made the largest donations but also because they often took the lead as the initiators or primary donors in fund-raising campaigns. *Jiao* played a very important role in local society in Taiwan and gradually became pillars of the community, with their members acquiring the status of social elites. This was quite different from the profile of their southern Fujian counterparts. The social role of *jiao* in Taiwan conferred legitimacy to their organization and contributed to their greater sense of belonging to local society.[54] Furthermore, they not only established powerful and good reputations in local society but also obtained respect from local governments prior to the emergence of the gentry in the early nineteenth century.

For merchant associations engaged in maritime trade, safety at sea was of paramount importance, and *jiao* were particularly keen to seek protection by worshipping deities of the sea. They often contributed to the construction of temples dedicated to the Goddess of the Sea and the Empress of Heaven (*Tian-hou*).[55] At the same time, while *jiao* did not have physical meeting places of their own, they generally conducted their business within the temples with which they had both religious and financial ties.

One manifestation of the association of *jiao* with temples was their adoption of the structure of temple associations as their own organizational model. *Jiao* members were called *luxia* or *lujiao* (sons of the incense keeper), and the members in charge of *jiao* affairs were given the titles *Luzhu* (incense keeper, executive official), *Jushi* (tax collector), *Jiaoshu* (secretary), and *Guanshi* (stewards or general staff). The *Luzhu* was selected annually by members by casting divination blocks at the Feast of Mazu, and oversaw in his one-year term all affairs of the *jiao* and sacrificial worship.[56] Working under the *Luzhu* were the *Jushi* and *Jiaoshu*. The *Jushi* was in charge of levying export taxes (*choufen*) on ships to maintain a provident fund for the *jiao*,[57] while the *Jiaoshu* was responsible for external liaisons and paperwork of the *jiao*.[58] Since many *jiao* merchants were not only merchants, but also landlords and members of the gentry, the *Jiaoshu* or *Jushi* were often selected from among those members of the *jiao* who were part of the gentry and held a relatively high official rank and enjoyed social prestige.[59] The *Guanshi* looked after general affairs and was responsible for collecting rents on fields and houses owned by the *jiao*.[60] Because of the similarities between *jiao* organization and temple groups, these merchant associations were sometimes mistaken for religious societies.[61] *Jiao* invested in real estate as a kind of endowment to support the activities of the organization; temple associations, lineages and other institutions also did so. In this respect, *jiao* were adopting a more general model for organizational behavior widespread in China.

Although *jiao* in Taiwan were organized in a similar manner, they differed slightly from each other in terms of scale, structure and naming conventions. For example, both the Three Jiao in Tainan and the Xia Jiao Jintongshun in Dadaocheng (Taipei) had directors in addition to the *Luzhu*. The Xia Jiao had four directors.[62] Working under the *Luzhu* and directors were *Gaoshu*, who were similar to *Jiaoshu*, and *Qianshou*, who were similar to *Jushi*. The greater complexity of their administrative structures reflected the greater organizational duties that these *jiao* faced.

Jiao affairs were settled through internal discussion and executed by the *Luzhu* and *Jiaoshu*. These two also represented *jiao* in all external liaisons. Issues that concerned all members had to be discussed and resolved at general meetings, rather than decided upon by the *Luzhu* alone. Unlike *huiguan* and *gongsuo* on the Chinese mainland, most *jiao* in Taiwan did not have exclusive venues for holding such meetings and hence they gathered in temples. In fact, these temples did not belong to the *jiao*; they were open to the public and not for the sole use of *jiao* members, although the *jiao* often managed them. The fact that small-scale *jiao* had no place of their own for meetings shows their relatively loose organization and weaker financial power; and their attachment to temples also reveals the importance of religious worship in fostering solidarity among members.

Another difference between the mainland *huiguan* and *gongsuo* and the Taiwanese *jiao* lies in the erection of monuments or engraving of inscriptions detailing the organization's ownership of properties to prevent encroachment by local governments.[63] These were popular and widely found on the mainland. On the contrary, there were no such monuments or inscriptions existing in Taiwan. This illustrates that *jiao* in Taiwan were very influential in local society and consequently had no need to take such elaborate measures to protect their property.

Conclusion

Jiao as merchant associations emerged due to the booming trade between Taiwan and mainland China. They first appeared in Taiwan, and the majority formed in port cities. Coastal trade inevitably involved a long sea voyage; hence, collaboration among merchants meant united efforts in seeking solutions to issues of navigation, sales, business and politics that most likely arose. Therefore, *jiao* were originally trade organizations navigating to the same areas and comprising merchants from both Fujian and Taiwan. Most of them were engaged in bilateral trade between Taiwan and Xiamen, or Taiwan and Quanzhou. As with the *huiguan* and *gongsuo* in mainland China, the *jiao* developed autonomously. In this sense, all these organizations were very different than the *shijŏn*, the government-patronized merchant communities of Chosŏn Korea described in Cho Young-Jun and Lee Hun-Chang's chapter in this volume.

Jiao rose and fell in accordance with the market situation and the products traded on the market. In central and northern Taiwan, the rice trade was dominant, so Quan Jiao and Xia Jiao, rice exporters to Fujian, were the most active. In the south, sugar was the main export, in exchange for daily essentials from mainland China; hence, the Northern Jiao, Sugar Jiao and Cloth Jiao ran most of the business and expanded gradually from Fucheng to Ben'gang and Yanshuigang.

From 1680 to 1740, Taiwan under the Qing was a developing region with much infrastructure still in the process of construction. Local public works and temple restoration projects were entrusted to local officials, members of various elites and landlords. Around the 1760s, merchant associations gradually became the backbone of local society, participating in and even leading different local undertakings in the eighteenth century. Hence, merchant associations maintained good relationships with the local governments.

Finally, merchants from Taiwan and Xiamen built the Dragon King Temple (*Longwang miao*) in Xiamen together and in general *jiao* donated much to the repair and construction of local temples to seek protection from deities associated with the sea for their maritime trade. This was the reason for the formation and growing popularity of *jiao* in ports all over Taiwan. *Jiao* in Taiwan also often used temples to hold meetings and seldom owned premises, which was a primary difference from *huiguan* and *gongsuo* in mainland China.

In sum, this chapter has focused on the formation of *jiao* in the eighteenth century. *Jiao* at this time undertook both social and economic functions to improve market development and raise their status in local society. Towards the nineteenth century, owing to the changing policies of the Qing government, the evolving market and social situations, and the growing presence of Western merchants in the Far East, the *jiao* underwent rapid and frequent reorganization and mergers. From a comparative prospective, the *jiao* show both similarities and differences with *huiguan* and *gongsuo* in China and *shijŏn* in late Chosŏn Korea. These differences came from the distinct political and economic environments in which each type of organization formed, as well as the separate cultures of their merchants.

Acknowledgements

This research was sponsored by the National Science Council (Project No.101–2410-H-001–066) and the RCHSS of National Cheng-kung University in Taiwan. I would like to thank Prof. Madeleine Zelin, Prof. Evan Lampe and Maura Dykstra, as well as two reviewers, for their useful comments on earlier versions of this chapter.

Glossary

Anhai jiao	安海郊	Luermen	鹿耳門
Anlan	安瀾	Lugang	鹿港
Ben Jiao	笨郊	lujiao	爐腳
Ben'gang	笨港	luxia	爐下
Cai Guolin	蔡國琳	Luzhu	爐主
Cai Yuanqie	蔡淵絜	Mazu	媽祖
Chaitou	柴頭	Mengjia	艋舺
Chen Zhiping	陳支平	Murakami Tamakichi	村上玉吉
Chiu Peng-sheng	邱澎生	nanbei	南北
choufen	抽分	Nanhao	南濠
chuanhang	船行	Nanshi	南勢
Dadaocheng	大稻埕	neijiao	內郊
Daniels, Christian	唐立	Penghu jiao	澎湖郊
Danshui	淡水	Puchi [Puzi]	朴子
De'an	德安	Puzaijiao	樸仔腳
dian	店	Qianshou	鐵首
Ding Jiao	鼎郊	Quan Jiao	泉郊
Ding Shaoyi	丁紹儀	Sanyitang	三益堂
Dongying Shilüe	東瀛識略	shangbang	商幫
duijiao	對交	shanghang	商行
Fang Hao	方豪	shanghao	商號
Fengshan	鳳山	shitu jiao	十途郊
Fu Yiling	傅衣凌	shuijiao	水郊
Fucheng	府城	South China Sea Putuo Temple	南海普陀寺
Gaoshu	稿書	Suwanli	蘇萬利
gongji	公記	Taiping Bridge	太平橋
gongsuo	公所	Tai-Xia Jiao	臺廈郊
Guanshi	管事	Tai-Xia Southern Jiao	臺廈南郊
hangdian	行店	Taotai [daotai]	道臺
hanghu	行戶	Tianhou	天后
Higashi Yoshio	東嘉生	Tu Zhaoyan	涂照彥
Hou Zongxing	侯宗興	waijiao	外郊
Hsinchu [Xinzhu]	新竹	Wang Shijie	王士傑
huiguan	會館	Wang Zhen	王珍
Jiang Yuanshu	蔣元樞	Xia Jiao	廈郊
jiao	郊	Xiang-Le-Xian-Shan jiao	香叻暹汕郊
jiaoguan	交關	Xinghua	興化
jiaohang	郊行	Xinzhuang	新莊
jiaohu	郊戶	yanghang	洋行
jiaopu	郊鋪	Yanshuigang	鹽水港
Jiaoshu	郊書	Yaoying	姚瑩
Jiayi	嘉義	yizhong	義塚
Jintongshun	金同順	*Yuanli Gazetteer*	苑裡志
Jinyongshun	金永順	Zhang Shixiang	張士箱
Jinzhenshun	金振順	Zhanghua	彰化
Jiucyonglin	九芎林	Zhangzhou	漳州

Jushi	局師	Zheng Chenggong (Koxinga)	鄭成功
Kurihara Jun	栗原純	zhengkou	正口
Lin Man-houng	林滿紅	Zhuqian	竹塹
Longshan si	龍山寺	Zhuo Kehua	卓克華
Longwang miao	龍王廟	Zongyue	總約

2 SEOUL MERCHANT COMMUNITIES IN LATE CHOSŎN KOREA

Cho Young-Jun and Lee Hun-Chang

The study of merchant institutions often includes a form of organization broadly grouped under the rubric of 'the guild'. Among merchants during the Chosŏn dynasty, the *shijŏn* was the only organization to fall within this category. *Shi* literally means market as well as city, and *chŏn* means shop; thus, the compound word *shijŏn* literally means 'shops in the city'. At their height, *shijŏn* could be found in a number of large cities, including P'yŏng'yang, Kaesŏng and Haeju.[1] However, it is only in the capital and largest city of Chosŏn Korea, Seoul, that we have sufficient data to explore the characteristics of this guild-like institution.

Shijŏn were an important organizational form in Seoul during the eighteenth and nineteenth centuries. They had both similarities and differences from the typical guild found in early modern Europe. The most significant difference was that the *shijŏn* was created and licensed by the government. *Shijŏn* were deeply embedded within the political economy of the Chosŏn dynasty. Thus, the difference in the political systems between Northeast Asia and Europe made a difference in guild institutions. We initially survey the political and economic environments of merchant communities. Then, we examine the organization and functions of the *shijŏn* in Seoul. Finally, we assess the economic performance of the *shijŏn*. By analysing a premodern Korean merchant institution, this chapter aims to shed light on the comparative study on merchant communities between East and West.

Political and Economic Environments of Merchant Communities

Market Size and Structure

The size of Korea since the sixteenth century has been about 221,000 square kilometres, of which roughly 20 per cent is arable land. The cultivated land was approximately 10 million acres, of which approximately 30 per cent was paddy field around 1800. Population estimates vary; however, a population of 16 million in the eighteenth century is a reasonable estimate. Korea developed an intensive agriculture and had a highly dense population.

Over 80 per cent of the population engaged in agriculture. The volume of hulled rice production was roughly 10 million Japanese *koku*, or approximately 15 million Korean *sŏm* around 1800,[2] which accounted for about 30 per cent of agricultural products and about 20 to 25 per cent of the gross domestic product (GDP).[3] The commercialization rate of agricultural products was roughly 20 per cent. Korean society was primarily agrarian, with most production coming from self-sufficient peasant families who produced grain and cloth mainly for subsistence and taxes.

The urbanization rate was extremely low. Around 1800, the proportion of the population that resided in urban centres of more than 10,000 people was only about 2.5 per cent, and in cities of over 5,000 people only 3.8 per cent.[4] The population of Seoul was slightly over 200,000, and this accounted for about one half of that urban 2.5 per cent. Wŏnsan, Masan and Kanggyŏng, which were prosperous port cities with a population of roughly 5,000 each, were the largest cites other than administrative centres. The number of local periodic markets increased to over a thousand in the mid-eighteenth century. After that, the number of markets per 10,000 square kilometres hovered around forty-five. The density of periodic markets was very high by pre-industrial standards. Around 1800, money stock over GDP was 2 to 3 per cent, which was much lower than found in Japan or China.[5] However, the traditional bill, *ŏŭm*, became widely used in the nineteenth century. The low urbanization rate and the small amount of large-denomination money reflected the weakness of domestic long-distance trade.

Korea had a small foreign trade for most of pre-industrial history despite its advantage as a small peninsular country. The main reason was its incorporation into the Chinese tribute system, which was the outcome of the geopolitics of Northeast Asia where one giant state, China, dominated.[6] The Chosŏn court initially wanted to prohibit all private trade with China; in the fifteenth century, it colluded with China in private trade attendant on tribute traffic. It authorized private trade in border-markets in the seventeenth century. Silver imports from Japan increased after the mid-sixteenth century. Korea exported silver to China, in return importing silk that was re-exported to Japan. Korea earned huge profits from this intermediate trade. The total sum of silver imported during the peak period from 1684 to 1710 amounted to 189 metric tons, and its value represented 58 per cent of total imports from Japan.[7] The cessation of silver importing around the mid-eighteenth century reduced private trade with Japan and China. The cultivation of ginseng, which grew wild in Korea, then rose to sustain private trade with China after the eighteenth century. In the mid-nineteenth century, the ratio of trade volume over GDP is estimated to have been at 1.5 per cent.[8] The Korean government allowed Koreans to trade overseas as late as 1882.

The Chosŏn Political System and the Principle of Economic Integration
Interestingly, the underdevelopment of the market had something to do with the
early development and long duration of the territorial state. The state institution
gradually developed in the long and continuous political history of Korea. Korea
had no experience of feudalism. The early Chosŏn dynasty established a centralized bureaucratic state comparable to the contemporary Chinese state.

Historically, around the world most economies have been composed of three
major allocation systems, namely, reciprocity, redistribution (or public finance)
and market.[9] The consolidation of the state in Korea from the Three Kingdoms
period (57 BC–AD 668) to the early Chosŏn period did not provide favourable conditions to market development. All the pre-industrial Korean states
preferred official international trade to private international trade, and often
suppressed the latter. This tendency was strengthened by Korea's incorporation
into the Chinese tribute system that subordinated trade to diplomacy. Setbacks
to external trade in pre-industrial Korea were instigated by the rulers' desire to
administer international trade and monopolize trade gains.[10] The new Chosŏn
state consolidated and expanded the redistribution system and suppressed trade
activities.[11] The Chosŏn state consolidated state finance in kind at an early stage
and developed famine relief, which had a crowding-out effect on the market. Per
capita grain storage to cope with famine was about five times bigger than that
of China in the 1790s, when grain storage was at its highest point in both Qing
China and Chosŏn Korea.[12]

The economy of the Chosŏn dynasty in its early period was mainly integrated by redistribution. In the eighteenth century, with the enforcement of
uniform tribute payment in rice (the *taedong* law) and the spread of copper coin,
both redistribution and the market played a significant role. In the nineteenth
century, with the dissolution of the state granary system (*hwan'gok*), the market
became the primary force for integration. Although the volume of the market
was larger than that of redistribution in the eighteenth century, the regulatory
power of state redistribution over the market was significant. Despite the relatively small scale of public finance, the Chosŏn dynasty was able to effectively
use it to achieve economic control and stabilize the livelihood of the commoners
through provisions such as famine relief programmes.[13]

Merchant Communities
Three types of major merchant communities existed in late Chosŏn Korea,
namely *shijŏn*, *pobusang* and Kaesŏng merchants. *Shijŏn* was the community of
shop merchants in large cities. *Shijŏn* as shops in Seoul were created by the government at the beginning of the early Chosŏn dynasty, following the precedent
of the former Koryŏ dynasty (918–1392). *Shijŏn* merchants seem to have gradually formed associations selling the same items. The government then came to
utilize the associations for maintaining market order and collecting commercial
taxes and to authorize their exclusive sale of designated goods.

The two other major merchant communities were groups of private merchants and bottom-up institutions. The first, the coalition of *pobusang*, mostly comprised local peddlers, whose main transaction place was the periodic market (*changsi*). Over a thousand periodic markets existed, and *pobusang* peddlers linked them with each other. The *pobusang* peddlers originally formed a coalition or a group for the purpose of a safe journey, and their community was eventually licensed by the government from the mid-nineteenth century. The organization of *pobusang* was volatile as its infrastructure was vulnerable to frequent changeover in individual peddlers. An analysis of the membership of *pobusang* indicates that mutual aid was their only function even in the mid-nineteenth century.[14]

Kaesŏng merchants, the final type of merchant community, were mostly engaged in long-distance trade, both domestic and international. They were known as the most innovative among Korean merchants because they used advanced accounting methods such as double-entry bookkeeping. In the eighteenth century, they also had loose credit communities offering low interest rates, mostly 1.5 per cent monthly. Kaesŏng merchants were basically independent of government, but one of their main sources of wealth lay in the international trade process regulated by government. They accompanied annual envoys to the emperor of China and obtained an opportunity to make much money through official trade. Although their legendary performance in commercial activity is famous, not much is known about the organization and functions of their community due to lack of evidence. Even the most recent research tells us little about these aspects of Kaesŏng merchants.[15]

Market Policy, Institutions and Governance
The literati elites of the new dynasty compiled a statutory code that would define the structure and functioning of the Chosŏn government, finally producing the National Code (*Kyŏngguk taejŏn*) promulgated in 1471. These literati continued to publish newly revised and enlarged editions. A researcher of legal history has argued that the early Chosŏn dynasty had an early modern level of legal institutions.[16] Similar to China, the Chosŏn dynasty put the penal code in good order, but it did not develop the civil code to settle private disputes on market transactions. No representative institution checked the arbitrary exercise of power by the king or government. No concept comparable to *universitas* existed; *universitas* was 'newly introduced to European law in the late eleventh and twelfth centuries', and its principle 'established the existence of fictive personalities that are treated as real entities in courts of law and in assemblies before kings and princes'.[17]

Despite the inefficiency of the formal legal system in settling private disputes on market transactions, market transactions encountered no severe hindrances. The reason is that the government protected these transactions. The penal code provided punishments for price manipulation, weights and measures manipulation, and coercive transactions. The Office of Market Regulation (*P'yŏngshisŏ*) had three functions, namely the regulation of prices, prevention of fraud and administration of market taxes in Seoul. Moreover, local governments had the same functions in administrative districts.

The ruling ideology of the Chosŏn state was Confucianism. The fundamental object of economic policy was to stabilize the economy and support the livelihood of the people; the object of market policy was deduced from this fundamental object. An early-nineteenth-century government manual (*Man'gi yoram*) noted: 'Since *shijŏn*s are concerned with the commerce of common people and at the same time provide goods needed by the state, the rulers of the country consider them to be important'.

The pre-imperial Chinese Confucian philosopher Mencius argued that to activate market trade the government should check and protect market transactions and should not levy commercial taxes. Consequently, Confucian bureaucrats were reluctant to impose commercial taxes. Commercial and industrial taxes were categorized as miscellaneous taxes (*chapse*). Given that Korean society was primarily agrarian, tax revenues from industry and commerce were extremely small. In the late eighteenth century, the total obligation of the people to government and offices including not only formal taxes but also informal burdens accounted for 5 to 10 per cent of GDP, and that from commerce accounted for 1 to 2 per cent of the total burden.[18] Most of the commercial burdens were not formally acknowledged by the state. Just like the Ming government, the Chosŏn government never considered foreign trade and industrial production as essential elements of public finance.[19] The government began collecting taxes from private international trade in the seventeenth century when private international trade was approved.

Confucian elites followed the teaching of Mencius that the state should not compete with people in seeking profit, and hence were reluctant to manage the profit-seeking business of the state. The strong Confucian culture was unfavourable to the exploitation of revenues from commerce. Furthermore, external peace and internal stability during the long-lasting Chosŏn dynasty weakened the incentive among bureaucrats for entrepreneurship and fiscal reform.

Although the tax rate defined by law was extremely low, similar to China, the tax system had a grave problem. Several government offices, local governments and members of the royal family and other powerful families engaged in rent-seeking, and the spread of miscellaneous taxes undefined by law (*mumyŏng chapse*) became an intense political issue in the nineteenth century.[20]

The government could not effectively remedy this problem. It did not have a strong incentive to do so because commercial taxes were only a small part of the state revenue. Moreover, it was a soft government. Confucian bureaucrats preferred rule by Confucian morals to rule by laws, and often were not faithful to abiding by laws. Therefore, merchants had an incentive to organize a community to cope with this situation. The typical case was the organization of a *pobusang* society.

Confucian elites considered agriculture as the main sector of the economy and commerce as an auxiliary one; hence, they wanted to promote agriculture and prevent commerce from flourishing. They believed that a vibrant commerce was harmful to agriculture and public morals. This Confucian ideology was unfavourable to the development of merchant communities, and hampered the emergence of any European-type mercantilism in Chosŏn Korea.

Organization and Institution of *Shijŏn* Guilds

Emergence of *Shijŏn* Guilds

At the beginning of the Chosŏn dynasty, the government constructed a series of *shijŏn* shop buildings for the purpose of procuring necessary materials for the everyday life of the court and for the daily business of government offices. In other words, *shijŏn*s in early Chosŏn Korea were procuring agencies rather than retail shops. They were initially called 'official' shops in a row (*kongnang*) attached to the government (see Figure 2.1). Therefore, originally, the listed operators of *shijŏn* shops were government-patronized merchants, and the *shijŏn* shops themselves were top-down institutions.

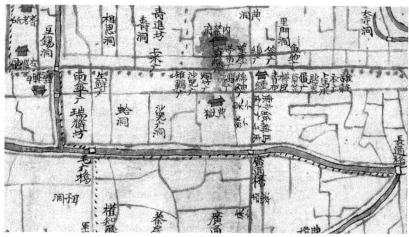

Figure 2.1: Major *shijŏn* shops in a row in the nineteenth century. The Chinese character *ŏm* in the map is an abbreviation of *chŏn*. **Source:** *Chŏnggu Yoram* (Tosŏngjŏndo), Kyujanggak Archive, Seoul National University.

Typically, the spatial organization of *shijŏn* was the '*chŏn, pang, k'an*' system. *Chŏn* was each *shijŏn* itself, as previously mentioned. *Pang* means the divisions (or shops) of each *chŏn*.[21] For instance, the hemp merchant guild (*p'ojŏn*) had five divisions in the early twentieth century. Divisions were numerically distinguished; every division (*pang*) had its own number, such as the first division (*ilbang*), the second division (*yibang*) and the third division (*sambang*). Every division of the hemp merchant guild had ten *k'ans*.[22] *K'an* has two meanings: the space enclosed by four pillars in the building, and a unit of area equivalent to 10 *tsubo* (approximately 33 square metres). Each merchant guild regularly imposed a fee (or rent) called *pangse* on all its *pang*.[23] *Pang* was a type of 'syndicate'. In principle, *shijŏn* merchants could individually buy and sell goods; however, all merchants engaged in a certain *pang* of a guild 'jointly' conducted their business, including purchase, investment and accounting.

As mentioned above, the association or guild institution of *shijŏn* members is considered to have gradually emerged after the beginning of the dynasty.[24] However, it remains uncertain how the association or guild was developed by the *shijŏn* merchants themselves until the sixteenth century. In the seventeenth century when the *taedong* law was enforced, the function of *shijŏn* expanded because rice, and not specialty products, began to be directly gathered into Seoul. In other words, tribute was no longer collected in kind. Instead, Seoul citizens, including civilians and members of the royal family, used rice as cash to buy their necessities. *Shijŏn* associations or guilds were organized to respond to the huge market demand that resulted from this change.

The exact number of merchant guilds is unknown; nevertheless, official records containing a list of major *shijŏn*s show the existence of 100 or more *shijŏn* guilds in the eighteenth and nineteenth centuries. Each *chŏn* was classified into two groups according to the requirement, or not, of corvée.[25] One group was *chŏn* with corvée duties (*yup'unjŏn*), and the other was *chŏn* without corvée (*mup'unjŏn*). Among *yup'unjŏn*s, six major *chŏn* guilds existed, which were called *yugjubijŏn*. *Yugjubijŏn* was also called *yugŭijŏn*,[26] and this is the *chŏn* best known to modern historians. *Yugjubijŏn*, or the Six Guilds, dealt in major commodities in frequent demand, such as cloth (i.e. silk, cotton, ramie, hemp), paper and fish.[27] *Yup'unjŏn*, including *yugjubijŏn*, had the responsibility of providing corvée labour for the royal family and public administration in return for having exclusive rights to sell their own commodities.

Table 2.1: The composition and numbers of *shijŏn*s in late Chosŏn Korea

	Numbers of *chŏn* guilds		Numbers of corvée share allocated	
	Eighteenth century	Nineteenth century	Eighteenth century	Nineteenth century
Yugjubijŏn (The Six Guilds)	6	6	48	54
yup'unjŏn (Guilds with corvée)	31	29	61	52
mup'unjŏn (Guilds without corvée)	55 + unlisted	59 + unlisted	–	–

Source: *Takchiji* (Oep'yŏn, Book 2, P'anjŏksa, P'andobu), *Man'gi yoram* (Chaeyongp'yŏn, Book 5, Kakchŏn).

The numbers and composition of these groups are presented in Table 2.1. Over a hundred *chŏn*s existed in eighteenth- to nineteenth-century Chosŏn, and the Six Guilds (*yugjubijŏn*) accounted for the largest portion of corvée labour. In addition, the number of *chŏn* guilds increased and changed as the market economy continued to develop. However, the relationship between the rising number of *chŏn* guilds and market development has not been empirically examined. To address this issue, the details of the organization and function of all *shijŏn* guilds should be explored.

The first academic research on the 'organization' of *shijŏn* guilds was conducted by a Japanese scholar, Kokushō Iwao, in the colonial period.[28] He concluded that the *shijŏn* – mainly *yugjubijŏn* – was a type of merchant guild, and it was not different from the guilds of other countries such as Japan or Western Europe, except for two factors. One factor is the origin of *shijŏn*, primarily its 'government-oriented' feature as previously mentioned. The other factor is the absence of relation with any religion. These two factors remain important. However, changes after the seventeenth century should be examined.

The first problem concerns a possible distinction between shops and guilds. The *shijŏn* 'shops' in early Chosŏn Korea were built by the government; nevertheless, evidence that clarifies whether *shijŏn* merchant 'guilds' were also government-oriented is inadequate. The merchant guilds might have been created as the market in Seoul changed after the seventeenth century, as discussed in the previous section. Kokushō might not have recognized the difference between the characteristics of *shijŏn* shops in early Chosŏn and the guilds (including shops) in late Chosŏn.

The second problem involves ascertaining the occurrence of religious activities. Extensive research demonstrates that the domestic silk merchant guild (*myŏnjujŏn*), one of the Six Guilds, performed a monthly memorial service for Kwanu.[29] Kwanu, a legendary general from the history of the Three Kingdoms in ancient China, was a well-known hero in the novel *The Romance of the Three Kingdoms* (*Samgukji*). Such a service was undertaken because he was believed to be a god of commerce (or wealth) in late Chosŏn Korea.

Temples or shrines were built for Kwanu in Seoul, such as Nammyo and Hyŏnsŏngmyo. Two Kwanu shrines are currently found in Seoul, namely, South Kwanu Shrine and East Kwanu Shrine. In front of East Kwanu Shrine is a stone lantern donated in the 1880s by the cotton cloth guild,[30] which indicates that Kwanu was worshipped not only by *myŏnjujŏn*, but also by most of the *shijŏn* merchant guilds. The ritual for Kwanu had several expressions such as a ritual for a god of wealth (*chaeshinje*), a ritual of shop defense (*shijŏn chinsuje*) and a ritual for a mountain spirit (*sanshinje*).[31] Furthermore, a semi-official survey (*Hankyŏng chiryak*) reported that the pork merchant guild (*chŏjŏn* or *chŏyukjŏn*) should serve as exorcists (*pangsangsi*) for the exorcism rite (*narye*) on occasions of national mourning. These aspects demonstrate that *shijŏn* guilds were also involved in religious activities.

Organization of Shijŏn Guilds

Shijŏn merchant guilds were called *tojung*. *Tojung* was a common expression for associations (or communities) in late Chosŏn Korea. The most well-known expression, *kye*, was often used by the administrative district of cities (e.g. Seoul) or rural communities for several purposes, including mutual aid; meanwhile, *tojung* was typically used by commercial associations, such as *shijŏn* merchants, tribute merchants, coastal brokers or maritime merchants, and international traders. Thus, the meaning of *tojung* may be deeply related with commerce.

Each *shijŏn* was supposed to have its own *tojung*; hence, 100 *tojung* might have existed in eighteenth- to nineteenth-century Seoul. Every *tojung* had the privilege of monopoly until the enactment of commercial liberalization (*Shinhae t'onggong*) in 1791. Immediately after the enactment, only *yugjubijŏn* had this privilege, which was finally terminated by the Kabo Reform in 1894. With such a privilege, called *kŭmnanjŏnkwŏn*, *tojung* could exclude any merchant who wanted to deal in the same commodities in the vicinity of Seoul.

Each *tojung* had an administrative office (or a guild hall) called *toga* or *toso*.[32] *Tojung* officials conducted the business of the guild at the office. The name of each guild office was distinguished with a prefix of the guild name. For example, *p'ojŏndoga* meant the main office of the hemp merchant guild. The area of *p'ojŏndoga* was 65 *tsubo* (approximately 215 square metres).[33]

Almost every document about the organization of *shijŏn* merchant guilds was written by *tojung*, and we discuss the organization based on those documents. However, the existing documents do not represent the entire reality of merchant guilds in Seoul at the time because the actual implementation of the regulations from those documents remains unascertained.[34] All of the information introduced below is based on raw documents from only a few *chŏn*s, such as the Chinese silk merchant guild (*sŏnjŏn*), the domestic silk merchant guild, the hemp merchant guild and so on. It is simply a selection of those guilds where the regulatory documents are particularly rich.

Gaining *tojung* membership was difficult. In principle, only sons or sons-in-law of the incumbent members could be candidates for membership; strict entry barriers to the guild were apparent. Still, although *tojung* was originally a kin-based organization, exceptions existed. For instance, a person who earned a certain prize from a *tojung* could gain the opportunity to be a candidate for membership if he obtained a recommendation from any of the existing members.

All candidates were to pay a membership fee (*yejŏn*), the amount of which varied according to kinship with existing members. If the candidate was not a family member of the existing members, the membership fee was typically high. For instance, twenty-eight *yang* was imposed on new members without blood ties, whereas sons or sons-in-law of the existing members might pay only fifteen *yang*.[35] In principle, *shijŏn* guild membership could not be transferred to anyone but sons and sons-in-law. In other words, an explicit nepotism existed.

Another significant form of nepotism, one related to social status, also emerges from the documents. Examples are as follows. Inheritance of goodwill (business rights) was prohibited for people whose mothers were untouchables in the case of the Chinese silk merchant guild. The child of a concubine could not succeed to goodwill in the case of the paper merchant guild (*chijŏn*). If a candidate was adopted, obtaining an authentication from the Ministry of Rites (*Yejo*) was necessary. If a son of an elder member (*sŏnsaeng*) gained another person's jural succession, he could not succeed to that member's goodwill.

These features could be different from those of the guilds in the Western world. Therefore, in principle, we can call the *shijŏn* guild an 'originally' kin-based organization.[36] The exclusiveness of membership (i.e. the entry barrier) apparently weakened in the late nineteenth century. Table 2.2 shows how the nepotism worked in the case of the Chinese silk merchant guild. Although some merchants could exceptionally gain membership, they had to pay more money to the community than did ordinary sons.

Table 2.2: Set-up fees (membership fees) by relationship in the case of the Chinese silk merchant guild

Relationship	Ties with incumbent elder member	Ties with former elder member
Sons and sons-in-law	Three yang	Six yang
Grandsons	N/A	Twenty yang
Sons of daughters	Twenty-five yang	Twenty-five yang
Grandsons-in-law (husbands of granddaughters)	Thirty yang	Thirty yang
Special fees (*myŏnhŭkryejŏn*)	Nothing	Twenty to twenty-five yang

Source: Ko Dong-Hwan, 'Chosŏn Hugi Shijŏn ŭi Kujo wa Kinŭng' [The Functions and Structure of the Licensed Shops (*Shijŏn*) during the Latter Half of the Chosŏn Dynasty], *Yŏksa wa Hyŏnsil*, 44 (2002), 65–99, on p. 69; Ko Dong-Hwan, 'Shijŏn Sang'in ŭi Chojik kwa Tosŏng Munhwa' [Organization of *Shijŏn* Merchants and Capital-Castle Culture], in Kuksa P'yŏnch'an Wiwŏnhoe (ed.), *Kŏsang, Chŏn'guk Sanggwon ŭl Chang'akkada* [Business Magnates who Gained Commercial Supremacy throughout the Country] (Seoul: Doosan Donga, 2005), pp. 87–167.

The personnel set-up in *tojung* comprised two layers. The details are evident in the case of the hemp merchant guild. In the upper layer (*taebang*) were four ranks of members; in the lower layer (*pibang*) were several types of members.

The four ranks in the upper layer comprised the following: In the first rank were officials, consisting of *toyŏngŭi, taehaengsu, sanggongwŏn*, and *hagongwŏn. Toyŏngŭi* was elected from the former officials, and it was a tenured post. This position functioned as an advisor of the guild. *Taehaengsu* was a secretary of the guild, and he or she was appointed by a general election of all guild members. A person in this position managed the overall official work. *Sanggongwŏn* was an official clerk, and *hagongwŏn* was a main cashier. Both were appointed by a general election of all members among three candidates shortlisted by the *taehangsu*. These three types of officials (*taehaengsu, sanggongwŏn* and *hagongwŏn*) were required to donate a certain amount of money to the guild under the name of 'clothing fee', which signified the act of wearing the official uniform. Their term in office was assumed to be two to six months only.

In the second rank were *sŏnsaeng*s, in the third *ojwa*s,[37] and in the fourth *shipjwa*s. *Sŏnsaeng* literally means elders, and *ojwa* and *shipjwa* refer to people who occupy the selected five (or ten) chairs (or seats).[38] In the case of the hemp merchant guild, the *sŏnsaeng*s totalled 20 to 30, and the *ojwa*s and *shipjwa*s totalled 50 and 100, respectively.[39] Overall, in the upper layer of the hemp merchant guild were 120 to 230 members. However, we do not have any information about the year of the document. Thus, we consider the number of merchants in the upper layer of the hemp merchant guild as a reference only.

Across the four ranks, promotion and age were fundamental standards for obtaining promotion to an upper rank. Table 2.3 shows the minimum age required to reach each rank in the paper merchant guild. Age pertained not only to the years lived, but also to the years of service as a guild member. Therefore, age denoted both seniority and term of service. However, age was merely a necessary condition; an additional condition was the obligation to pay money to the guild. The amount of money varied from guild to guild (see Table 2.3).

Table 2.3: Age and fee needed to get into an upper rank

	Age	Fee	
	Paper merchant guild	Chinese silk merchant guild	Knife merchant guild (*tojajŏn*)
Advisor (*yŏngŭi*) or elders (*sŏnsaeng*)	Over sixty	Five yang	N/A
Five chairs (*ojwa*)	Over fifty	Twelve yang	Seven yang
Ten chairs (*shipjwa*)	Over forty	Eighteen yang	Ten yang
Incumbent secretary in the lower layer (*shihaengsu*)	Over thirty-seven	Twelve yang	N/A

Source: Ko, 'Chosŏn Hugi Shijŏn ŭi Kujo wa Kinŭng', pp. 71–2.

The lower layer also comprised several types of members, namely, *shihaengsu, haengsu, sang'im, haim, kunjung* and so on. They were typically younger than the members in the upper layer, and most of them were unmarried. For instance, member candidates of the paper merchant guild were supposed to be under twenty-four years of age. Age and marital status were crucial limitations in the *shijŏn* guild because the community followed the Confucian ideology, mimicking that of the *yangban* elite group. Even if individuals did not necessarily adhere to Confucianism, almost everyone in premodern Korea believed in the propriety of following an elders-first and married-first discipline.

One primary source reported the existence of 500 to 1,000 ordinary members with no position (*kunjung*),[40] but the figure is extremely large and is contrary to another study that estimated the number of *kunjung* at 40 in the case of the domestic silk merchant guild.[41] If the latter is correct, the figure raised by the former might pertain to the entire number of *shijŏn* guild members, not that of a certain guild. This presumption is plausible based on recent research that reported 193 members of the domestic silk merchant guild in 1832.[42]

The exact number of *shijŏn* guild members cannot be directly determined from the primary documents; nevertheless, certain clues for estimating the figure emerge. One method is to use the guild's share of corvée labour. However, numerous guilds called *mup'unjŏn* had zero share; thus, this form of estimation is unreliable. An alternative can be found from official government records (*Pibyŏnsa tŭngnok*). In 1784, King Chŏngjo (r. 1776–1800) lent cash to *shijŏn* merchants and tribute merchants to resolve an insolvency problem. The amount of money lent was presumed to be roughly proportional to the business volume of each guild.[43] If we accept the maximum number of hemp merchant guild members to be 250, considering the foregoing discussion, we can extrapolate the number to every other guild.

Table 2.4: Numbers of each guild's members in 1784, roughly estimated through extrapolation

chŏn	A	B	*chŏn*	A	B	*chŏn*	A	B
sŏnjŏn	10	600	sŏgangmijŏn	0	15	ryangdaejŏn	0	10
myŏnp'ojŏn	9	500	map'omijŏn	0	15	chapch'ŏljŏn	0	14
myŏnjujŏn	8	500	yugijŏn	2	200	paektangjŏn	0	2
naeŏmuljŏn	5	350	ŭnjŏn	2	20	pogmajegujŏn	0	7
chŏngp'ojŏn	3	250	ŭijŏn	2	50	naesegijŏn	0	7
chijŏn	7	500	rijŏn	2	110	sŭnghyejŏn	0	50
chŏp'ojŏn	6	500	hwap'ijŏn	1	70	sanghamokkijŏn	0	10
p'ojŏn	5	250	yinsŏkchŏn	1	30	tŭngjajŏn	0	7
yŏnch'ojŏn	5	220	chinsajŏn	1	50	paengnipchŏn	0	5
oeŏmuljŏn	4	350	ch'ŏngmiljŏn	1	50	choripchŏn	0	10
mangmunsangjŏn*	3	100	kyŏng'yŏmjŏn	1	30	hŭngnipchŏn	0	7
shinsangjŏn*	2	100	ch'egojŏn	1	50	oesegijŏn	0	7

chŏn	A	B	chŏn	A	B	chŏn	A	B
myŏsangjŏn*	2	100	naejangmokchŏn	1	25	ch'imjajŏn	0	10
tongsangjŏn*	1	100	ch'ŏlmuljŏn	1	50	chogdurijŏn	0	5
sujinsangjŏn*	1	70	yŏnjukchŏn	1	30	ch'igyejŏn	0	16
p'osangjŏn*	0	10	naeshijŏjŏn	1	40	manggŏnjŏn	0	5
ch'ŏlsangjŏn*	0	10	oeshijŏjŏn	1	40	chŏnnipchŏn	0	17
p'ilsangjŏn	0	7	ujŏn	1	7	koch'ojŏn	0	12
nammunsangjŏn*	0	10	majŏn	1	7	rijŏjŏn	0	10
yŏmsangjŏn	0	10	oejangmogjŏn	0	10	chŏnjogjŏn	0	5
chŏngnŭngdong-sangjŏn	0	10	soch'aejŏn	0	5	tojajŏn	0	5
kurigaesangjŏn*	0	10	songhyŏnmojŏn	0	15	p'ajajŏn	0	7
chisangjŏn*	0	10	chŏngnŭngdong-mojŏn	0	15	chongjajŏn	0	2
saengsŏnjŏn	3	200	munoemojŏn	0	15	yŏmsujŏn	0	2
chapkokchŏn	3	180	sangmojŏn	0	15	haphoejŏn	0	2
myŏnjajŏn	3	100	hamojŏn	0	15	nammunoeyŏmjŏn	0	7
sangmijŏn	3	200	chŏnmojŏn	0	15	map'oyŏmjŏn	0	7
hamijŏn	3	180	hyejŏnggyo-chabjŏn	0	7	yongsansimokchŏn	0	7
munoemijŏn	2	180	semuljŏn	0	10	Total	109	6,873

Note: A is the share of corvée labour regulated. B is the number of members estimated. See the appendix for the Chinese rendering of each guild. * Thirteen branches of the miscellaneous items merchant guild (*sangjŏn*). Source: *Takchiji* (Oep'yŏn, Book 2, P'anjŏksa, P'andobu). *Pibyŏnsa Tŭngnok* (21 March 1784).

As the results in Table 2.4 indicate, the entire number of *shijŏn* guild members was at least 7,000. This figure is quite reasonable because a narrative of chronicles recounted that 400 to 500 merchants comprised the miscellaneous items merchant guild;[44] meanwhile, another estimate indicates that the minimum number of guild merchants was over 6,000 in the eighteenth century.[45] We can surmise that approximately 10,000 people were engaged in the merchant guild in Seoul in late Chosŏn Korea. If we include their family members, the number of people in merchant households is roughly 40,000. Considering that the population in the capital city Seoul in the eighteenth century was about 200,000, almost 20 per cent of citizens were related with the activities of merchant guilds.

Institution of *Shijŏn* Guilds

The *shijŏn* guild had several functions.[46] These functions include the following: (a) management of relations with the government, particularly in terms of tax and other duties; (b) protection of the privileges of the guild merchants against outside competition; (c) promotion of mutual benefit and friendly relations among merchants, and mediation in any dispute; and (d) in *shijŏn* that combined production and trade, *tojung* officers oversaw the purchase of raw materials and the manufacture and sale of finished products. To understand the multiple facets of merchant guilds, we divide the functions into two aspects, namely, privileges and obligations.

With the political authorities, the *shijŏn* guild had both privileges (or benefits) and obligations (or responsibilities). Privileges came in three forms. First, *shijŏn* merchants had shops to sell commodities every day, whereas other merchants did not have the opportunity to formally open shops in Seoul. The second and major privilege was the monopoly right over the commodities that were dealt in by each *chŏn*. As will be discussed in the next section, the government protected the business district of each merchant guild. The third privilege was the provision of government emergency relief to each merchant guild in case of fire.[47]

Among the obligations, the first and most important one was the regular procurement of commodities for the courts and government offices, called *chinbae*. In a certain sense, this obligation could be considered a privilege when the government budget was favourable; however, it could be a burden when government revenue was in deficit. The procurement process involved several steps. First, the government office in need of certain commodities sent the request list to the relevant *shijŏn* guild. After confirming the list, the corresponding *tojung* allocated the procurement amount to its member merchants who conducted their business in each *pang*. A recent study highlighted the systematic process and well-organized document structure in the procurement process in royal finance.[48]

The second obligation of a *shijŏn* guild was the provision of corvée labour called *kugyŏk*. Corvée labour consisted of various forms of manual work. The three major types of corvée labour were wallpapering, building maintenance and stitchery. *Shijŏn* merchants repaired government office buildings and royal palaces and completed the wallpapering of those buildings, which was the most important task.[49] Female merchants typically did stitchery when Chinese envoys were present. Minor types of corvée labour were also provided. For instance, merchant guild members shouldered a bier during a royal funeral, and several merchants provided ice-storing. Such corvée labour was a burden to *shijŏn* merchants, but it could also be an opportunity to show off their status.[50] No one except *shijŏn* guild merchants could access the inner part of the royal court. Therefore, King Yŏngjo (r. 1724–76) even called them 'the core people in the capital city'.[51]

The third obligation was tax payment to the government. *Tojung* also paid taxes as a collective responsibility.[52] Unfortunately there is inadequate information detailing this obligation. However, the expression *jubi* might be related with this collective tax payment, because *jubi* in rural society is widely believed by a number of researchers to have been a unit of taxation.[53]

The most important aspect is that all these privileges and obligations (or burdens) were assumed by merchant guilds, not by individual merchants. If the government did not force merchants to form such guilds, we should explain why they organized the guilds. In other words, a crucial question arises: why did the *shijŏn* merchants organize their own guilds?

Originally, the merchant guilds were kin-based, as previously discussed; nevertheless, the kin-based feature was not the determining factor because members outside the original lineage also existed. Another probable explanation could be the provision of mutual aid among members. During ceremonies such as weddings, funerals and memorial services for the members and their families, the *tojung* might give cash or lend money at a low interest rate. Such aid was partly conducted by the guild itself, and sometimes it was managed by *kye*, which were composed of its members.[54] However, mutual aid was not the main reason for creating guilds, but an additional function that arose due to the creation of the guild.

Therefore, we should understand the relationship between the guilds and government to explain the reason why the merchants organized guilds. Although *shijŏn* guilds had a significant role in late Chosŏn Korea, their key function was far from that of Western guilds. As for the functions of *shijŏn* guilds, the relationship between merchants and government was more important than the merchants' mutual (or multilateral) relationship(s) if we consider *shijŏn* guilds were always under government control. The root cause might be that the *shijŏn* guild was not initially organized for the benefit of its members. Thus, the role of *shijŏn* guilds could be somewhat different from those of other countries from the viewpoints of market regulation, market growth and economic development.

Evaluation of the Economic Performance of *Shijŏn*

Shijŏn as a community had both social functions and economic functions. Mutual aid was an important centre of their activities. However, the more meaningful function of these merchant communities was the role they played in market development and economic growth, especially in the transitional period to a modern economy.

Debates about the economic performance of European craft guilds are ongoing. Stephen Epstein argued that the aggregate social benefits of European craft guilds outweighed their costs.[55] However, Sheilagh Ogilvie contended that 'guild rent-seeking imposed deadweight losses on the economy'.[56] Ogilvie added that 'distributional conflicts provide a better explanation than efficiency for the core economic institutions of pre-industrial Europe' including guilds.[57] Using game theory, Avner Greif verified the role of merchant guilds in protecting the property rights of foreign merchants from the state.[58]

What was the economic performance of *shijŏn* in the Chosŏn dynasty? We have not found any study evaluating *shijŏn* to be efficient. Most existing studies on *shijŏn* have only emphasized the distributional conflicts generated by their monopoly right to trade specified commodities and their right to prohibit illegal traders of the commodities (*kŭmnanjŏnkwŏn*).

However, the positive aspects of the *shijŏn* should be recognized. A number of government offices, local governments and members of the royal family and other powerful families were engaged in rent-seeking; the *shijŏn* community helped protect the interests of its members from such rent-seeking in some degree. The government bought the goods it demanded from the *shijŏn*, and this procurement system reduced the problem of high-pressure sales. When Greif emphasized the role of merchant guilds in securing property rights, these rights were for foreign merchants engaged in international trade.[59] Although this context differs from that of Korea, the role of *shijŏn* in securing property rights is interesting. Greif pointed out the contract enforcement function of merchant guilds in medieval Europe.[60] Considering that the Chosŏn government had the role of contract enforcement in domestic trade, *shijŏn* did not have a substantial need for such a function. However, *shijŏn* could have a role in contract enforcement with the trading government. Moreover, the central government tried to mobilize *shijŏn* to establish order in the Seoul market.[61] The government absorbed the commercial surplus through *shijŏn* by levying tax and corvée labour, which was cost-saving. In sum, we should consider both the distributional and efficiency approaches.

Which was larger, aggregate social benefit or the cost of *shijŏn*? *Shijŏn* had a weak role in contract enforcement, and generated distributional conflicts. *Shijŏn* had no active role in the development of the market institution. The social costs of *shijŏn* seem to have outweighed its social benefits in the eighteenth century when the trade volume of private merchants grew and the *shijŏn* monopoly right to trade the specified commodities was strongly enforced. However, we are not sure which was larger before the seventeenth century when the *shijŏn* monopoly right was absent or was not strongly enforced. We need to pay attention to the evolution of *shijŏn* in response to institutional change. *Shijŏn* evolved while responding to the needs of the economy. According to Greif, 'a merchant guild that had facilitated trade in the late medieval period was transformed into a monopolistic organization and hindered trade expansion during the pre-modern period'.[62] We also argue that Korea's *shijŏn*, which had facilitated trade in the early Chosŏn dynasty, transformed into a monopolistic organization and hindered trade expansion in the late Chosŏn dynasty. *Shijŏn* were built for promoting urban commerce, and grew as the Seoul market expanded. The monopoly right was strengthened in the late seventeenth century, and was weakened by the policy to further liberalize urban commerce, namely the enactment of *Shinhae t'onggong*, in 1791.

Shijŏn also had positive roles similar to those of the European merchant guild, but lacked their economic significance. Why were the roles of merchant communities in Korea different from those in Europe? We argue that the main reasons were the differences in the political system, economic integrating principle and international environment. Eighteenth-century Korea had a centralized bureaucratic state and a small international trade. *Shijŏn* was a top-down institution created and licensed by the state, and it engaged in domestic trade in which contract enforcement was guaranteed by the state. Under such conditions, *shijŏn* had little incentive to seek innovation and build efficient institutions. Though *shijŏn* had internal regulations, those seldom included penal provisions on unfair or illegal trading activities.[63]

As mentioned in the first section, Kaesŏng merchants, who engaged mostly in long-distance domestic and international trade, were innovative. They were independent of government. Private merchant communities seem to have had a more positive role in economic development than government-patronized merchant communities. If the Chosŏn state had not been able to provide a stable environment for trade, Kaesŏng merchants might have organized a bottom-up institution similar to the guild of medieval Europe, and played a similar role.

We presume that the merchant communities of Japan, China and Taiwan had more positive roles than those of Korea. The expanding domestic market of Japan in the eighteenth century fostered numerous merchant houses. Competition among domains and between domains and the *bakufu* (shogunate) made possible the relative autonomy of merchant groups. *Daimyōs* (domain lords) initially attempted to establish self-contained economic units, much as had the Chosŏn rulers; however, under the system of alternate residence and the expanding national market, they had no other choice than to act like the mercantile rulers of Europe. The role of *daimyōs* in pouring the surplus of peasants into the national market contributed to market expansion. They promoted import substitution and export to gain hard currency from a trade surplus. The early modern Japanese economy shared with early modern Europe the important advantage of being a 'world economy' and could be called a 'small world economy'. Within such a prosperous small world economy, a multilateral reputation mechanism by the merchant guilds, *kabu nakama*, could be successfully enforced.[64] Tokugawa Japan achieved dramatic economic development on the basis of this small world economy in spite of its prohibition on overseas trade and its extremely small foreign trade. In contrast, the same system of managing foreign trade imposed a serious disadvantage in market development on Korea, where a different economic integrating principle prevailed.[65]

China had the same political system as Korea, but it had a larger domestic market. This huge market size was favourable to the development of merchant communities. Chinese merchants' communities (*hang* or *hanghui*) show a parallel pattern with those of Chosŏn, that is, the two-sided character of a top-down institution created by the state and an association formed through merchant initiative in order to protect themselves from the government's arbitrary exploitation. However, they had developed voluntary merchant associations such as *huiguan* or *gongsuo* in the sixteenth century. Compared to Chosŏn Korea, Qing China had many more merchant communities which performed economic functions for trade more actively. The Chosŏn government, like the Qing government, came to recognize some merchant associations officially. However, no merchant association in the three Northeast Asian countries acquired a legal status such as corporation before the introduction of Western laws.[66] The merchant communities in Taiwan seem to have been more vigorous than those of Korea around the eighteenth century, which is credited to the vigorous trade between Taiwan and mainland China, as explained in Lin Yu-ju's chapter in this book.

Should we say, then, that the Korean case is peculiar? We do not think so. We argue that the Korean case was a typical Northeast Asian type. The political system of Tokugawa Japan was different from that of premodern China in the respect of rule by a warrior caste and decentralization, which resembled the European feudal system. The huge domestic market size of China reduced the harm of the tribute system to market development. Therefore, we argue that, compared to their counterparts in China and Japan, the Korean merchant communities better reflected the influence of the Northeast Asian characteristics of a central bureaucratic political system and an international environment governed by the Chinese tribute system.

The key hypothesis behind the 'Great Divergence' debate is that up to that point, the levels of economic development at the two ends of Eurasia were much more equal than previously assumed.[67] For this reason, we need to pay attention to not only differences but also similarities between East and West. Though the merchant communities of Chosŏn Korea were significantly different from those of Western Europe in many respects, the former also had some of the same positive roles as the latter. Several conditions of institution, culture and international environment in Western Europe were favourable to the take-off to modern economic growth. The economic development of Korea lagged behind that of China and Japan in the eighteenth century, but the gap was not substantial. Although Korea had a low urbanization rate and low money stock per GDP, it had a high density of population and local periodic markets. Korea developed a culture of record-keeping, and had about 10,000 private elementary and middle schools, namely *sŏdang*, around 1800; this was similar to the numbers of *terakoya*, their Japanese counterparts also known as 'temple schools'. Moreover, *sŏdang* served a smaller number of students than did *terakoya*. A few scholars have argued that eighteenth-century Korea may be called early modern. It had achieved a considerable degree of agricultural technological development, market growth, institutional development and human capital accumulation, thus paving the way for the transition to modern economic growth. These were the internal factors behind the catch-up and economic development of Korea in the twentieth century.[68]

Appendix: List of *Shijŏn* Guilds in Alphabetical Order

ch'egyejŏn	체계전	髢髻廛
ch'igyejŏn	치계전	雉鷄廛
ch'imjajŏn	침자전	針子廛
chŏjŏn	저전	猪廛
chŏyukjŏn	저육전	猪肉廛
ch'ŏlmuljŏn	철물전	鐵物廛
ch'ŏlsangjŏn	철상전	鐵床廛
ch'ŏngmiljŏn	청밀전	淸蜜廛
chapch'ŏljŏn	잡철전	雜鐵廛
chapkokchŏn	잡곡전	雜穀廛
chijŏn	지전	紙廛
chinsajŏn	진사전	眞絲廛
chisangjŏn	지상전	紙床廛
chogdurijŏn	족두리전	簇頭里廛
chongjajŏn	종자전	種子廛
chŏngnŭngdongmojŏn	정릉동모전	貞陵洞毛廛
chŏngnŭngdongsangjŏn	정릉동상전	貞陵洞床廛
chŏngp'ojŏn	청포전	靑布廛
chŏnjogjŏn	전촉전	箭簇廛
chŏnmojŏn	전모전	典毛廛
chŏnnipchŏn	전립전	氈笠廛
chŏp'ojŏn	저포전	苧布廛
choripchŏn	초립전	草笠廛
hamijŏn	하미전	下米廛
hamojŏn	하모전	下毛廛
haphoejŏn	합회전	蛤灰廛
hŭngnipchŏn	흑립전	黑笠廛
hwap'ijŏn	화피전	樺皮廛
hyejŏnggyochabjŏn	혜정교잡전	惠政橋雜廛
koch'ojŏn	고초전	藁草廛
kurigaesangjŏn	구리현상전	九里峴床廛
kyŏng'yŏmjŏn	경염전	京鹽廛
majŏn	마전	馬廛
manggŏnjŏn	망건전	網巾廛
mangmunsangjŏn	망문상전	望門床廛
map'omijŏn	마포미전	麻浦米廛
map'oyŏmjŏn	마포염전	麻浦鹽廛
munoemijŏn	문외미전	門外米廛
munoemojŏn	문외모전	門外毛廛
myŏnjajŏn	면자전	綿子廛
myŏnjujŏn	면주전	綿紬廛
myŏnp'ojŏn	면포전	綿布廛

myŏsangjŏn	묘상전	妙床廛
naejangmokchŏn	내장목전	內長木廛
naeŏmuljŏn	내어물전	內魚物廛
naesegijŏn	내세기전	內貰器廛
naeshijŏjŏn	내시저전	內匙箸廛
nammunoeyŏmjŏn	남문외염전	南門外鹽廛
nammunsangjŏn	남문상전	南門床廛
oejangmogjŏn	외장목전	外長木廛
oeŏmuljŏn	외어물전	外魚物廛
oesegijŏn	외세기전	外貰器廛
oeshijŏjŏn	외시저전	外匙箸廛
p'ajajŏn	파자전	笆子廛
p'ilsangjŏn	필상전	筆床廛
p'ojŏn	포전	布廛
p'osangjŏn	포상전	布床廛
paektangjŏn	백당전	白糖廛
paengnipchŏn	백립전	白笠廛
pogmajegujŏn	복마제구전	卜馬諸具廛
rijŏjŏn	이저전	履底廛
rijŏn	이전	履廛
ryangdaejŏn	양대전	涼臺廛
saengsŏnjŏn	생선전	生鮮廛
sanghamokkijŏn	상하목기전	上下木器廛
sangjŏn	상전	床廛
sangmijŏn	상미전	上米廛
sangmojŏn	상모전	上毛廛
semuljŏn	세물전	貰物廛
shinsangjŏn	신상전	新床廛
soch'aejŏn	소채전	蔬菜廛
sŏgangmijŏn	서강미전	西江米廛
songhyŏnmojŏn	송현모전	松峴毛廛
sŏnjŏn	선전	立 廛 or 縇廛
sujinsangjŏn	수진상전	壽進床廛
sŭnghyejŏn	승혜전	繩鞋廛
tojajŏn	도자전	刀子廛
tongsangjŏn	동상전	東床廛
tŭngjajŏn	등자전	鐙子廛
ŭijŏn	의전	衣廛
ujŏn	우전	牛廛
ŭnjŏn	은전	銀廛
yinsŏkchŏn	인석전	茵席廛
yŏmsangjŏn	염상전	鹽床廛
yŏmsujŏn	염수전	鹽水廛
yŏnch'ojŏn	연초전	煙草廛
yongsansimokchŏn	용산시목전	龍山柴木廛
yŏnjukchŏn	연죽전	煙竹廛
yugijŏn	유기전	鍮器廛

Source: *Takchiji* (Oep'yŏn, Book 2, P'anjŏksa, P'andobu)

Glossary

bakufu	ばくふ	幕府
chaeshinje	재신제	財神祭
changsi	장시	場市
chapse	잡세	雜稅
chinbae	진배	進排
chŏn	전	廛
Chŏnggu yoram	청구요람	靑邱要覽
Chŏngjo	정조	正祖
Chosŏn	조선	朝鮮
daimyō	だいみょう	大名
gongsuo		公所
Haeju	해주	海州
haengsu	행수	行首
hagongwŏn	하공원	下公員
haim	하임	下任
hang		行
hanghui		行會
Hankyŏng chiryak	한경지략	漢京識略
huiguan		會館
hwan'gok	환곡	還穀
Hyŏnsŏngmyo	현성묘	顯聖廟
ilbang	일방	一房
jubi	주비	注比
k'an	칸	間
Kabo Reform	갑오개혁	甲午改革
kabu	かぶ	株
kabu nakama	かぶなかま	株仲間
Kaesŏng	개성	開城
Kanggyŏng	강경	江景
kit	깃	衿
koku	こく	石
kongnang	공랑	公廊
Koryŏ	고려	高麗
kugyŏk	국역	國役
kŭmnanjŏnkwŏn	금난전권	禁亂廛權
kunjung	군중	軍中
Kwanu	관우	關羽
kye	계	契
Kyŏngguk taejŏn	경국대전	經國大典
Man'gi yoram	만기요람	萬機要覽
Masan	마산	馬山
Mencius	맹자	孟子
mumyŏng chapse	무명잡세	無名雜稅

mup'unjŏn	무푼전	無分廛
myŏnhŭkryejŏn	면흑례전	面黑禮錢
myŏnju	면주	綿紬
Nammyo	남묘	南廟
narye	나례	儺禮
ojwa	오좌	五座
ŏm	엄	广
ŏŭm	어음	於音
p'ojŏndoga	포전도가	布廛都家
P'yŏng'yang	평양	平壤
P'yŏngshisŏ	평시서	平市署
pang	방	房
pangsangsi	방상시	方相氏
pangse	방세	房稅
pibang	비방	裨房
Pibyŏnsa tŭngnok	비변사등록	備邊司謄錄
pobusang	보부상	褓負商
sambang	삼방	三房
Samgukji	삼국지	三國志
samjwa	삼좌	三座
sang'im	상임	上任
sanggongwŏn	상공원	上公員
sanshinje	산신제	山神祭
Seoul	서울	漢城 or 漢陽
shi	시	市
shihaengsu	시행수	時行首
shijŏn chinsuje	시전진수제	市廛鎭守祭
shijŏn	시전	市廛
Shinhae t'onggong	신해통공	辛亥通共
shipjwa	십좌	十座
so	소	所
sŏdang	서당	書堂
sŏm	섬	石
sŏnsaeng	선생	先生
taebang	대방	大房
taedong law	대동법	大同法
taehaengsu	대행수	大行首
Takchiji	탁지지	度支志
terakoya	てらこや	寺子屋
to	도	都
toga	도가	都家
tojung	도중	都中
toso	도소	都所
toyŏngŭi	도영위	都領位
tsubo	つぼ	坪
Wŏnsan	원산	元山
yang	양	兩

yangban	양반	兩班
Yejo	예조	禮曹
yejŏn	예전	禮錢
yibang	이방	二房
Yŏngjo	영조	英祖
yŏngŭi	영위	領位
Yŏnjo Sillok	영조실록	英祖實錄
yugjubijŏn	육주비전	六注比廛
yugyŭijŏn	육의전	六矣廛
yup'unjŏn	유푼전	有分廛
za	ざ	座

3 RICE, TREATY PORTS AND THE CHAOZHOU CHINESE LIANHAO ASSOCIATE COMPANIES: CONSTRUCTION OF A SOUTH CHINA–HONG KONG–SOUTHEAST ASIA COMMODITY NETWORK, 1850S–1930S

Choi Chi-cheung

From the mid-nineteenth century to around the 1960s, a Xiang-Le-Xian-Shan *jiao* (Hong Kong-Singapore-Bangkok-Swatow trading network) existed. It was established by Chaozhou merchants who were mainly engaged in transnational rice trade.[1] Until the mid-nineteenth century Chaozhou merchants played an essential role in the rice business in Hong Kong and Southeast Asia. According to Suehiro Akira, three of the five rice exporters in the late nineteenth century, and five out of eight in the first half of the twentieth century in Bangkok were merchants from Chaozhou.[2] Chen Shouzhi shows that in the 1950s and 1960s in Hong Kong, more than 50 per cent of the rice was imported from Thailand, where 80 to 90 per cent of the rice mills were run by the Chaozhou Chinese. Not only were the majority of licensed rice importers Chaozhou Chinese, but rice distributors, wholesalers and retailers were also mostly Chaozhou natives[3] (see Table 3.1).

Table 3.1: Number and percentage of Chaozhou rice merchants in Hong Kong in the 1950s

Year	No. of licensed importers	No. and % of Chaozhou importers	No. and % of Chaozhou wholesalers	No. and % of Chaozhou retailers
1950–4	17	10 (59%)	–	–
1957–60	38	19 (50%)	10/39 (26%)	1895/2400 (80%)

Source: Chaozhou Chamber of Commerce in Hong Kong, *Xianggang Chaozhou Shang-hui Chengli Sishi Zhounian ji Chaoshang Xuexiao Xin Xiaoshe Luocheng Jinian Tekan* [A Special Volume Commemorating the Fortieth Anniversary of the Hong Kong Chaozhou Chamber of Commerce and the Completion of the New Building of the Chaozhou Merchant School] (Hong Kong: Chaozhou Chamber of Commerce, 1961), pp. 12–13, 40, 41.

This trading network required three elements, namely the product, the consumer and the trading agents. This chapter will first discuss where the supply of rice came from; whether Swatow (hereafter, Shantou) and its hinterland, the prefecture from which many Chaozhou merchants hailed, provided a sufficient consumer base; and whether rice, being the sole product, could sustain the trade. The second part of the chapter will focus on the organization and trading network of one of the earliest transnational Chaozhou rice import-export companies. Rice is a subsistence commodity, and profit from its sale relies on various factors, ranging from the taste of the consumers to natural conditions, many of which cannot be controlled by the trading firm. This chapter therefore attempts to point out that it was important for the firm to establish an integrated business strategy in order to reduce risk and maximize profits. The Shantou treaty port, the Chaozhou migrants and the trading network provided a nested trading environment for the development of successful rice merchants in the late nineteenth and early twentieth century.

Trading Environment: Shantou Treaty Port in the Late Qing Period

Before the 1920s the business environment in Shantou can be summed up as follows: it was a transit port that did not sustain itself as a consumption centre. Weak control by the state facilitated competition between two major financial factions in the local Chamber of Commerce. Finally, trading relied heavily on trading networks that linked the area with Hong Kong and Southeast Asia as well as with Shantou's hinterland.

The Area under the Jurisdiction of Shantou
Shantou, located on the eastern coast of Guangdong province, was not a prime trading port that colonial empires sought to open before the mid-nineteenth century. As pointed out by a contemporary writer,

> Europeans were first attracted to the neighborhood of Swatow shortly after the opening of the Port of Amoy [Xiamen] in 1842, but the first attempt at forming a trading depot was made at the island of Namoa [Nan'ao], where opium-vessels were anchored for several years.[4]

The treaty port opened by the Tianjin Treaty in 1858 was not in Shantou but in the wealthier Chaozhou-fu, the prefectural seat thirty-five miles north of Shantou. When the Shantou port was legally opened to foreign trade in 1860, replacing the strongly anti-foreign Chaozhou-fu, it was not an ideal consumer centre nor was there a strong pre-existing trading infrastructure to facilitate the city's rapid growth.

In 1860, Shantou was a city of less than 1.08 square kilometres.[5] On 29 May 1860, John E. Ward of the Legation of the United States in Shanghai reported to Lewis Cass, the Secretary of State, that the trade in Shantou was increasing.

> Swatow, long before it was opened by [the Tianjin] Treaty, was the resort of Chinese pirates, and foreign opium smugglers. No mandarin of high rank had ever resided there, and the petty officials were easily induced for a very small sum to permit the trade to go on, without any treaty rights. It was of course very irksome to these traders and officials to be compelled to pay the duties required by treaty, and to lose the profits of the illicit trade.[6]

The absence of a high-level official and traditional indigenous power in its early days encouraged competition among rival sub-dialect groups (different varieties of Chaozhou), dialect groups (Chaozhou and Hakka) and business factions. It also encouraged merchants to seek alternative trading routes that might reduce the cost of transportation and allow them to pay lower transit taxes.

As a treaty port, Shantou was not itself a consumption centre of subsistence commodities. Even as late as the beginning of the twentieth century, the entrepôt had a population of less than 30,000.[7] The *Decennial Report* of the Maritime Customs for the decade 1882 to 1892 noted that

> facing the sea-front are long rows of roomy godowns, where incoming and outgoing merchandise finds temporary rest. But away from the waterside there are only an insignificant collection of houses, a few shops where pewter is beaten into various shapes, and here and there a temple or a guild-hall.[8]

Therefore, rice, like other consumption commodities, was re-exported to inland consumers. Until the late nineteenth century, trade was constrained by the port's limited facilities and hindered by the competition presented by alternative trading routes.

In 1919, the US Department of Commerce reported that Shantou lacked modern financial facilities. Banking and exchange had to rely on Hong Kong.[9] Therefore, Shantou was not one of the four southern Chinese cities recommended to American businessmen by the Department of Commerce.[10] Its geographical size and limited number of warehouses also disallowed long-term storage of commodities. The British consul reported in 1863 that

> [The above-mentioned] vessels average from 150 to 300 tons and are better suited to the coasting trade under Chinese charter than our larger vessels, which require more cargo than can be stowed at Swatow, where there is a paucity of godown room; goods have, therefore, to be retained up country until the vessel is ready to take in her cargo, when it is sent down in boats which go at once alongside to put it on board. Nearly all the vessels employed in the trade of the port, exclusive of course of steamers, are chartered by Chinese merchants, who much prefer these smaller crafts; which are besides chartered at a lower rate than either British or American vessels.[11]

Though Shantou was the primary maritime port in the region, serving a huge hinterland, the port also faced tremendous competition with other native ports, like Zhelin and Zhanglin, along the south-eastern coast of China. In 1907, along the coast of Chaozhou prefecture there were fourteen native transit stations and substations where many Chinese vessels anchored.[12] (see Figure 3.1). The rate paid at these stations was about half of that levied at the Shantou Maritime Customs. These ports were easily accessed by small Chinese vessels, and their cargo could reach inland consumers much faster and cheaper than through the Shantou port.[13]

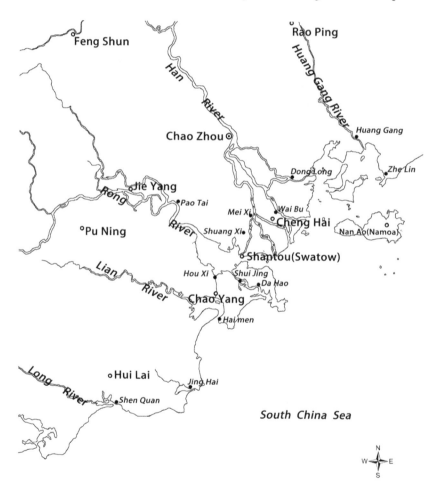

Figure 3.1: Location of the fourteen transit stations in 1907.

From the perspective of trade and taxation, British consuls at Shantou never failed to point out the disadvantages foreign merchants encountered. Nicholas Dennys described the situation thus:

> Proximity to Hong Kong enables the large native firms to conduct their own importing business more cheaply than it can be done for them by Europeans, whilst the staple trade of the Port – the importation of Beancake coastwise from the North and the export of Sugar – is also conducted in correspondence with Chinese agencies at Newchwang [Yingkou], Chefoo [Yantai] and Shanghai. Hence the foreign firms established at Swatow are chiefly occupied in obtaining charters and insurance for Chinese principals ... The merchant-princes of former days are being superseded by astute and cheaply-living Cantonese or Singapore Chinese.[14]

He stressed that 'trade is almost entirely in the hands of native or Singapore Chinese, the foreign community is very small'.[15] Many Chinese also chartered vessels under flags of continental (non-British) states at a cheaper rate.[16] As Chinese citizens, they could dispose of their cargo in ports between Hong Kong and Shantou, choose a shorter and more direct route to the corresponding inland markets and pay lower transit dues at the native customs stations.[17]

The inaccessibility of Chaozhou prefectural city, where many wealthy merchants lived, and the hostility of the inland Chinese towards Westerners forced foreign importers and exporters to hire native agents to conduct business inland. In addition to this, transit taxes had to be paid a few times more on foreign commodities when they left the treaty port area. Hence, the price of foreign goods was higher than that of native products.

The British consul, on the one hand, emphasized that the spirit of the treaty was such that all foreign goods, whether transported by the foreigners themselves or by their Chinese agents, should be exempted from all kinds of taxes, transit dues or *baoxiao* donations, after tariff payment at the treaty port.[18] On the other hand, they argued that the treaty port area should include the Chaozhou prefectural seat and that the Chinese government should not collect any *lijin* or transit dues (sometimes known as *likin*) within the treaty port area.[19] When the city area of Shantou expanded rapidly in the early twentieth century, the Maritime Customs extended its jurisdiction to include coastal native customs and interior cities that were also accessible to foreign merchants. However, before 1934 when a strong state stepped in,[20] the local political economy was dominated by merchant factions.

Merchants and Factions

Shantou is an alluvial sandbank situated at the southern exit of the Han River. The trading port was founded in the nineteenth century. Most of its merchant guilds were established after the 1860s. The first commercial guild, the Zhang-Chao Huiguan (Association of the Zhangzhou and Chaozhou Merchants), was established in 1854 by Fujianese and local Chaozhou merchants. The association was the centre for various kinds of transactions, including shipping, Chinese medicine, rice and food, matches, and remittance and exchange.[21] In 1867, as the influence of the Fujian merchants shrank, the Chaozhou merchants established their own Association, Wan Nian Feng (literally, prosper for ten thousand years). The Association dominated most of the businesses in Shantou. For example, the Maritime Customs reported as follows:

> In 1881 some Swatow merchants were heavily fined for disregarding a Custom rule affecting the examination of cargo. The guild took the matter up with spirit. And an anonymous note called upon merchants to cease all import and export trade unless their demands were complied with. In that particular instance the guild was unable to gain the point for which it was fighting, but trade was kept completely at a standstill for 15 days, pending its decision to submit.[22]

It was this group that formed the Shantou Chamber of Commerce in 1901. The Association's membership was composed of many occupational guilds. The dominant guilds were those for remittance and money exchange. The Association was also called Liuyi Huiguan (Association of Six Counties) as it was founded by merchants from six Chaozhou counties.

The Association was divided into two equally influential cliques: the first was formed by merchants from Haiyang (or Chao'an), Chenghai and Raoping, all of whom spoke with a Chaozhou accent. The second was formed by merchants from Chaoyang, Puning and Jieyang, most of whom spoke with a Chaoyang accent. Each clique had its own organization, regulations and ritual celebrations.[23] The Association had a board of forty-eight member firms representing equally the two cliques. Every month each clique would choose two employees from its twenty-four representative firms to run the Association's daily affairs and accounts. The two cliques continued to compete for control of the Association until the 1930s.[24] Their rivalry was further enhanced in the early twentieth century when the Shantou Chamber of Commerce was given the power to regulate the issuing of private notes by local firms; this practice continued until 1934 when the central government made illegal the use of private notes, and enforced state-issued tender as the only legal currency.[25]

Competition occurred not only between the two Chaozhou cliques, but also among different dialect groups. There were two non-Chaozhou associations established before 1891, namely the Guangzhou Association (1871) and the Hakka Association (1882). Both Associations were small and not especially influential, and they were mainly involved in business negotiation and welfare for members.[26] During the late nineteenth to early twentieth century, fourteen regional associations (*tongxianghui*) were founded. Besides one created by Cantonese speakers from Guangzhou and Zhaoqing prefectures, ten were established by the Chaozhou dialect group and three by those from Meizhou. Most of the associations established in Shantou, at least until 1925, were dominated by Chaozhou dialect speakers.

In 1925, in order to balance the Chaozhou/Shantou merchants' power, the Nationalist Party united the middle and small merchants in Shantou to found a *shangmin xiehui* (association for the merchants and the people). One year later, chambers of commerce of different counties in the Chaozhou and Meizhou regions together founded a joint association in Shantou. According to a directory published in 1934, there were in total sixty-nine guilds and twenty regional associations in Shantou. They controlled 4,465 firms engaged in eighteen different types of business.[27]

In other words, before the intervention of the central government, the treaty port was dominated by the merchants and their alliances. Whereas rivalry between the two Chaozhou cliques centred on control of local finance, that between the Hakka and the Chaozhou merchants was instigated by three inter-dialect group disputes which occurred in the early twentieth century.[28] In 1902, the Hakka association, which represented merchants from the eight hinterland Hakka dialect counties, announced publicly that they belonged to a different ethnic group, and therefore should be exempted from the *baoxiao* contribution which was levied only on Chaozhou merchants.[29]

Rivalry among the Shantou merchants demonstrated a complementary oppositional relationship (see Figure 3.2). For instance, the Chaozhou merchants established an alliance that allowed them to dominate the commercial sector in Shantou, and on the other hand the cliques strove to control the guild (later the Chamber of Commerce). Such a relationship was further enhanced by not only the dialect/accent they spoke, but the type of business in which they engaged.

Shantou City

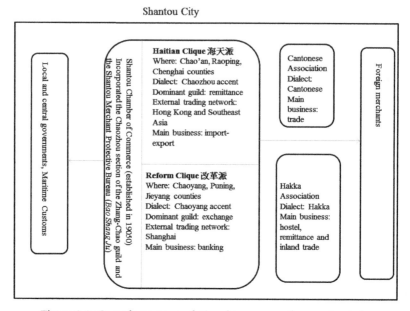

Figure 3.2: Complementary relationships among the merchants in Shantou before 1934.

The Trade

Shantou was a commercial city. Its prosperity relied heavily on shipping, remittance and exchange, and on import and export.[30] Besides embroidery (Chaozhou *chousha*, a kind of drawn work on silk products), industry was not significant. These four dominant businesses – shipping, remittance and exchange, import-export and embroidery – linked Shantou's fate with its hinterland and with Hong Kong and Southeast Asia.

Shipping, Import and Export

Shipping can be divided into two categories, that is, the transportation of human beings and the transportation of goods. The number of ferries and junks entering or leaving the Shantou port increased from 161 ships carrying 59,236 tons in the 1860s, to more than 2,000 ships transporting over 2,000,000 tons in the 1920s, and then to 4,010 ships handling 5,735,828 tons of cargo by the 1930s (see Table 3.2). These figures indicate that the number of legal transactions, as well as the amount of goods imported and exported and the movement of people, all increased rapidly, especially from 1890.

Table 3.2: Movement of goods and passengers

Year	No. of ships	Tonnage	Customs (Total customs, in taels)	No. of immigrants	No. of emigrants	Total over-seas settlers
1860	161	59,236	6,176,293	–	–	
1870	414	204,968	9,455,850	–	22,282	
1880	866	627,886	21,275,667	28,013	38,005	9,992
1890	1,649	1,573,542	25,070,981	50,062	65,475	15,413
1900	2,127	2,185,554	40,030,734	71,850	93,640	21,790
1910	2,592	2,960,744	54,014,382	108,833	132,928	24,095
1920	2,496	2,921,531	65,497,958	68,525	109,251	40,726
1930	4,010	5,735,828	108,879,407	94,726	123,724	28,998

Sources: Zhongguo Haiguan Xuehui Shantou Haiguan Xiaozu and Shantou Shi Difang Zhi Bianzhuan Weiyuanhui Bangongshi (eds), *Chao Haiguan Shiliao Huibian* [Collection of Historical Documents Relating to the Chaozhou Maritime Customs] (Internal reference, 1988), pp. 136–279; hereafter, *Chao Haiguan Shiliao Huibian*.

Before Shantou was established as a treaty port, smuggling was a way of life for the people who lived in the region. Opium, which occupied about 75 per cent of the revenue from imports until 1910, was gradually replaced by the importation of cotton yarn, sugar and canned food. In 1926, the major commodities imported from overseas were rice, sugar, cotton and charcoal. The major goods exported to overseas countries were paper and peanut oil. Major goods imported from other parts of China included bean cake, cotton yarn, beans and peanuts; goods exported to other ports of China included paper, sugar and clothes. Products were transported inland by local steamship companies. As we can see from Table 3.3, the Shantou–Hong Kong–Southeast Asia trade occupied about 70 per cent of the total trade return. This trade route was mainly dominated by the Haitian clique (merchants from Chao'an, Chenghai and Raoping) of the Shantou Chamber of Commerce. However, trade with Shantou's hinterland and Shanghai was mainly in the hands of the Reform clique, which included merchants from Chaoyang, Puning and Jieyang. This situation continued until the 1930s.

Table 3.3: 1926 trade returns of Shantou port (Haiguan tael)

	Import	Export	Total	Percentage
Hong Kong	4,436,535	733,911	5,170,466	16.90
Siam	3,776,891	2,929,592	6,706,483	21.90
Straits settlements	307,728	4,819,929	5,124,657	16.80
Vietnam	2,097,286	2,223,188	4,310,474	14.10
Sub-total	10,605,460	10,706,620	21,312,080	69.7
Other China ports	8,641,133	678,359	9,319,492	30.3
Total	19,246,593	11,384,979	30,631,572	100

Source: *Xin Shantou* [New Shantou] (Shantou: Shantou Shi Shizhengting, 1928), p. 10

Shipping also transported large numbers of Chaozhou and Hakka people over-seas and brought them back. In the 1850s, Shantou replaced Xiamen as the major port for transporting coolies. Coolie trade agents ran hostels and coolie kens, sent their brokers to Shantou's hinterland to recruit coolies, and trans-ported these recruits to Shantou via local steamships. The coolies were kept waiting in the hostels until the day for departure. From 1852 to 1853, more than 3,450 coolies were sent through the coolie business. In 1855, the number increased to 6,300. After Shantou became a treaty port, more and more Chi-nese from inland districts went overseas via this port. The Chaozhou merchants, mainly from the Chaozhou accent district, acted as agents of foreign shipping companies or themselves were owners of ships. They provided an efficient infra-structure to assist these new emigrants; services ranged from transporting them from their hometowns to assisting them to settle in the host country. According to a set of 1935 statistics, there were about two million Chaozhou Chinese living in Southeast Asia (see Table 3.4). They constituted 40 per cent of the Chaoshan region's population of five million.[31] The large number of Chaozhou people liv-ing overseas resulted in a great demand for Chaozhou goods as well as the need for sending back remittance through various agencies.

Table 3.4: Number of Chinese in Southeast Asia

	Chaozhou	Hakka	Hainanese	Cantonese	Hokkien	Other	Total	Year (note)
Malaya (including Singapore)	364,232	437,407	157,649	641,945	827,411	(a) 71,850 (b) 48,094 (c) 12,754 (d) 17,065 (e) 36,260	2,614,667	1947 (1)
(Singapore)	157,188	40,036	52,192	157,980	289,167	(a) 742 (b) 9,477		1947 (2)
Indonesia	87,812	200,736		136,130	554,981	188,409	1,190,014	1930 (3)
Burma				33,990	50,038	(f) 67,691 (e) 41,875	193,594	1931 (4)
Siam	1,297,000	370,000	278,000	162,000	162,000	46,000	2,315,000	1955 (5)
Vietnam	30%			50%	20%			1936 (6)
(Cholon)	41.12%	10.6%	3.4%	41.12%	7.8%			1950 (7)

(a)= Guangxi (b)= Fuzhou (c)= Fuqing (d)= Xinghua (e)=Other (f)=Yunnan

(1) *Nanyang Nianjian* [Directory of Southeast Asia], section 10, 'Huaqiao' (Singapore: Nanyang Baoshe, 1951), p. 77.

(2) *Nanyang Nianjian*, section 10, 'Huaqiao', pp. 78–9.

(3) *Nanyang Nianjian*, section 10, 'Huaqiao', p. 140.

(4) *Nanyang Nianjian*, section 10, 'Huaqiao', p. 168.

(5) V. Purcell, *The Chinese in Southeast Asia* (London: Oxford University Press, 1965), p. 82.

(6) Huaqiao Zhi Bianzuan Weiyuanhui, *Huaqiao Zhi: Yuenan* [Gazetteer of Overseas Chi-nese: Vietnam] (Taipei: Huaqiao Zhi Bianzuan Weiyuanhui, 1958), p. 51. Estimated percentage of total ethnic Chinese in Vietnam. According to *Nanyang Nianjian*, the

Indochinese peninsula, including Vietnam, Cambodia and Laos, had a total of 418,000 Chinese in 1931. Most of them lived in Cholon and Saigon (p. 211).

(7) Percentage of ethnic Chinese in Cholon, Vietnam. See *Huaqiao Zhi: Yuenan*, p. 51. In 1949, Cholon had a Chinese population of around 400,000.

Remittance and Exchange

Before the Second World War, there were only a few modern financial organizations in Shantou. Local native banks played an important middleman role in small-scale transactions. They were able to minimize the influence of large-scale financial institutions such as the Shanxi remittance banks before the 1911 revolution and foreign banks such as the Hong Kong and Shanghai Banking Corporation until the late 1930s.[32] The only foreign bank, the Japanese Taiwan Bank, did not play an active role in foreign exchange and remittance. The Bank of China (Zhongguo Yinhang) and Bank of Guangdong Province (Guangdong Sheng Yinhang), both of which established branches in Shantou in the 1920s, did not have any branches in Thailand, from where most of the remittances came (see Table 3.5). The agencies that managed remittance before 1934 were always the *xinju* (letter bureaus), *yinhao* (traditional Chinese banks), *shanghang* (business companies) and *shuike* (individual agents). A publication of 1933 describes the situation before the Second World War thus:

> The most convenient and safe method is to ask an individual agent to bring back the money. The remittance agents founded by different counties in Shantou are as many as the fish in the river. The remittance business is very prosperous in Shantou. It is the major power in the Chaoshan economy.[33]

Table 3.5: 1933 remittances (in millions of dollars)

	Siam	Singapore	Vietnam	Other	Total	% of national share
1930	40	30	10	20	100	
1931	35	28	10	17	90	22
1932	32	25	6	12	75	21.9
1933	27	25	6	12	70	20.5
1934	20	18	4	8	50	20.2

Wu Chengxi, 'Shantou di Huaqiao Huikuan' [Shantou's Overseas Chinese Remittances], *Huaqiao Banyuekan* (Nanjing), 99–100 (16 January 1937), pp. 13–14.

Yinhao or native banks were important as they had more capital. They usually assisted the remittance houses whenever the latter had financial difficulties. Of the remittance sent from Thailand, 90 per cent was sent through the Chaozhou *yinhao* via Hong Kong to Shantou. Before 1934, many of these *yinhao* could issue paper notes themselves. In 1946, there were in total eighty-five remittance agents, of whom fifty-five belonged to the remittance guild. Of these eighty-five agents, thirty handled more than four billion yuan a month or forty-eight billion yuan a year.[34]

In 1933, there were seventy-one agencies that could issue paper currency. They were closely related to the two merchant cliques in the Chamber of Commerce, one controlling the remittance guild and the other the banking guild (see Table 3.6). These included seventeen traditional Chinese banks registered with the remittance guild (*qianye gonghui*); twenty-three business firms registered with the remittance guild; eighteen traditional Chinese banks registered with the banking guild (*yinye gonghui*); and thirteen business firms registered with the banking guild.

Table 3.6: Competition between the Haitian group and the Reform group

	Haitian	Reform
Region	Chao'an, Raoping and Chenghai counties	Chaoyang, Puning and Jieyang counties
External connection (remittance, trade)	Hong Kong and Southeast Asia	Hinterland and Shanghai
Financial guilds	Yinye gonghui	Qianye gonghui
Number of paper currency agencies registered with the guild	18 native banks 13 business firms	17 native banks 23 business firms
Business scale	Transnational merchants	Many petty merchants

Sources: Xie Xueying, *Shantou Zhinan* [Handbook of Shantou)] (1933; repr. Shantou: Shantou Shishi Tongxunxie, 1947), pp. 82–3; *Xin Shantou* (Shantou: Shantou Shi Shizhengting, 1928), pp. 19–20; reports in *Nanyang Siang Pau* [Nanyang Shangbao], 3 March 1934, p. 13; 16 November 1934, p. 14; 17 November 1934, p. 14; 29 November 1934, p. 12; 8 December 1934, p. 12; 10 December 1934, p. 12; *Nanyang Siang Pau Sunday Edition*, 30 December 1934, p. 1; Imperial Maritime Customs, *Decennial Report, 1882–91*, pp. 537–40.

In brief, before 1934, the local government in general was weak and not able to manage the monetary system. The local economy and socio-political affairs were controlled by two major cliques, founded on the basis of dialect, place of origin and occupation. These two groups, which either had close ties with Hong Kong and Southeast Asia, or with Shanghai and Shantou's hinterland, competed for control of the city through influence over the Shantou Chamber of Commerce. Most businesses in Shantou were of small scale (see Table 3.7). To influence the local society, they had to affiliate with large corporations, such as Yuan Fa Hang and Kin Tye Lung, which had the major portion of their businesses in Hong Kong and Southeast Asia. Shantou was only one of their many branches.[35] These companies and the local banks associated with them enjoyed the liberty of issuing paper notes until 1934. Instead of sending the capital back to Shantou to settle business transactions or as remittances, they could use the accumulated foreign currency or currency by weight to reinvest in other areas in Hong Kong and Southeast Asia. The reputation of the firm, the social credit of the merchants and real estate holdings functioned as guarantees, allowing capital circulation backed only by a small amount of currency by weight. As a result, most of the business firms in Shantou operated on the basis of a comparatively small amount of capital (see Figure 3.3).

Table 3.7: Average capital of major firms in 1933

Type of firm	No. of firms	Total capital(yuan)	Average capital of firms
Exchange	256	1,024,000	4,000
Remittance	55	1,100,000	20,000
Native bank	58	14,500,000	250,000
Import-export	70	7,000,000	100,000

Sources: Rao, *Chaozhou Zhi Huibian*, section 4, 'Shiye Zhi: Shangye', pp. 1299–300.

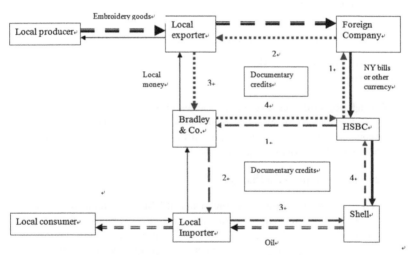

Figure 3.3: Transactions with special notes on the flow of currency and bills.
Source: F. H. H. King, *The History of the Hong Kong and Shanghai Banking Corporation, vol. 2, The Hong Kong Bank between the Wars and the Bank Interned, 1929–1945* (Cambridge: Cambridge University Press, 1988), pp. 496–7.

The central and local governments had never successfully implemented a strong and efficient financial mechanism in Shantou. Even after 1921 when Shantou became an administrative city, the city was always under the influence of the merchants, many of them engaged in the import-export business. Before the Great Depression, plantations and the trading of rice and other local products in Southeast Asia had attracted many Chinese from this region either as contract labour or as members of a family-run trading firm. Shipping of goods and passengers and the remittances sent back from overseas members were major businesses affecting the livelihood of the city and its hinterland. Business firms opened by the Chaozhou merchants in Southeast Asia also provided financial services, particularly in remittance and production. After the First World War, some of them established modern banks that were tightly affiliated with their family businesses. Before China adopted a legal tender with gold as its standard in 1934, they took advantage of favourable exchange rates between silver and gold. By issuing paper notes, they did not need to provide currency by weight to settle their transactions in Shantou. Moreover, because of their social credit and their overseas connections, these companies expanded the volume of their transactions with only limited reserves of currency by weight. To make this possible, a transnational integrated trading strategy was needed. Shantou's trading environment before the twentieth century was the foundation that shaped the business formation of the Chaozhou transnational merchants who, on the books, were rice importers and exporters.

Rice Trade in Shantou: A Historical Review

The Maritime Customs in Shantou stated in its *Decennial Report* for the years 1902 to 1911 that

> although rice is cultivated to a considerable extent in the surrounding districts, the supply does not suffice to meet local requirements, and large quantities of this cereal are consequently imported each year, principally from the Yangtze ports, but also at times, as in 1910, when the Yangtze crop failed, from Siam.[36]

Ten years later, it reported a change.

> [L]ess rice is now imported, both from Siam and Wuhu, than formerly, but more flour; the local rice crops are, owing to the hilly nature of the hinterland, never sufficient for the needs of the large population, but the area under cultivation is smaller than it was at one time, as the cultivation of fruit and vegetables is more profitable, and they are in great demand among emigrants abroad ... Swatow rice is preferred to any other on the market.[37]

We learn from these two reports that the district itself was not only an area that consumed rice, but was also an area that produced it. The supply and demand of imported rice therefore relied on the harvest of the grain, the population and the utility of land. We also learn that at least until the beginning of the twentieth century, most imported rice came from central China. Southeast Asian rice, particularly from Thailand where the majority of the Chinese and the Chinese rice merchants from Chaozhou were based, constituted only a small percentage of imported rice.

Various factors contributed to the amount of rice imported through Maritime Customs. When a good harvest was reported, there was no need to import rice.[38] However, Chaozhou is a district prone to typhoons in the summer, when the second cropping of rice is about to yield. This poses a threat to the rice crop. Before the twentieth century, the Chaozhou region was reported to have experienced three serious natural disasters respectively in 1864–5, 1885–6 and 1898.[39] Typhoons brought heavy rain. As a result, '[in 1864] immense embankments were broken down, and fields and villages inundated in all directions'.[40] In response to the bad harvest, rice importation increased in the subsequent year.

The second reason was social unrest, in particular, the Taiping rebellion from 1850 to 1865. The rebels forced many capable cultivators to leave their land, and with certain cities threatened by the rebels, rice dealers were not motivated to distribute rice even though it would sell at a good price. Disruption of inland trade routes as well as the bankruptcy of hinterland farming encouraged importation of rice from Southeast Asia. It also encouraged illicit importation through alternative routes where rice and other subsistence products could reach the consumer directly. Political decisions regarding rice production in central China also affected the amount of rice imported as well as the decision to import rice from Southeast Asia.[41]

The third reason was related to land utilization. In the 1880s and 1890s, two important trends in the Chaozhou district could be observed. Firstly, cultivable land was switched over from producing rice to growing sugar cane,[42] and later, when the sugar market was threatened by Java in the global and domestic markets,[43] to fruits and vegetables.[44] Sugar was always one of the major export items from Chaozhou. 'While there will be more sugar to export, there will be more rice to import'.[45] In 1885, when many farmers in Sichuan province used their fields to grow opium, more Chaozhou farmers moved to plant sugar cane. Even in 1889 when the London market for sugar diminished, there was still a high demand locally because sugar was widely used in festivals and rituals in the Chaozhou district. Exports of sugar gradually became insignificant in the late 1880s. However, during the same period there was higher demand for local goods, fruits, vegetables and other foodstuffs needed by overseas populations.[46] In other words, the farmers were responding to the changing global market. Hence, land utilization made way first for sugar cane and later for fruits and vegetables. The scarcity of cultivable land for growing rice was perhaps the result of the importation of rice even though no serious natural disasters, except in 1885 and 1886, were reported during this period.

The second trend was that people in Chaozhou started to change their preference in rice from the late 1890s. This was probably because of the dwindling confidence in the supply and quality of native rice, and the changed eating habits that accompanied returning migrants. The Sino-Japanese War in 1894 forced the closure of Yangtze ports. The price of rice was further elevated by the fact that many local dealers engaged in speculation. In 1897, it was reported that importers from northern ports wet the grain in order to increase weight.[47] As a result, local people lost their trust in native grains. In 1898, importing from Yangtze ports stopped completely, driving local suppliers to look for alternatives from Bangkok and Saigon.[48] It was also during this period when many early migrants, merchants or coolies, returned home after ten to twenty years overseas. These two factors – forced changes in eating habits combined with new tastes brought back by returned members of the community – facilitated the rice trade with Southeast Asia (see Table 3.8).

Table 3.8: Rice imported through the Maritime Customs

Year	Quantity (picul)	Value (Haiguan tael)	Price per picul	Page in source
1865	644,621	1933,863	3	p. 193
1870	3,654	5,280	1.44	p. 194
1875	0	0	0	p. 195
1880	22,902	31,437	1.37	p. 196
1885	80,033	105,963	1.32	p. 197
1890	128,388	188,214	1.47	p. 198
1895	248,752	403,589	1.62	p. 199
1900	72,520	181,202	2.5	p. 200
1905	8,521	0	0	p. 201
1910	1,116,936	0	0	p. 202
1915	391,882	0	0	p. 202
1920	6,578	0	0	p. 203
1920	736,896	0	0	p. 203
1930	1,397,872	0	0	p. 204

Source: *Chao Haiguan Shiliao Huibian*, pp. 193–204. Note: information about the value of commodities is given for some years before 1900 and not provided after that year.

In brief, as a subsistence commodity, rice in Chaozhou came from three sources: local production in Chaozhou, central China and Southeast Asia. The increase of grain importation was not necessarily because of rice yield failure. The rapid decrease in local rice production was due to a growing interest in planting sugar cane, vegetables and fruits, which were cheaper to grow, less labour intensive and more profitable. These changes in land utility worked well with the population landscape where many capable men preferred to seek their fortunes overseas. The supply of rice also changed from central China to Southeast Asia by the end of the nineteenth century. This was probably because of the long-term high price of the former and the decreasing quality and quantity of native rice in the 1890s. It was, however, also related to the altered eating habits introduced by the return of the overseas Chaozhouese, who had learned to prefer Southeast Asian fragrant/jasmine rice.[49]

Maritime customs in Shantou levied a higher tariff on goods imported through the treaty port, compared with native transit stations at which Chinese vessels could anchor more easily and where it was easier for dealers to have access to consumers. As a result, the rice trade was unstable, high in risk and probably less profitable. Yet, many large transnational Chaozhou merchants in the mid-nineteenth century engaged in the rice import and export business. The following section examines their trading strategy, which was devised in response to the trading environment in Shantou.

The Chaozhou Transnational Rice Merchants and the Structure of their Trade

After 1684, when the Qing court lifted its ban on maritime trade, many villagers from the Chaozhou area engaged in the business of importing rice from and exporting local products to Southeast Asia.[50] Along with the blooming of maritime trade and the loosening of Chinese emigration policy in the mid-nineteenth century, many Chaozhou villagers established trading companies and settled in Hong Kong and Southeast Asia. Kin Tye Lung (hereafter KTL), the oldest existing Chinese import and export company in Hong Kong, was one such example.

KTL was founded in the early 1850s by Chen Xuanyi and his brother Xuanming, who came from the Chen lineage of Qianxi village in Raoping county, Chaozhou prefecture.[51] The Chens in Qianxi claim to be descended from the same founding ancestor. In the 1840s, members of the Chen extended family, including Xuanyi, left the village to work as crew on ships owned by the Yuan Fa Sheng company.[52] A few years later, Xuanyi, probably with his brother and cousins, accumulated enough money to set up their own import-export business in Hong Kong. The company, KTL, imported rice from Siam to Hong Kong and Guangdong province and exported local products to Southeast Asia.[53] From rice import-export, the company expanded its operations to Shantou and Southeast Asia[54] and into rice milling, remittance, shipping and banking. The business was very successful, partly because of the demand for local Chinese products by Chinese immigrants; for remittance services for the Chinese labourers in Southeast Asia; and for rice in southern China.

In the last quarter of the nineteenth century, the Chens quickly rose, both socially and economically. The family continued to acquire land in their hometown and in Shantou,[55] joined Chinese high society in Hong Kong and southern China,[56] and established associate companies respectively in Bangkok (Wanglee, 1871), Singapore (Tan Seng Lee, 1885; later renamed Tan Guan Lee), Shantou (Tan Wan Lee) and Saigon (Kien Guan Lee). By the turn of the century, they were one of the wealthiest families in the Chaozhou region. Members of the family enjoyed high social status in Shantou, Hong Kong, Singapore and Bangkok.[57]

The expansion of KTL's external business network and internal structure was closely related to the trading environment in Shantou. In the 1870s and 1880s when the two Chen brothers dispatched their sons to open associate companies[58] in Saigon, Bangkok and Singapore, they were looking to establish a vertical business network, integrating rice production and distribution. As shown in Figure 3.4, unhusked rice was collected by the associate company's agents in Bangkok and Saigon and brought to the rice mills owned by the company. The milled rice was then exported to Singapore and Hong Kong, where part was auctioned by the wholesalers for local consumption, and the remaining part re-exported to Shantou where KTL's associate company redistributed it to local wholesalers. While the importer controlled the source (that is, the physical production of the rice), he/she could not control the wholesale and retail markets. They had to sell the rice on receipt of the goods. It was the wholesalers who benefited more as they could wait for a good buying price before purchasing and a good selling price before putting the goods onto the market. Therefore, many of the staff of the rice importing company also participated in the wholesale business. Usually, the credit term the rice importer gave the wholesaler was one month. Thus, the wholesaler had better flexibility in managing their finances.

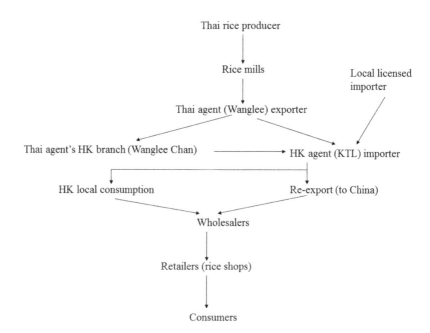

Figure 3.4: Vertical expansion: KTL's position in the rice trade

For example, in the 1930s, at least three rice wholesalers in Singapore were regular clients of Tan Guan Lee. These three wholesale companies, Wu Rong, Chang Xing and Qian Xing, were owned by staff of the financial section of Tan Guan Lee. Wu Rong was founded by the five major shareholders of Tan Guan Lee: besides Chen Ken'gou, they were Chen Shouzhen, Chen Shouming and Chen Shouhe of the Wanglee company in Bangkok and Chen Shouzhi of KTL in Hong Kong. Chang Xing was founded by the sons of Chen Liangchen, the treasurer, while Qian Xing was founded by the daughter and son-in-law of Chen Lizhi, general manager of Tan Guan Lee. Managers of these companies were professionals who 'had good brains and good knowledge of the rice market'.[59] However, like Tan Guan Lee, the respective financial sections of these wholesale companies were controlled by close agnates of the managing directors. For instance, Wu Rong's general director was Chen Ken'gou. Its rice manager, though surnamed Chen, was not a member of the Chen lineage in Qianxi, but Wu Rong's treasurer, Chen Chengqu, was.[60]

Though these related wholesalers had to compete with other wholesalers at public auctions, they had two advantages: first, they had inside information on the quality and quantity of the rice, and second, they possessed better credit terms, for they could prolong their payment as they were also in control of the accounts of the rice importer, Tan Guan Lee. Moreover, members of the financial department had a special account with their names registered in Tan Guan Lee's account books. For instance, Chen Ken'gou's account name was Gouji, and Chen Lishan's was Shanji and Qiongji. Having internal accounts enabled the members to benefit from the transfer of capital between the importer and the wholesaler.

To reduce transaction costs, KTL, like other transnational import-exporters, engaged in businesses related to rice transaction. For instance Wanglee, founded in 1871, expanded within a few years from being a company that provided milled rice to KTL, to having its own import-export business. It also acted as an agent for the Norway BK Steamship Company, transporting cargo and passengers from the ports of Bangkok, Singapore, Haikou (in Hainan), Hong Kong and Shantou.

Figure 3.5 shows the internal structure of Tan Guan Lee, KTL's associate company in Singapore. Before the Japanese occupation, the company employed more than fifty regular employees. The company was headed by a general manager, who was assisted by a managing director. Four managers (geteo; Mandarin, *jiazhang*) managed four respective sections of the company. These were rice, Southeast Asian products, miscellaneous products (from China) and shipping. Rice and shipping were the most important. Under the section managers were four clerks, responsible for writing letters and reports, and four stock keepers, responsible for the company's warehouses. Besides the manager, the shipping section had a separate team of five clerks who handled documents written in English. The company was the agent for more than twenty-five types of rice, salted fish, salt, sugar, spices, tea and dried fruits. It was also the agent for Thoresen & Co. Ltd. In the 1930s, KTL and its associate companies ran a fleet of four cargo ships, which plied the waters between Bangkok, Singapore and Malaya, and two cargo and passenger ships, which shuttled between the ports of Xiamen, Shantou, Hong Kong, Haikou, Rangoon and Singapore.

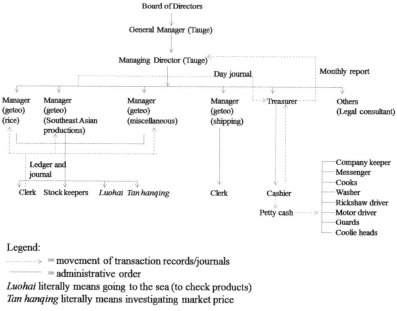

Legend:

--------> = movement of transaction records/journals

———— = administrative order

Luohai literally means going to the sea (to check products)

Tan hanqing literally means investigating market price

Figure 3.5: Internal structure of Tan Guan Lee. Source: Interview with Mr Chen Songrui, 28 December 1995. Songrui was the son of Ken'gou, who was Managing Director (Tauge; Mandarin, *toujia*) of the company from the 1920s to 1946. Songrui was cashier and treasurer of the company until the 1970s, when he retired.

The associate companies also ran insurance companies in Bangkok and Hong Kong, owned warehouses in all port cities and engaged in remittance as well as native banking in Shantou. As mentioned in the previous section, passenger traffic was one of the most profitable businesses beginning in the late 1870s. The British consul in Shantou pointed out that the 'Chinese passenger was an important branch of the business of the port'.[61] The large quantity and importance of passenger trade was mentioned, without exception, almost every year in the consular trade report. Figures 3.6 and 3.7 show the rapid growth of passengers and vessels entering and departing from the port. For the import-export companies, it was essential to integrate these different sectors of business in Shantou as well as overseas. In Shantou they imported rice and Southeast Asian products; they exported sugar, fruits and vegetables; and they conveyed passengers to and from Shantou. To facilitate these transactions, they founded their own financial establishments and built storage space. To serve the passengers' needs, KTL, like the Chinese herbal medicine company Eu Yan Sang,[62] became involved in remittance.

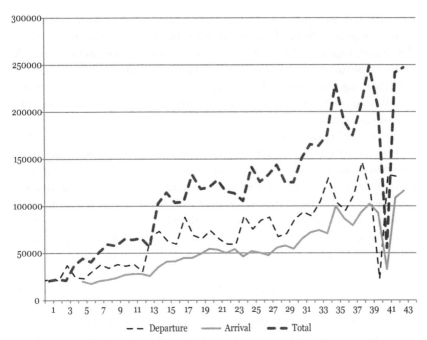

Figure 3.6: Number of passengers arriving at and departing from the Shantou port, 1873–1933. Source: *Chao Haiguan Shiliao Huibian*, **pp. 238–51 (passengers to and from Hong Kong, the Straits Settlements, Bangkok, Saigon, Sumatra and other places).**

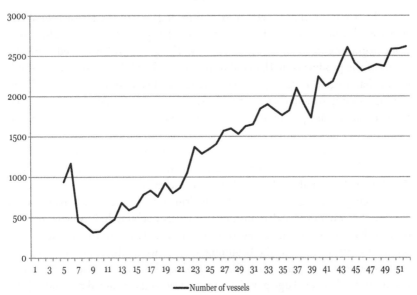

Figure 3.7: Number of vessels entering and leaving the Shantou port, 1861–1910. Source: *Chao Haiguan Shiliao Huibian*, **pp. 136–40.**

After 1933, many Southeast Asian countries tightened their immigration procedures. Migration from China to Southeast Asia was not as easy as before. For this reason, together with the restriction of rice exportation and the unstable economic situation in southern China, Chinese firms that were headquartered in Hong Kong, Singapore or Bangkok reoriented their business focus. This withdrawal from the Shantou business sector allowed them to survive through the 1934 financial crisis.

Before 1934, small-scale businesses with little capital were established through mutual guarantee and through their affiliation with various associations. They had strong networks with their hometowns and their business included the transportation of passengers, sundries and remittance between inland areas and the treaty port. For them, the damage of the 1934 financial crisis was mitigated because they were able to retreat inland with only a very limited loss. The business environment in Shantou before 1934, including weak political governance, strong factional politics, reliance on overseas financial organizations, the small scale of capital and the freedom to issue paper notes provided a vital means for the economic growth of the city. However, these factors did not provide any roots for development. Therefore, when the economic crisis occurred and when a strong central government stepped in, business firms in Shantou with strong affiliations to either overseas or inland parties could simply retreat from the business arena because they had little to lose.

Conclusion

The Chaozhou merchants, who were mainly engaged in the transnational rice trade, established a Hong Kong–Singapore–Bangkok–Shantou trading network beginning in the nineteenth century. The grain, which moved from the hands of the producers in Thailand to the stomachs of the consumers in South China, had to go through various commercial and technological systems. From milling to shipping and then to storage, rice merchants needed a well-informed network to contain potential risks and reduce transaction costs. With limited capital, they needed trusted cross-border partners to handle advances and guarantee credits. Under these conditions, a system of *lianhao* associate companies was founded. These are companies whose shares are cross-owned by close relatives but are financially and administratively independent.

This chapter, using a Chaozhou family firm and its associate companies as an example, has attempted to demonstrate that it was 'rice' and the businesses derived from it that facilitated the success of this trading network in the second half of the nineteenth century to the beginning of the twentieth. Importation of rice from Southeast Asia, particularly Siam, was shaped by (1) the yields in Shantou's vast hinterland, whose large population produced and consumed rice and (2) the supply of rice from central China. As a subsistence commodity, the price of rice was closely monitored by the government, which meant that the trade alone was not always profitable. To reduce risk and increase trading efficiency, 'rice' importers in Shantou engaged in various business activities; they organized shipping agencies; imported and exported other goods and transported passengers; managed godowns and warehouses for temporary storage; and established financial institutions. This integration of business activities required the efficiency of a well-structured trading network. Shantou, before 1934, provided an environment that made this integrated and structured business network possible.

Acknowledgements

The first draft of this paper was presented at the 16th World Economic History Congress, 9–13 July 2012, Stellenbosch University, South Africa. The author is grateful for the support of the Hong Kong Research Grant Council CRF project (CUHK5CRF11G) led by Prof. Leung Yuan-sheng and the 'Intra-Asian Trade during the "Long 19th Century"' panel led by Prof. Shiroyama Tomoko.

Glossary

baoxiao	報效
Chang Xing	長興
Chao'an	潮安
Chaoyang	潮陽
Chaozhou	潮州
Chaozhou-fu	潮州府
Chefoo [Zhifu]	芝罘
Chen Chengqu	陳成渠
Chen Ken'gou	陳肯構
Chen Liangchen	陳良臣
Chen Lishan	陳立珊
Chen Lizhi	陳立植
Chen Shouhe	陳守河
Chen Shouming	陳守明
Chen Shouzhen	陳守鎮
Chen Shouzhi	陳守智
Chen Songrui	陳松銳
Chen Xuanming	陳宣明
Chen Xuanyi	陳宣衣
Chenghai	澄海
chousha	抽紗
Cizong	慈宗
Da Hao	達濠
Da Shi Ji	大事記
Dong Long	東隴

Eu Yan Sang [Yu Ren Sheng]	余仁生
Fujian	福建
Fuqing	福清
Fuzhou	福州
geteo [jiazhang]	家長
Gouji	構記
Guangdong Sheng Yinhang	廣東省銀行
Guangxi	廣西
Guangzhou	廣州
Haiguan	海關
Hai Men	海門
Haikou	海口
Hainan	海南
Haitian	海天
Haiyang	海陽
Hakka [Kejia]	客家
Han River	韓江
Hokkien [Fujian]	福建
Hou Xi	後溪
Huang Gang	黃岡
Huaqiao	華僑
Hukou	戶口
Jieyang	揭陽
Jing Hai	靖海
Kien Guan Lee [Qian Yuan Li]	乾元利
Kin Tye Lung [Qian Tai Long]	乾泰隆
lianhao	聯號
likin [lijin]	釐金
Liuyi Huiguan	六邑會館
Luohai	落海
Mei Xi	梅溪
Meizhou	梅州
Namoa [Nan'ao]	南澳
Nanyang Nianjian	南洋年鑑
Newchwang [Niuzhuang]	牛庄
pao hsiao [baoxiao]	報效
Pao Tai	砲台
Puning	普寧
Qian Xing	乾興
Qianxi	前溪
qianye gonghui	錢業公會
Qing	清
Qiongji	瓊記
Raoping	饒平
shanghang	商行
shangmin xiehui	商民協會
Shanji	珊記

Shantou [Swatow]	汕頭
Shen Quan	神泉
Shiye Zhi	實業志
Shuang Xi	雙溪
Shui Jing	水井
shuike	水客
Sichuan	四川
Tan Guan Lee [Chen Yuan Li]	陳元利
tan hangqing	探行情
Tan Seng Lee [Chen Sheng Li]	陳生利
Tan Wan Lee [Chen Wan Li]	陳萬利
tauge [toujia]	頭家
Tianjin	天津
Tongwen	同文
tongxianghui	同鄉會
Wai Pu	外埔
Wan Nian Feng	萬年豐
Wanglee [Hong Li]	黌利
Wei Tai Hou	蔚泰厚
Wu Rong	五榮
Wuhu	蕪湖
Xiamen [Amoy]	廈門
Xiang-Le-Xian-Shan jiao	香叻暹汕郊
Xinghua	興化
xinju	信局
Yangtze River [Yangzi jiang]	揚子江
Yantai	煙台
Yingkou	營口
yinhao	銀號
yinye gonghui	銀業公會
yuan	元
Yuan Fa Hang	元發行
Yuan Fa Sheng	元發盛
Yunnan	雲南
Zhang-Chao Huiguan	漳潮會館
Zhanglin	樟林
Zhangzhou	漳州
Zhaoqing	肇慶
Zhelin	柘林
Zhongguo Yinhang	中國銀行
Ziyin	子因

4 THE RISE OF CHINESE COMMERCIAL DOMINANCE IN EARLY MODERN SOUTHEAST ASIA

Kwee Hui Kian

Scholars of Southeast Asia have been baffled by the economic dominance of Chinese sojourners and settlers during the colonial era as well as that of the ethnic Chinese in the postcolonial period. They usually explain the phenomenon as a result of sponsorship by European regimes or because of Confucian-derived business characteristics and practices among the Chinese or a combination of both factors.[1] In recent years, more attention has been paid to the workings of the *gongsi* and other socio-religious organizations and their effects on Chinese entrepreneurship in Southeast Asia from the late eighteenth to early twentieth centuries. Several scholars including myself have argued that these allowed for the pooling of capital and labour, mutual loans at low interest rates and a platform for the settlement of internal disputes among people of the same surname as well as home village and/or district.[2]

In other words, similar to the Sephardic Jews, Greeks, Maghribi Arabs, Armenians, Chettiar Indians and other longstanding diasporas in global history, the Chinese appear to have built their commercial empire in Southeast Asia by utilizing kinship, home-region ties and religious institutions. These forms of symbolic capital enabled a system of trust and sanction, mutual assistance, knowledge sharing and business networking among these trading communities.[3] Although their ventures, unlike those of European merchants and companies, were not supported by home governments, these 'merchants without empire' could apparently boost their commercial activities in the host societies through what Douglass North calls 'informal institutions'.[4] In fact, various historians have argued that the European counterparts could only gain an edge over them by using political and military power to create monopolies or near-monopolies.[5]

But before we dwell on an over-celebration of the significance of these informal institutions, it is worthwhile to consider the argument of Jonathan Israel. In his study of the Sephardic Jews in the early modern Atlantic, Israel proposes that their success had little to do with 'traditional Jewish forms of community and social organization'. Instead, it was the confluence of historical events – the rise of early modern European maritime empires, the resettlement of large numbers of Sephardic Jews in the Ottoman Empire and their subjection to religious persecution by the Spanish Inquisition from the late fifteenth century – which enabled them to develop an 'unmatched capacity to span religious and cultural divides as well as continents and oceans' in the sixteenth century. Israel concludes that, '[n]o matter how important structural characteristics [read: communal and social organizations] were, historical context, as always, was decisive'.[6] Israel's statement thus serves as a useful reminder when assessing the success of trade diasporas: how much merit should be given to their socio-cultural institutions? How far did developments and conjunctures in history enable the dominance of certain commercial groups over others?

With these research questions in mind, this chapter examines the Chinese economic expansion in pre-nineteenth-century Southeast Asia. It particularly seeks to understand how the Chinese came to predominate over their erstwhile mercantile rivals including the Indians, Arabs, Javanese, Bugis, Malays and other communities by the eighteenth century. In its analysis, this chapter discusses both the historical development of the regional commerce as well as the forms of symbolic capital of these migrant entrepreneurs. It argues that although the latter factors did render the Chinese strong players, the peculiar trajectories of the political economy gave these sojourners and settlers decisive advantage over other regional and long-distance traders in early modern Southeast Asia.

The Southeast Asian Commercial World before the Late Seventeenth Century

At the advent of what Anthony Reid calls the 'Age of Commerce' (1450–1680), various groups were trading actively in Southeast Asia.[7] Some were indigenous to the region, such as the Javanese, Malays, Mons, Chams and other Austronesians. Others hailed from further regions, including the Gujaratis as well as the Arabs and their creoles who were mostly based in north-western parts of India. The Coromandel Indians also expanded their mercantile activities from south-eastern India to the Malay Peninsula and north coast of Java during the later Chola dynasty (1070–1279). These western and southern Asians primarily brought a range of Indian cotton textiles and opium to exchange for the fine spices of clove, nutmeg and mace as well as commodities such as tin, gold and elephants. Meanwhile, merchants from South China started sailing to Southeast Asia from the twelfth and thirteenth centuries, importing earthenware, iron products and other manufactures and buying up pepper, aromatic woods and other exotics.[8]

During the fifteenth and sixteenth centuries, while the long-distance merchants handled the trunk trade from their home regions to Southeast Asia, those indigenous to the region specialized in inter-island and coastal trade. In fact, a kind of division of labour was at work: regional shippers would ferry local commodities from the production regions to Melaka and other emporia where long-distance merchants usually stationed themselves. The latter would buy up these products for export to their home regions and also sell the regional traders the goods they imported.

Because of their knowledge of the wider world and trans-regional commerce, prominent Chinese, Indian and West Asian merchants, as well as their creole descendants, enjoyed special patronage from the indigenous rulers. They were often appointed as royal agents to handle the kings' shipping trade with their home regions. From the second half of the sixteenth century, long-distance traders also started venturing beyond the entrepôt region to the secondary ports and the production areas of the coveted commodities. Tamil traders were gaining dominance in tin-yielding areas in Kedah, Perak, Ujung Selang (today's Phuket) and neighbouring Bangeri. They and their Gujarati counterparts had also become active on the north coast of Java and in South Sulawesi and the Moluccas region buying spices and other products. To acquire pepper more efficiently, Chinese traders were not only calling at the secondary ports of Jambi, Palembang and Patani but also taking up residence in pepper-growing uplands in the interior of south Sumatra by the turn of the seventeenth century.[9]

For their supplies of fine spices and other Asian merchandise, the European markets had thus far depended on the trade connections between western India, the Arabian Peninsula and the Mediterranean Sea. In their quest for cheaper sources of Asian products, Portuguese explorers discovered the route to Asia via the Cape of Good Hope during the late fifteenth century. Within a few decades they captured the entrepôts in the Persian Gulf, western India and Southeast Asia – namely Hormuz, Goa and Melaka – as well as a handful of secondary ports. Although the Portuguese initially attempted to shut out the Muslim traders – their enemies in the Crusades – this religious animosity was quickly abandoned in the interests of trade. There was in fact more concern to keep out rival European traders who would compete in the sales of Asian goods in the home market. Asian traders now had to buy *cartazes* (passes) at Portuguese-controlled ports to avoid harassment from the armed European cruisers. Otherwise, they could carry on their business as before.

Following in the trail of the Portuguese, other Europeans also started arriving in Southeast Asia from the mid-sixteenth century. The Spanish and Dutch set up their bases in Manila and Batavia respectively. As was the case with the Portuguese, they encouraged Asian traders to call at their enclave settlements and also instituted the pass system. By contrast, the English, French, Danes and other northern Europeans operated as one among many trading groups. During the late sixteenth and early seventeenth centuries the European presence did not cause major shifts in the Southeast Asian trade but only made it more flourishing.[10]

If we were to take a snapshot of the Southeast Asian commercial world in the mid-seventeenth century, the picture would be as follows. In the trans-regional sector, Chinese junk shipping remained unrivalled in the trunk trade between China and Southeast Asia in spite of the bases the Portuguese and Dutch had established in Macao (1557) and Taiwan (1624) respectively. Although a part of the European supplies for Asian goods were now channelled through the southern African coast, the South and West Asians were still actively carrying out trade between the Indian subcontinent and Southeast Asia. The European injection of military force did little to curb the intra-Asian trade. In fact, the Portuguese, English, French and Danes commonly freighted ship space to these operators and sold them passes, enabling their trade with Southeast Asia with little harassment.[11]

Within Southeast Asia, the European enclave settlements of Melaka, Manila and Batavia might have had greater preference for Asian traders, but entrepôts under the control of indigenous rulers had a more cosmopolitan outlook. Ayutthaya, Banten, Makassar and Aceh were multi-regional and multi-ethnic hubs which welcomed all merchants, not only those from within Southeast Asia but also those hailing from Europe, the Middle East and both South and East Asia. By this time, the long-distance Asian traders were not only calling at these emporia but also the feeder ports. While Indians and Arab creoles tended to concentrate in the Bay of Bengal, the Malay coasts and Indonesian islands, the Chinese and other East Asian traders were clustering around port towns along the littoral zone of the South China Sea.

Nevertheless, the spread of their mercantile activities did not threaten those of their Southeast Asian counterparts. The general modus operandi for most long-distance merchants was to rely on the regional traders to market their imports and gather products from Sumatra, the Moluccas and other parts of the archipelago. Although the Mons and Bandanese had disappeared from the scene because of domestic political troubles, Malay and Javanese shippers continued to reign over the waters of island Southeast Asia from the eastern end of Nusa Tenggara to the western end along the Melaka Straits. Joining their ranks were the Acehnese, Bugis and other South Sulawesians as Aceh and Makassar developed into thriving entrepôts after the Portuguese conquest of Melaka. The Chams, Luzons and Bruneians also dominated the coastal trade of the Indo-Chinese peninsula and the Philippines islands.[12]

Chinese Commercial Expansion in the Late Seventeenth and Eighteenth Centuries

The Southeast Asian commercial scene experienced drastic changes from the late seventeenth century. For one thing, the Dutch East India Company (Vereenigde Oost-Indische Compagnie, henceforth VOC) engaged in multiple military actions in Makassar (1667), Mataram Java (1677, 1741–3), Banten (1682) and other polities and effectively imposed a monopoly over fine spices. In the course of the seventeenth and early eighteenth centuries, its personnel also extended its influence over other parts of the Malayo-Indonesian archipelago by interfering in internal politics in Jambi, Palembang, Johor, Padang and other polities. Their chief objective was to drive out unwanted trade competition or to install cooperative princes in ruling positions. Although the Company administrators did not exert direct control over most areas, they obliged the local kings and lords to deliver tin, pepper, rice, sugar and other commodities as tribute or at depressed prices. At times the Dutch also demanded that these rulers declare certain trade items as Company monopolies or close their ports to various groups of traders.

Outside the forced deliveries and circumscribed monopolies of the VOC, local rulers as well as traders from within and outside Southeast Asia could engage freely in commercial activities. During the late seventeenth and eighteenth centuries, the most phenomenal development was the extension of Chinese mercantile activities. Their junk shipping was at its nadir during the Ming-Qing transition but it recovered rapidly in the 1680s.[13] From the late seventeenth century, the Chinese migrants and their mixed-blood and localized descendants (*peranakan, mestizo, baba*) not only dominated the trade between China and Southeast Asia but also gradually came to play a key role in the inter-insular and coastal commerce. They also became the paramount mercantile force in most of the entrepôts and secondary ports and penetrated the hinterland markets in many parts of the region.

In the realm of inter-island trade, although the South Sulawesians, Malays and Javanese still enjoyed a strong presence, the shipping activities of the Chinese migrants and creoles increased rapidly in the course of the 1700s. By the end of the century they came to challenge the dominance of these regional trading communities. In Nusa Tenggara, for instance, the share of the Chinese in terms of shipping volume increased from less than 10 per cent in the 1720s to one-third, equivalent with the Malays and South Sulawesians, six decades later.[14]

As for littoral trade, although they could not rival the Bugis and Malay shippers on their home turfs, the Chinese and their mixed-blood descendants were more successful elsewhere. They effectively replaced the Chams along the Vietnamese coastline and Gulf of Siam.[15] Although they were not as numerous as the Javanese shippers on the northern *pesisir* (coastal area), the Chinese were the most important carriers in terms of shipping volume by the 1770s.[16] In the second half of the eighteenth century, the Spanish authorities might have shut out immigrant Chinese with six pogroms and other prohibitions but local-born mestizo Chinese who had converted to Catholicism were now presiding over the trade in Philippine waters.[17]

All the entrepôts in eighteenth-century Southeast Asia came to boost a substantial Chinese mercantile presence. Many lost the plural character of the previous centuries and underwent sinicization where the Chinese presided over the trade of all of the main commodities in the locale. The process was particularly palpable in the port towns that came under Dutch control such as Banten, Makassar and Melaka.[18] Among those which remained under indigenous rule, the ones located in the Indo-Chinese peninsula were also increasingly dominated by Chinese merchants. This included Ayutthaya, which had been among the most cosmopolitan cities in Southeast Asia in the previous century. Its Siamese rulers kept aloof of the Europeans after their participation in the 1688 coup and welcomed only Asian traders. Whereas many Indian and other foreign merchants used to serve as port-masters (*krom tha*) and foreign ministers (*phra-khlang*), by the early 1700s they had lost these positions to the Chinese.[19] During the eighteenth century, Ayutthaya became increasingly 'an outpost of the Chinese trading network rather than a major international entrepôt'.[20]

Besides harbour activities, the Chinese penetration into the trade of the hinterland and more isolated seas of Southeast Asia was nothing short of spectacular. By the early eighteenth century the rice bowl regions had practically fallen under their sway. They included central and east Java as well as the Mekong delta, Tonle Sap, Chantaburi and Trat. These spaces drew thousands of Chinese migrants from the 1660s. By assuming lordship or leasing whole districts in these regions from the local authorities, these traders were able to gain control over the rice trade.[21] Through their hold over the primary commodity they could also extend a trade monopoly over other key local products. In central and east Java, these included cotton textiles, tobacco and timber as well as cane and palm sugar. By the third quarter of the eighteenth century, they also rivalled the Malays in the trade of salt as they increasingly took up revenue farming in Pasuruan, Pamekasan, Sumenep and other salt-producing areas.[22]

The Chinese mercantile links also extended effectively into places producing commodities in demand by the China market. We have seen how the Chinese quest for pepper had brought them into the uplands of south Sumatra during the late sixteenth and early seventeenth centuries. The list expanded in the eighteenth century to include sea cucumber, tortoiseshell, seaweed, birds' nests, sandalwood and tin. Let us take maritime products for instance. In the seventeenth century, the Chinese were getting these sea products from the eastern Indonesian archipelago by working with Bugis, Makassarese and Malay middlemen. The latter would use the capital advanced by the Chinese to liaise with and buy the products from the Bajo people, who specialized in hunting turtles and gathering seaweed and sea cucumber. A century later, the Chinese started dealing directly with the Bajos, exchanging old iron or lengths of cloth in return for the marine commodities.[23]

In other words, there was a gradual development from multi-ethnic collaboration to a Chinese-dominated trading network. Similar transitions could be observed in the Chinese acquisition of birds' nests in Java and sandalwood in Timor.[24] In the tin fields of Ujung Selang and Ligor, where Coromandel Indians had previously dominated the purchase of the mineral in these Siamese vassal states, the Chinese replaced them as lessees of these tin fields and did smelting there while the Malays and Thais dug for the tin.[25]

So great was the demand for pepper, tin and other minerals that Chinese merchants also liaised with indigenous rulers to introduce Chinese workers where a local labour force was lacking. From the 1680s, and especially during the eighteenth century, these coolies were migrating by the thousands, growing pepper – sometimes together with gambier – in Hatien, Chantaburi, Trat, Brunei, Trengganu, Kelantan, Riau, Mentok, Melaka and Penang. Others undertook copper and zinc mining in North Vietnam and Burma, tin mining in Bangka and parts of the west coast of the Malay Peninsula, and gold mining in Pulai (Kelantan) and West Borneo. Naturally, the needs for provisions and tools of these miners and agriculturalists and other supplies were serviced by the Chinese traders, who also marketed their yields.[26]

Hence by the end of the eighteenth century, the Chinese and their creoles not only continued to preside over the shipping trade between China and Southeast Asia but had also gained a prominent position in the commercial world of the latter region. In terms of the inter-insular trade, their share was equal to, if not greater than, that of the Malays, Bugis and other regional players who had dominated the sector in the previous centuries. They also became paramount in the littoral trade of the South China Sea and also on the north coast of Java. On land, the Chinese were able to reign over other trading groups in most of the entrepôts in Southeast Asia and extended their networks into the hinterland of central and east Java, south Sumatra, west Borneo and the southern parts of the Indo-Chinese peninsula. Whereas there had been a more plural character in the intra-regional trade of Southeast Asia before the mid-seventeenth century, subsequent centuries saw the tremendous growth of the mercantile activities of the Chinese immigrants and creoles. They were gaining an edge over both long-distance traders and those from within the region.

Superior Commercial Methods and Institutions?

Various reasons have been proposed to explain the phenomenal expansion of the Chinese economic activities in Southeast Asia in the early modern period. Leonard Blusse argued that the symbiotic relationship elite Chinese merchants established with the indigenous rulers facilitated their ventures greatly. Chiefly by means of tax farming and leases of entire villages and districts from the political authorities, they were guaranteed first entry to rural markets and were also free to organize the production process in west Borneo, central and east Java, south-eastern Sumatra, the Malay Peninsula and the Riau archipelago.[27]

Other historians emphasized the Chinese readiness to integrate with the host society and itinerant trading methods. In her discussion about their ease in penetrating the upstream regions of Jambi and Palembang, Barbara Andaya notes that Chinese traders commonly picked up local languages and underwent religious conversion. They also married native women who not only helped take care of their shops but also occasionally accompanied the traders on their trips to buy up pepper and sell textiles in the interior. Andaya further remarked on the Chinese willingness to settle for slimmer profit margins and their peddling methods of operation. The latter enabled them to reach the producers and consumers directly and to gauge more accurately their tastes and preferences for textile designs.[28]

It is also observed that to lock in their access to commodities, the Chinese often offered goods and money to the producers and gatherers several months prior to the harvest periods and deliveries. This had become a common practice for securing rice, tobacco and other commodities in central and east Java by the turn of the eighteenth century. Similar provisions were extended to the hunters and gatherers of tortoiseshell and birds' nests in east Borneo and south Sulawesi during the eighteenth century.[29]

Besides these commercial methods, Chinese socio-cultural mechanisms aided their extension of networks into the hinterland and more remote parts of Southeast Asia. Chinese merchants based in coastal towns frequently gave low-interest loans or advanced goods to smaller-scale traders to retail imported goods and gather local products in the interior towns as well as more rural and isolated regions. Usually they entrusted the loans and goods to traders from the same home village and district or to those with identical surnames as these forms of symbolic capital allowed for social sanction against cheating behaviour and if necessary for appeals of adjudication by the elders (*gongqin, zuqin*). Should the debtor default on the loans or lose the advanced goods, village and surname ties made it more possible to track down his family members and demand compensation from them.

From the Batavia and Semarang Chinese Council archives, it can be seen that these native-place and clan ties were oftentimes formalized into urn-worship, temples and clan associations. These institutions further fostered affinities among the members by hosting regular occasions for socializing on the twice-monthly *zuoya* worshipping sessions, deities' birthdays, ancestral sacrifices during spring and autumn and in other festive seasons. They also provided low-interest loans from their coffers and temporary lodgings for member-traders on their premises – facilities that were most empowering for people with little means and connections.[30]

It is undeniable that these socio-economic practices aided the Chinese commercial activities considerably; however, they were not exclusive to the Chinese. Other mercantile actors engaged in similar methods. Since the fifteenth century, the Indian and Arab merchants had maintained close ties with the royal families in the Malay states and in Ayutthaya and Aceh, serving as their trade agents, *syahbandars* (port-masters) and tax farmers. These long-distance traders also customarily intermarried with the locals to aid their ventures in Southeast Asia.[31] In the seventeenth and eighteenth centuries, Gujarati and Coromandel merchants based in Kedah dispatched their agents in tin-rich Perak to secure prior access to the mineral supplies.[32] The Bataks, Malays, Acehnese, Minangkabaus, South Sulawesians, Javanese and other regional traders also did itinerant trade into more remote regions and similarly generated advanced credit to secure agricultural products and other commodities.[33]

Although they were latecomers to the regional commerce, the Europeans developed these small-scale trading skills over time as well. By the mid-seventeenth century English and Danish vessels would sail along the north coast of Java, putting their traders ashore at each harbour to sell textiles and opium to the local market vendors and fetching them upon return after several weeks.[34] During the eighteenth century the Portuguese and mestizos from Macao who sailed yearly to Goa, Malabar and Coromandel would also call at tin-producing regions on the west coast of the Malay Peninsula. They left money or merchandise there on credit, picking up the mineral on their return journey.[35]

In terms of symbolic capital and socio-cultural strategies, various Asian mercantile communities appear to have possessed institutions comparable to the Chinese native-place and clan bonding. One example was the Chulias – Tamil Muslims from the Coromandel coast – who had operated successfully for centuries in the Bay of Bengal and Melaka Straits. Accounting for why they had been able to compete effectively against the English private traders in the eighteenth century, Sinnappah Arasaratnam credited their cost-effective shipping operation that hinged on kinship and communal ties.

> Owners of ships and many of the crew had an interest in the cargo carried. The entire operation of equipping a ship, launching it and sailing it to its destination and back was a communal operation with most persons involved belonging to a clan network. Many of those who sailed in a ship would be linked in this way, others, in any case, were members of the broader Chulia community. The crew and laskars employed on

the ship were paid less in wages and permitted to engage in small ventures of their own. When a vessel was at anchor in a port, these people were engaged as labourers and artisans who worked as carpenters, caulkers, riggers and so on. In this way, the outfitting of a ship was considerably less expensive to the owner. Consequently the Chulias were known for their ability to operate with small profit margins and were difficult to compete against.[36]

Coromandel Hindu traders also had effective ways of resolving disputes among themselves. If both parties were members of the same caste, the heads of that caste were the arbitrators. Where they belonged to different castes, each party would choose three arbitrators to hear the case.[37]

Within Southeast Asia, regional peoples had also maximized their commercial potential by developing institutional innovations. In the early eighteenth century, the *matoas* (leaders) of the Wajorese – one of the Bugis entrepreneurial diasporas hailing from South Sulawesi – met in Makassar to ratify a set of legal codes to regulate Wajorese commerce and navigation in the Indonesian archipelago. So effective was this form of customary (*adat*) governance in facilitating, regulating and financing trade that large segments of the Wajorese society – elite and commoner, rich and poor alike – were able to engage in commerce overseas.[38]

In sum, the employment of revenue farming, itinerant trading, advanced credit and assimilation with local society to foster commercial activities were not peculiar to the Chinese traders. Many mercantile groups operating in Southeast Asia – whether they hailed from this or other parts of the world – engaged in similar practices. On closer scrutiny, the Chinese utilization of close affinities based on common clan and home regions to extend marketing networks also does not bear an exclusive stamp. Their Indian counterparts as well as other regional entrepreneurial communities possessed equivalent if not the same socio-cultural resources and used them adeptly towards commercial objectives. To explain the increasing dominance of the Chinese in the Southeast Asian economy, it is necessary to look beyond their trading methods and institutions. The following section delineates several historical developments which greased the way towards the Chinese ubiquity in regional commerce.

Wider Contextual Workings

It is well-acknowledged that in comparison with the Iberians, the arrival of the northern Europeans created more upheavals for intra-Asian trade.[39] In pre-nineteenth-century Southeast Asia, the VOC enjoyed the largest sphere of influence among the European powers. With the largest amount of operating capital, its personnel not only set up the most factories but also possessed the greatest willpower to impose monopolies. In Southeast Asia, their primary target was to gain control over the sales of fine spices and they did so through a series of military actions in the Moluccas and the Java Sea. But they did not stop there. Great efforts were also taken to ensure that the Company was the sole supplier of Indian textiles and opium – its key imports in the region – and the exclusive buyer of tin, pepper and other products.

Since the marketing of these commodities had been the main commercial pursuit of various communities for several centuries, these monopolies came into direct conflict with their trade interests. Being denied entry of their main imports of piece goods and opium in the VOC spheres of influence, Indian and West Asian merchants found themselves welcomed mainly in the Bay of Bengal, and the western and northern flanks of the Malayo-Indonesian archipelago, areas which were still largely under the indigenous ruling authorities in the seventeenth and eighteenth centuries. In face of the Company prohibitions, the Malays, Makassarese, Bugis, Javanese and other traders who specialized in ferrying fine spices and Indian textiles in the archipelago resorted to smuggling instead. The Dutch retaliated by imposing further restrictions. Once the VOC administration subjected the north coast of Java and South Sulawesi to its authority, it forbade all these regional traders to sail to the Moluccas. It also tried to restrict them within the local shipping trade to pre-empt them from establishing links with other European and regional traders in the Sulu Seas, Melaka Straits and western Sumatran coastal waters and from dealing in Indian textiles, opium and other goods over which the VOC had tried to establish exclusive sales rights.[40]

It was impossible to shut out all Asian shipping, however. The VOC dispatched the most sailors and vessels in the East Indies among the European companies during the seventeenth and eighteenth centuries. Between 1602 and 1796 it sent almost a million Europeans to work in the Asia trade on 4,785 ships, most of them operating in Southeast Asia.[41] Nevertheless, even including the private shipping trade of *burghers* (mostly retired VOC administrators), it lacked the personnel and resources to ship foodstuffs and other supplies to all its outposts in the Malayo-Indonesian archipelago and to gather the required local products for export purposes.

In this regard, the Dutch found it most expedient to work with the Chinese. Although Company administrators were still wary that the Chinese might engage in spice smuggling, they were seen as the lesser evil compared to the other regional traders. Besides the VOC and Dutch *burghers*, they were the only group of traders allowed to bring provisions to Ambon and Banda. Indeed, the Company regarded the Chinese rice imports to these spice-producing islands as an indispensable service.[42] By the late seventeenth century they were servicing much of the inter-island transportation of food and other supplies for the VOC. Dutch administrators also came to rely greatly on the Chinese to both distribute their imports and gather commodities for export to Europe.[43]

The Chinese mercantile links were also useful for another reason. It was difficult for the Europeans to gain a permanent foothold in their trade with China. Of their southern Chinese bases, only the Portuguese managed to retain their hold over Macao whereas the Dutch had lost Taiwan by 1662. To get their supplies of Chinese porcelain, tea and silks, other Europeans could either acquiesce to conduct commercial activities through the Canton system – as stipulated by the Qing regime – or trade with the Chinese junks visiting the different Southeast Asian ports.[44] This situation persisted until the outbreak of the Opium War (1839–42) and the consequent opening of treaty ports along the southeastern coast of China. In the early modern period, the Dutch, Spanish and English obtained most Chinese manufactures from Fujian traders who brought them to Manila, Batavia, Bengkulu and other ports. Similar to the region's indigenous rulers, the Europeans tried to attract Chinese shipping to ports under their control.[45] The Dutch company did likewise, which was a far cry from how they treated the Indians, West Asians and regional traders.

Thanks to their role in service shipping and as a commercial intermediary among the Asian traders, the Chinese were able to operate the most freely in the Dutch zone of influence or practically the whole of the Malayo-Indonesian archipelago. Hence it was possible for them to conduct a kind of relay shipping trade especially for those with restricted freedom to trade in the archipelago. For instance, based on the agreement with the Dutch, the Palembang ruler was obliged to sell all the local tin and pepper to the Company. But the prices paid were consistently below market prices. To obtain higher returns, Palembang rulers and aristocrats commonly worked with resident Chinese to transport tin and pepper to harbours outside Dutch control such as Riau, Trengganu, Siantan, Hatien, Siam, Cochinchina, Magindanao and other coastal towns at the rim of the Dutch sphere of influence. Chinese based in the latter ports would also sail to Palembang to buy these products. These commodities would in turn be purchased by the Chinese, Bugis, English and other shippers plying the waters of the Melaka Straits, the Gulf of Siam and the South China Sea whether for local sales or to be brought further afield to China, Europe and other markets. Similar transactions were conducted by other 'Company's kings' such as the sultans of Jambi and Banten. The VOC personnel found it difficult to obstruct these types of dealings without jeopardizing diplomatic relationships with the Southeast Asian rulers, especially since they were sometimes unable to adhere to their part of the agreement to buy up *all* the products.[46]

Because of their ease to traverse the VOC-controlled realms, the Chinese traders were attractive to all harbour polities that remained outside Dutch influence. As they were prohibited to sell certain types of Indian piece goods in the Java Sea and eastern Indonesian archipelago, the English, French, Portuguese and South and West Asian merchants would dispatch these to the Chinese and other smugglers in the Malay and other outlying ports.[47] As the VOC often sold similar imports at highly inflated prices, the above venture was still lucrative even though it involved more intermediaries. For these non-VOC mercantile operators, it also became more convenient to buy all kinds of products – including those the Company had banned – at the neighbouring ports rather than venturing to Dutch-Batavia where they were charged higher prices and imposts.[48]

In other words, the VOC reliance on the Chinese to operate as suppliers and distributors had given rise to their commercial freedom in the realms under Dutch influence. This in turn made them desirable trade partners for the indigenous rulers and other Asian merchants, as well as lesser European powers such as the English and Portuguese. The Chinese were hence welcomed in every Southeast Asian port polity, whether it was under a European or indigenous authority. The overall effect was to generate the Chinese inter-island dominance in the region during the eighteenth century.

Furthermore, the Chinese had come to lay hands on the rice bowl areas of Southeast Asia – central and east Java as well as Trat, Chantaburi, Mekong Delta and Tonle Sap – by the turn of the eighteenth century. In the case of Java this was partly because of the sponsorship of the VOC, which had exerted authority over the north coastal region since the late 1670s.[49] As for the rice production in the south-eastern parts of Thailand, Cambodia and the Mekong delta, because its main market was South China from the 1720s and the main exporters were the Chinese, they also began to prevail over the domestic rice trade.[50]

The eighteenth century saw a growing commercialization in the Southeast Asian production. In some cases these changes were connected to the burgeoning demands for regional commodities in the European, South Asian and Chinese markets. For instance, the Minangkabaus, Bantenese and Banjarese progressively converted forests and jungles into agricultural lands for pepper growing in Sumatra, west Java and south-eastern Borneo because of the rise in international demand in the seventeenth and eighteenth centuries.[51] Meanwhile, other developments of market production such as that of Southeast Asian textiles were due to regional economic readjustments. As the Europeans were buying up Indian cloth for the European and other markets, the prices of these commodities became inflated. Unwilling to pay higher prices for the same types of Indian cloth, various Southeast Asian regions including central and eastern Java, Bali, Sumbawa and southern Sulawesi intensified indigenous textile production both for local consumption as well as export to other parts of the archipelago.[52]

The proliferation of market production generated greater necessities for food imports. In the context of increasing commercialization in many parts of the region, having control over these rice-producing regions was tantamount to having your hands on the throat of the Southeast Asian economy. In the course of the eighteenth century, it became even more difficult to dislodge the Chinese as inter-insular traders since they handled the essential provisioning networks.

In the face of the restrictions and challenges posed particularly by the VOC, regional traders and other long-distance operators such as the South and West Asians did not disappear. Some chose to resist the monopolistic claims, as evidenced by the unceasing complaints of smuggling activities found in VOC correspondence. Others decided to readapt themselves, whether by shifting their trading routes or by opting out of dealing with certain commodities. Even though the shipping volume of these traders did not decline and even increased at times, it became clear that most of the commercial expansion was absorbed by the Chinese traders and their mixed-blood descendants. The latter could navigate the Southeast Asian seas most freely, whether they were under European or indigenous spheres of influence. They were at liberty to extend their trading networks, both maritime and overland – so long as they stayed away from goods declared as Dutch monopolies. The room for expansion was enormous and the Chinese networks grew to dominate large parts of littoral Southeast Asia and its interior.

Conclusion

In the history of the Southeast Asian political economy, the mid-seventeenth century was a crucial turning point. Whereas they were one among many mercantile communities in the period before the mid-seventeenth century, the Chinese and their creole descendants became active in practically every port polity of Southeast Asia by the late eighteenth century. Besides their extensive maritime activities, these traders had also gained entry into the hinterland of south Sumatra, central and east Java, west Borneo, the Gulf of Siam and other parts of the region. Because of their omnipresence, they were the distributors of imported goods and acquirers of commodities for export purposes par excellence, serving not only their own mercantile needs but also those of traders hailing from other regions of the world.

When considering the reasons for the spectacular economic expansion of the Chinese, it is clear that their skilful utilization of tax farming, advanced payment and the peddling trade, as well as clan- and native-place networks, helped boost their economic activities. Nonetheless, although these commercial methods and socio-religious institutions had put them in good stead, the Indians, South Sulawesians and other mercantile communities also deployed the same strategies and possessed equivalent symbolic capital. Hypothetically speaking, these latter groups would have acquired a larger share and rivalled the Chinese in the intra-regional trade had they not encountered the Dutch interdiction in the late seventeenth and eighteenth centuries.

Historical developments and their confluence are thus fundamental to explain the rise of the Chinese as the pre-eminent commercial players in Southeast Asia during the late seventeenth and eighteenth centuries. Thanks to the VOC endorsement of their intermediary services as suppliers of local commodities and distributors of imported goods, and in part also because of the needs of South China for overseas rice provisions, the Chinese came to dominate not only the China–Southeast Asia trunk trade but also the inter-insular commercial world of the latter region. This development further fostered their abilities to penetrate the hinterland and more isolated waters in Southeast Asia. In the early modern period, they largely focused on the goods in demand by the China markets. From the mid-nineteenth century, the Chinese also came to service the needs for raw materials and to market the manufactures of the European and American industries. At this point, their commercial networks reached maximal potential on the basis of eighteenth-century developments, extending to practically all the markets in Southeast Asia, on land and at sea.

5 THE MERCHANTS OF THE KOREA–CHINA GINSENG TRADE IN THE LATE NINETEENTH CENTURY

Ishikawa Ryota

Chosŏn Korea (1392–1910) had restricted its trading partners only to China and Japan from the seventeenth century, and imposed strict regulations on the style of trade, participants and commodities to be transacted. However, new diplomatic relationships from the late nineteenth century changed the system of foreign trade drastically.

The first commercial treaty was sealed with Japan in 1876. It requested Korea to open three ports and declared that '[both Korean and Japanese] subjects may freely carry on their business without any interference from the authorities of either Government' (Clause 9).[1] Major Western powers also concluded treaties with Korea in the 1880s. They enjoyed the right of trade given to Japan on the basis of favoured-nation clauses and tried to get additional rights. For example, the Korea–Britain treaty in 1883 allowed British merchants to advance into interior markets to buy local goods, and prohibited any taxation on goods for import and export besides a customs duty. Through these treaties, foreign powers forced Korea to enter into a so-called 'free-trade' regime more deeply than China and Japan, in the sense of the thorough exclusion of interference by indigenous authorities in trade.[2]

However, the domestic commercial system did not change immediately upon the conclusion of treaties with foreign powers. As is often the case in premodern polities, Korean governmental offices and members of the royal family had gained income from merchants in return for various privileges, such as the rights of taxation and monopoly over a specific commodity or place. Income from commerce became more important to state finance, as the amount of land tax almost stagnated after the seventeenth century.[3] On the basis of such a fiscal structure, commercial privileges given to domestic merchants lasted (or increased) even after the opening of treaty ports,[4] and sometimes clashed with the rights granted to foreigners by the treaties. From the historical records of frequent protests by foreign merchants over 'unfair' taxation, we can see not only the aggressive attitude of foreigners but also the persistence of the traditional commercial system.[5]

Moreover, when we estimate the actual impact of opening ports on the Korean market, the degree of continuity of the existing commercial system should not be overlooked. To make clear the process of transition in Korean traditional commerce, this chapter will focus on the case of the 'red ginseng' (steamed ginseng) trade in the late 1880s. Red ginseng had long been one of the traditional export goods from Korea to China, and here we examine the adaptation of that trade following the opening of the treaty ports.

From the seventeenth century, Korea had been a 'vassal state' of Qing China (1644–1911). Even after the conclusion of treaties with Japan and Western countries, Korea continued to present tribute to the Qing court until the outbreak of the Sino-Japanese War in 1894. However, on the economic front, China requested that Korea give it the same rights as those granted to Japan and Western countries. In other words, China took part in a 'multilateral imperialism' centred on Korea.[6] Before that, Korea had banned Chinese merchants from entering her territory, but permitted limited numbers of Korean officials and merchants to trade with China through overland routes.[7] However, from 1882, on the basis of new regulations approved by the Qing emperor,[8] Chinese people were allowed to live in treaty ports and travel to interior markets (i.e. those outside the treaty ports) in Korea, like merchants from other countries. The Chinese formed the second-largest group of foreigners in Korea, after the Japanese, and gathered in the capital Seoul and its neighbouring port of Inch'ŏn.[9] Chinese merchants rapidly enlarged the trade between Korea and Chinese seaports like Shanghai,[10] whereas the traditional overland trade declined.

However, red ginseng was an exception to this 'free-trade' system. It was the only commodity that all treaties and regulations prohibited foreigners to export,[11] and it continued to be traded by licensed Korean merchants or officials via traditional overland routes until the Sino-Japanese War. Chinese merchants could take part in its export only by collaborating with Korean license holders, unless they engaged in smuggling. These cases show not only Chinese merchants' adaptability but also the transformation (not collapse) of the traditional system in response to the new environment.

This chapter will discuss in detail how merchants of both sides, Chinese and Korean, tried to export red ginseng, using two actual cases of Chinese firms in Korea. One is Tongshuntai, a firm founded by a Guangdong merchant in 1885. Its commercial correspondence, which constitutes the only surviving set of managerial records of Chinese merchants in Korea, shows its trading activity in detail.[12] The other is Yuzengxiang, a Shandong firm. The records of civil cases relating to the firm, which are included in the documents of the Chinese delegation in Seoul, tell us about its attempt to export ginseng.[13] These correspondence and records are valuable for learning about not only Chinese merchants but also Korean ones at that time, because materials from the Korean side on actual commercial transactions are very few.

Institutional Overview of Ginseng Export

After two invasions by the Manchus (the founders of the Qing dynasty) in the early seventeenth century, Chosŏn Korea became a tributary state. Henceforth, Korea–China trade was conducted at the time of periodic missions by the Korean government to the Qing court.[14] Missions for tribute and other diplomatic affairs were dispatched once or twice a year by overland route from Seoul to Beijing. Members of the mission, especially official translators and merchants, had the right to trade at their quarters in Beijing. Furthermore, in the Chinese-side border town of Fenghuang-cheng, fairs called *chaekmun-hushi* (literally, 'market behind the border-gate') were held when missions passed through.[15]

Red ginseng, the product made by steaming raw ginseng roots, became the main export commodity to China after the late eighteenth century. Ginseng had been a well-known product of Korea for centuries. As long as only wild ginseng was available, the government had restricted its export for fear of resource depletion. However, after the development of cultivation techniques in the late seventeenth century, the supply of ginseng became stable and increased.[16]

Before that, the members of the mission to China, many of whom were official interpreters (*yŏkkwan*), had brought silver with them to cover the cost of their trip. But in 1797, they were permitted to bring red ginseng to trade, instead of silver. At first the amount was only 120 *gŭn* (1 *gŭn* is about 500 grams), but it was increased to 40,000 *gŭn* by 1851. Of that amount, 10,800 *gŭn* was allotted to official interpreters and 29,200 *gŭn* to merchants from the Korean-side border city of Ŭiju. In return for this privilege, Ŭiju merchants undertook official work such as collecting taxes on border trade and enforcing controls over smuggling.[17] The amount of export permitted by the government changed frequently. For example, it was 15,000 *gŭn* in 1867, but the amount smuggled was not small.[18]

Export of red ginseng was targeted by the government as a source of tax revenue. At the beginning of red ginseng export in 1797, the amount of tax was 200 *nyang*[19] per 1 *gŭn* of ginseng. It decreased gradually to about 14 *nyang* in the 1850s. The tax was distributed to the Office of Interpretation, the Sayŏgwŏn, to meet the cost of tribute missions, for which this office was responsible. However, from 1841, a part of the tax was transferred to the Ministry of Finance, the Hojo. The office collecting tax from border trade in Ŭiju, the Kwanse-ch'ŏng, was called 'the outer cashbox of the Hojo' in the 1850s.[20] This means that the tax on ginseng had turned out to be a major source of income for the state. This change paralleled the fixing of the total amount of the land tax (see n. 3).

After the ascension of King Kojong (Yi Hŭi, r. 1863–1907), his natural father, Hŭngsŏng Taewŏn'gung (Yi Haŭng, 1820–98) gained power as the regent of the young king. He tried to enhance the royal power against other noble families and expand the military, while rejecting requests to trade from Western countries.[21] Some part of the income from the ginseng tax was diverted to fund military expansion.[22]

King Kojong began his personal rule in 1873 and changed his father's foreign policy to conclude treaties with Japan and Western countries. However, as mentioned before, red ginseng was an exception to the system of free trade at the treaty ports and continued to be exported under the existing control system. As his father had done, Kojong used the tax income from ginseng as a resource for military reform. For example, in 1881 a new regulation granted 85,000 *nyang* of tax revenue from red ginseng to Muwiso, the newly established royal guard, out of a total of 105,000 in such revenue.[23] Kojong also tried to put the process of export under his direct control. From 1884, Kojong took 10,000 *gŭn* of red ginseng every year into his own property. He sent officials to the producing area of red ginseng to control the production process and commanded official interpreters to export it and deliver the proceeds back to the king's treasury. This ginseng was called *byŏlbu*, which means 'the special share for the king'.[24] As these cases show, Kojong used red ginseng as a flexible source of income to enforce the state's power and improve his own political status in the midst of change.

Cases of Red Ginseng Export by Chinese Merchants

The red ginseng trade was strongly controlled by the political authorities even after the opening of the treaty ports, as discussed above. However, it is not easy to comprehend the actual trading system – for example, the features of the merchants involved, the terms of payment, and so on – from the extant records of the Korean side of the trade.[25] Instead, we can find two cases of the trade from the Chinese side's documents. Both occurred in 1889 and were related to Chinese merchants who entered Korea in the 1880s. They were not allowed to export red ginseng officially, but engaged in it by supporting Korean agents who were entitled to take part in the trade. This section provides an overview of these two cases; the detailed discussion appears in the following sections.

The Case of Tongshuntai
Tongshuntai was established by a merchant from Guangdong, Tan Jiesheng, in 1885. The firm was based in Seoul and had a branch in the port of Inch'ŏn, which was opened in 1883. Tongshuntai traded mainly with Shanghai through Inch'ŏn but also carried out transactions with Koreans in Seoul. We find evidence of the firm's engagement in the red ginseng trade through the correspondence sent from the Inch'ŏn branch to the headquarters during January and February of 1889.[26]

In late 1888, Tongshuntai was asked by a Korean official named Hyŏn Hŭngt'aek to export 3,500 *gŭn* of red ginseng to Shanghai. The firm was to receive the red ginseng at Ŭiju, convey it overland to the port of Yingkou in southern Manchuria and sell it in Shanghai. Tongshuntai was to pay Hyŏn in kind, in the form of 2,000 piculs of copper and lead to make copper cash.[27] As we shall see below, Hyŏn may have been chartered to mint currency. The red ginseng was entrusted by the king to Hyŏn and four other officials in July 1888. Hyŏn and these others had already paid the king 15.7 *nyang* of silver per *gŭn* of ginseng.[28]

Tongshuntai agreed to these conditions and planned to have its clerks carry the ginseng from Ŭiju to Yingkou and there pass it on to a partner Chinese firm, Yuanfahao, to send it to Shanghai for sale.[29] After Hyŏn had obtained a needed 'document' (perhaps the permit to export the ginseng) from the king's palace on the eleventh day of the first month of 1889,[30] two clerks from Tongshuntai and the broker from the Hyŏn side, Sin Ch'anghŭi, departed together from Seoul the next day.[31] They got to Ŭiju on the twenty-fourth day of the second month and found the ginseng. However, they could not start for Yingkou because Hyŏn telegraphed them from Seoul to stop the transaction.[32] Ordering them to stay in Ŭiju, Hyŏn requested Tongshuntai to increase the amount of copper and lead he would receive, on the grounds that the price was decreasing in the market abroad. Tongshuntai rejected the request because the original agreed price was not so high and the firm wished to keep the original price.[33]

At the beginning of the second month, Tongshuntai was told by Sin Ch'anghŭi and another Korean broker Kim Sang'u that Hyŏn Hŭngt'aek had dropped out from the transaction; instead, O Kyŏng'yŏn was now in charge. Sin and Kim asked Tongshuntai to agree to the change of the counterparty and to drop the price of the copper and lead.[34] Tongshuntai rejected the request and started to search for other buyers for the metal, which they had already imported. Sin and Kim alerted the firm that no one would dare to buy the metal without permission from O Kyŏng'yŏn.[35] In fact, on the thirteenth of the month, a Korean merchant in Inch'ŏn who bought copper from Tongshuntai was taken into custody by the Korean local office.[36] Tongshuntai protested to the office and learned that Sin had pulled strings to create this incident. Tongshuntai became concerned about keeping contact with O Kyŏng'yŏn.[37]

The Case of Yuzengxiang

Yuzengxiang was a firm managed by Shandong merchant Sun Zhaoji. In September 1889,[38] just several months after the case of Tongshuntai, Hyŏn Hŭngt'aek requested that this firm export 6,000 *gŭn* of red ginseng to Shanghai. As in the Tongshuntai case, this transaction also resulted in a conflict. According to the court claim made by Yuzengxiang and handed in to the Chinese Commercial Commissioner in Seoul, the outline of the case was as follows.

Yuzengxiang contracted to export red ginseng for a price paid in silver. At first, the firm agreed to pay 13 silver *liang* per *gŭn* of ginseng.[39] Afterwards, Hyŏn requested to increase the price to 15 *liang* per *gŭn*. Yuzengxiang accepted this change, but made Hyŏn promise not to export additional ginseng without notifying the firm, due to fear of a drop of the price in the market. Yuzeng-xiang paid the agreed price to Hyŏn in advance: 20,000 *liang* of silver and 7,000 *liang* in promissory notes for the red ginseng. Yuzengxiang conveyed the ginseng to Shanghai via Yingkou, and found that the price in Shanghai had dropped unexpectedly. Yuzengxiang learned that another shipment of ginseng from the Korean king had been brought to Shanghai first by Hyŏn's subordinate Ch'oe Sŏgyŏng. Yuzengxiang re-exported its ginseng to Hong Kong but suffered a big loss. Yuzengxiang brought suit against Hyŏn to compensate them for the loss, on the grounds that extra export by Hyŏn resulted in the fall in value in Shanghai.[40]

In January 1890, the case was heard at the office of the deputy-governor of Seoul.[41] Hyŏn admitted that he had exported 2,600 *gŭn* of ginseng separately from the original 6,000 which he had asked Yuzengxiang to sell. But he denied that he had promised the firm not to export additional ginseng and disclaimed his responsibility for the deficit, on the grounds that he had only acted as the agent of the king. Additionally, Hyŏn insisted that the price was originally 15 silver *liang* per *gŭn*, not 13 *liang*. The court found in favour of Yuzengxiang, and ordered Hyŏn to repay 4 *liang* of silver per *gŭn* of ginseng.[42]

Although Yuzengxiang won the lawsuit, the firm experienced further damage. A portion of the promissory notes which Yuzengxiang had paid to Hyŏn, worth 46,000 *liang* of silver, went to the Korean government and was used to repay a loan provided by Zhaoshangju, a shipping company supported by the Chinese government. The Chinese government requested Yuzengxiang to refund the notes, but the firm could not accept them due to the loss it had suffered from the red ginseng trade.[43]

It is possible that the ginseng that Yuzengxiang traded was the same shipment which Tongshuntai had been asked to export some months before, because both were originally entrusted to Hyŏn by the king. King Kojong tried to put the ginseng trade under his control, as explained before. It is notable that the king's ginseng was exported via the traditional overland route, but by means of Chinese merchants who entered Korea after the opening of the treaty ports.

It is also worth noting that the case in 1889 was not Yuzengxiang's first experience to export ginseng. According to the documents relating to the case above, the firm had already contracted to export 15,000 *gŭn* of the king's ginseng in 1887 at the request of O Kyŏng'yŏn, who appeared in the case of Tongshuntai in 1889. The agreed price was 15 *liang* of silver per *gŭn* of ginseng, for a total price of 225,000 *liang*.[44] This example shows that the involvement of Chinese merchants in trading the king's ginseng started before the cases of 1889.

Agents for the Korean Side and their Backgrounds

The traditional export system of red ginseng, which had been characterized by privileged agents and overland trading routes via Ŭiju, was basically maintained, even after the opening of treaty ports. However, one change that cannot be overlooked is the deepening involvement of the king in the distribution of export rights and tax income. To provide a detailed image of this change, this section will discuss the backgrounds of the agents of the Korean side, O Kyŏng'yŏn and Hyŏn Hŭnt'aek.

O Kyŏng'yŏn was born in 1841. He was a son of O Ŭnhyŏn, who was an official interpreter of Chinese.[45] He had three brothers, all of whom passed the civil examination for interpreters.[46] O Kyŏng'yŏn passed the examination in 1876, and went to Beijing as a member of the tribute missions in 1881 and 1882.[47]

In the early 1880s, the Chosŏn government tried to introduce modern technologies from China, as well as from Japan. In the process of this project, official interpreters of Chinese played a significant role. For example, O Kyŏngsŏk, one of O Kyŏng'yŏn's brothers, is famous for diffusing information from abroad through books brought from China. O Kyŏngsŏk died early, in 1879, but his son O Sech'ang also became a Chinese interpreter and contributed to the modernization policy.[48] O Kyŏng'yŏn also took part in this policy, mainly from the financial side. For example, he went to Tianjin at the end of 1883 and paid 20,000 *liang* of silver to the military factory founded by Li Hongzhang for military machines.[49] Moreover, in 1887 he was ordered to go to Tianjin and Shanghai again to sell 15,000 *gŭn* of red ginseng to obtain funds for purchasing machines.[50]

O Kyŏng'yŏn engaged in the modernization efforts inside the country, too. In February 1888, he began managing one of the mints in Mallich'ang, Seoul, as an official of the Chŏnhwanguk, the Bureau of the Mint, which was founded in 1885 to provide funds for the modernization policies.[51] In August of the same year, he was ordered to hold an additional position in the Kwangmuguk, the Bureau of Mines.[52] These positions explain why he requested Tongshuntai to hand over copper and lead in payment for red ginseng in 1889. His influence in official circles was considerable, judging from the fact that he urged the local office in Inch'ŏn to detain a merchant who traded with Tongshuntai without O's permission, as mentioned in the previous section.[53]

Compared to O Kyŏng'yŏn, much less personal information is available on Hyŏn Hŭngt'aek. His dates of birth and death are not clear, nor his family background. The first mention of his career in the historical record is as a member of the diplomatic mission to the United States in 1883, which was known as the first mission to the Western countries from Korea.[54] Min Yŏng'ik (1860–1914), the central person of the mission, was a close relative of Queen Min and played an important role in the government, along with other clan members.[55] It is not clear how Hyŏn got the position in the mission, but the relationship with Min Yŏng'ik would be critical for his career after that. After returning home from the United States, Hyŏn was sent to Shanghai in 1883 with unknown objects, and in 1886 again as a messenger of the king.[56] He was also appointed to official positions in the Bureau of Mines[57] and the Bureau of Transport, Chŏnunguk,[58] in 1887. Both were founded in the 1880s as part of the modernization policies.

Hyŏn's deep involvement in the red ginseng trade can be confirmed through Korean records. According to a list of export right holders of red ginseng in October 1888, he held the right for 15,200 *gŭn* out of a total of 25,735 *gŭn*, which was the lion's share among the thirty holders.[59] In addition, Hyŏn held 8,000 ginseng fields in Suan county, where he had once been a magistrate.[60]

Gossip like that found in a newspaper article in 1914 can also be a collateral form of evidence of Hyŏn's engagement in the king's ginseng trade, mediated by Min Yŏng'ik. After the Sino-Japanese War, Min was in Shanghai in exile. According to the article, the sales proceeds of red ginseng from before the Sino-Japanese War were still there and under Min's control. The former king, Kojong, who had abdicated in 1907, asked Min to repay the money in 1909, but Min rejected the request. During this dispute Hyŏn Hŭngt'aek played the role of messenger between the former king and Min.[61]

O Kyŏng'yŏn and Hyŏn Hŭngt'aek had different backgrounds, but both had experiences of going abroad and were involved in the implementation of modernization policies from the fiscal side. As mentioned above, Kojong used red ginseng as a flexible source of income to strengthen the state and his own power. The careers of the two officials who directly engaged in the trade imply that the king's ginseng was aimed especially to procure funds for modernization, an effort which the king and those surrounding him led from the 1880s.

The Chinese Side's Agents and their Networks

O Kyŏng'yŏn and Hyŏn Hŭngt'aek had to export red ginseng by the traditional overland route, because it was exempted from the objects of free trade at treaty ports. Actually, however, they relied on Chinese merchants to convey it and sell it in Shanghai. This differentiated the business of O and Hyŏn largely from the traditional trading system. Presumably, they intended to use the market information or trading knowledge of Chinese merchants. It must be noted that the transaction networks of Chinese merchants, which supported their cross-border business, had different geographical breadths and functions, depending on factors such as their native places. This section will compare the backgrounds of Yuzengxiang and Tongshuntai, and discuss how their networks were related with Korean-side agents.

Yuzengxiang

The headquarters of Yuzengxiang was located in Fenghuang-cheng, which is on the south-eastern edge of Manchuria. The manager, a Shandong merchant named Sun Zhaoji, had five other affiliate firms in the neighborhood, which engaged in various businesses like grain trading, brewing and banking.[62] This multi-faceted style of business was typical of Shandong merchants in Manchuria from the mid-Qing period: they connected immigrant farmers with the market outside Manchuria by buying their agricultural products and providing consumer goods.[63]

In the case of Yuzengxiang, the location of the headquarters was significant for its engagement in the Korea trade. Fenghuang-cheng, as the Chinese-side border city on the traditional overland route between China and Korea, had long been a trading post with Korea. A periodic fair had been held there from the seventeenth century whenever tribute missions went through.[64] After the opening of Yingkou in 1863 as the first treaty port in Manchuria, Fenghuang-cheng merchants began exporting Western goods like cotton textiles to Korea.[65] Yuzengxiang also had branches in Yingkou, Yantai and Shanghai, besides Seoul, through which the firm traded Western textiles, Chinese sundries and Korean ginseng.[66]

Ŭiju merchants were granted the right to export red ginseng by the Korean government, in exchange for their services in checking and collecting taxes on the border trade.[67] Chinese merchants in Fenghuang-cheng obtained red ginseng from them.[68] One way to do this was to pay the tributary mission expenses for the Korean government on behalf of the Ŭiju merchants responsible for them. Yi Ŭngjun, a Korean official sent to China in 1882, reported that the cost of tributary missions had been covered by Chinese merchants in Fenghuang-cheng for 'two hundred years', and Ŭiju merchants refunded the money by selling a 'medicinal herb', that is, red ginseng.[69]

In Yuzengxiang's case, the firm began to trade with Ŭiju merchants by 1865 at the latest.[70] One of its trading partners, Kim Ŭng'o, had ginseng fields in Kaesŏng, a major area of red ginseng production.[71] Yuzengxiang also lent money to the Office of Tax Collection, the Kwanse-ch'ŏng, which was actually managed by Ŭiju merchants under the name of covering travel expenses of tribute missions.[72] These facts imply that Yuzengxiang had accumulated both experience of and personal connections to the traditional trading system of red ginseng.

With the conclusion of the Korea–Japan treaty in 1876, trade in Fenghuang-cheng declined rapidly, because the route of import of most foreign goods changed to the treaty ports.[73] Yuzengxiang's founding of a new branch in Seoul shows the firm's ability to react to the change in economic and political circumstances. Besides their experience with traditional trade, this kind of ability explains the firm's positive attitude to the business opportunity presented by the king's ginseng trade, even though it turned out to be a failure.

In addition, some of the Korean merchants who had been based in Ŭiju and Fenghuang-cheng moved to treaty ports after 1876.[74] In the records of lawsuits between Chinese and Korean merchants in Seoul, we find examples of Korean brokers or interpreters who had moved from Ŭiju.[75] Some of the Korean partners of Yuzengxiang also moved to Seoul after the failure of their business in Ŭiju.[76] They supported the trade of Chinese merchants who entered Seoul and Inch'ŏn after the 1880s. These cases highlight the continuous side of Korea–China trade before and after the opening of the treaty ports, with respect to human resources.[77]

Tongshuntai

In contrast to Yuzengxiang, which had experience in the traditional Korea–China trade, Tongshuntai gained access to Korea after the opening of the treaty ports. Tongshuntai was established in Inch'ŏn in July 1885 by a Guangdong merchant named Tan Jiesheng. He got the start-up capital from his sister's husband, Liang Lunqing, a prominent Guangdong merchant who operated in Shanghai. As the import trade from Shanghai to Inch'ŏn grew rapidly from the late 1880s, Tongshuntai imported manufactured goods like Chinese silks and Western cottons from Liang Lunqing's firm, Tongtaihao. By the outbreak of the Sino-Japanese War in 1894, Tongshuntai had become one of the most well-known Chinese firms in Korea.[78]

When Tongshuntai first began doing business in Inch'ŏn, the firm transacted mainly with the Korean broker Son Kyŏngmun. The next year, 1886, Tongshuntai moved its headquarters to Seoul, where it rented a room in the shop owned by Son Yunp'il, who was Kyŏngmun's brother.[79] Tongshuntai made an agreement with Son Yunp'il that all commodities would be sold through Son Yunp'il, while Son would take responsibility for transactions that he mediated. For example, in the case of failure to pay by the buyer, Son would indemnify for the loss.[80] This contract shows the typical style of commission merchants, called *kaekchu* in Korean; the term means 'hosts of peddlers'. These merchants arose in commercial towns and local ports from the eighteenth century, and transacted with foreign merchants at treaty ports after their opening.[81] They can be compared with compradors in Chinese treaty ports, in the sense that both mediated and ensured transactions for foreign merchants.

The support of *kaekchu* was crucial for foreign merchants to access the indigenous market of Korea. Yet, as the relationship between them deepened, commercial disputes increased. One of the reasons was the commercial privileges given by the authorities to *kaekchu*, who were permitted to monopolize (or collect tax from) specific commodities or places, which contradicted the foreign merchants' right as stated in the commercial treaties to trade without any interference and taxation other than the customs duty.[82] However, the privileges of *kaekchu* could be profitable for foreign merchants if they collaborated with each other, as shown in the following case of Tongshuntai. The firm's trading partner, Son Yunp'il, had the right to deliver copper to the mint.[83] Tongshuntai increased its imports of copper from Japan and China because the firm could secure customers through Son Yunp'il.[84] Besides, Tongshuntai established personal relationships with the officials in the mint through the offices of Son Yunp'il.[85] Tongshuntai may also have gotten the chance to export red ginseng through Son Yunp'il as well, judging from the contract terms requiring payment in the form of copper and lead to the mint.

Tongshuntai was aware of its own weakness, that is, its lack of experience in the traditional trade of red ginseng. In 1890, after the dispute with Hyŏn Hŭngt'aek, Tongshuntai was again offered the opportunity to export 15,000 *gŭn* of the king's ginseng by a Korean official,[86] but Tongshuntai rejected it on the grounds that the firm had insufficient information about overland trade via Ŭiju.[87] On the other hand, the breadth of the trading networks established by Guangdong merchants, which stretched across East Asia, was one of the advantages of Tongshuntai. Besides Tongtaihao in Shanghai, Tongshuntai's main trading partner, the firm had partner firms in Hong Kong, Guangzhou, Yantai, Kobe, Nagasaki, Yokohama and Vladivostok.[88] Tongshuntai collected a variety of market information through these associates. In the case of copper, Tongshuntai could import it more cheaply than Japanese merchants, because the firm decided from where to import it on the basis of the price information from each port, whereas its Japanese rivals imported mainly from Osaka.[89]

Based on market information collected through trading networks, Tongshuntai tried to find market niches for new commodities. Tongshuntai sent a clerk to Kaesŏng, a city in central Korea that was famous for ginseng products.[90] The main object was to buy 'white ginseng' (*paeksam*), which is processed by drying. This was originally consumed in the Korean domestic market, although 'red ginseng' (*hongsam*) had long been a main export commodity to China, as mentioned above. Tongshuntai was informed by its trading partner in Hong Kong that white ginseng could be sold there as a substitute for American ginseng. Before that, no Chinese merchants had taken notice of white ginseng, so Tongshuntai tried to obtain a monopoly on it by collaborating with a Korean merchant in Kaesŏng, Yu Kyŏngnyan, who claimed to hold the privilege to deal exclusively with white ginseng there.[91] This case shows that Tongshuntai made use of traditional commercial privileges that restricted open competition in the market, in order to secure market niches.

However, reliance on privileges of Korean merchants involved risk because of the uncertainty of such rights as well as the firm's ignorance about them. As for the white ginseng, Tongshuntai could not know from where the privilege of Yu Kyŏngnyan originated. In June 1892, Tongshuntai was informed that Yu's right to collect white ginseng was not in fact his own, but only rented from Kim Chong'u. Tongshuntai was surprised to hear that Kim would change the contractor from Yu to another person.[92] At the beginning of July, Tongshuntai got further information that Kim Chong'u was also not the original holder of the privilege, but himself a contractor from one of the queen's relatives.[93] Just a few weeks later, Tonghshuntai learned that the king intended to abolish the privilege itself.[94]

Conclusion

Korea was included into the international 'free-trade' regime after its opening of treaty ports. However, even after that, red ginseng continued to be exported through the traditional trading system, that is, by specific privilege holders via the overland route for tributary missions. The king, Kojong, secured a certain part of the export rights for himself from the 1880s. This chapter has discussed two cases of commercial disputes relating to the king's ginseng, both of which occurred in 1889. In these cases, the ginseng was entrusted to Chinese merchants to sell in Shanghai, and the transaction mediated by specific Korean officials who were involved with modernization policies. It can be supposed that the king wanted to use the income thus obtained to enlarge the fiscal resources available to fund the modernization policies he led, at a time when the revenue derived from the land tax had stagnated. Chinese merchants were likely expected to be able to support the trade by their market information or by their transacting networks in China.

In respect to the continuity of the commercial system in Korea after the opening of the treaty ports, this case study suggests two implications. The first point is the continuity of human resources from the traditional trade. The example of O Kyŏng'yŏn shows that official interpreters, who had been the main agents of tributary trade between Korea and China, were engaged deeply in the red ginseng trade after the opening of the treaty ports. On the Chinese side, the firm Yuzengxiang had experience in the trade with Korea from the Chinese border city of Fenghuang-cheng. Although not all the figures had been involved in the traditional trade, this ongoing dimension of Korea–China trade before and after the opening of treaty ports has been overlooked in previous scholarship.

The second point is the question of how foreign merchants reacted to the traditional commercial system in Korea. By collaborating with the privileged merchants of the Korean side, Chinese merchants tried to secure a kind of 'rent', or profit from non-market factors. Tongshuntai did not have experience in the traditional trade, which made it different from Yuzengxiang, but the firm tried actively to contact these privileged merchants in order to secure market niches. However, such relationships could be risky due to the uncertainty of various factors. The attitude of foreign merchants to the traditional commercial system was not just antagonistic, but rather multi-faceted.

Glossary

Korean names and terms

chaekmun-hushi	柵門後市
Ch'oe Sŏgyŏng	崔錫榮
Chosŏn	朝鮮
Chŏnhwanguk	典圜局
Chŏnunguk	轉運局
gŭn	斤
Haeju	海州
Hojo	戶曹
hongsam	紅蔘
Hŭngsŏng Taewŏn'gung (Yi Haŭng)	興宣大院君 (李昰應)
Hyŏn Hŭngt'aek	玄興澤
Inch'ŏn	仁川
kaekchu	客主
Kaesŏng	開城
kan	間
Kim Chong'u	金鍾佑
Kim Sang'u	金相愚
Kim T'aegyŏng	金澤榮
Kim Ŭng'o	金應五
Kim Yunsik	金允植
Kojong (Yi Hŭi)	高宗 (李熙)
Kwangmuguk	鑛務局
Kwanse-ch'ŏng	管稅廳
Mallich'ang	萬里倉
Min Yŏng'ik	閔泳翊
Min Yŏngmuk	閔泳默
Muwiso	武衛所
nyang	兩
O Ŭnhyŏn	吳膺賢
O Kyŏngsŏk	吳慶錫
O Kyŏng'yŏn	吳慶然
O Sech'ang	吳世昌
paeksam	白蔘
Pusan	釜山
Sayŏgwŏn	司譯院
Sin Ch'anghŭi	申昌熙
Son Kyŏngmun	孫景文
Son Yunp'il	孫允弼
Suan	遂安
Sŭngjŏngwŏn Ilgi	承政院日記
Tongsunt'ae Wangbok Munsŏ	同順泰往復文書
Ŭiju	義州
Yi Ŭngjun	李應俊
yŏkkwan	譯官
Yu Kyŏngnyan	劉敬良

Chinese names and terms

Donglaifu	東来福
Fenghuang-cheng	鳳凰城
liang	兩
Liang Lunqing	梁綸卿
Sun Zhaoji	孫兆吉
Tan Jiesheng	譚傑生
Tongshuntai	同順泰
Tongtaihao	同泰號
Yingkou	營口
Yuan Shikai	袁世凱
Yuanfahao	源發號
Yuzengxiang	裕增祥
Zhaoshangju	招商局
Zhu Han shiguan dang'an	駐韓使館檔案

6 TRANSCENDING BORDERS: THE STORY OF THE ARAB COMMUNITY IN SINGAPORE, 1820–1980s

Stephanie Po-yin Chung

Starting from the 1990s, we have witnessed the rise of a new paradigm for study-ing Southeast Asia. This research emphasizes networks of trade mediated by nodal centres of power rather than state structures.[1] The resulting debates high-light the role of various diaspora merchant groups, and their interactions with emerging state powers.[2] The Arab diasporic communities in Singapore provide an important case study.

Long before the Dutch and Portuguese set up colonial footholds in South-east Asia, the Arabs already played a dominant role in trade in Southeast Asia. Most of these Arabs traced their ancestry to Hadhramaut on the southern tip of the Arabian Peninsula, in the present-day Republic of Yemen. At the crossroads of Africa, the Middle East, and Asia, Hadhramaut had been an important post on the ancient spice routes. Its harsh and lawless desert environment drove many Hadhramis to seek their fortunes elsewhere.[3] Moreover, it continued to shape their economic and religious life even after they left the Arabian Peninsula.[4]

Many of these traders from Hadhramaut had ventured into the lands of Java (Indonesia) before migrating to Singapore. In other words, most of them came to Singapore with wealth. They were familiar with local customs. They contrib-uted to the young colony in several ways. For instance, they pioneered the 'Haj/ Pilgrimage Services', provided retail services and imported native goods from the Middle East. They also ventured into shipping and moneylending. Soon, many Arab traders stood out as wealthy merchants in the infant colony. Notable among them were the Alsagoffs and the Alkaffs. Both were major landlords in Singapore and had substantial properties held in the form of a religious endowment known as the *waqf* (plural, *awaqf*); the British officials always regarded *awaqf* as trusts. When these Hadhramis migrated, they brought their belief in family and small group loyalty, and the institutions, such as the *waqf*, that supported it.

Background

In 1819 the island of Singapore was a thinly inhabited domain, populated by a few Orang Laut and Malay Muslims and situated in a far corner of the Johor Empire. In 1824, under British rule, there were only 15 Arabs in a total population of 10,683. Although they were few in number, Arabs were important in the migrant merchant community. For centuries, they had been influential in economic, political, social and religious developments in the region. Over the centuries of Hadhrami trade diaspora, Hadhrami seafaring traders settled in countries around the Indian Ocean and in Southeast Asia, especially in places where Islam was observed. The Hadhramis were influential not only as traders but as religious authorities among Muslims in the 'Malay World' (Alam Melayu).[5] They were respected for their education and their spiritual authority, and this respect facilitated their business connections as well.[6] Their religious-based business connections were strengthened by their ability to sustain their family networks across oceans and territories.[7]

From the beginning Sir Stamford Raffles of the British East India Company encouraged Arabs to settle in the new colony, and the first arrived in 1819.[8] Since the Arabs had close ties with Malay leaders through marriage and trade, and an influence on local culture through the practice of their religion, it made sense for them to serve as intermediaries between the British and the Malays and other Muslims. Yet, at that time, there was no unified Muslim community. Muslims were divided along ethnic lines into two main groups: those from the Malay Peninsula and nearby archipelago; and those from more distant lands, such as South Indians and Hadhrami Arabs. The Malaysian immigrants usually brought their wives and children with them, but the Arabs married local Muslim women, forming their own communities of Malay-Arabs of Hadhrami descent. They were the elite of the Muslim population because of their wealth and alleged kinship to the Prophet. Regarded as the inheritors of the wisdom of Islam and exemplars of religious piety, they were held in high esteem by local Muslim communities, both Malay and Indonesian, in the young colony.[9]

Accumulating Wealth in Landed Property

While the pilgrimage to Mecca (Haj) had connected the Mediterranean and the Indian Ocean world economies through the practice of Islam a thousand years before Western capitalism was able to do so, the rise of the British East India Company, and corresponding demise of Dutch influence, opened up new business opportunities for Arab traders in Southeast Asia.[10] As the Dutch lost their grip on the spice trade in Southeast Asia (with growing British influence in the region), the Hadhrami traders gained a bigger share of the spice trade. With established bases in Java, Hadhrami traders remigrated to Singapore with readily available wealth. Colonial Singapore was a legal safe haven for them to do business and to amass greater wealth in the form of landed property. They emerged as one of the largest landowners among all ethnic groups in Singapore.[11]

With accumulated wealth based upon landed properties, the Hadhramis set about preserving their family estates through a traditional Muslim institution known as the *waqf*. As an ideal, a *waqf* ties up property in perpetuity by transferring its ownership to God, or endowing it for the sake of God in perpetuity, so that it is withdrawn from circulation. It should be noted that in Shari'a law only a third of a person's fortune is allowed to be passed on through a will. The rest should be divided. The *waqf* became a mechanism among Muslims for keeping capital together.[12] In general, there are two types of religious endowments or *awaqf*: the public *waqf*, which is dedicated to a religious or charitable institution; and the familial *waqf*, which provides a way to pass on property to descendants without the property being divided into many small shares under Islamic inheritance law. For many Arab merchants in Singapore, the *waqf* was an attempt to maintain their scattered assets for a far-flung web of descendants in the Middle East and Southeast Asia.[13]

In Singapore, Arab traders tended to set up *awaqf* (in the form of landed property) to preserve family wealth, but in indigenous Malay thought, land was not regarded as a commodity.[14] Yet, under British colonial rule, systematic land surveys were gradually carried out in Singapore. Land was divided into small lots, numbered and auctioned off. Under such arrangements, land became an alienable, marketable commodity protected by British laws. A land-owning class came into being, making Singapore unique in the Malay world.[15] Notable among this land-owning class were the Alsagoffs and the Alkaffs.[16]

The Story of the Alkaff Family

The Alkaffs were from the Hadhramaut coast of southern Arabia. According to the official family history, they belonged to the Shafei school of the Sunni sect. The family had little fame in the region up till the mid-nineteenth century. Only several members of the family became judges (*qadi* and *faqih*) in their hometown. Looking for more economic opportunities, the Alkaffs sailed to various cities and towns along the coast of the Indian Ocean. It was after they reached Southeast Asia that the fortunes of the family started to turn.[17]

In the early nineteenth century, Syed Abdulrahman bin Ahmed Alkaff (d. 1863) settled in Southeast Asia, building up a business network with his relatives in the region. Three of his sons, Syed Mohamed (Syed Mohamed bin Abdulrahman Alkaff, d. 1900), Syed Abdallah (Syed Abdallah bin Abdulrahman Alkaff, d. 1879) and Syed Shaikh (Syed Shaikh bin Abdulrahman Alkaff, 1839–1910) gradually settled in Singapore. The Alkaff brothers were born and grew up in

Tarim, South Yemen and were educated there in Arabic. In the 1850s, the eldest of these three brothers, Mohamed, arrived at Singapore, where he took over the family business from his father. His father 'was weighed down by his responsibility for a family of six children'.[18] Mohamed's brother Abdallah soon joined him. The two brothers started to engage in trade between Europe, India and Southeast Asia. One of their trading partners was the British East India Company.[19] Mohamed then moved to Surabaya in Java, where he also carried on his father's business, trading items such as spices, sugar, coffee and cloth. Another brother, Shaikh, who had just entered his twenties, also settled in Singapore. Under these three Alkaff brothers, the family business gradually expanded. The Alkaffs also became well-known traders who carried on a lucrative business in spices, coffee and sugar between India and Indonesia.

In 1863, the three brothers inherited a good fortune from their half-brother Husayn, who died in Java in 1863 or 1864 without any heirs. This enabled the Alkaff brothers in Singapore to expand their trading substantially between Java and the Malay Peninsula. They engaged in the spice trade, and then turned to scrap iron. At the same time, Shaikh started to invest in real estate in Singapore while Abdallah acquired farmland in Hadhramaut.

After Abdallah's death in the late 1870s, Mohamed returned to Hadhramaut as head of the family. The youngest of the brothers, Shaikh, became the head of the family's ventures in Southeast Asia. Shaikh established several settlements on properties that stretched from Beach Road to South Bridge Road for the benefit of his descendants. After Shaikh returned to Hadhramaut in 1883 or 1884, his nephew Abdalrahman bin Abdallah (i.e. son of Abdallah) bought a valuable piece of land in Singapore. In 1888, the land was used to build a shopping arcade and garage. Through this garage, carriages (and later cars) were hired out to the public. The Alkaffs also built an old Moorish-style arcade in Raffles Place, with offices and shops located on the first storey and the ground floor reserved for horsedrawn carriages. In the same year, the Hotel de l'Europe, which became a famous hotel for Europeans and distinguished visitors to Singapore, was built. In addition, near to the city area (what is now off the MacPherson Road), the Alkaffs developed the Alkaff Lake Gardens, a Japanese tea garden with a high-class restaurant and an artificial lake.

During the period from 1892 to 1940, the family business was consolidated in real estate, particularly when the business was registered as Alkaff & Company in 1907. That year, the area where seventeen warehouses along the Singapore River owned by the Alkaffs were located was given the name Alkaff Quay. Alkaff & Company became a major property owner in Singapore. Starting from 1908, it was also one of the biggest taxpayers.[20]

As they amassed their fortune, the Alkaffs made plans for its future. In 1888, the family began to invest much of the family wealth in a *waqf* to secure income for the family and for charity, mainly for the rebuilding of their hometown in Tarim. Another family trust was established in 1893. Shaikh stipulated that the properties had to be held in trust for seventeen generations. The beneficiaries were all males of his line and those of his brothers, Mohamed and Abdullah. Females were to inherit only in the absence of a male heir. The Alkaffs used *awaqf* as a means to manage and preserve family wealth acquired in the colony.

The Story of the Alsagoff Family

The Alsagoffs traced their descent from Syed Abdul Rahman Alsagoff, a Hadhrami spice trader from Mecca.[21] In 1824, he moved to Singapore with his son Syed Ahmad. In 1848, father and son established Alsagoff & Company for spice trading within the islands of the archipelago. By the 1850s Alsagoff & Company was a famous wholesaler, supplying a wide variety of foodstuffs to Arab retailers in the region. Under Syed Ahmad, the family business diversified to include shipping and retailing.[22]

The Alsagoffs became more influential and more securely rooted in Singapore when Abdul's son Ahmad married Raja Siti, the daughter of the Bugis Sultana Hajjah Fatimah. Fatimah was also from a well-known Malaccan family.[23] The marriage of Ahmad and Fatimah's daughter linked the families and their trading ventures. With the addition of Fatimah's fleet of Bugis sailing vessels, Alsagoff & Company enlarged their trading network substantially.

The combination of the Bugis and Alsagoff businesses brought extensive trade connections and a veritable fleet of ships. Ahmad's only son, Syed Mohamed bin Ahmad Alsagoff (1836–1906), was half-local. Syed Mohamed and his nephews were popular and influential in Malay circles, not only because they were wealthy Arab merchants with 'Syed' titles, but also because they were maternal descendants of Fatimah.[24] In 1878 Sultan Abu Bakar gave Mohamed a gift of land in Kukup, a fishing village on the Strait of Malacca. With the sultan's approval, Mohamed cleared land for agriculture. From 1878 to 1895 about 3,400 acres of land were planted with black pepper, nut palm, sago palm, coconut, cocoa and pineapple. Mohamed also opened a port on Kukup Island for ships bound for Singapore or Malacca. He developed the area by employing a large number of labourers from the Middle East, the Malay Peninsula and Indonesia. Many of these men worked for the Alsagoff family to pay their passage on his ships for Mecca, to make the Haj.[25]

As well as engaging in Haj transport and moneylending, Mohamed diversified his investments by buying land in Singapore. By the 1890s, Mohamed's properties included about 1,000 acres of plantation land in Geylang Serai, and many houses and shophouses around Jalan Sultan, North Bridge Road, Kallang Road and Jalan Besar. With such extensive property holdings, the Alsagoff family was anchored to the British colony.[26] Wealthy and well-connected, Mohamed also travelled frequently to Europe. In 1906 he had a heart attack and died in Singapore. Since his three sons were still very young and living with their maternal grandfather in Jeddah,[27] Mohamed's nephew Omar relocated from the Middle East to Singapore to take charge of the Alsagoff business in Southeast Asia as well as the Middle East.[28]

As the new patriarch, Omar had to deal with the powerful European shipping monopolies that had moved into the Haj business and begun to be serious competitors with the Hadhramis. By the early twentieth century, the European shipping companies were building enormous vessels that could combine pilgrim and cargo transport. Some Singapore shippers protested publicly against the European shipping monopolies, but Omar's strategy was different; he worked with his European rivals.[29] Omar had cultivated his trading networks in Jeddah and the Dutch East Indies for decades. As early as 1896, he had organized a syndicate for the pilgrim traffic in alliance with the British-owned Alfred Holt & Co. (also known as the Blue Funnel Line), Mansfield (who were Singapore-based agents for the Ocean Steamship Company and for John Swire's China Mutual Steam Navigation), and for several Dutch shippers. By the 1910s, in the face of rising competition from British and Dutch shipping giants and increasing British legislative control on Haj traffic, the Alsagoffs gradually withdrew from the Haj business, becoming a ticket agent for other shippers instead.[30]

Omar died in 1927 in Java but his body was brought to Singapore and interred in the Alsagoff family burial grounds.[31] His sons inherited his social standing as well as his economic power. Omar had arranged for his sons to have very dissimilar educations, reflecting his ties with both the British and the Arab communities. Omar's eldest son, Syed Mohamed bin Omar Alsagoff (1890–1931), graduated from Christ's College, University of Cambridge. He could read, write and speak six languages and was known as one of 'the most versatile men of his time, equally at home in arts and in sports, in business and in society'. He was a Justice of the Peace and a Municipal Commissioner in Singapore, owned a string of race horses, frequented the Singapore and Malay Turf clubs, and travelled around the world several times before he died in an accident in England in his early forties.[32] The second son, Dato Syed Ibrahim bin Omar Alsagoff (1899–1975), was born and raised in Mecca and educated in Mecca and Egypt, where he was friends with the Arab aristocracy. In 1926 he went to Singapore to assist his father with company business; when his elder brother died, Ibrahim was made senior partner of S. O. Alsagoff, Landowners, Merchants and Commission Agents, which his father had founded, and became the sole proprietor of Alsagoff & Co. Within six years after he had settled in Singapore, he had become fluent in English and a spokesperson for local Muslims, having made the pilgrimage to Mecca at least seventeen times and holding positions in many religious institutions.[33]

Like the Alkaffs, the Alsagoffs set up a number of *awaqf* to preserve their family fortune. In 1875, for instance, Syed Ahmed established a 'Waqf Syed Ahmad bin Abdul Rahman Alsagoff', with fifty-three properties in Singapore along Arab Street, North Bridge Road, Beach Road, Jalan Sultan, Aliwai Street, Jalan Pinang and Kandahar Street, including the land where the famous Raffles Hotel was erected.[34] In 1904, his son Syed Ahmed established 'Waqf Syed Mohamed bin Ahmed Alsagoff' with a property in Kukup in the State of Johore.[35] One-third of the income from the fund was set aside for charitable works, which included the maintenance of the Alsagoff Arab School and Muslim orphanages.

An Arab Landowning Community

By the turn of nineteenth century, the Arabs owned around 75 per cent of the private land alienated by the British. Arab land ownership peaked in the 1920s when Arabs owned 80 per cent of the large estates, including the prestigious Raffles Hotel (by the Alsagoffs) and the Hotel de l'Europe (by the Alkaffs).[36]

Politically and economically British Singapore was comparatively stable, while most of the Middle East was in political turmoil. Given its rising value under British legal protection, Singaporean real estate attracted Hadhrami money from far away. Many Arabs with fortunes made in the Dutch East Indies and India invested in Singapore property, as did Hadhramis residing in Hadhramaut. This created a need for property agents, and some Arab landowners in Singapore became real estate managers as well. As moneylenders, they were able to use real estate as collateral for loans instead of asking for interest payments; in this way they also could avoid the Koranic ban on usury. Within this context, in the 1910s Syed Omar expanded Alsagoff & Company's involvement in real estate management in Singapore and Johor. A British judge observed that the company

> was a very well-known and prosperous business. Among other things it had a monopoly of the sale of tickets of pilgrim ships to Jeddah. The firm also sent produce, chiefly timber, to Jeddah, carried on the business of land and house agents in Singapore and Johore; under power of attorney or letter, of administration from this Court, managed large estates of Arabs absent from the colony or deceased, and had trade connections with portions of the Dutch Indies.[37]

Based on these foundations, Omar set up his own company, the S. O. Alsagoff, Landowners, Merchants and Commission Agents, to manage property and collect rents for a number of wealthy merchants in the region.[38] The Arab community had become a significant land-owning class in British Singapore.

In Singapore, most of the land in today's central business district was once owned by Hadhrami *awaqf*. These *awaqf* properties, bearing the family names, gave considerable prestige to the Arab community in the colony. In fact, the Arabs were not only a dominant merchant group in Singapore but were influential in other parts of Southeast Asia. The early land concessions for the Alkaffs and Alsagoffs came from two major sources: land granted from the British East India Company and that secured through marriage with local Malay/Bugis royalty. Both the Alkaffs and Alsagoffs maintained connections and marriage ties with the Sultans in Sumatra, as well as with wealthy Malay/Bugis traders. In the late 1870s, the Alkaff family was awarded a large concession in Upper Serangoon Road by the East India Company. It was the large estates inherited via marriage with local families in Java, however, that cemented and expanded the sizes of their *waqf* properties. The Alsagoffs likewise inherited a large amount of land from a maternal grandmother, a wealthy Bugis/Malay trader and landowner, as well as receiving a land concession from the Sultan of Johor. These properties became the core foundation of their fortune. As part of their endeavour to contain scattered assets within a border-crossing web of polygamous family ties, the Arab families stored their wealth in the form of *waqf* property.

Changing Government Land Policy

The British East India Company was more interested in trade than in governance, so their land development policies were flexible, aimed at attracting immigrants and opening up virgin territories.[39] When Straits Settlements administration was transferred from the East India Company to the India Office in the 1830s, and then to London in 1867, land-usage policies changed.[40] By the turn of the twentieth century, the colonial office wanted more control over land use in Singapore.

As some of the largest landowners in Singapore, Arabs were greatly affected by such policy changes. To complicate matters, *awaqf* properties were seen as fostering slum conditions. In 1906, to forestall complaints about the mismanagement of religious trusts, a Mahomedan and Hindu Endowments Board was set up to supervise properties under Muslim and Hindu religious endowments.[41] As housing and slum clearance became a priority, a housing commission was established in 1918 to review living conditions in central Singapore, where overcrowding in shophouses and squatter settlements had led to widespread disease and civil unrest. Following the recommendations of the commission, a Singapore Improvement Trust (SIT), composed of professional architects and contractors, was set up in 1927 to build affordable public housing.[42]

These urban renewal projects targeted a number of immovable properties in the city centre, including *awaqf* properties that belonged to the Alkaffs and the Alsagoffs. The family was asked to give up their land, which instigated a number of legal disputes in the 1930s.[43] At the same time, a new breed of Malay Muslim leader, mostly men who had been educated in England, was becoming influential in the Muslim community. They not only challenged Arab leadership of the Muslim community in Singapore but also wanted more land for the Malay community.[44] Land became an increasingly sensitive political issue in colonial Singapore.

Post-War Changes

When Britain resumed its rule over Malaya after the Second World War, competition for land was fierce.[45] To alleviate widespread hardship as many Malays returned to Singapore from rural areas, the British introduced a rent control act in the late 1940s that proposed freezing the rents of properties bought before the war.[46] The Hadhramis were still an impressive landowning class in the lucrative central and southern areas of the island, but their properties and most of the *awaqf* holdings were pre-war purchases, and the rent control act promised to lead to a long-term decline in real income for private Arab landlords and most *awaqf*.[47]

Newspapers reported widespread approval for the rent control proposal, especially in the poor Malay communities. The general public believed that much of the Arab-owned land in Singapore belonged to absentee owners in Hadhramaut, India and China,[48] and that rental costs drained wealth out of Singapore to these other countries. A 1947 report in the *Straits Times* pointed out that such assumptions were somewhat mistaken – about half of these owners still lived in Singapore:

> The total Singapore rent roll, particularly that of the shophouses area, is split up among a surprising number of people. There were many thousands of people in Singapore whose incomes from real estate ranged from $10 to $50 a month. The practice of bequeathing shares in house property to various members of a family results in [the property being] divided into shares the number and smallness of which will astonish anyone who is able to undertake research into this system. Take, for example, the case of a certain firm in Singapore which control[s] eight hundred houses. The public associates the name of that firm with the wealthiest landlord interests in the city, but if the total rent from those eight hundred houses is divided among all the beneficiaries who are entitled to share in it, the average amount received by each beneficiary does not exceed $50 a month. Another surprising fact is that half of those beneficiaries live in this country, which suggests that the drain of wealth from Singapore to absentee property owners in China, India, the Hadhramaut and elsewhere may not be as great, in proportion to that which stays in Malaya, as is generally supposed.[49]

During debates over the Rent Control Act, Dato Syed Ibrahim Alsagoff (the son of Syed Omar) was a spokesman for discontented landlords. He condemned the Rent Control Act, and claimed that it would 'impose undeniable injustice on the small property owners and would benefit tenants of business premises'.[50]

After rent control went into effect, Syed Ibrahim held a meeting with the Municipal Commissioners, in which he claimed that the 'most extraordinary economic fact in Singapore today [1950] is that rents are actually lower than they were twenty years ago' and proved his point with a list of properties on the books for the Alsagoff Estates, with their rental prices in 1929 and 1950. The newspaper report noted Syed Ibrahim's information that

> [the] landlord has to accept lower rents for his property than he got twenty years ago, and to accept those rents in money which is worth three times less than its value twenty years ago, while the cost of repairs is three times what it was before the war ... so far from landlords exploiting tenants, it is the tenants who are exploiting the landlords.[51]

Syed Ibrahim suggested that the government would do better to supervise the chief tenants, who sublet their spaces without consent of the landlord.[52]

During the drafting of the Rent Control Acts, landlords in Singapore had tried in vain to convince the government to include a clause to enable landlords whose properties had been bought before the war to evict tenants in order to house family members or beneficiaries of the trusts. Without the clause, it was extremely difficult to evict an undesirable tenant. All the large landowners lost money through rent control, but without the clause there were repercussions along ethnic lines, since most shophouse tenants were Chinese and most landlords Arab.[53] These landlords claimed that the Rent Control Act had indirectly transferred a huge amount of income from the Muslim owners to the Chinese tenants. Due to inflation and loss of revenue, the *awaqf* could not refinance and redevelop dilapidated properties as the government required, and this allowed the rising Chinese merchant class to buy the shophouses themselves.[54]

An Independent Singapore Government

By the time Singapore attained self-government in 1959, the housing shortage had become critical. In 1960, under Lee Kuan Yew's People's Action Party (PAP), SIT was dissolved and replaced by the Housing and Development Board (HDB) to provide low-cost public housing on a large scale. PAP was keen on building a new Singapore with stronger government control, particularly over land usage.[55] In 1966, the Lands Acquisition Act granted the HDB the power to purchase any private land required for housing development. Compensation was based on a predetermined formula and was far below market value.[56]

In 1966 the Singapore Parliament passed the Administration of Muslim Law Act (AMLA), paving the way for the formation of the Singapore Muslim Religious Council (also called Majlis Ugama Islam Singapura, or MUIS) in 1968. MUIS was a corporate body with the power to oversee *awaqf* administration in Singapore. After decades of operation, as the senior family members who had managed them passed away, most *awaqf* in Singapore were mismanaged. There were legal disputes among family members and in many cases professional trustees had to be appointed. After MUIS, fewer *awaqf* were created. MUIS undermined the Arabs' authority over their *waqf* properties; once *awaqf* administration was institutionalized, it became impersonal, and the Arab benefactors less socially visible.[57]

As a newly independent republic, the government in Singapore set out to reorganize the state. Land and housing policies, such as the Land Acquisition Act, became tools to achieve these aims. The Land Acquisition Act in 1966 challenged the holding of *awaqf* by the Arab community. Pre-war properties were the major target for acquisition as Singapore underwent a modernization programme. Since rent control had left the Arab landlords without enough revenue to modernize their holdings, the government was able to acquire significant properties owned by Arab *awaqf* for modest compensation.[58]

Between 1960 and 1979, the percentage of land owned by the Singaporean government rose from 44 to 67 per cent (see Table 6.1 in the Appendix to this chapter). By 1976, more than 50 per cent of the population was living in HDB flats, a significant increase from the 8.8 per cent in SIT flats in 1959. In the late 1960s, urban Muslim villages in Geylang Serai and other areas of Singapore where Malays, Arabs and Acehnese resided were cleared for redevelopment. Muslims, as well as other Singaporeans, moved from their traditional neighbourhoods into housing estates. In 1960 less than 10 per cent of the population lived in public housing. By 1988, HDB apartment complexes housed 86 per cent of the population. Many mosques, and the Muslim communities that had surrounded and supported them, were lost in this urban redevelopment. Further disintegrating the Arab communities were government policies to promote ethnic integration. The government set maximum proportions for the various ethnic groups in each HDB block and in each HDB neighbourhood, and did not approve the sale of a new, or resale of an existing, flat to a member of a particular ethnic group if that ethnic group's limit had been reached.[59]

In present-day Singapore, the Arabs are no longer major landowners. A survey carried out in 1980 revealed that before the 1920s, an estimated 80 per cent of Arabs in Singapore lived on rental revenue; by the early 1960s, this had fallen to somewhere between 30 and 40 per cent. Most Arab families were unprepared for the drastic drop in their income. S. O. Alsagoff, Landowners, Merchants and Commission Agents downsized its property management business, and moved into the import and export of rubber and timber in the mid-1960s.[60] As the glory of the Arab families faded in Singapore, events in Hadhramaut triggered an even more drastic change.

Although Haj traffic between Southeast Asia and the Middle East gradually resumed after the Second World War, political change in the Middle East weakened and finally severed familial and economic ties between Singapore and Hadhramaut when, after years of bloodshed, the British pulled out of South

Yemen in 1967. A communist government in the newly formed People's Republic of South Yemen put an end to the Singapore Hadhramis returning home. The Suez Canal was closed, depriving Aden of economic resources. Under communist rule, the new Yemen government took control of a massive public sector, nationalized private fixed property, and drove political rivals and entrepreneurs abroad. All *waqf* properties were confiscated and their assets nationalized. Co-operatives were set up to redistribute land and small boats. All schools were taken over and given a national curriculum.[61]

The result was that the Singapore Hadhrami community lost its connection with its homeland. The Hadhramis no longer sent their sons back to Hadhramaut to be educated. The younger generations living in Singapore now have no affiliation or contact with Hadhramaut and few of them speak any Arabic at all, which some claim as major factors in the loss of Arab identity among Singapore residents. The post-war rise of the independent nation-state in both Singapore and Yemen transformed the Hadhrami Arabs and their descendents' relationship to the Indian Ocean world.

Conclusion

The Arab community was a small but influential merchant community in Southeast Asia. The history of the Alkaffs and the Alsagoffs illustrates vividly the ups and downs of this community in Singapore. In 1819, when British Singapore was founded, Sir Stamford Raffles encouraged Arab merchants to settle in the new colony. Most of those who came were Hadhramis who had accumulated wealth in Java and remigrated to Singapore. Using their assets and cultural capital, they pioneered the 'pilgrim services', taking Muslims from Southeast Asia on the Haj and expanding into pilgrim-related businesses like shipping and moneylending. In the age of the steamship, Singapore became the hub of an expanding pilgrim trade from Southeast Asia, especially as it enabled pilgrims to avoid Dutch discriminatory measures.

For many Arab migrants, colonial Singapore was a legal safe haven for conducting pilgrim business and building fortunes. With the wealth they made through trading, shipping and pilgrim-related businesses, the Arabs invested in land in Singapore, which became a hot commodity in the market protected by British law. An Arab landowning class sprang up in Singapore. Notable among these landowners were the Alkaffs and the Alsagoffs. In their heyday, they sent their sons back to Hadhramaut to be educated, and made frequent visits themselves. The Arab community in Singapore also maintained their culture and Hadhrami identity by sending money back to their homeland and by setting up *awaqf* to preserve family estates.

From their rise in wealth and influence to the gradual shrinking of their fortunes following the Japanese occupation of Singapore during the Second World War, South Yemeni independence under a communist government, and the post-war emphasis on the nation-state that led to changes in land and housing policies in Singapore, the history of the Arab land-owning class stands witness to how the Arab community responded to decades of political and socio-economic transformation in colonial and postcolonial Singapore. During this century-long process of change, the Alkaffs and the Alsagoffs maintained their Arab identity even as they became more assimilated in Southeast Asia. Their intermarriage with local women led to their absorption of local traits (and genes) and a hybrid identity. The Alkaffs and the Alsagoffs, like other prominent Hadhramis, adapted to and prospered under colonial regimes even as they forged and maintained connections in the Arab world. Over the course of a diaspora that continued for over five generations, their family identity became more diverse and multi-stranded: they sent their sons to be educated in the Middle East and in Britain, and they lived in multiple residences around the Indian Ocean. The traditional institution of the *waqf* became an important mechanism helping them to preserve the family estate amassed in British Singapore. Yet, with the demise of British colonial rule after the Second World War, and the rise of Singapore as a secular city-state with an expressed mission to use 'state land' for all of its citizens, the influence of this merchant community has gradually been eroded by a series of high-handed modernist government policies.

Appendix

Table 6.1: Ownership of land in Singapore, 1949–90

Year	State ownership (%)	Private ownership (%)
1949	31.0	69.0
1960	44.0	56.0
1965	39.3	50.8*
1970	60.0	40.0
1975	65.5	34.5
1980	76.2	23.8
1990	80.0	20.0

Sources: P. Motha and B. Yuen, *Singapore Real Property Guide* (Singapore: Singapore University Press, 1999); O. J. Dale, *Urban Planning in Singapore: The Transformation of a City* (Shah Alam, Selangor Durul Ehsan, Malaysia and Oxford: Oxford University Press, 1999).

* In 1965, the British military owned about 9.9 per cent of state land.

7 SPANISH COLONIAL POLICY TOWARD CHINESE MERCHANTS IN EIGHTEENTH-CENTURY PHILIPPINES

Tina S. Clemente

Chinese merchants[1] were central to Spain's colonial policy for the Philippines. While domestic Chinese commerce serviced the colony, the government became increasingly conflicted over increases in the Chinese population and their perceived rise in economic influence. This struck a sensitive chord with the local colonial administration, a relatively small number of Spaniards composed of government authorities and clerics who ran the islands, albeit in a constant state of contestation.

Fears over conspiracies and uprisings exacerbated tensions over what the Spaniards considered commercial success at the expense of economic and political security. Various state policies were meted out against Chinese traders to limit their numbers and their trade, and even to replace them in commerce with Spaniards, *mestizos* or the indigenous. On one hand, the commerce that the Chinese brought into the Spanish realm through the galleon trade financed the colonial administration. On the other hand, the commerce cultivated by the Chinese merchant community[2] in various goods and services, and later in the wholesale-retail trade, provisioned the colony. In both cases, Chinese commerce became both a boon and bane for the Spanish colonial government, which saw how entrenched and indispensable the Chinese merchants seemed to be.

Institutional action in the colonial period was exemplified through trade restrictions and financial impositions; seizure and destruction of property; control of population and movement through expulsions and segregation. Various works also refer to 'massacres' as the extreme form of institutional action.[3] The use of the word 'massacres' is in the context of abuses against the Chinese, the suspicion of violent plots and how these fuelled what was deemed as excessive armed force against the Chinese.

By focusing on the eighteenth century, a reform era in Spain's Empire, this chapter analyses the relationship between the Spanish colonial government and Chinese merchants through the policy of Chinese expulsions and makes reference to other containment policies as they relate to expulsions. The chapter explores the complicated policy tensions that accompanied the centrality of Chinese commerce in Spanish Philippines. Through an analysis of Chinese expulsions, we learn about the socio-economic and political contexts of colonial governance, the push and pull of vested interests and institutional change in the imperial programme. The chapter contributes to the scholarship of transnational merchant communities by providing the case of Chinese traders with minority status in a colonial paradigm within the context of empire, in which issues of political economy played out across a vast realm. The persecution of Chinese traders in eighteenth-century Philippines presented here is an important part of merchants' narratives and, in a larger view, of comparative history and global history, allowing the reader to draw similarities and differences in regard to the exploits of Chinese traders in the rest of Asia.[4]

Spanish Colonial Context

Beyond the commercial traffic birthed by the galleon trade from 1565 to 1815, of which the Manila port was integral, the Spanish considered the Philippines a financial burden that functioned merely as a military detachment. Notwithstanding the archipelago's natural resources and suitability for agriculture, Spanish Philippines operated on subsistence levels. Various authors posit that the colony was kept afloat by an annual subsidy from Acapulco which officially commenced in 1606, consisting of duties paid on merchandise entering Acapulco through the galleons. Recent scholarship has challenged this notion, pointing out that the subsidy was not as significant as estimated, except when military threats to the colony were severely felt. Further, other sources of internal income such as indigenous tribute payments, import-export duties and revenue from Chinese residence permits were not negligible.[5] Nevertheless, the colony still suffered from underdevelopment of the domestic economy, which rendered the Philippines unprofitable.

The contrast of prosperity from Spanish success in the galleon trade and Philippine underdevelopment is therefore a perennial puzzle. The dominant producers of silver – Latin America and Japan – sold to China, which absorbed world silver output. China's demand for silver highlighted Manila's sole purpose as a conduit in the trade of silk and silver between China and the Americas,[6] furthering disincentives in the archipelago's economic development.

While domestic Philippine products were part of the galleon shipments, their value did not even reach 10 per cent of the entire cargo value.[7] Furthermore, local produce was not really considered for export to the Americas and Europe, as the Americas had plantations of their own to maximize. Prior to the liberalization of the Philippines under the reforms that began in the eighteenth century, the domestic economic output was therefore insignificant. This seemingly puzzling state of economic backwardness that persisted for a long period was consistent with the Spanish Empire's mercantilism. That is, Spain drew from the surplus of productive colonies, while unproductive ones were supported and kept surviving, protected from conquest attempts by other powers.[8]

However, by the eighteenth century, calls for more productivity from the Philippine colony intensified. The Manila galleon trade and Acapulco subsidy eventually ended in the early nineteenth century and the Royal Philippine Company did not succeed, officially closing shop in 1834. The consequent entry of foreign commercial houses in turn resulted in Anglo-Saxon domination of the colony's plantation economy and wholesale-retail trade. The Chinese again played a major role amidst these changes in the economic landscape.[9]

Wickberg specifies three economic systems that coexisted in Spanish Philippines. First was the Western economy, which hinged on the galleon trade and rendered local products into mere marginal goods. Second was the native economy, which operated largely on a subsistence basis. Third was the Chinese economy, which was comprised of the various artisan trades and wholesale-retail trade that provided supplies to the Spaniards. These three systems were interrelated, with the Chinese merchants an important linkage. The Chinese distributed imports throughout the islands while gathering up supplies for the Spanish settlements.[10]

Although the existence of the Spanish government in Manila brought with it many economic opportunities, the Chinese faced obstacles in taking advantage of them. Their commercial activity had to carry on despite many forms of state-sponsored and informal discrimination. For instance, from 1581 to 1850, the colonial government imposed numerous and varied financial assessments – tariffs on Chinese goods, an annual tribute, a residence tax, fees for moving the entire Parian district and a head tax. These assessments were deemed onerous and oppressive.[11] The Chinese were also not permitted to sell their goods at retail. Instead, a system of wholesale trade, called *pancada*, was established whereby Spanish authorities set prices and collected the goods for reselling at retail.[12] This led to the underpricing on premium goods, which in turn encouraged the Chinese to hoard. When caught, the Chinese had to pay heavy fines, and at times, endure flogging.[13] In 1777, Carlos III officially put an end to the *pancada* after years of 'benign' implementation.[14]

A number of violent suppressions – termed and acknowledged as 'massacres' in the literature – occurred in 1603, 1639, 1662,[15] 1696[16] and 1762[17] as Spanish reactions to periodic Chinese revolt. The 1603 incident has various estimates ranging from 15,000 to 30,000 Chinese deaths on record, while the 1639[18] massacres resulted in contested estimates in the range of 13,000 to 24,000 Chinese deaths.[19] While the number of Chinese killed in these incidents remains unsettled, the

1603 incident was most notable for the arrival of a strongly worded diplomatic letter from China. While it seems a weak response considering the many lost lives, we point out two important considerations. First is the commercial motivation for maintaining friendly relations with the Philippines, which facilitated the global silk–silver exchange. Second, Chinese authorities had low regard for the Chinese community in the Philippines.[20] This was consistent with isolationist Ming policy banning private overseas trade and its bare tolerance towards overseas traders who remained abroad.[21] As a result, the Chinese community faced economic pressure not only from Spanish policies, but also from their homeland.

The Spanish found themselves in a bind. While they perceived the Chinese as beneath them, they found assimilation relatively difficult to carry out. The Chinese acquiesced to Catholic conversion as a utilitarian measure to reduce political, economic and cultural transaction costs. However, they persisted in their affinity with China and its culture. Assimilation problems would have been less of an issue if Spain had not depended on the growing Chinese community for commerce, but the large Chinese population had always raised Spanish anxieties over possible insurrection. Policies later instituted by the colonial administration consistently reflected the tensions and unresolved issues among the government, merchants, clerics and the public in advancing their own interests with regard to the Chinese.[22] Where the clerics were concerned, for instance, protecting the Chinese in support of missionary potential in mainland China added to the dynamics.

Colonial Policy of Containment in the Eighteenth Century: Expulsions, 1700s–1740s

Spanish colonial rule at the turn of the eighteenth century was marked by protracted expulsion debates, which had come to a head with the official expulsion order of 14 November 1686, an order opposed both by the non-Christian Chinese and the public. The Spanish authorities themselves who facilitated the royal order could also not help but concur that the colony depended on Chinese commerce. The timing of the orders before the onset of the monsoon also added to the difficulty.[23]

In a formal letter appealing the order, the Chinese underscored the importance of their commerce as well as the revenue derived from residence permits in keeping the colony afloat. The colonial administration regularly battled solvency issues because of delays in remittance of the royal subsidy coming from the Acapulco government. Expulsion efforts, however, proceeded until 6 April 1700.[24]

The atmosphere of oscillating policy and sentiment towards the Chinese is exemplified in a reproach addressed to Governor-General[25] Domingo Zabalburu on 7 October 1701 and written by Villa, Santa Ynes, Lopez, Morales and

Santissima Trinidad – respective provincials of the provinces of Santissimo Rosario, St. Francis, St. Augustine, Society of Jesus and the Discalced Recollects of St. Augustine. The letter illustrated the existence of policies restricting trade as well as basic interaction between the Chinese with the indigenous. However, these restrictions were neither enforced nor accepted.

The distinctions made among Sangleys – the term for Chinese merchants – are noteworthy. 'Infidel or heathen' male Sangleys, who happened to be married to indigenous women,[26] faced relative leniency in regard to residence and freedom of movement. On the other hand, Christian (i.e. Catholic) Sangleys benefitted from the protection of the clerics. This is evident in the clerics' argument that the Christian Sangleys should not pay the same tribute as unbaptized Sangleys. Below is a relevant excerpt from the provincials' letter.

> The experience of many years with the Chinese nation has made it very evident that it was necessary to prohibit to the Sangleys, especially the infidels, trade and intercourse with the villages and provinces of Indians, and keep them out of Indian houses and grain-fields, and thus it is provided and ordained; but unfortunately this prohibition is neither obeyed nor respected. It is, however a fact that only when they are married, and compelled to make their abode in the chief town [of the province], where the *alcalde-mayor* resides, or when they are settled in a certain Parian, does his Majesty permit them to reside among the Indians – who from communication with the Sangleys obtain only superstitions, frauds, and the loss of habits of morality in which we are trying to instruct them. The administration of the Christian Sangleys is in charge of the two holy religious orders of St. Dominic and the Society of Jesus; and as these people are for the most part the poorest [of the Sangleys], we do not consider it foreign to our obligation to attend to them, in such manner as is possible and right. It is only just to direct your Lordship's attention to a custom introduced within the last few years, which is that the tribute that they pay for licenses [to remain in the country] has been increased – although it appears that the laws favor the Christian Sangleys, providing that their tribute shall be only ten reals; but at present they are paying the same amounts of tribute as do the infidel and heathen Sangleys. Your Lordship, with your clear judgment and ready comprehension, will be pleased to consider whether it is in accordance with the lofty purposes which his Majesty has for propagating the faith, and for lightening the burdens of those who are converted to it – in which his Catholic piety has so earnestly striven – that the said tributes should be extended and increased among the Christians; and whether they do not deserve to be relieved from so grievous a burden.[27]

This shows how policies toward the Chinese were also contingent on the specific dynamics between Church and State within the twin tenets of colonial rule and missionary evangelization. Conversion often became a matter of pragmatism, which reduced the risk of anti-Chinese predation. But on the part of the clerics, increasing Chinese conversion was in accordance with encouraging submission; spreading Catholicism and extending it to the Chinese mainland; and facilitating integration.[28] To achieve these aims, Chinese and indigenous intermarriages were encouraged. Table 7.1 shows the number of applications for such unions in selected years of the eighteenth century.[29]

Table 7.1: Number of intermarriages between Chinese men and local Philippine women, 1742–81

Year	Number of marriage applications
1742	10
1748	5
1757	24
1758	1
1767	4
1772	0
1781	4

Source: R. T. Chu, *Chinese and Chinese Mestizos of Manila: Family, Identity, and Culture, 1860s–1930s* (Mandaluyong City: Anvil, 2012), p. 159.

Governor-General Conde de Lizarraga arrived in the Philippines in 1709, five years following his official appointment to head the colony. Juan de la Concepcion, a historian and Augustinian cleric who produced a fourteen-volume work on Philippine history, describes Lizarraga as possessing the favorable qualities of fairness and uprightness. Concepcion contends that the Governor-General deemed the Chinese population in the archipelago excessive and proceeded to deport many, while others were able to stay by securing paid licenses.[30]

A royal order dated 30 May 1734 made the issue of expulsion again the subject of heated discussion.[31] The Real Audiencia of Manila (Audiencia de Manila hereafter) – the supreme court – strongly favoured Chinese expulsion, confident that any commercial void could be filled by the non-Chinese, comprised of Spanish, indigenous and Chinese *mestizos*.[32]

In a 1741 statement, Justice Pedro Calderon Henriquez not only advocated the complete expulsion of Chinese plying their trades in Manila. In 1742, an order was released specifying the steps toward expulsion, which included repatriation of provincial Chinese to Manila after a year; Chinese withdrawal from wholesale trade and provisioning the public; and the settlement of affairs, after which deportation to China would be carried out. By 1743, the case against the Chinese resulted in a hearing in Madrid by the Council of the Indies.[33]

Late 1740s–1750s: Expulsions, Power Dynamics and Commercial Void

In 1747, the new Archbishop Pedro de la Santisima Trinidad Martinez de Arizala arrived in the Philippines. Arizala, who became an ecclesiastic during his time as counsellor of the Indies, was mandated not only to carry out his royal appointment as interim governor, but to implement the royal order calling for absolute Chinese expulsion. This expulsion order had already been sent to Manila. Arizala observed that then current Governor General Arrechedera's interests were too attached to the Chinese, rendering expulsion difficult to carry out. As a result, Arizala could not put the royal order into effect.[34].

In July 1750, Francisco José de Ovando assumed the position of Governor General in Manila. The expulsion of Chinese again became a pressing concern as Ovando immediately received orders from Arizala specifying the expulsion order shortly after his arrival. However, due to an argument with Arizala concerning protocol and official etiquette, the expulsion was not implemented. When the council was called to order to discuss the issue, the Archbishop demanded the honour to be seated on Ovando's left side, but Ovando preferred otherwise. Neither did Ovando permit the guards to make a public display of official respect towards the Archbishop. This conflict in protocol put the expulsion order on hold. The incident had to be reported to the council, and favour tipped towards the Archbishop.[35] The conflict demonstrates that weak implementation of expulsion orders not only resulted from vested interests in the Chinese but also from power plays among officials, who regarded public representation as an important legitimizing element of contested authority.

Contested authority is best understood in the context of John Leddy Phelan's concept of multiple hierarchies with conflicting standards in Spanish colonial bureaucracy, which emphasized the flexibility in subordinates' response to changing colonial objectives and innovative opportunities as opposed to mere observance of the rules. Although the system allowed officials to adapt to changing circumstances in colonial rule, it led to the coddling of vested interests while policies remained unenforced and tensions rose in jurisdictions within and across hierarchies. Notorious tensions often involved the State and Church throughout colonial rule.[36] While the Ovando-Arizala quarrel was related to protocol, it was merely the tip of the iceberg in State–Church animosity.

In 1754, Pedro Manuel de Arandía y Santisteban became Governor General. Arandía carried out mass expulsion in 1755. Arandía also restricted travelling Chinese traders in Manila's business activity to the San Fernando market until their vessels were ready to sail from the islands. Only Christian Chinese and Chinese studying Catholic doctrine as a precursor to baptism (i.e. cathechumens) were permitted to remain in the Philippines and only as long as they pursued agriculture.[37]

Arandía would not be swayed by Spaniards who pointed out the commercial void that would result from Chinese absence. Arandía believed that the Chinese were superfluous and went on to establish an enterprise run by Spaniards and *mestizos*, which failed after a year. Business failure only increased criticism of Arandía from the community.[38]

1760s–1780s: British Occupation, Anti-Chinese Aftermath and Demise of the Expulsions Era

The aftermath of the British occupation (1762–4) became particularly difficult for the Chinese. Simon de Anda y Salazar was made Governor General during the British occupation. In March 1763, a decree ordered treasonous Chinese to be put to death with a conciliatory note of pardon. Below is an excerpt of the decree, dated 3 March 1763:

> Notwithstanding the heavy damages that have attended his Majesty's party in these Provinces upon account of many Chinese having gone over to the Faction of the English Enemies and helped them to invade the Country from which have sprung all the evils and losses which they have experienced and acknowledged, however as it appears from true and sincere information that the principal Chinese who reside at the Parian and other Villagers in the District of Manila have not intervened in the execrable proceedings of the Guilty, that they were concerned for the disorders, that were committed, and prudently endeavoured to dissuade them, besides it is well known that the Guilty and promoters have already repented: upon account of the fatal consequences which have happened, and calling to mind that those were punished with Death, who were apprehended and were found guilty of said Crimes, whereby the public revenge is sufficiently satisfied and being desirous for the future to avoid Broils and destruction and that the good harmony and commerce between the Chinese, Spaniards, and Indians should be put upon the ancient footing in all the Provinces; By these presents, and in the name of His Catholic Majesty (whom God preserve) a general pardon is granted for the lives of all such Chinese as still remain and had sided with the English and likewise a free commerce in the Villages of Provinces belonging to these islands, upon the following conditions:
>
> That such as may reside in any Village, or Province, whether married men or Bachelors, must be furnished with License from this Superior Government, and registered, that it may be known who they are.
>
> That without said License they cannot go to the Provinces, nor remain in them longer than may be permitted.
>
> That they shall not aid, assist or obey the Enemy so as to take up Arms against Spain since the present war is not against the Chinese and they should continue neutral, and the English cannot oblige them by Laws of Nations to do anything else.[39]

The deaths that Anda mentioned in the decree referred to the hanging of about six thousand Chinese in 1762, implicated for supporting the British occupation of Manila, which occurred towards the end of the Seven Years' War (1756–63). Chinese support for the British is attributed to Spanish excesses that consisted of cultural discrimination, excessive taxes, killings and expulsions spanning nearly two hundred years.[40] In regard to the killings, four prior incidents had taken place in the seventeenth century: in 1603, 1639, 1662 and 1696. The incident in 1762, the fifth, is the only one occurring in the eighteenth century. While the deaths reflect the hard-line stance of the colonial administration, the provision of pardon still makes the decree somewhat conciliatory toward the Chinese, even at the height of tensions. Here, Anda pushed for the strict control of movement and residence through the documentation of identity and the use of licenses. In the context of clemency, Anda clarified that the conditions were to also apply to Chinese mestizos. Despite the implementation of the decree, Anda's note of pardon highlighted the administration's interest in maintaining favourable relations, trade, personal security and property protection as they had existed before. This demonstrated that between extremes, which were often motivated by reactionary sentiment, policy slipped back to the status quo.[41]

In his 1899 work on Anda's memorial, Pardo de Tavera contends that Francisco Leandro de Viana, Attorney-General of the Audiencia de Manila, ordered on 9 July 1765 the expulsion of Chinese who stayed in the Parian and Alcaiceria. Confiscation of the traders' goods was also advocated as additional punitive action for siding with the British. Viana reiterated an old proposal that married Chinese traders in the Parian should now be restricted to the penal colony of Santa Ynes for the purpose of labouring in the mines and the nearby fields.[42]

At face value, Viana's position on the expulsions does not seem different from the stance of earlier officials. An exploration of Viana's major reports lends insight. On 10 February 1765, Viana wrote a detailed memorial. In this meticulous work, Viana evaluated the state of the colony and analysed the viability of keeping the islands. He argued that it was not only possible for the Philippines to be self-supporting; trade profits could be maximized by improving navigation (through the Cape of Good Hope, in particular) and, invoking the royal decree of 23 March 1733, establishing a 'Royal Company of the Philipinas'[43] with a detailed plan he himself proposed. Nearly twenty years prior to Viana's memorial, Justice Henriquez had in 1748 proposed a trading company in the same vein as those of the Dutch and British, overestimating their successes and underestimating the institutional challenges. In contrast, Anda in 1768 supported the idea of Manila–Cadiz direct trade but disagreed with the proposed royal company.[44] On 10 July 1776, Viana wrote a very pointed report on the financial affairs of the Philippines and outlined how self-sufficiency could be achieved by applying prudence in certain items of spending.[45] In 1767, a year before Anda's memorial, Viana wrote a letter to Carlos III and did not mince words when he raised various matters on governance.[46]

What is consistent in Viana's thoughts is the overarching perspective that the colony needed to be a productive colonial asset, rid of its dependency on the annual silver subsidy from Acapulco, or of its survival, at best, on subsistence mode. In keeping with this objective, Viana's ideas, which were considered radical at the time, attempted to advocate reforms on governance, trade, navigation and Philippine financial stability. Within this perspective of promoting the interests of the indigenous for the ultimate utility to the monarchy, his stance in favour of Chinese expulsions was rationalized. Marciano de Borja writes that Viana was a reformer whose ideas ruffled many feathers, including Arandía's and those of the powerful Consulado.[47] While Arandía also favoured expulsions and was even partial to the establishment of a Spanish company, the divide between him and Viana was deep on all other issues. As far as the Consulado was concerned, it took forced cessation of the galleon trade in 1815 during Mexico's war of independence for Viana's prescriptions to be taken seriously.

On 17 April 1766, a royal decree of Carlos III was handed down which stipulated that Chinese who sided with the British, even if they were Catholic, should be expelled and only true Christian Chinese should be permitted to stay. Again the decree included the proviso that the remaining Chinese should be restricted to designated areas where they could labour in agriculture and needed industries. Leaving the localities without permission was punishable with expulsion.[48] The decree described these new restrictions:

> Consequently, on the recommendation of the Supreme Council of the Indies, I order the total and absolute expulsion of all married or unmarried Chinese, who during the war had either apostasized or had committed seditious acts, either by helping the enemy or by fomenting the rebellion of the natives in the provinces. Children under twelve years old may remain in the Islands with their mothers and those older who repent could also stay. Those who left voluntarily with the British and those about to be banished should not be allowed to return under penalty of death, and any officials or ecclesiastics who violate this order under any pretext will be deprived of their respective offices. Chinese who sail regularly to Manila for trade could continue as usual as provided by the laws. They have to stay at the Alcayceria of San Fernando (silk market) and return to China after the fair. No one will be allowed to remain, and trading in other ports is absolutely forbidden.[49]

In the decree, exceptions to the 'total and absolute expulsion of all married or unmarried Chinese' were for those who travelled to temporarily reside in the islands on account of trade, for which previous laws supposedly stipulated residence in designated locales. The other exception regarded those allowed to stay for the purpose of undertaking agriculture or mechanical arts, and who were required to accomplish religious obligations. As before, their residence had to be registered and assigned, while movement was allowed only with express permission from the *alcalde-mayor*. Despite post-war tensions, absolute expulsion could never be truly carried out due to the recognized commercial need for the Chinese. The seriousness of the decree is evident in its inclusion of married Chinese in the expulsion order, although they had already been baptized into Catholicism (a precondition to marriage) and were hence regarded as assimilated.

To understand the position Anda took a few years after the British siege, it is worthwhile to refer to his memorial to the Spanish government dated 12

April 1768. This memorial specified nineteen abuses and their corresponding remedies. Anda discussed troubles regarding the Chinese in the section on the eleventh abuse, drawing attention to several critical issues. First, he took issue with clerical protection of the Chinese even while the clerics themselves acknowledged the so-called ill character of the Chinese. Clerical protection, Anda argued, worked to the detriment of the Spaniards, who were driven away from the provinces. Anda pointed this out as precisely the reason why Spanish settlements were not found in the provinces, the indigenous people remaining distant from and hostile to them.

> It is an abuse that the fathers have in every way defended and protected, from the time of the conquest, the Chinese idolaters, apostates, traitors, and sodomites, without any benefit to the community, but with considerable harm in spiritual and temporal affairs; and that they have persecuted the poor Spaniard with so great rancor and eagerness. For it is seen that if any Spaniard goes, on account of misfortune, to the provinces to gain his livelihood, the father immediately orders him to leave, even if he does not lash him, etc.
>
> This is the reason why, after so long a time, there is not other settlement of Spaniards than that of Manila; for in the provinces rarely or never does one see a Spaniard. And, pursuing the same reasoning, after the lapse of so many years we are as strange to the Indians as in the beginning, and even more so, as one can see in the history of the conquest compared with what we all saw during the war.[50]

But the root of the problem, Anda posited, was that the discrimination against Spanish settlements in the provinces was legally supported. In the passage below, Anda underscored that both the law and the ecclesiastical perspective were outdated. The law prevented Spaniards from exerting positive influence in the provinces, leaving only the ecclesiastics with the indigenous, who in turn grew more hostile toward Spain through the instruction received by the clerics. Anda made mention that 'intelligent Catholics weep', denoting a rift in the philosophy of governance between administrators and ecclesiastics.

As a precursor to the themes about which Anda later wrote in his memorial, Viana reported that the ecclesiastics, by suppressing the teaching of the Spanish language, wished to continue the 'despotism with which they govern[ed] the Indians in both spiritual and temporal matters'.[51] To Viana, this was a clerical attempt to preserve power by keeping doctrine out of the hands of the indigenous people. Below is another excerpt of the same memorial to the Spanish government.

> I venerate, as I ought, the justness of the laws (xxi and xxii, book vi, titulo iii, and law I, book vii, titulo iv, of the Recopilacion) which prohibit, in the words of the laws, 'Spaniards, negroes, mulattoes, or mestizos from living in the villages of the Indians, for it has been found that some of the first are restless fellows, of evil life, robbers, gamblers, and vicious and abandoned people'. However, conceding for the present whatever crimes and stigmas these laws impute to the Spaniards, I declare and affirm

that, with that ban, the regulars have committed more havoc in America and Filipinas than all the locusts together. These (laws) the regulars order posted in the tribunal houses of the villages, and obey them with such rigor that if the laws concerning the missionaries were observed in the same way there would be no Christianity equal to that of those countries.

Let the evil Spaniard be punished; that is but justice: but the good man cannot and ought not to be punished. The fact is that by means of the said laws the father puts all [the Spaniards] on the same footing, and persecutes and punishes all without distinction until he drives them out of the country. In this way, he is left alone in the village, and without witness for what only God knows, and the intelligent Catholics weep; and the Indian grows more alien every day, and becomes hostile to the Spaniard through the instruction which he receives from the father.[52]

Preventing 'Spaniards, negroes, mulattoes, or mestizos from living in the villages of the Indians'[53] reflected a benevolent principle of protecting the indigenous from potential abuses by the settlers. This shifted power to the religious orders, on whom the colonial administration depended for rearing the indigenous in the Catholic faith. Clerical influence became more and more established at the grass-roots level. In the context of Iberian social history, the concept of *limpieza de sangre* or blood purity referred to ancestral lineage that did not include Muslim or Jewish forebears. This concept was carried into Spanish colonial governance, in which mixed or indigenous races were restricted from taking positions of government or religious authority. In the Philippines as in other Spanish colonies, blood purity became the basis for social hierarchy. But in terms of colonial administration, racial segregation served two purposes. One was to prevent abuses of the indigenous and the other was to simplify taxation imposed on the different races.[54]

Elsewhere in his memorial, Anda framed the issue of Chinese expulsion in the rubric of what was supposed to be sound colonial policy of Spanish integration. Here, he underscored the need for the latter by presenting two options: it was either advantageous to keep the Chinese or not. The mutual exclusivity of the alternatives was clear: if there was no advantage in keeping the Chinese, then this would entail freedom for the Spaniards and abandonment of the Chinese. The memorial proceeded by criticizing the non-teaching of the Castilian language among the indigenous and the fact that the policy of Spanish-indigenous intermarriage, which would have encouraged assimilation, was not carried out. Theoretically, these two approaches would have resulted in better colonization outcomes. Anda reiterates the modification of the old laws in 'favour of the nation', with a special mention of the need to restrict the powers of the ecclesiastics.[55]

In 1769, Jose Raon attempted to carry out expulsion orders, with only partial success.[56] Upon the death of Anda in 1776, the intense anti-Chinese sentiment relaxed. Two years later, in 1778, a significant number of Chinese returned with the recall of the expulsion order, only to again face a resumption of immediate expulsion activities in February 1785 – the last of the expulsions. The small number of Chinese who were allowed to remain had to stay at a designated place under watch outside of Manila. In April of the same year, a Chinese colony with 200 people was established by decree in Pampanga.[57] The era of expulsions came to an end as expulsions were ruled out as a way to deal with the Chinese. The application of financial levies became the preferred approach.

Imperial Reform and the Drive towards Productivity

The shift from expulsions to Chinese taxation is best understood in the context of continuing Bourbon reforms in the second half of the eighteenth century. When Carlos III assumed the Spanish throne in 1759, he applied Enlightenment ideas to reforms not just in Spain itself but also in its colonies. While Governor Generals Ovando, Arandía and Anda all attempted to advance reforms in the Philippines, it was Jose Basco y Vargas who exemplified the major break from tradition with his proposed 'General Economic Development Plan.'[58] Aside from attempting to rationalize colonial administration to improve operational efficiency, Basco was known for his critical views of the galleon trade. He believed that it was not a sustainable economic plan and instead laid out radical plans for the development of the domestic economy through agriculture, manufacturing and trade. Basco planned to restrict the import of foreign goods, only allowing needed raw materials to enter the Philippines. In addition, Basco had two institutions in mind as the forefront of development – the Economic Society of the Friends of the Country and the Royal Philippine Company, established in 1781 and 1785 respectively. As an economic society, the former focused on exploring critical ideas, resulting in proposed policies and enterprises for economic development. The latter executed the Society's proposed projects to spur Philippine export commerce with Spain and Europe. Basco supported Chinese immigration as he recognized their utility in domestic commerce. Basco's development plans did not materialize, but they created a blueprint with bold attempts at execution. In 1778, the prior expulsion order was revoked[59] and Basco encouraged Chinese farmers and artisans to enter the Philippines with a cap of 4,000 – a number that would not be difficult to contain in case of an uprising. But Chinese immigration did not hasten as hoped, and by 1788 there were only 1,500 living in Manila, comprised of baptized Chinese and those studying Catholic doctrine.[60]

Even if taxation was not efficient due to corrupt activities by the collectors, the importance of capitalizing on Chinese commerce and taxation became more apparent as economic output was envisioned beyond subsistence. In the seventeenth century, Governor General Sebastian Hurtado de Corcuera had observed annual collections and claimed that revenue from Chinese residence permits alone could bring the colonial government in Manila out of its budget deficit.[61]

Basco wanted to do more to usher the Philippines into productivity; he did not see the Chinese as antithetical but as complimentary to economic development. Basco, who was compelled to pursue alternative sources of internal income, even acknowledged gambling as a lucrative opportunity; he decriminalized cockpits in five provinces in 1784.[62]

Although the Bourbon reforms did not effect sweeping change in Spain or in colonial administration in the eighteenth century, they emphasized the need to raise the colony's efficiency in order to improve royal income.[63] The need for productivity in the colonies for the sake of bolstering Spain's agriculture and industry as well as finances was still the mode of colonial economic policy, its urgency reaching its height during the years of war with France (1793–5) and Britain (1796–1802 and 1804–8), when Spain was on deficit financing. In the late eighteenth century, colonial revenues still made a significant contribution to the treasury, albeit a declining share. In 1792, they made up a fifth of treasury receipts but only registered 9 per cent on average in the years from 1793 to 1807.[64]

Eventually, colonial revenues ceased to be a factor in peninsular economic development. Although the Philippines was considered unproductive beyond subsistence and did not contribute to peninsular financial relief through repatriated public funds, the drive towards productivity especially in the late eighteenth century fits into the larger context of imperial reform.[65]

Chinese in the Philippines entered into a new era of trade in the nineteenth century. The galleon trade was over, the Royal Philippine Company discontinued operations and foreign merchant firms set up shop in the Philippines. It was during this time that Chinese traders transitioned into large-scale middleman traders in the import-export business. This was the pattern in the second half of the nineteenth century[66] vis-à-vis a more extensive trade through cross-border networks akin to Choi Chi-cheung's analysis of the Chaozhou merchants.[67] It is important to note that it was only largely in the twentieth century after the end of Spanish colonialism that many Chinese traders moved beyond the roles of purchasing and distribution agents for foreign firms. For instance, Chinese-owned rice mills in Central Luzon – a rice-producing region – started to be identified in 1919 while the 1920s and 1930s saw a significant rise in their number.[68] The 'expediency' that the Dutch recognized in utilizing the Chinese as trade intermediaries and later, conduits in the import-export commerce for the Dutch East India Company, as Kwee Hui Kian points out,[69] was only realized in the Philippines late in the Spanish colonial era. This late shift in Spanish policy was necessarily intertwined with particular issues of political economy involved in managing the Philippines in light of the rest of the Spanish empire's concerns.

Concluding Remarks: Expulsion Policy and Institutional Change

In the eighteenth century, the pattern of constant oscillation in institutional action to deal with the Chinese in the Spanish Philippines continued. These shifts reflected policy issues that were never resolved. Actions were ultimately determined by what factional interest prevailed, with crucial adjustments during extreme times such as uprising or war. Institutional improvement occurred in small iterations, and expulsions were gradually ruled out over the course of two centuries. What later prevailed was the application of financial impositions as the institutional approach. In this sense, a pragmatic utilitarian consensus won over other bases for institutional action.

While policy oscillation characterized colonial policy from the beginning of conquest, we see major shifts in the eighteenth century. The approach of the Hapsburg rulers with regard to colonial administration in the Philippines was that of utmost flexibility, 'which depended on decentered and heterogenous forms of authority in constant flux and negotiation'.[70] Due to Spain's constrained resources to carry out a systematic application of authority, the loose frontier system prevailed until the Hapsburgs fell from power and were replaced by the Bourbons. The transition from the Hapsburgs to the Bourbons ushered new views into the philosophy of governance, specifically that colonial rule was contingent on indigenous consent, and that it should be pursued with a specific socio-economic and political agenda.[71] Expulsion policy was advocated along the lines of aggressive reform to spur non-Chinese economic development. The efforts of Viana did not materialize and even the efforts of Governor General Jose Basco y Vargas, who undertook more concrete actions toward reform, did not see fruition in the midst of broader Spanish political vagaries. Hence, restricting Chinese participation in the domestic economy could not be sustained.

Contemporary studies of the role of the Chinese in the domestic economy such as those by Edgar Wickberg and Kwok-Chu Wong[72] show how the nineteenth century saw yet another major shift where Philippine modern society itself took shape, with the Chinese contingent securing its place in commercial life and other dimensions of society. However, it must be noted that explanations of Chinese commercial success in contemporary Philippines draw from the achievements of the ethnic Chinese and emphasize intermarriage and assimilation of Chinese *mestizos* into Filipino society, which began earlier in colonial times, as well as the relatively recent migration beginning in the nineteenth century due to increasing labour demand and kinship-motivated immigration. What this chapter underscores is that the critical adjustments in colonial governance, economic development policy and the reframing of the Chinese concern started in the eighteenth century. These adjustments were intertwined with each other and later impacted the political, economic and social fibre of modern society.

As an area for further research, subsequent investigations into expulsions of Chinese should attempt a deeper examination of the victims' perspectives regarding Spanish containment policies in the eighteenth century. Chinese traders in the Philippines began as a despised minority; they were not formally organized until the nineteenth century and their perceived success intensified resentment towards them. Hence, voicing objections to Spanish policy was almost impossible for them. Instead, such objections were made by sympathetic clerics, government administrators, Spanish merchants or citizens who saw the benefits of protecting the Chinese.[73] Further study of such sources may help us reconstruct this crucial victims' perspective.

Acknowledgements

The research for this chapter was supported by the PhD Incentive Grant Year 2, Office of the Vice Chancellor for Research and Development, University of the Philippines-Diliman.

Glossary

Alcaiceria	silk district
alcalde-mayor	a local government official in the Spanish realms, with administrative and judicial authority over a district-size territorial area
Christians	individuals who are baptized into Catholicism
Consulado	guild of merchants established in 1769 for the express function of overseeing the galleon trade and settling conflicts among merchants
ecclesiastic	member of a religious order
indigenous	inhabitants of the Philippine islands with native lineage; the pejorative form is *indio*
galleon trade	the prized trade between Manila and Acapulco using large ships from 1565–1815
Governor General	highest official in a colonial realm, governing on behalf of the king
memorial	A memorial is an archaic reference to a written report containing facts or a petition addressed to a major government authority or branch of government. During the Spanish colonial period, for instance, Simon de Anda's 1778 memorial was addressed to the Spanish government.
mestizos	individuals with Spanish and indigenous lineage or offspring of Spanish and indigenous unions.
pancada	system of wholesale trade in which Spanish authorities set prices and collected goods for reselling at retail
Parian	locale designated for Chinese residence or a temporary stay by visiting Chinese traders
Provincial	head of an ecclesiastical province or a major territorial subdivision of a religious order

Real Audiencia of Manila	the Supreme Court, which held authority over the Spanish East Indies, with the Governor General of the Philippines at the helm
Sangley	a term used by the Spanish in referring to a Chinese trader in the Philippines; derived from the Hokkien term 'siong lay', which means 'frequent visitor'. See *Tsinoy: The Story of the Chinese in Philippine Life* (Manila: Kaisa Para Sa Kaunlaran, 2005), p. 47.

8 MERCHANT COMMUNITIES IN A QASBA (MARKET TOWN) OF WESTERN INDIA IN THE LATE MARATHA AND THE EARLY BRITISH PERIOD (1760s–1840s)

Ogawa Michihiro

India underwent great changes by colonization from the eighteenth century to the nineteenth century. British colonial rule has been a major topic in Indian history for a long time. Studies that justified the process of colonization in India tended to present the eighteenth century as a 'Dark Age' marked by political chaos and economic decline. Opposing this view, two edited collections of essays, P. J. Marshall's *The Eighteenth Century in Indian History: Evolution or Revolution?* and Seema Alavi's *The Eighteenth Century in India,* both published at the beginning of this century, have prompted a reconsideration of eighteenth-century India.[1]

Discussions on 'the eighteenth-century problem' begin with the collapse of the administration of the Mughal Empire after the death of Aurangzeb (1707). The Mughal satrapies such as Nizam, and new polities such as Marathas, emerged in the early eighteenth century. This decentralization led to economic development in rural villages and towns.[2] In the same context, P. J. Marshall explained economic development in the eighteenth century by discussing a proliferation of market towns (*qasbas*).[3] Seema Alavi pointed out that a vibrant cross-caste mercantile sector emerged and was involved in administration through tax farming. Tax farming, which united merchant and agrarian interests, resulted in the emergence of a new class of intermediaries. They derived their power from a variety of portfolios in the eighteenth century,[4] leading Sanjay Subrahmanyam and C. A. Bayly to call them 'portfolio capitalists'. They were great merchants who came from the merchant caste, had cultural links with smaller merchants, and maintained direct connections to the rulers of new polities through revenue collection.[5]

This last relationship with political authorities has been amply discussed in the literature, but thus far, the scholarship has only focused on these great merchants. Yet as seen above, rural towns (*qasbas*) developed in eighteenth-century India. For a more comprehensive understanding of Indian economic history, it is necessary to consider not only the great merchants but also the small merchants who worked in these rural towns and whose role has been neglected, primarily due to a lack of primary sources. Fortunately, exceptionally rich indigenous sources survive for the Marathas in western India. This chapter concentrates on small merchant communities under the Marathas to explore small merchants in towns and their relationship with political authority.

The Tax System and Merchants in Qasba Indapur under the Marathas

The territory of the Marathas in the eighteenth century was divided into thirteen provinces called *subhas*, which were subdivided into several districts called *parganas*. A district (*pargana*) consisted of villages, and each district had a town called *qasba* as its centre. The district called *pargana* was not only a higher-level administrative unit but also an area of the local economy. A town (*qasba*) was both the administrative and economic centre of the local economy under the Marathas. Within the *qasba* was located the market area called the *peth*, where various traders, artisans and even farmers gathered and conducted business. The remaining area was rural and agricultural. Except for the work of a few scholars,[6] previous research on towns and cities in Indian history has overlooked the fact that towns included a rural area.

This chapter considers the role of merchant communities in the local economy of western India. However, it is difficult to 'find' or precisely identify merchants in this premodern rural Indian economy, because many of them were unprofessional or part-time merchants who also worked as farmers or artisans. In this study, those communities which the government defined as merchants for purposes of tax collection will be discussed. Within this western Indian context lies Indapur Pargana, whose various tax documents between the 1780s and 1840s provide the information for this chapter. Indapur Pargana had a town called Qasba Indapur as its centre. Within Qasba Indapur was the market area called Peth Indapur.

The public office (*kacheri*) of Indapur Pargana, which was the centre of the *pargana* administration, was located in Peth Indapur. Peth Indapur was both the administrative and economic centre of Indapur Pargana, and it was separated off from the remaining area by a streamlet. The remaining area was rural and quite similar to the surrounding villages. Peth Indapur and this agricultural swathe were clearly separated, and their accounts were also different. The tax collection of both areas needs to be analysed separately.

The Rural Area of Qasba Indapur

The land tax was the chief revenue in the rural area of Qasba Indapur, and agriculture was its main industry.[7] Judging from the area of Qasba Indapur (see Figure 8.1), Qasba Indapur was the largest crop-producing area in Indapur Pargana.

Next to the land revenue, two headings of tax called *balute* and *mohtarfa* were important. *Balute* means 'a share of the corn and garden-produce assigned for the subsistence of the twelve public servants of a village.'[8] A village under the Marathas was supposed to have twelve servants called *bara-balutedars.*[9] According to Grant Duff, these servants consisted of a carpenter, a blacksmith, a shoemaker, a *mahar*, a *mang*,[10] a potter, a barber, a washerman, a priest of the village-temple, an astrologer, a goldsmith and a Muslim jurist.[11] They were said to live traditionally. The Peshwa government[12] levied a tax on the professions of these servants (*balutedars*) called *balute*.

Mohtarfa means 'a tax or taxes levied on traders and professions, on the artificers of a village or their implements, as upon the weaver's loom, upon tradesmen and their shops and stalls, and sometimes upon houses.'[13] In other words, *mohtarfa* was levied not only on merchants but also on artisans. It is therefore possible to identify the merchant community by analysing the *mohtarfa*. The names of the taxpayers of *balute* and *mohtarfa* are found in the lists of taxpayers of the rural area of Qasba Indapur, which are attached to the lists of the payers of the land revenue and are in the accounts of the rural area of Qasba Indapur.

In the lists of taxpayers,[14] the payers both of *balute* and of *mohtarfa* are entered together. According to these lists, various communities such as those of carpenters, weavers and oilmen paid *balute* or *mohtarfa*. The British report shows that some artisans such as oilmen and weavers sold the goods they produced,[15] so there is a possibility that the artisans in the lists were engaged in commercial activity. In the 1786 list of taxpayers,[16] the names of a *gujar* and a weaver are entered under the title of a trader (*wani*). It can thus be said that at least a trader called *wani* and a merchant from Gujarat, who was called *gujar*, were merchants. There is a possibility that weavers also took part in commercial activities.

In the accounts of the rural area, *balute* and *mohtarfa* are written down separately, although it is not clearly mentioned in the account who paid *mohtarfa* as merchants. This tax often has the subcategory of *mohtarfa-dukan* (shop), which means the tax levied on a shop. In this subcategory, a *gujar*, a *wani* and a weaver are included. In other words, *gujars*, *wanis* and weavers kept shops in the rural area.

It is found from the accounts that *wanis*, *gujars* and weavers were merchants in the rural area of Qasba Indapur. In the accounts, the name *gujar* is always entered under the heading *mohtarfa-dukan* (shop). No shops in the rural area of Qasba Indapur were owned consistently by any other community, although weavers and *wanis* had shops there temporarily. This indicates that the *gujar* community constituted the most important shopkeepers among the above merchants in the rural area.

Peth Indapur

In Peth Indapur, the land tax was not levied because there was no cultivated land. The revenue accounts of Peth Indapur consisted of a list of taxpayers of *balute* and *mohtarfa*. This indicates that these two items were the main revenue of Peth Indapur. The lists of taxpayers that are available in the Pune Archives cover the 1780s and 1810s only. Payers of *balute* and of *mohtarfa*, who are entered together in the lists, are as follows:

Table 8.1: The payers of *balute* and *mohtarfa* in Peth Indapur

Type of taxpayer	1784	1788	1789	1811	1814	1816	1818
Bakal (shopkeeper)	81	80	87	41	42	46	46
Saraf (money-changer)	10	10	10	10	8	9	9
Bajaj (cloth merchant)	24	26	25	9	13	17	21
Sonar (goldsmith)	18	19	16	6	7	11	11
Kasar (brazier)	19	20	18	3	4	5	5
Seti Burkul (?)	4	3	4	0	0	0	0
Burkul (?)	18	16	17	0	0	0	0
Dhangar (shepherd)	5	5	6	17	15	13	12
Balgade Koshti (weaver)	6	6	6				
Kande Koshti (weaver)	6	6	6	11	15	18	18
Bagwan (Muslim gardener)	7	9	8	4	4	4	4
Miscellaneous payers	10	10	8	7	7	9	11
Tamboli (betel-leaf seller)	3	4	3	4			
Atar (perfumer)	2	3	2	2	7	7	6
Darji (tailor)	23	24	22	0	0	0	0
Khartik (butcher)	11	9	10	8	8	7	7
Teli (oilman)	22	23	21	5	8	9	10
Mali (gardener)	12	14	12	13	13	13	12
Majur (waged labourer)	44	64	44	6	11	24	48

Sources: Hiseb Peth Indapur (Shuhur 1184, 1188, 1189, 1211, 1214, 1216, and 1218), Pune Jamav Rumal no.716, MSAP.

The *mohtarfa* in Peth Indapur was collected partly according to occupation, although it was collected according to the community in Qasba Indapur. To be precise, a shopkeeper (*bakal*), a money-changer (*saraf*) and a cloth merchant (*bajaj*) are the names of occupations, not communities, whereas the remaining heads are the names of the communities. In the list of shopkeepers, the names of a *gujar*, a *wani* and some artisans such as a goldsmith and a shepherd are found, and in the list of shopkeepers, the names of a *gujar* and some artisans such as a tailor are found. This indicates that not only *gujars* and *wanis* but also some artisans such as tailors and shepherds were involved in commercial activities.[17] In Table 8.1, the number of shopkeepers in the 1810s is much less than that in the 1780s. In spite of this decrease, the number of shops belonging to *gujars* remained constant at eight to eleven in both periods, while that of other communities' shops decreased. It can be said that the *gujars* were one of the most important merchant groups in Peth Indapur in the 1810s, although the number of their shops itself was not large.

As Table 8.1 shows, various merchants, artisans and money-changers resided in Peth Indapur and were engaged in their professions. Thus, handicrafts, commerce and banking were the main industries of Peth Indapur. Administratively, the land revenue, which was collected in kind in some villages or in money in other villages, in the region of Indapur Pargana was gathered into the *pargana* office called *kacheri*, located in Peth Indapur. Grain was finally sold at shops in Peth Indapur. Money was exchanged for remittance to the central government. In addition to grain, many goods were traded. Peth Indapur was the centre of the economy of Indapur Pargana.

Merchants and Artisans in Qasba Indapur

Artisans and traders in Qasba Indapur can be divided into three groups. The first group was that of the traditional twelve servants called *bara-balutedars*, who paid *balute*. The second consisted of artisans other than these twelve servants, who paid *mohtarfa* for their professions as artisans. Some of them were called *alutedars*, which means irregular or occasional village servants.[18] They most likely came to villages after the *bara-balutedars* had established their businesses. Whereas *balutedars* were recognized as regular members of a village, *alutedars* were not, in spite of paying the *mohtarfa*. The third group was made up of merchants, who paid *mohtarfa* for their commercial activities. It is impossible to grasp the whole picture of these merchants. Because there is a possibility that artisans sold the goods they produced in various ways, it is very difficult to sort out the third group from the second group. However, the documents on tax collection provide one way to classify them clearly. In the accounts both of Peth Indapur and of the rural area, *mohtarfa* has a subcategory for shopkeeping. Accordingly, the third group in Qasba Indapur has the sub-group 'shopkeepers'. In the British period, the British officer classified artisans and traders into four groups: shopkeepers, artisans other than traditional servants, traditional servants and others.[19] In other words, this officer considered shopkeepers to be one separate group.

It is clear from the accounts of Qasba Indapur who the shopkeepers were. Weavers, *wanis* and *gujars* kept their shops in the rural area, and *gujars*, *wanis*, goldsmiths and some artisans such as tailors and shepherds did so in Peth Indapur. The above analysis makes clear that *gujars* were very important among these shopkeepers, both in Peth Indapur and in the rural area of Qasba Indapur. Interestingly, *gujars* were not originally local merchants but came from Gujarat Province. Studying their activities may shed light on how merchants from outside settled and became important in Qasba Indapur.

Gujars in Qasba Indapur

Gujar is a subdivision of *wani*. The term *wani* was originally a functional term meaning a merchant in western India, known elsewhere in India as *bania*. The community of *wani* had some subdivisions, which, according to British reports, included forty separate sub-communities. For example, *wani* who were said to come from Gujarat in the seventeenth and eighteenth centuries were called *Gujarat wani* or *Gujarati vania*. *Gujar* was a sub-caste of *Gujarat wani*.[20]

In Indian history, Gujarati merchants were one of the largest merchant communities, as were Marwari merchants. Their commercial activities spread all over the Indian Ocean, as well as within India itself. For example, Meshra Vania, or the subdivision of *Gujarat wani*, to which the *gujars* belonged, went as far as Karnatak and Madras in southern India, and they were called *gujar vanias*.[21] There is, therefore, a high possibility that the term *gujar* means not only one sub-caste of Meshra Vania but also merchants from Gujarat more broadly. According to Sumitra Kulkarni,[22] Gujarati merchants began to be distinctly visible in Pune from the 1760s onward and came to the region around Indapur Pargana in the 1760s. Because Gujarati merchants migrated southward successively, *gujars* in Qasba Indapur may have come from Gujarat together with other Gujarati merchants in the 1760s, or else they may have settled in Indapur Pargana prior to this point.[23]

Gujarati merchants greatly developed their trading and banking businesses in the British Empire, especially after the late nineteenth century. Many moved to Southeast Asia and to the British territories in East Africa. In Southeast Asia, Gujarati merchants developed a financial system and operated as merchant bankers there.[24] In western India also, Marwari and Gujarati immigrants settled and ran rural businesses under British rule. They engaged in moneylending and accumulated capital and land in Pune District, including Indapur Pargana, and in Ahmandagar District, which caused the Deccan Riots of 1875.[25]

The influential position of Gujarati merchants in the economy of western India of this period makes it vital to investigate their activities, including those of the *gujars*. This study utilizes documents on the collection of taxes in Qasba Indapur to describe the various activities of the *gujars* in Qasba Indapur. Their commercial, agricultural, financial and cultural undertakings are discussed here.

Commercial Activities
According to its tax records, Peth Indapur had eight to eleven *gujars* in the 1780s. They worked as shopkeepers or as cloth merchants. In Peth Indapur, the

gujars sold various groceries in their own shops. The rural area of Qasba Indapur had six to eight *gujars*. All the names of the *gujars* on whom *mohtarfa* was levied for shopkeeping in the rural area are included in the shopkeeper (*bakal*) category in Peth Indapur. In other words, all the *gujars* in the rural area had shops in Peth Indapur also. They appear to have taken agricultural produce such as sorghum from the rural area to the market in Peth Indapur, and brought the goods traded in the market to the rural area. Shopkeepers in Peth Indapur other than *gujars* did not keep shops in the rural area of Qasba Indapur. *Gujars* thus played an important role in connecting the urban and the rural areas in Qasba Indapur commercially.

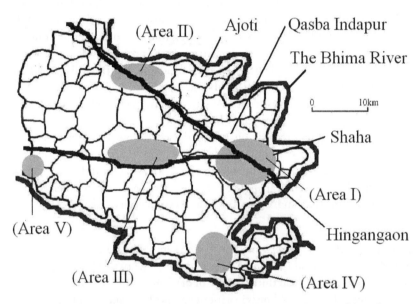

Figure 8.1: **Indapur Pargana and its market places. Source:** *Map of the Indapoor Pargana of the Poona Zilla,* **1875, Maps, I.S., Map Collection, BL.**

Zooming out to observe the villages surrounding Qasba Indapur, none of the *gujars* who did business in Qasba Indapur are visible. Some of these villages had other merchants belonging to the *gujar* community, and some villages appear to have had no merchants at all. Other villages had merchants belonging to other communities, including that of the Marwari.[26] It seems that the businesses of *gujar* merchants varied from village to village across Indapur Pargana. As Figure 8.2 shows, Indapur Pargana had four additional marketplaces, each of which had more than five *gujars*. In the remaining villages, however, there was at most one *gujar* merchant doing business, and in some cases none.

The tax records on transit duties called *jakat* under the Marathas[27] offer another notable detail. Maniram Gujar, who was the only *gujar* cloth merchant in Peth Indapur, carried his cloth to the nearby village of Hingangaon. This village, located on the bank of the Bhima River, was an outport of Qasba Indapur. This river was one of the major trade routes which connected Indapur Pargana with other *parganas*. In other words, it can be seen that he was engaged in exporting cloth that he stocked in Peth Indapur to other *parganas*. A *gujar* from another village also participated in this trade between Hingangaon and Peth Indapur. *Gujars* in Qasba Indapur brought groceries and sorghum[28] from the villages of Ajoti and Shaha on the bank of the Bhima River. *Gujars* from outer villages carried out the trade in cloth and groceries between Qasba Indapur and other marketplaces, in particular, the villages of Gotwadi (Area III in Figure 8.1) and Tawashi (Area V in Figure 8.1). According to the records on transit duties in Tawashi, a *gujar* who originally came from Peth Indapur resided in Tawashi and participated in the trade between Qasba Indapur and this village.[29] These cases indicate that some of the *gujars* who came from Qasba Indapur but moved to other villages kept business relations with persons in Qasba Indapur, though it is not clear with whom these *gujars* had dealings.

According to these records on transit duties, various communities other than *gujars* also participated in the trade between Qasba Indapur and other villages. *Gujars* were only one of the merchant communities in Indapur Pargana. Unfortunately, it is not clear if *gujars* in Qasba Indapur and in other villages cooperated in the trade in Indapur Pargana as a community.

Agricultural Activities

Interestingly, a few of the *gujar* merchants who kept shops either in Peth Indapur or in the rural area held land and paid a land tax in the rural area. For example, Mukund Seth Gujar[30] held thirty *bigha*[31] of dry land in the rural area. The earliest reference to his landholding is in a list of payers of the land revenue in 1782.[32] No names of other *gujars* are found in the earlier lists. To be concrete, Mukund Seth Gujar, who was the first landholder among *gujars* in Qasba Indapur, gained thirty *bighas* of land in the rural area around 1782 and kept it continuously.[33] He often hired two peasants to cultivate part of his extra land,[34] while he always cultivated the original land which he gained around 1782 himself. In this sense, Mukund Seth Gujar was not an absentee landlord, unlike Gujarati merchants in the late nineteenth century. Other *gujars* in the rural area managed agricultural land in the same way.[35] In short, a few of the *gujars* in Qasba Indapur were actually cultivators as well as merchants, and some landholders in other communities also kept shops in Peth Indapur. These landholders, including *gujars*, connected agriculture in the rural area to commerce in Peth Indapur.

Financial Activities

The accounts of Peth Indapur and of the rural area of Qasba Indapur indicate that *gujars* lent money to the local government in Qasba Indapur, which consisted of the village headman and village officials of Qasba Indapur, as well as to residents there. *Uchapat*, lending and financial support for the local government are discussed here.

Uchapat

The expenditures in the accounts of Peth Indapur and of the rural area include a heading called *uchapat kharch*. *Uchapat* is a Marathi word which means taking goods on credit,[36] and *kharch* means expenditure. The local government took goods on credit from *gujars* and *telis* (oilmen) and then paid the money to them by installment later without interest. This expenditure was called *uchapat kharch*. In the local administration, oil was an essential item that was used not only for various rituals at Hindu temples such as Shiddheshwar temple (see Figure 8.1) but also for lights in various offices such as the *kacheri* of Indapur Pargana.[37] The local government purchased oil directly from *telis* on credit.[38] In the accounts of Qasba Indapur, the local government often paid *uchapat kharch* to *gujars* for village expenditures.[39] In other words, the *gujars* paid the expenses of the village of Qasba Indapur on behalf of the local government, and the government paid them back later. Similarly, the *gujars* prepaid for Hindu festivals such as Diwali and Sankranti[40] and sometimes for religious celebrations at Shiddheshwar Temple.[41] They purchased the stationery such as paper and ink used at *kacheri* in Peth Indapur,[42] and sometimes provided the horses of local officials and soldiers with sorghum as feed.[43] *Gujars* made all the payments on behalf of the local government. They also financially assisted the local government with cultural, administrative and military functions in Qasba Indapur.

Lending

In addition to *uchapat*, gujars lent money directly to the local government,[44] which the government paid back with interest. *Gujars* lent money to military commanders called *sardars* in Indapur Pargana[45] and also to residents in Qasba Indapur. The following figures show how *gujars* lent money to residents in Qasba Indapur.

RIM5340

Shuhur 1188 (AD 1788)

1) Name: Khandu Setya
2) Land Tax: **Rs.12-8**
   levied on 30 Bigha of dry land

1) Re.1   3 Moharam (The 1st month of Islamic year)
2) Rs.2   16 Safar (The 2nd month of Islamic year)
   borrowing from **Mukund eth Gujjar**
3) Rs.3   3 Rabiilawal (The 3rd month)
4) Re.1   11 Rabilakhar (The 4th month)
5) Re.1   8 Jamadilawal (The 5th month)
6) Re.1   22 Jamadilakhar (The 6th month)
7) Re.1   7 Saban (The 8th month)
8) Re.1   5 Jamadilawal (The 5th montl (AD1789)
9) Rs.1-8 1 Jamadilakhar (The 6th month)
Rs.12-8

Figure 8.2: The schedule of the payment of a land tax by Khandu Setya (1788).
Note: Re. stands for Rupee, and Rs. is for Rupees. Source: Jama Khandu Setya
(Shuhur 1188), Qasba Indapur, Rumal no. 709.

RIM5334

Shuhur 1188 (AD1788)

Rs.130-4	Safar (the 2nd month)
Rs.12	Vyankatrao Bhidhe
Rs.13	Mahadu Niv Mali
Rs.2	Santu Malhari Mali
Rs.5-12	Harbhat Aba
Rs.31	Atuba Trigul
Rs.2	**Khandu Setya**
Rs.8	Kashiram Hajari
Rs.8-8	Nagoba Trigul
Rs.6	Bapu Hajari
Rs.27	Radhu Mali and Seti Mali
Rs.130-4	

Rs.8	18 Rabilakhar (The 4th month)
Rs.5	Subhana Holkar
Rs.3	Khanaji Ghat (?)
Rs.8	

Rs.13	14 Jamadilawal (The 5th month)
Rs.8	Jalisant Mali
Rs.5	Radhudav Mali
Rs.13	

Figure 8.3: The schedule of moneylending by Mukund Seth Gujar (1788).
Source: Kharch Mukund Seth Gujar (Shuhur 1188), Qasba Indapur, Rumal no. 709.

RIM5298

Shuhur 1188 (AD1788)

1) Name: Joti Teli
2) Land Tax: **Rs.9**
   levied on 15 Bigha of dry land

1) Re.1   5 Moharam (The 1st month)
   borrowing from **Apa Sonar**
2) Rs.2   16 Safar (The 2nd month)
   borrowing from **Motiram Gujjar**
3) Rs.2   29 Safar
   borrowing from **Motiram Gujjar**
4) Re.1   5 Rabilakhar (The 4th month)
5) Re.1   3 Jamadilawal (The 5th month)
6) Re.0-8 11 Safar (The 2nd month)
7) Re.0-8 22 Safar (The 2nd month)
   borrowing from **Kadari Teli**
8) Re.0-8 12 Rabilawal (The 3rd month)
9) Re.0-8 15 Saban (The 8th month)
Rs.9

Figure 8.4: The schedule of the payment of a land tax by Joti Teli (1788).
Source: Jama Joti Teli (Shuhur 1188), Qasba Indapur, Rumal no. 707, MSAP.

According to Figure 8.3, Mukund Seth Gujar loaned Rs. 2 to Khandu Setya in the month of Safar. Figure 8.2 confirms that Khandu Setya borrowed Rs. 2 from Mukund Seth Gujar on 16 Safar in order to pay the land tax. By comparing these schedules, it is found that *gujars* lent money to residents of Qasba Indapur for their tax payments. As Figure 8.3 shows, one *gujar* simultaneously lent money to different persons belonging to different communities. As Figure 8.2 shows, the land revenue was paid by installments, and taxpayers did not always borrow money from *gujars*. For example, Joti Teli borrowed money from not only Motiram Gujar but also from Apa Sonar and Kodari Teli (see Figure 8.4). As this case shows, some taxpayers borrowed money from more than one person in Qasba Indapur, and not only *gujars* but also various communities[46] engaged in moneylending.

The above cases show *gujars* clearly worked not only as merchants but also as moneylenders in Qasba Indapur. The local government procured its immediate funding exclusively from *gujars*, while various communities got involved in private moneylending. Moneylending by *gujars* was obviously quite important for the functioning of the local administration there. This made the relationship between the *gujars* and the local government in Qasba Indapur strong.

Financial and Administrative Support for the Local Government
The phrase 'Govind Seth Gujar-*vidyamane*' is found in documents on the collection of taxes such as the land revenue and *mohtarfa* from the late 1780s onward.[47] *Vidyamane* is a Marathi word which means 'in the presence of'.[48] In other words, taxes were collected in the presence of Govind Gujar in Qasba Indapur. It is inferred from this phrase that this *gujar* was in charge of supervising the collection of taxes in Qasba Indapur. Some *gujars* were thus directly involved in revenue administration as well as supporting the local government financially.

The expenditure in the account of Indapur Pargana in 1789 provides an interesting case.

> Rs. 20: Water in an irrigation pond [in the rural area of Qasba Indapur] dried up. So the bushes were broken. And Badekhan Jakatdar and Mukund Seth Gujar gave money in order to plant a melon and chickpeas. This payment amounted to Rs. 20.[49]

In 1789, Badekhan Jakatdar and Mukund Seth Gujar paid Rs. 20 for the reclamation in the rural area due to a water shortage. This money was lent or given to the local government. This case also shows that *gujars* were involved in the local administration.

The earliest reference to a *gujar* in Qasba Indapur is in the schedule of a land tax paid by Ranu Teli, to whom Khushali Gujar lent money in 1761.[50] This schedule indicates that a *gujar* was there in at least as early as the 1760s and already worked as a moneylender. *Gujars* then began to prepay money on behalf of the local government under the name of *uchapat* in the 1770s.[51] In the 1780s, *gujars* loaned money directly to the local government,[52] and one *gujar* was in the charge of supervising the collection of taxes in Qasba Indapur. The financial activities of the local government enabled the *gujars* outside of Indapur Pargana to get involved in the local administration.

Cultural Activities
Gujars paid some local taxes at festivals such as Dasara,[53] as this was one of the ends to which tax revenue was used.[54] In the late 1780s, *gujars* started to pay a local tax for this festival.[55] This indicates that they participated in social events like festivals in Qasba Indapur from the late 1780s onward. In the 1770s, they had not paid any festival-related taxes because they were still outsiders. During this decade, as seen above, they began to pay the village expenditure on behalf of the local government. Part of this expenditure was used for festivals such as Dasara. In other words, they started to get financially involved, albeit indirectly, in cultural activities in the 1770s. In the late 1780s, probably, they were allowed

to take part in festival activities. This suggests that *gujars*, who were originally outsiders, had become not only economically but also socially admitted to a community in Qasba Indapur by the late 1780s. As village servants could be divided into two categories (*balutedars* and *alutedars*), a village community in eighteenth-century western India did not consist of homogenous groups. Thus the admission to festivals did not always mean *gujars* became regular members of a community in Qasba Indapur. However, it can be said that *gujars* were gradually included in the public or social sphere of the community in Qasba Indapur in the 1780s.

In the 1760s, *gujars* in Qasba Indapur were not only merchants but also moneylenders. They prepaid expenses for, and loaned money to, the local administration in Qasba Indapur. It seems this moneylending made their positions in Qasba Indapur strong. By the late 1780s, they had settled into a secure socio-economic niche in Qasba Indapur. As a result, *gujars* got involved in various activities in Qasba Indapur at the end of the eighteenth century.[56]

Gujars' Activities in Qasba Indapur in the Nineteenth Century

Indapur Pargana saw a great change at the beginning of the nineteenth century. In 1803, Holkar, one of the chiefs who had joined the Maratha Confederacy, invaded Pune Subha, in which Indapur Pargana was located,[57] and in 1804 the failure of rain heavily damaged crops in this Subha.[58] The following passage from a contract (*kaulnama*) in 1814 mentions that these disasters also hit Peth Indapur.

> Contract: Mokadam [village-headman], Shete [leader of a market], Mahajan [accountant of a market] in Peth Indapur, Shuhur year 1214 [= AD 1814] merchants in Peth Indapur had gone out because of a disorder by [Holkar's] invasion. So *zamindars* [the local hereditary officers of Indapur Pargana] petitioned the government to give a contract of *istawa* of a tax.[59] Concerning this petition, a contract, which amounted to Rs. 1684–12, was issued. But it was impossible for merchants in Peth Indapur [to pay the whole amount]. For some merchants died and others were in other villages. So Sadashiv Pant living in Tembhrni[60] received a contract to manage Peth Indapur [and to collect taxes there]. *Mohtarfa* will be collected after seeing the families living there. After he visited and inspected Peth Indapur by himself, a contract was finally concluded.[61]

This passage mentions that merchants died or left Peth Indapur after the disasters in 1803 and 1804 and that merchants could not pay the *mohtarfa* even a decade later. In other words, the disasters devastated Peth Indapur and it does not appear to have recovered smoothly. According to Table 8.1, however, some merchants paid the *mohtarfa* despite the severe situation. Analysing the accounts in detail reveals that the number of *gujar* shops there did not change between the 1780s and the 1810s, while the number of the shops of other merchant communities greatly decreased. In short, the *gujars* could keep their businesses in Peth Indapur in the face of disaster and subsequent unrest, and even as various other local merchants abandoned their businesses. *Gujars* survived probably because of their administrative and financial links to the local government.

According to the accounts of Qasba Indapur in the 1810s, *gujars* continued to prepay the local government's expenditure under the name of *uchapat*.[62] *Gujars* also got involved in the remittance to the central government. The local government had to remit part of the revenue in Qasba Indapur. This payment was called *bharna*. The names of some *gujars* are found together with the amount of remittance in the list of *bharna* in the 1810s.[63] This means some *gujars* remitted money to the central government on behalf of the local government. Under conditions of disorder, *gujars* got more deeply involved with the local administration, especially revenue collection. When cavalry divisions came from Tembhurni and from Pune to Qasba Indapur, *gujars* paid to feed their horses daily.[64] Even after the disasters hit Peth Indapur, financial support from the *gujars* continued in various ways, and became essential to managing the local administration. Probably this close relationship with the local government enabled the *gujars* to obtain a special position in Qasba Indapur at the beginning of the nineteenth century.

Documents in the Pune Archives tell that *gujars* continued to hold and cultivate land in the rural area of Qasba Indapur,[65] to loan money to taxpayers[66] and to pay money for festivals such as Dasara in the 1810s.[67] In other words, *gujars* in Qasba Indapur carried on through the last phase of the Maratha period much as they had in the late eighteenth century, even while Qasba Indapur as a whole underwent great change and many villagers ran away.[68] The special position *gujars* held in Qasba Indapur due to their financial support for the local administration accounts for this difference. In this period, *gujars* gained a very high status in Qasba Indapur society.[69]

In 1818, the English East India Company defeated the Maratha Confederacy in the Third Anglo-Maratha War, and British rule started in western India. As far as Marathi documents in the British period show, *gujars* still paid money on behalf of the local government under British rule.[70] The relationship between the *gujars* and the local government did not change even after the colonization of western India.

Under British rule, *mohtarfa* was levied in Qasba Indapur as it had been under the Marathas. In 1825, the Assistant Collector, who was the British officer in charge of Indapur Pargana, checked how much *mohtarfa* was collected in Peth Indapur and settled the new amount of *mohtarfa* there.[71] In the 1830s, the *gujars* continued to pay the new amount.[72] This means they kept their businesses as shopkeepers in Peth Indapur under the British. The pattern of their activities continued. *Gujars* continued to pay *mohtarfa* until it was abolished in 1844,[73] although detailed data on the payments after 1835 is no longer available. It is impossible to confirm whether they continued their businesses after 1844. In 1847, the road between Pune and Peth Indapur was improved, becoming an Imperial Highway.[74] We may infer that colonial rule directly affected the rural economy in Indapur Pargana, including the *gujars*, in the late nineteenth century.

Conclusion

This chapter has offered a window into the functioning of the rural socio-economy of Indapur Pargana in western India by focusing on the activities of a particular community of local merchants called *gujar*. Five marketplaces served the rural economy of Indapur Pargana, each with more than five *gujars*; among them, Qasba Indapur had the largest number of *gujars*. Within Qasba Indapur some *gujars* kept shops both in Peth Indapur and in the rural area, and a few of them held land in the rural area and brought crops to Peth Indapur. Some *gujars*, therefore, played an important role in connecting the rural and the urban areas. However, landholders from other groups in the rural area also kept shops in Peth Indapur and played a similar role in the local economy. In this context, *gujars* were only one of the merchant communities in Qasba Indapur.

Gujars did not, however, carry out only commercial activities. The earliest reference to a *gujar* in Qasba Indapur comes from a loan in 1761. The *gujars* lent money to various communities in Qasba Indapur chiefly for payment of taxes, so by this time they already functioned not only as merchants but also as moneylenders. In the 1770s, they began to lend money to the local government. This business of *gujars* was fundamental to the functioning of government and unique among the merchant communities in Qasba Indapur. In the late 1780s, the *gujars* became even more deeply involved in administration in Qasba Indapur by supervising the collection of taxes.

Although *gujars* were originally outsiders, their relationship with the local government gave them a special position among the communities of merchants and moneylenders in Qasba Indapur. From the late 1780s onward, *gujars* paid a local tax for a festival and participated in cultural activities in Qasba Indapur. This indicates they had become social members of Qasba Indapur at least by the late 1780s. Probably their financial support of the local government enabled the *gujars* to settle not only economically but also socially in Qasba Indapur. Previous studies of the migration of Marwari and Gujarati merchants have rarely focused on their social relations in the destination areas.

Throughout the devastation of 1803 and 1804 and the ensuing unrest, *gujars* alone were able to keep their businesses in Peth Indapur and continued to financially support the local government under the Marathas as other merchants fled.

The special position their ties to the government gave them raised their status in Qasba Indapur society and strengthened their place in the market. Even after British rule began in 1818, little change is seen in the activities of the *gujars*. At least up to the 1840s, *gujars* maintained their businesses in Qasba Indapur.

This complementary relationship between the *gujars* and the local government grew ever tighter in the political and economic divergence of the early nineteenth century. Under British rule, the Assistant Collector, who was in charge of Indapur Pargana, worked at the *kacheri* in Peth Indapur. He could not change this situation, and the continued role of the *gujars* in Qasba Indapur, at least in the early nineteenth century, was necessary in order to administer this area smoothly. Sanjay Subrahmanyam and C. A. Bayly have shown that in many places English traders took the place of Indian portfolio capitalists in the process of the colonization and that the English East India Company finally replaced revenue farming with direct collection.[75] However, no English merchants emerged in Qasba Indapur who could take the place of *gujars*, and the Assistant Collector could not exclude them because they propped up a declining state and kept local government finance functional. Great changes introduced by colonization from the late eighteenth to the early nineteenth century consequently gave some small merchants like *gujars* firm positions as local merchants and moneylenders even as they robbed some great merchants of their positions as portfolio capitalists. The *gujars* did this by establishing ever closer relations with local government in a period of upheaval caused by the decline of the central government, and they successfully retained their position under the new colonial rulers at least through the early nineteenth century.

It is said that the Imperial Highway and railways connected rural towns such as Qasba Indapur to the outer world in the late nineteenth century. In this period, Marwari and Gujarati merchants accumulated capital and land as moneylenders on a scale quite different from the *gujars* in the period between the 1760s and the 1840s. It is possible that the emergence of these powerful merchants changed the relationship described above between the local government and *gujars*, and so altered the nature of their activities in the late nineteenth century. A discussion of the activities of Marwari and Gujarati merchants in the late nineteenth century must, however, be left for another occasion.

Glossary

alutedar(s)	village servants secondary to balutedars
balute	a share of the corn and garden-produce assigned for the subsistence of the twelve public servants of a village, or a tax levied on these servants.
bharna	paying or remitting money in full

Dasara	a popular festival for Durga who is a warrior goddess. It starts on 10 Ashwin (the seventh month of the Hindu year), which overlaps September and October.
Diwali	the feast of lights, a popular festival of the Hindus, which is held on the last two days of the dark half of Ashwin and the new moon and the four following days of Kartik (September to October).
Gujar	traders and dealers from Gujarat, a province in northwest India
hundis	bill of exchanges
kacheri	a court, a hall, a public office
koshti	weaver and spinner
mahar	a type of untouchable in western India. *Mahars* carried out various kinds of work. For example, they worked as guardians of a village and public servants of a village headman.
mang	a type of untouchable in western India. They worked as scavengers, sweepers and skinners; as tanners, they supplied leather materials like ropes. They also acted as watchmen.
Maratha Confederacy	the alliance of the Maratha chieftains, which formed to enlarge the territory of Marathas in the early eighteenth century. It ruled the greater part of western, central and northern India. Its centre was the Peshwa Government.
mohtarfa	a tax levied on traders and professions, on the artificers of a village or their implements
pargana	a district, a province, a tract of country comprising many villages
peshwa	the prime minister of the Maratha Confederacy
peth	a market, part of a town where shops are assembled, a trading or manufacturing town
qasba	a small town, or a large village, the chief or market town of a district
Sankranti	the passage of the sun from one sign of the zodiac to another, and the day of the transition of the sun into Makar (Capricorn) (14 January), which is celebrated in almost all parts of India.
sardar	a chief, or a military commander
subha	a province, a division comprising from five to eight *parganas* or *tarafs* (a subdivision of a *pargana*)
uchapat	taking goods on credit
wani	a trader, a grocer or corn-chandler

9 MID-NINETEENTH-CENTURY NAGASAKI: WESTERN AND JAPANESE MERCHANT COMMUNITIES WITHIN COMMERCIAL AND POLITICAL TRANSITIONS

Robert Hellyer

In the first half of the nineteenth century, Nagasaki, as it had throughout the Edo period (1603–1868), served primarily as a point of trade with Chinese merchants, who brought silver and medicinal goods to barter for Japanese marine products and copper. Dutch traders, stationed on the man-made island of Dejima in Nagasaki harbor, also exported copper, obtained in exchange for a variety of European and Asian products. Historians of Japan often give less focus to events in Nagasaki in the 1850s, instead highlighting the visits of US Commodore Matthew C. Perry. Following negotiations with Perry, leaders of the Tokugawa *bakufu* (shogunate), the central authority of the Japanese state, signed the US–Japan Treaty of Peace and Amity of 1854. Also known as the Treaty of Kanagawa, the pact established provisions for US ships to obtain wood, coal, water and other supplies at the ports of Shimoda (near Edo, today's Tokyo) and Hakodate (on the southern coast of Hokkaido). It also created protocols for the repatriation of US castaways and for limited trade at the two ports.

Yet even with the new interactions permitted at other ports, Nagasaki remained a key venue for diplomacy and trade. During the Crimean War (1853–6), British, French and Russian military and diplomatic envoys called, aiming to gain military advantages in East Asian waters over their European rivals. They also sought concessions along the lines of those granted to the United States by the Treaty of Kanagawa. As diplomatic historian William McOmie has shown, these visits to Nagasaki represent an alternative narrative to the better-known Perry missions on the role of Western diplomatic and military pressure in Japan's revision of foreign relations in the early 1850s.[1]

In 1858 another US envoy, Townsend Harris, negotiated a more expansive commercial agreement: the US–Japan Treaty of Amity and Commerce. As with the Treaty of Kanagawa, the 1858 pact spurred Tokugawa officials to sign similar agreements with Britain and other European states. The treaties designated Nagasaki, Kanagawa (later Yokohama) and Hakodate as treaty ports to be established the following year, with Niigata and Kobe (Hyogo) to be added several years later. Of the three ports 'opened' in 1859, Nagasaki held the most lucrative trade links with China, carefully protected by the *bakufu*, which directly ruled the city. This chapter will examine three merchant groups in Nagasaki during the 1860s, defining 'community' differently with each. The first is the Tokugawa clearing-house (*kaisho*), which prior to 1859 dominated trade at the Kyushu port by directing that all imports and exports flow through it. The clearing-house functioned as the main organ of an 'institutional' merchant community. Created by Tokugawa caveat, the institutional community gained cohesion around the goals of implementing *bakufu* directives and maintaining the clearing-house's dominant position on the Nagasaki commercial scene.

The chapter also considers a 'domain' merchant community comprised of representatives of feudal domains (*han*; the Japanese state included roughly 250 domains until the early 1870s), as well as individuals with loose affiliations to particular domains. More organic than its institutional counterpart, the domain community coalesced around common commercial agendas of military and economic strengthening. The community also gained cohesion because of the need for domain representatives to share information and cooperate in what were, for most, new situations of negotiating and trading with foreign partners. To consider the domain perspective, the chapter will focus on Tosa, on the southern portion of the island of Shikoku, whose leaders sent representatives to Nagasaki to pursue trade. Tosa's commercial agenda will be presented primarily through the activities of Iwasaki Yatarō, a domain representative, who became a leading businessman in the Meiji period (1868–1912).

Western traders, especially from Britain, compose the third merchant community formed in Nagasaki in 1858.[2] Like its domain counterpart, this was an organically formed group composed of traders who chose to venture to Nagasaki, most in hopes of obtaining wealth through commerce. Yet akin to the institutional community, the Western merchant group was also defined by Tokugawa directives, in this case the *bakufu* policy that restricted foreign merchants to a contained enclave. This physical factor, combined with sharp linguistic and cultural differences from their Japanese counterparts, enhanced the ideal of a distinct Western merchant community. The community competed against the clearing-house for Japanese-Chinese trade, and many of its members developed commercial partnerships with counterparts in the domain merchant community. The perspective of Western merchants will be considered primarily through the case of William Alt, a British merchant who arrived at Nagasaki in 1859 at the age of nineteen. Alt founded an import/export firm that traded with the *bakufu* but also notably established extensive commercial ties with Tosa, as well as a personal relationship with Iwasaki.[3]

As its larger themes, the chapter will consider the three communities within political currents during the tumultuous 1860s, a decade marked by peasant rebellions, urban popular protests and armed conflicts within domains (to name just a few trends). It will focus on the role of the movement to expel foreigners from the Japanese state, and the related effort of many domains to increase their military and economic positions in a fluid, domestic political landscape. It will also trace the intersection of those political trends with two commercial ones: a burgeoning trade in ships and arms that resulted from the expulsion movement, and a gradual but consistent move away from long-established trade links with China.

As more specific points, the chapter will explore first, the ability of *bakufu* officials to adroitly navigate the initial years of Nagasaki as a treaty port, channelling through their hands the most lucrative sectors of Japanese-Chinese trade while also manipulating to their advantage the flows and use of bullion. Second, through the experiences of Alt, it will consider the formation of the Western merchant community and detail the political factors whereby trade in ships and arms came to upstage Japanese-Chinese trade, thereby weakening the position of the institutional merchant community. Third, it will examine how the goal of enhancing domain economic and military strength brought Iwasaki and Tosa representatives to Nagasaki, where they traded with Alt and other Western merchants. Finally, the chapter will chart connections into the Meiji period by outlining how the commercial enterprises created by Alt and Iwasaki in the 1860s developed into established companies that capitalized in different ways as Japanese foreign trade grew to become more centred on Western markets.

The Durability of Established Trade Patterns in East Asia

Although identifying the institution of the treaty port system as a watershed in the economic history of East Asia, historians have observed that the new system did not bring an immediate end to established patterns of trade. In his study of maritime trade in mid-nineteenth-century China, John K. Fairbank noted that the regime of 'free' trade imposed with the Treaty of Nanjing of 1842 brought only a temporary reversal of the pre-Opium War pattern of silver flowing into China to purchase tea and silk.[4] In a trend more fully explored by economic historian Lin Man-houng, British and US merchants found it difficult to obtain enough tea and silk to meet growing home demand by trading solely opium and Western manufactured goods, such as British Lancashire textiles, of limited interest to Chinese consumers. In a turnabout to the marked outflow of silver in the years after the start of the new treaty regime, British and US ships therefore brought more silver to China during the 1850s and 1860s.[5] Exploring late nineteenth-century Korea in this volume, Ishikawa Ryota offers the Korea–China ginseng trade as another example of the durability of established trading patterns even after the implementation of the treaty port regime in Korea in the 1870s.[6]

In Japan as well, the imposition of the treaty port system in 1859 was marked by the continued vitality of an established, China-centred maritime trading system dominated by the Tokugawa *bakufu*. Since the mid eighteenth century, *bakufu* leaders had focused on shipping copper and marine products – kelp, sea cucumbers, abalone and shark fins – to China as substitutes for silver in order to obtain chiefly medicinal goods from China. The *bakufu* developed Nagasaki into a collection point for marine products harvested especially in Ezo (today's Hok- kaido). In the decades prior to the start of the treaty port system, *bakufu* leaders consistently protected the marine product trade, in 1832 issuing decrees prohibit- ing non-sanctioned exchanges to assure a steady flow of those goods to Nagasaki.[7] In the 1840s, they staved off a challenge from the Satsuma domain (on the south- ern portion of Kyushu) to gain a share of the trade at the port. In negotiations in the 1850s, *bakufu* officials also refused entreaties by Dutch merchants to permit the purchase of marine products directly from Nagasaki merchants.[8]

The clearing-house acquired profits as the sole middleman in transactions between Chinese and Dutch merchants and their Japanese counterparts. It also collected tariffs, royalties from various barter arrangements, and assorted lev- ies. With its combined revenue, the clearing-house would first pay its expenses, chiefly personnel costs for a staff that numbered 1,565 persons in 1830. It also allocated revenue in the form of annual payments to the districts of Nagasaki, a practice that began early in the Edo period, with the remainder deposited into the *bakufu* treasury.[9]

A string of Russian, Dutch and British diplomatic and military envoys in the first half of the 1850s altered the methods of exchange at Nagasaki. For exam- ple, Europeans could acquire Japanese goods at 'Dutch' and 'Russian' bazaars established in the port area as venues for foreign visitors to obtain Japanese wares.[10] Sherard Osborne, a British naval captain who visited Nagasaki along with British ambassador Lord Elgin in the summer of 1858, was impressed by the well-crafted European-style clocks, knives and microscopes available for purchase at the bazaars, at prices far lower than in London. Nonetheless, Toku- gawa officials asserted their authority by dictating that Osborne and his party exchange their foreign coins into paper script to use in purchases. The Briton noted that the *bakufu* profited from the 6 per cent transaction fee levied on his exchange of dollars (presumably Mexican silver dollars, a standard currency of mid-nineteenth-century Pacific trade), and also garnered tax proceeds when bazaar merchants exchanged their accumulated script for Japanese silver coins.[11]

C. Pemberton Hodgson, the interim British consul at the time of Nagasa- ki's official 'opening' on 1 July 1859, described a continued reluctance on the part of Tokugawa officials to allow for widespread use of Japanese currency. He detailed how on 1 July, British merchants brought thousands of Mexican dollars to a *bakufu* office in hopes of obtaining silver *ichibu* to use in trade. Much to the frustration of the British, Tokugawa officials allowed for only limited exchanges. The resulting dearth of currency, Hodgson concluded, retarded trade for several months.[12]

The nascent Western merchant community also faced the challenge of breaking into the existing Japanese-Chinese trade links dominated by the Tokugawa clearing-house. In his report on trade from June to December 1859, British consul George Morrison (who replaced Hodgson) noted that most of the commerce through Nagasaki involved exports tailored for Chinese consumers. 'The produce exported is principally for the China market, consisting largely of sea weed (used as food) [probably kelp], bicho de mar [sea cucumbers], dried shell-fish [probably abalone], peas, beans, &c.' As for imports, he described them as 'consisting mainly of sapan wood, Chinese medicinal herbs, indigo, &c, and a certain amount of manufactured goods, the latter re-exported from Shanghae [*sic*]'.[13]

Kenneth Mackenzie, the Nagasaki agent for the China-based British firm, Jardine, Matheson and Company (hereafter Jardine), also noted the dominance of trade with China in his correspondence with Jardine offices in Shanghai and Hong Kong. He repeatedly mentioned imports of sappanwood (used as red dye) and rhubarb (for medicinal uses), bartered for seaweed (probably kelp), shark fins, vegetable wax and camphor. On 11 October 1859, he wrote of exchanging rhubarb for seaweed, and asked to receive woollen manufactures and piece goods to begin developing a market for those products.[14] Yet Mackenzie soon lamented the lack of interest in what were then staples of British trade in much of the world, writing that 'dealers do not appear inclined to invest in piece goods and woolens and have little other produce than seaweed to give in payment'.[15] A few days later, he underscored the key role of 'produce', in the form of commodities for the China market, lamenting, 'I am getting somewhat disgusted with matters here, the more especially as I do not see prospect of early improvement and so long as we do not get produce, [we] cannot expect to realize imports.'[16]

Mackenzie also expressed his displeasure with Tokugawa policies that prohibited him from purchasing goods directly from Japanese merchants, and compelled him to change dollars into silver *ichibu* at rates dictated by the *bakufu*. Like other British merchants at the time, he asserted that Chinese merchants bribed clearing-house officials to gain commercial privileges.[17] He later expressed pessimism about obtaining camphor for export, stressing that the clearing-house held a tight grip on a good that had long been in the panoply of Nagasaki exports.[18]

To serve as his residence and business, Mackenzie first rented a farmhouse, one of the few existing buildings in the area designated for the Western settlement by Tokugawa officials. Through his additional position as French consul, Mackenzie helped to plan the development of the Ōura commercial district. Completed in the early summer of 1861, Ōura became the nucleus of the Western merchant community. Merchants set themselves up on waterfront lots reserved for business establishments, while proprietors of retail shops and hotels took lots in the rear quarter.[19] Yet just as merchants began to move into Ōura, Mackenzie, perhaps out of frustration with the trading situation at the port, chose not to return to China, where he had previously worked in the tea trade in Shanghai and Hankou.[20]

Alt's and Iwasaki's Journeys to Nagasaki

William Alt had also gained experience in Shanghai before coming to settle permanently in Nagasaki in the autumn of 1859. Born in Greenwich, England, at the age of thirteen Alt secured a position on *Charlotte Jane*, a ship noted in the annals of British imperial migration as the first to deliver men and women to the colony of Canterbury in New Zealand in 1850.[21] He grew up on-board during the ship's voyages between London and points such as Adelaide and Bermuda.[22] When *Charlotte Jane* called at Shanghai in October 1857, through his captain, Alt made the acquaintance of D. de Barros, a Portuguese merchant who had apparently acquired significant profits from the tea trade. Looking for help with his commercial enterprises, de Barros proposed that the seventeen-year-old Alt remain in Shanghai and work for him, receiving free lodging and a salary of £120 per year, which would double after two years. As a further enticement, de Barros offered £100 for Alt to begin trading on his own. Alt found the package appealing but lamented that it would prevent him from returning to Britain for several years. On *Charlotte Jane*, he had a stable position and the potential to make first mate in three years and become a captain of his own vessel in roughly six years. As his captain advised him, however, obtaining command of his own ship would mean at most £300 in annual income. After much vacillation, Alt chose to accept the word of his new acquaintance and stay in Shanghai in pursuit of personal fortune.[23]

Although contractually obligated for three years beginning on 1 January 1858, it is unclear how long Alt worked for de Barros, as sometime in 1858, he accepted a position in the Customs House in Shanghai. Alt may have taken the new post because de Barros encountered financial problems; the Portuguese consulate in Shanghai reported on 3 March 1860 that 'the accounts of the estate [of de Barros] being now finally closed' would thereafter 'be open for the inspection of the Creditors', suggesting a drawn-out demise of the firm.[24]

In a letter to his mother in February 1860, Alt explained that he 'had nothing to do in Shanghai' and 'not being able to lead an idle life' had decided to settle permanently in Nagasaki several months earlier. Alt received roughly $400 in severance from the Customs House, and in exchange for a one-third share of future business, a loan of $1,500 from the captain who transported him from Shanghai. Perhaps the captain saw potential in Alt's enterprises because the young Briton held a letter of recommendation from Jardine's Shanghai office, and had secured a position as the Nagasaki agent for Shanghai's *North-China Herald* newspaper.[25] To announce his intentions, Alt ran an advertisement in the *North-China Herald* stating that from 6 January 1860 he would serve as 'a *General Commission Agency* at this port [Nagasaki]'.[26] He soon established his own firm, Alt and Company.

Iwasaki Yatarō, descended from low-ranking 'country samurai' (*gōshi*) in Tosa, also visited Nagasaki for the first time in 1859. Yoshida Tōyō, a high-ranking domain official, dispatched the twenty-six-year-old Iwasaki with samples of domain goods – shiitake mushrooms, medicines and white sugar – to gauge the interest of Western merchants.[27] Like his contemporaries in other domains, Yoshida had strengthened domain monopolies to allow Tosa to obtain a larger share of profits from domain products sold not only in Osaka, the central marketplace of the Japanese state, but also potentially to foreign merchants at Nagasaki. As historian Brian Burke-Gaffney notes, Iwasaki seized opportunities during his Nagasaki sojourn, such as arranging meetings with resident Chinese merchants. In addition, he marvelled at examples of Western technology, which he saw close-up during a tour of a British steamship offered by John Major, a British merchant. Before the tour, Major invited Iwasaki to a lunch of cheese and ham (among other foods) and treated him to European alcoholic beverages at his home that evening.[28]

In the years following Iwasaki's visit, within Tosa opposition grew to Yoshida and his policies, particularly from Takechi Zuizan, the leader of a group that sought to demonstrate fealty not simply to the lord of the Tosa domain, Yamauchi Toyonori, but also – in line with a growing loyalist movement – to the emperor in Kyoto. Takechi and others in the domain objected to Yoshida's reforms that had equated to less autonomy and profit for rural leaders. In May 1862, a band of assassins organized by Takechi killed Yoshida, an act that soon led to the dismissal of Yoshida's appointees from the domain government, and a downgrading of commercial initiatives at Nagasaki.[29] Although a Tosa official did travel to the Kyushu port the following year in an effort to sell domain camphor, Japanese paper (*washi*), and whale oil and bones (the latter used for fertilizer), his primary goal was to obtain weapons, instead of developing sustained trading ties.[30]

Alt's Commercial Success

We do not know if Alt met Iwasaki or other Tosa representatives in 1859 but by the following year, the Briton had become an active participant in Nagasaki trade. Alt apparently avoided the frustrations experienced by Mackenzie; in early 1860, he reported hiring 'three to four Chinese' as well as Japanese servants and described garnering commissions from the sale of two vessels.[31] Available figures list Alt as the consignee of six British and US ships that arrived in Nagasaki between June and September 1861. Only one other firm, Adrian and Company, consigned more vessels (eight) during that period.[32]

In a letter from early 1863, Alt offered insights on the process of selling a ship to a Japanese customer, describing the sale of *Sir Charles Forbes*, a steamship, to the Tokugawa regime.[33] As the agent, Alt received a commission of £230 and arranged for the *bakufu* to pay the ship's owner '11,400 tons of the best Japan coals'. He hoped the owner would decline receiving the coal directly and instead allow Alt's firm to sell it at Shanghai, a transaction he anticipated would bring an additional £2,000. He also loaned $20,000 to the *bakufu*, which he believed would bring in another £1,250 in interest. Alt had decided to make the loan in order to help secure future contracts for 'muskets and machinery' and for a 'government steam factory'. In addition, he detailed the sale of the steamer, *City of Nantes*, to an undisclosed buyer for which he would receive camphor and lumber as partial payment.[34]

Alt reported these details in letters home and we should therefore consider that at times he may have exaggerated his successes to allay any fears of his mother, whom he had not consulted about his decision to leave the *Charlotte Jane* or to move to Nagasaki. Indeed, in his report to London, the acting British consul at Nagasaki recorded the sale of *Sir Charles Forbes* but not the *City of Nantes*.[35] Although it is unclear how many ships he sold during his first few years in Nagasaki, it is certain that Alt quickly achieved financial success, evident in his decision to construct a personal yacht launched in July 1861.[36] Records of the foreign concession also indicate that a prosperous Alt and Company rented several lots that apparently served as residences for its Western and Chinese employees.[37]

Alt's two-storey office in Ōura became a centre of activity for the Western merchant community, for example as the site of a meeting of the Chamber of Commerce in July 1861. The Briton also became the chairman of the Municipal Council, which oversaw discussions concerning plans to improve drains, provide lighting and develop a police force in the foreign concession.[38] In addition, Alt served as one of the first of two trustees of the Nagasaki Club, a men's social organization founded in 1861.[39]

Meanwhile, British consul Morrison spearheaded negotiations for further additions to the foreign settlement, for example sites that became cemeteries for Westerners. Disastrous fires prompted Morrison, other consuls and Western residents to form a fire brigade which *bakufu* officials directed should only fight blazes breaking out within the foreign concession. In 1861, an English-language newspaper, the *Nagasaki Shipping List and Advertiser*, began to publish twice-weekly, primarily providing information about Nagasaki trade but also news of events in Japan, China, Europe and the United States. To communicate more effectively with other treaty ports in Japan, a mail service was instituted. As venues for their social lives, in addition to the Nagasaki Club, Western merchants could recreate at a bowling alley or participate in sailing regattas in the harbour.[40]

Social events were no doubt important venues for Americans and Europeans to meet and consult about business affairs in what remained, throughout the 1860s, a small merchant community composed primarily of British and Americans. In 1862, the Western community included eighty-four souls; of that number thirty-one were British subjects and thirty-seven American citizens. By 1868, official registries counted 184 Westerners: seventy-two British and forty Americans, with seventy-two others from various European nations. The vital role of Chinese merchants and employees in the enterprises of Western merchants is evident in the fact that Chinese always outnumbered Westerners: 98 were listed on the Nagasaki registers in 1862, a number that rose to 296 in 1868.[41]

Nagasaki as a Centre of Domain Trade

In her chapter, Tina Clemente details how in the eighteenth century fear of uprisings and conspiracies prompted Spanish authorities to actively debate the role of the Chinese merchant community in the Philippines. Key officials urged the expulsion of all Chinese from the colony, advocating instead for a combination of Spanish, indigenous and Chinese *mestizo* merchants to be entrusted with the colony's foreign trade. Following the brief occupation of Manila by the British in 1760s, some Spanish leaders also called for expulsion to extract retribution from Chinese merchants alleged to have colluded with the British.[42]

In Japan, the expulsion movement was largely political, emerging soon after Western merchants began to live and trade at the treaty ports in 1859. Many advocating a restoration of imperial power viewed the presence of Westerners as an affront to the sanctity of the Japanese realm, and began to attack not only Westerners but also Tokugawa officials they viewed as facilitating the detrimental foreign presence. As tensions with Western nations rose, *bakufu* leaders deemed it necessary to take measures to improve Japanese maritime defenses. To that end in the summer of 1862, they no longer required that domain lords request Tokugawa permission to acquire warships and large vessels, but permitted the lords to instead freely obtain them from Westerners through the mediation of magistrates' offices at the three treaty ports.[43] As will be detailed below, the policy change would, in the long run, prove a boon for Alt and other Western merchants at Nagasaki.

Nonetheless, in the short term, the expulsion movement gained momentum with the support of Emperor Kōmei. In June 1863, the Chōshū domain in western Honshu honored an imperial order for expulsion and shelled Western vessels passing through the straits between Honshu and Kyushu. The following month, French and US naval squadrons engaged Chōshū ships and batteries near the port of Shimonoseki, but domain forces managed to effectively close the straits to maritime traffic. In August 1863, British warships bombarded Kagoshima in retaliation for the killing of a British merchant by a Satsuma samurai the previous year.[44]

Fearing a possible attack, Western firms in Nagasaki suspended trading and as a precaution, moved their files to ships in the harbour. During anxious moments, the British community gathered at Alt's office, apparently judging it a particularly safe building in the foreign concession.[45] In a letter to his mother in October 1863, Alt tried to assuage any concerns about the turbulent political situation. He wrote that despite the recent events (which he anticipated she had read about in the British press), Nagasaki was safe, protected by three to four men-of-war in the harbour and patrols that kept out any 'lawless characters'.[46]

Yet in one of the twists that defined the fluid political landscape of the 1860s, the expulsion movement proved fleeting. In Chōshū, the bastion of the cause, pro-expulsion leaders suffered a key setback when a domain military foray in Kyoto was repulsed in August 1864. Moreover, domain forces were outmatched by a combined fleet of warships from Britain, France, the United States and the Netherlands that forcibly removed Chōshū's batteries in September 1864. As the *bakufu* later readied forces to punish Chōshū for its military adventures, advocates of expulsion lost power, replaced by men more willing to work with Edo, prompting Tokugawa leaders to cancel the planned military expedition. Thereafter while sporadic attacks continued, the threat of military clashes between Westerners and Japanese domains waned.[47]

Nonetheless, by removing restrictions on the sale of ships, the *bakufu* had opened the proverbial floodgates. Consequently Nagasaki became an emporium for the sale of ships; between 1863 and 1870, 106 ships were sold there, compared to just 14 at Yokohama.[48] Economic historian Sugiyama Shinya calculates that the trade in ships made up 48 per cent of all imports by value in 1864, well exceeding cotton manufactures which occupied 20 per cent. Ships, when combined with a smaller trade in arms and ammunition, continued to make up roughly 40 to 50 per cent of all imports by value into Nagasaki until 1868. The importance of trade in ships and arms is further illustrated by the fact that annually, their value well exceeded that of tea, a prominent export. Alt and Thomas Glover, another British merchant who arrived in 1859, had developed tea-processing plants in the port area, shipping Japanese green tea to Britain and especially to the United States. Tea proved a steady export, occupying just over 20 per cent of the trade by value between 1863 and 1868. Yet the value of tea exported failed to match that of imported ships and arms. For example in 1865, over $157,000 of tea was exported but imports of ships, arms and ammunition that year totalled close to $915,000.[49]

Domains in Kyushu and western Honshu had long maintained offices in Nagasaki; for the Kyushu domains of Saga and Fukuoka this stemmed from their roles in defending the city against possible foreign attacks. For Satsuma and Tsushima, an island domain between Kyushu and Korea, domain offices facilitated foreign trade ties; Tsushima with Korea and Satsuma with the Ryūkyū Kingdom (today's Okinawa Prefecture).[50] Beginning in 1863, however, representatives from domains throughout Japan made their way to the port city. Many sought to obtain sail and steam ships for commercial, transport and military uses, while also expanding markets for domain goods. As a result, the domain merchant community grew over the next few years.

Domain representatives began to trade in earnest with Western merchants. Glover became especially active, notably selling ships and, against *bakufu* wishes, arms to Chōshū.[51] Through the trade, he developed strong business and personal ties with prominent Chōshū samurai such as Kido Takayoshi. The Briton also established a trading relationship with Satsuma, which in 1866 made a secret pact with Chōshū to challenge Tokugawa rule. Thanks to his success in the ships and arms trade, by 1866 Glover's firm surpassed Alt's in size and commercial stature at Nagasaki.[52]

As historian Sidney Brown has detailed, Chōshū used weapons and steamships obtained from Glover to equip its military forces. Glover sold technologically advanced Minié rifles to the domain in the autumn of 1865. Due in part to these acquisitions, Chōshū developed effective fighting forces that defeated a punitive Tokugawa military expedition dispatched against it in 1866.[53]

The military strengthening of Chōshū and also Satsuma is a key component of a central political narrative of the 1860s: the ability of the two domains to develop forces that toppled the Tokugawa *bakufu* in 1868. Yet the surge in trade in ships and weapons also indirectly weakened the institutional merchant community of Nagasaki. I have previously explored how Western merchants gradually siphoned off the flow of marine products into Nagasaki, preventing the clearing-house from profiting from a still viable sector of trade.[54] The inability of the clearing-house to potentially profit from transactions between domains and Western merchants proved another area of weakness. Proposed reforms to help the office compete more effectively with Western merchants brought little success, and the clearing-house faded from commercial significance in the years prior to the Meiji Restoration.[55]

Moreover, trade in ships and arms proved a catalyst in the development of significant, personal connections between domain leaders and Western merchants, such as the aforementioned ties between Glover and Kido. Although this is an area requiring further research, it appears that Tokugawa officials, while also involved in purchasing ships from Alt, Glover and other Western traders, never developed the rapport that emerged between British merchants and domain representatives at Nagasaki.

Iwasaki Returns to Nagasaki

Early in 1867, Iwasaki was again dispatched to Nagasaki, and his activities on behalf of Tosa exemplify the commercial agendas and aspirations of many in the domain merchant community in the port city. As had transpired in Chōshū, factions advocating the expulsion of foreigners and a greater political role for the emperor began to lose influence in Tosa in 1864. The domain lord tapped Gotō Shōjirō, a high-ranking samurai and protégé of Yoshida, to assume the lead administrative role. Gotō revived some of Yoshida's key initiatives, notably establishing the Kaiseikan in the spring of 1865. The multi-division office aimed to expand the domain's share of profits from commerce conducted both in Tosa and in Nagasaki, and thereby provide the domain government with much needed revenue. It included a medical school where English and French were taught; offices to expand whaling and mining; and an industrial department to promote the production of camphor, paper, sugar and tea, with the goal of exporting those goods in greater volume through Nagasaki. In the summer of 1866, Gotō led a group to Nagasaki, where he met with Alt, Glover and representatives of other Western firms. The Tosa official subsequently travelled to Shanghai, where he negotiated purchases of a warship and Armstrong guns, a kind of breach-loading, heavy gun.[56]

Gotō relied on Iwasaki to run the Nagasaki branch of the domain's trading arm, the Tosa Trading Office (*Tosa shōkai*). It was in this capacity that he came to associate with Alt. In the first entry of his official diary on 14 June 1867, Iwasaki describes how the domain had previously purchased the steamer *Yūgao* from Alt, paying in installments over several months. The next day, Iwasaki, Gotō and another Tosa representative called at Alt's office and began negotiations to purchase another steamship.[57] The following month, Iwasaki met again with Alt to continue negotiations, offering as a possible model a contract for the purchase of ship from a Western firm by the Ōzu domain (in today's Ehime prefecture).[58] On 15 July, Iwasaki noted a contract had been signed for the purchase from Alt of a sailing ship, the *Daigoku Maru*. Just over a week later Alt gave him a tour of 'the very sturdy ship, *Osaka*', another barque that Tosa would purchase and rename *Otome*.[59]

Iwasaki sought to pay for these purchases with domain goods, especially camphor, a product which, as we have seen, Alt had received as partial payment in an earlier transaction for a ship. Iwasaki repeatedly visited Alt and other Western merchants concerning camphor sales, underscoring the importance of that good in Tosa's trading schemes.[60] In addition Ike Michinosuke, a Tosa samurai working under Iwasaki, recorded delivering 180 blocks of camphor to Alt's office, presumably as payment for an earlier purchase.[61]

Ike also provides titbits about social interactions between Tosa representatives and Alt. He mentions Alt coming to the Tosa office one evening where drinks were shared. He records that on another evening, domain representatives provided entertainment for Alt and four unidentified men and women.[62] Tosa officials apparently hosted many meals for Alt and other Western merchants. Another Tosa official assigned to Nagasaki, Sasaki Takayuki, recorded that over seventy *ryō* was spent to entertain Alt, while fifty-five *ryō* was allocated for meals with a Belgian merchant, Charles Comte de Montblanc.[63]

Moreover, Alt assisted Iwasaki in a plan to create opportunities for Tosa in commerce between Kyushu, Korea and Tsushima. In June 1867, Iwasaki recorded meetings in Nagasaki between Tosa representatives and a Tsushima official.[64] These meetings no doubt involved conversations about possible trade with Korea, as Tsushima was officially sanctioned by the *bakufu* and the Korean court to monopolize Japanese–Korean commerce. With Gotō's backing, also in June 1867 Iwasaki chartered a steamship from Alt and sailed to Ulleungdo, an island that is today part of South Korea. It is likely that the 'development' (*kaitaku*) he envisioned on Ulleungdo and on the nearby island of Takeshima involved a domain outpost that could capitalize on trade across the Korea Strait. Iwasaki did not record the events of the approximately five-day voyage, which ended at Karatsu, a port in northern Kyushu. Following up on a visit there several months earlier, he discussed with Karatsu officials the acquisition of coal, which Iwasaki apparently planned to use in his trading schemes.[65]

Iwasaki's dealings with Karatsu and Tsushima officials underscore how Tosa's initiatives relied not only on obtaining ships from Alt but also in cultivating commercial ties with other members of the domain merchant community in Nagasaki.[66] Additionally the Tosa Trading Office had links with the Kaientai, a group formed by the Tosa *rōnin* (lordless samurai) Sakamoto Ryōma. Composed primarily of men from Tosa, the Kaientai aimed to capitalize on domestic trade from its base in Nagasaki. During his time in the Kyushu port, Sakamoto established commercial ties with merchants and samurai in Satsuma and Chōshū, discussing with them several trading proposals, including expanded trade with Ezo.[67]

A few months later Alt served as a liaison between Tosa officials and British diplomats after two British sailors from the warship HMS *Icarus* were murdered in Nagasaki's Maruyama pleasure quarter on 16 August 1867. The next day, Alt requested Iwasaki to visit his office, where he related British suspicions that members of the Kaientai were responsible for the murders.[68] A ship carrying Kaientai members had sailed hurriedly from Nagasaki harbour around the time of the murder and returned the following day. Many British merchants and diplomats viewed this as circumstantial evidence that a Tosa samurai had murdered the sailors and fled on the ship. Alt relayed to Iwasaki the anger of the British consul-general, Harry Parkes (then visiting Nagasaki), and accompanied him to the British consulate to meet with Parkes.[69] Tosa and British representatives continued negotiations for several weeks, but it was not until months later that the culprit was identified as a samurai from Fukuoka domain.[70]

Although recording the details of numerous meetings with Alt (we have no letters from Alt mentioning Iwasaki directly), Iwasaki offers little about their personal relationship. Perhaps he never developed a friendship with the younger Briton, but it is clear that Iwasaki and his Tosa colleagues found Alt a reliable business partner, with whom they traded on a consistent basis.

Trade Moves Away from Nagasaki

During the summer and autumn of 1867, leaders from powerful domains met in Kyoto and increasingly put pressure on the shogun, Tokugawa Yoshinobu, to return power to the court, which he did in November. Intense negotiations also centred around the establishment of Kobe as a treaty port, which had been stipulated in the 1858 treaties but delayed due to opposition from many quarters, notably Emperor Kōmei. When Kōmei died suddenly in early 1867, the court changed its position, and in June 1867 issued a decree allowing the 'opening' of the port on 1 January 1868.[71] On 3 January, the Chōshū and Satsuma alliance accomplished a coup at the Kyoto imperial palace, 'restoring' the Emperor Meiji to dominant political power.

After Yokohama, Kobe became the most prominent port for foreign trade, notably in tea, which emerged after silk as Japan's second largest export. (Yokohama had served as the primary port for silk exports since 1859.) During the 1870s tea production increased in central and western Honshu and more tea was exported through Kobe, boosting commerce at that port at the expense of Nagasaki.[72] In addition, the end of military confrontations between domains in western Honshu and Kyushu following the January palace coup saw other ports emerge as emporia for the arms trade. During the Boshin War (1868–70), several domains fought the new government established by the Chōshū- and Satsuma-led alliance. Imitating the actions of Chōshū just a few years earlier, anti-government forces in Echigo (today's Niigata Prefecture) acquired weapons at the port of Niigata from Eduard Schnell, a Dutch merchant whom Harold Bolitho dubbed 'the Glover of the north'. Thanks in part to the flow of arms, anti-government units held off Satsuma and Chōshū forces for several months in 1868.[73]

Iwasaki and Alt realized the growing commercial importance of Kobe, and transferred a large share of their operations to that port and nearby Osaka in 1868. Over the next few years, Iwasaki supervised Tosa's trading enterprises, which continued to use domain ships and as before, sought to direct profits from the sale of Tosa-produced goods into domain coffers.[74] In 1871, the central government abolished the domains, replacing them with prefectures administered by a governor dispatched from Tokyo [formerly Edo], the new national capital. Iwasaki thereafter came to control many of the domain's former businesses and in 1873 founded Mitsubishi, developing it into a shipping firm. Benefiting from government assistance, Iwasaki rapidly expanded the size of Mitsubishi and adroitly undercut competitors, allowing him by 1877 to own 80 per cent of all commercial ships in Japan and to effectively control coastal trade.[75]

During the half decade after 1868, Alt began to work more at Osaka, assigning supervision of the Nagasaki office to Henry Hunt and Frederick Hellyer, a nephew who had arrived from Britain the previous year. Having amassed a sizable fortune but battling ill health, Alt decided to return to Britain in 1872. Just thirty-two years of age, he settled into a comfortable life, purchasing a home in Surrey (near London) and later, a villa in an Italian coastal city.[76] Alt and Company remained in existence until 1881, when Hunt and Hellyer split the firm, each developing independent companies.[77] Both came to specialize in tea, emerging as two of the more prominent Western tea export firms in Japan over the next few decades.[78]

By contrast Glover sought new commercial opportunities by purchasing a coal mine on the island of Takashima in Nagasaki harbour. Beginning in the late 1860s, steamship companies came to value Kyushu coal, finding it especially suitable to fuel ship engines. Shanghai subsequently became a key destination for coal from Takashima and other Kyushu mines: 25,000 tons of Kyushu coal, 50 per cent of all the coal entering Shanghai, was imported in 1876.[79] Although achieving initial success, the mine failed to sustain a high volume of production. Glover, saddled with debts primarily resulting from previous short-term and speculative deals for ships with various domains, was forced to sell his interest in the mine and declare bankruptcy in 1870. He continued to work at Takashima and by 1877, had paid off his debts. Thanks to Iwasaki, Glover subsequently found employment in Tokyo, serving as a consultant for Mitsubishi.[80] Iwasaki also arranged for Frederick Hellyer's brother, Thomas, to become an English teacher in Tosa's castle town of Kōchi in 1870, a position he held for three years.[81]

Conclusions

Over the course of the 1860s, Nagasaki's commercial profile changed dramatically: from a port dominated by Japanese–Chinese trade, to an emporium for ships and weapons, to finally, a purveyor of coal for steamships plying routes in East Asian waters. Given the fluid landscape, it is perhaps not surprising that one merchant community, the institutional, proved unable to adapt. As this chapter has detailed, *bakufu* officials at the clearing-house, while adeptly handling trade in the years around 1859, were dealt a blow by the decision to allow domains to independently purchase ships, creating a trade that brought the trading office little direct financial benefit.

It was therefore a political trend, the expulsion movement, which proved a key factor in recasting commerce through Nagasaki during the 1860s, and brought profit to Western merchants like Alt and Glover. The domain community also contributed to the surge of commerce at Nagasaki by making it a venue to advance their military and economic agendas.

Yet while the political trend of expulsion transformed the port during the 1860s, a larger economic trend – the move to export trades focused on Western markets – meant that Nagasaki, while still a trading hub, would not rival Kobe and Yokohama as the chief venues for Japan's foreign trade during the Meiji period. Alt and Iwasaki clearly realized this and moved their bases of operations to Osaka and Kobe. They also focused their firms to capitalize on emerging sectors: Iwasaki on shipping, and Alt and his company's successors on tea (and also Glover on coal). A look at Japan's foreign trade in 1877 confirms the prominence of goods for Western markets: tea occupied 20 per cent of all Japan-produced exports, ranking second behind silk at 47 per cent, with coal making up around 10 per cent. Previous mainstays of kelp, abalone, sea cucumbers and shark fins made up just over 3 per cent of all foreign trade.[82] Japan had definitely entered a new period in its foreign trade.

Acknowledgements

I thank first, the editors of this volume, Lin Yu-ju and Madeleine Zelin, for assistance at many stages in the writing of this chapter. I also thank Luke Roberts for his suggestions about sources and Ellen McGill for her editorial assistance. I also wish to acknowledge the valuable feedback received from attendees at the November 2013 National Tsing Hua University conference, 'Dialogues between European and Asian Commercial Documents: Trade, Cultural Exchanges, and Knowledge Making in Modern East-Asia'.

Glossary

bakufu	shogunate; central political authority of Japan during Edo period	幕府
Boshin War	1868–70 conflict between newly established Meiji government and Tokugawa supporters	戊辰戦争
Daigoku Maru	Tosa ship purchased from Alt	大極丸
daimyō	lord of feudal domain	大名
Dejima	artificial island and base for Dutch merchants in Nagasaki harbour	出島
Edo Period	1603–1868	江戸時代
gōshi	country samurai; lowest rank of samurai in the Tosa domain	郷士
han	feudal domain	藩
ichibu	silver coin; a standard currency of the Edo period	壱分
Kaientai	Naval Auxiliary Force; Tosa-supported enterprise of Sakamoto Ryōma involved in domestic maritime trade	海援隊
Kaiseikan	Tosa Office for Domain Economic Expansion	開誠館
kaisho	Tokugawa clearing-house for Nagasaki trade	会所
kaitaku	development	開拓
Otome	Tosa ship purchased from Alt	乙女
rōnin	lordless samurai	浪人
ryō	gold coin; a standard currency of the Edo period	両
shiitake	mushroom	椎茸
Tosa *shōkai*	Tosa Trading Office; Nagasaki branch administered by Iwasaki Yatarō	土佐商会
washi	Japanese paper	和紙
Yūgao	Tosa ship purchased from Alt	夕顔

Personal names of Japanese mentioned in text

Emperor Kōmei	孝明天皇	1831–67, r. 1846–67
Emperor Meiji	明治天皇	1852–1912, r. 1867–1912
Gotō Shōjirō	後藤象二郎	1838–97
Ike Michinosuke	池道之助	dates unknown
Iwasaki Yatarō	岩崎彌太郎	1834–85
Kido Takayoshi	木戸孝允	1833–77
Sakamoto Ryōma	坂本龍馬	1835–67
Sasaki Takayuki (Sanshirō)	佐々木高行 (三四郎)	1830–1910
Takechi Zuizan	武市瑞山	1829–65
Tokugawa Yoshinobu	徳川慶喜	1837–1913, shogun 1866–7
Yamauchi Toyonori	山内豊範	1846–86, lord 1859–69
Yamauchi Toyoshige, aka Yōdō	山内豊信、容堂	1827–72, lord 1848–59
Yoshida Tōyō	吉田東洋	1816–62

Place names

Chōshū Domain	長州藩
Edo	江戸
Echigo	越後
Ehime Prefecture	愛媛県
Ezo	蝦夷
Fukuoka Domain	福岡藩
Hakodate	函館
Hankou	漢口
Hokkaido	北海道
Honshu	本州
Hyogo	兵庫
Kagoshima Prefecture	鹿児島県
Kanagawa	神奈川
Karatsu Domain	唐津藩
Kobe	神戸
Kōchi	高知
Kyoto	京都
Kyushu	九州
Maruyama (Nagasaki Pleasure Quarter)	丸山
Nagasaki	長崎
Niigata	新潟
Okinawa Prefecture	沖縄県
Osaka	大阪
Ōura (Nagasaki district)	大浦
Ōzu Domain	大洲藩
Ryūkyū Kingdom	琉球王国
Saga Domain	佐賀藩
Satsuma Domain	薩摩藩
Shanghai	上海
Shikoku	四国
Shimoda	下田
Shimonoseki	下関
Takashima Island (Nagasaki harbour)	高島
Takeshima Island (aka Dokdo or Tokto)	竹島 (독도/獨島)
Tokyo	東京
Tosa Domain	土佐藩
Tsushima Domain	対馬藩
Ulleungdo Island	鬱陵島/울릉도
Yamaguchi Prefecture	山口県
Yokohama	横浜

10 THE PROBLEM OF THE SAILORS: POWER, LAW AND THE FORMATION OF THE MERCHANT COMMUNITY IN TREATY PORT CHINA, 1842–60

Evan Lampe

During the First Opium War (1839–42), the British brig *Kite* violently ran aground near Shanghai during a voyage through the South China Seas, from Singapore to the Yangzi River. As the *Kite* drew ten feet, the crew learned it was unusable for the surveying mission and they went back toward Shanghai on 12 September 1840. They did not face enemy ships, but the crew of the *Kite* observed signs of war and endured almost total incapacitation due to an outbreak of dysentery. The greatest devastation happened on 15 September when the ship struck a sandbar and broke apart, killing some of the crew, including the captain and his five-year-old son. Most survived, to the shock of the common seaman J. L. Scott, who recorded these events. An earlier epidemic had left the crew weakened and Scott was convinced that the crew 'had now nothing but death to look forward to'.[1] Before long, the Chinese captured the sick and dying survivors of the *Kite* and led them to confinement in a Chinese prison near Ningbo. The survivors were treated harshly, placed in irons, and abused by the Chinese 'lower orders', including other prisoners, as they were hauled on the long overland trek to Ningbo. There the crew was united and introduced to other prisoners from the war, including a battered Englishman and eight 'Lascars'. As Scott reported:

> We were placed in the small divisions, the coops being ranged round three sides of each compartment, the fourth side being the entrance. A chain was passed through each cage, and between our legs, over the chain of our irons; the two ends being padlocked together, we were thus all fastened one to another, and also to our cages.[2]

One of the prisoners died that night. After much suffering, humiliation and fear, the survivors of the accident and the captivity were freed.

Scott's narrative of his captivity and the simultaneously published account by the captain's widow, Anne Noble, convinced the British public and those that would later live and work in the five treaty ports 'opened' by the Opium War that they would need to create their own institutions of justice. This is not to suggest that the British had much to be proud of. Their own use and misuse of capital punishment and forced emigration remained in the collective memory of the British working class.[3] Yet, the British public was reminded, if they did not already know, that the Chinese judicial system was brutal. Works like G. H. Mason's *The Punishments of China* – illustrated in graphic detail – contributed to the Enlightenment-era conversations about the proper treatment of prisoners.[4] What emerges from Scott's account is the indiscriminate and randomness of violence in Chinese jails and its total effect on its victims.

> [O]ne of the marines that we had left in the prison walked in, looking stout and well; but after him came, or rather was carried, the other, a most horrid spectacle, a moving skeleton, with the skin stretched tightly over his bones; his eyes were sunk deep in his head, and his voice was awfully hollow; he was the most melancholy sight I ever saw. When on board the ship he was a stout, well-made man, and now how dreadfully changed! He had come up merely to die with his old companions.[5]

Scott's emphasis is not on the sufferings that the British felt at the hands of the Chinese. His perspective as a sailor, working closely with people from many parts of the world, perhaps informed his more international perspective. Scott carefully documents how Lascars, English sailors and Chinese shared a similar fate at the hands of jailers. His temporary delight in Chinese traditions such as the New Year and his sharing of Christmas with even his jailor suggests his capacity to form a transnational community in one of the world's most horrible places.[6]

I retell some of Scott's story so we do not forget the importance of the prison in the important transition from the Canton trade to the treaty port system. Scott was not the last Westerner to spend some time in a Chinese jail, but his story did help make the case for the extraterritoriality laws that would give jurisdiction over Western criminals in treaty ports to the imperial powers. When trade was exclusively with Canton, the Chinese defended their judicial rights. The tense Terranova case of 1821, when a Western sailor was executed for the killing of a Chinese civilian, was just one of many examples of the triumph of Chinese justice. The Opium War changed this. The Treaty of Nanjing (1842) gave extraterritorial rights to European powers in the treaty ports. But to make this meaningful, the Europeans and Americans would need the institutions under their authority, first courts, then jails and finally prisons. We know little about life in these jails and prisons or even if their conditions were much better than those of the Chinese alternatives, but they were at the heart of this transition.

This chapter argues that the prison was a central but by no means singular institution of power created by the foreign community in Chinese treaty ports. And while we cannot deny that these courts were used to enforce the 'rights' of foreigners in China, they were also used to discipline and control working people, particularly sailors who were no less liberated in their activities in China than were the victorious merchant community. Consuls and other agents of state power worked alongside the treaty port merchant community to create prisons and manage the maritime working class that inevitably came with commerce. By controlling the activities of sailors, disputes, brawls, riots, property crimes, smuggling and other activities that could potentially harm the smooth functioning of trade could be minimized. In other words, the problem of the sailors worked alongside the problem of Chinese justice to create the treaty port institutions of power.[7] This chapter also suggests that maritime history too often focuses exclusively on merchant communities' economic activities, while sidelining their role in class discipline and the formation of institutional power, as well as their function as empire builders. One corrective to this myopia is to discuss more broadly 'maritime communities' instead of 'merchant communities'. Maritime communities include sailors, stevedores, naval marines, shopkeepers who benefited from maritime commercial activity, customs agents, police, ship captains and prostitutes. The very diversity of this group made it problematic and difficult to control. However, the largest – and most troubling for the elite – members of this motley crew were the sailors.

The Lessons of Canton

Canton had no shortage of problems brought on by the mobile, flexible, rowdy and savvy maritime working class. Sailors got drunk, brawled, smuggled goods and daily broke the rules against illicit commercial activities between Chinese and foreigners. Officially all trade had to take place between specific Western merchants and the Chinese monopoly known as the hong merchants.[8] Of course, in practice it was impossible to sustain these rules, particularly when it came to the day-to-day needs of sailors. However, geography mitigated the damage that sailors could inflict on the delicate relations between the Qing empire and the major European traders. As the Pearl River delta, which housed Canton, was extremely shallow, all ships had to stay at an anchorage miles south of the city, called Whampoa.[9] Whampoa was not a free zone. Ship masters did what they could to sustain the disciplinary regimen of the ship in Whampoa, giving crews numerous tasks and never failing to use the irons and the lash to maintain proper order. The anchorage was not a place of total anarchy, but it was evidence that the Canton system, with its massive regulations and 'Thirteen Factories', was not all it appeared to be. In Whampoa, sailors hired prostitutes, purchased rice liquor, patronized washerwomen, and in general pushed the limits of the Canton system and the labour regimen of the ship. When missionaries, captains and merchants worried about the sailors, it was Whampoa that sparked their concerns. Of course, Whampoa was an extension of the maritime community of Canton.

The well-documented voyage of the *New Hazard* (1810–13), which was involved in the Pacific-wide sea otter fur trade before arriving in China, suggests how the labour and disciplinary regime extended itself into the Whampoa anchorage. The author of our major source on this voyage, the common sailor Stephen Reynolds, provides a detailed description of the daily labours and common punishments inflicted on sailors by the officers. He also shows how the captain travelled to Canton regularly, leaving most of the crew behind to prepare sails, caulk, stay masts or fetch provisions. During their free time, the sailors brawled, drank, met sailors from other nations or simply bided their time. For the most part, Canton was closed to sailors.[10]

The history of the Western presence in Canton exposes an important conflict that sits at the heart of much of world history, particularly the history of global capitalism. This was the dilemma between openness (for the merchants, missionaries and elite) and control (for working people). On the one hand, the elite required and often demanded total liberty of mobility and absolute liquidity for their goods and funds.[11] On the other hand, the same elite feared working people and preferred the safety and comfort of walls. In Canton, the years 1845 to 1848 saw these tensions reach a near breaking point. It started when the Chinese attempted to maintain the tradition of preventing foreigners from entering the walled section of the city of Canton despite the broader opening of the other four treaty ports of Shanghai, Ningbo, Amoy (Xiamen) and Fuzhou. One of the first to test this, initially unsuccessfully, was the American missionary I. J. Roberts. As the Governor General of Canton Ch'i-Ying [Qiying] explained, the situation in Canton made the opening of the city unnecessary.

> At Canton the shops and markets are comparable to the teeth of a comb, the many residing in the suburbs ... do not equal the most worthy mass without its walls. If the Chinese people who reside in the city desire to trade to advantage, they must also necessarily go out of the city to do their business and this they can do and still be able to add something to their capital.[12]

He also mentions that the entrance into the city is likely to cause problems. Through lobbying, pressure and, finally, 'gunboat diplomacy', the Chinese agreed to open up the city to foreigners. This meant missionaries and merchants could walk the streets, but it also opened the city up to sailors. There was one less wall keeping the Western workers from the streets and people of the city.

The costs of openness are strongly suggested by the 8 July 1846 riot in Canton. This created, for the foreign merchants in the city, the greatest threat to their survival since the outbreak of the Opium War. The *Chinese Repository* reported on this event in detail equal to the riot's importance in the minds of the foreign community. The disturbance occurred directly in front of the 'Thirteen Factories'. Calling for the death of the foreigners, the mob threw rocks at the windows of the factories and even constructed a battering ram to smash the door to the factories. They tried to set the dwellings on fire. In all of this, the Chinese police were silent, out of either indifference or fear. The violent protests gathered support as well. The newspaper reported: 'Hundreds of the basest of men were already collected and many hundreds more were hastening to the scene of the riot'.[13] In response to this threat, the foreigners took over police functions and 'moved in mass against the crowd'.[14] Eventually, the Chinese state aided the foreigners in clearing the streets and the riot died down.

If we take the *Chinese Repository* as a serious reflection of the values of the elite members of the foreign community in China, we cannot help but notice the centrality of class to their interpretation of the riot. The authors of the article blamed the failure of the Chinese 'to keep all idlers and vagrants away from the vicinity of the factories' as the root of the problem. Such restrictions were agreed to during the treaty negotiations between the United States and the Qing empire in 1844. They are worth looking at in detail.

1 The foreign residents in Canton were permitted to build walls between the factories and the 'citizens' shops' to prevent risk of fire.
2 Another wall should be created 'to avoid the Chinese, in passing and repassing, looking through the fence, causing disturbances and quarrels'.
3 Walls could be established on three other streets.
4 'Chinese and foreigners being mixed up together, it is easy for trouble to arise; hereafter, therefore, at the six gates of the three streets, it is right to establish a military station and posts for sentries, who shall constantly dwell there, and keep guard. Men bearing things about upon their shoulders to traffic with (pedlars [*sic*]), are not permitted in front and on the right and left of the Factories, to expose for sale melons, fruits, cakes, et cetera; and likewise all quacks, fortune-tellers, beggars, and showmen and all idlers, and the like, are not permitted to pass and repass in front and on the right and left of the Factories, obstructing the way, and collecting a crowd of idlers. Whoever violates this shall be searched out, and pursued to the utmost. In the event of any quarrel, or of the calamity of fire, these six gates shall be immediately shut and locked, and the idlers shall not be permitted to look through; and should any bandits insist on violently entering, and wrangle with the guards and soldiers, the bandits shall be rigorously seized and punished to the utmost. If the soldiers and guards are remiss in expelling them, they shall be severely punished.'
5 A high-ranking officer should stay near the factories to keep watch.
6 The streets in front of the factory were not to be used as a 'thoroughfare'.
7 Any shops selling liquor to foreigners should be shut down.
8 The streets should be kept 'pure and clean'.[15]

In short, the *Chinese Repository* argued that if the area around the factories had been kept clear for the elite, the riot could not have happened. While they demanded, with the use of force, the opening of the city of Canton for exploitation, conversion and commerce, the best response to the attempts by the working people of Canton to seize for themselves a living was higher walls, more guards and isolation.

The lesson of Canton, made clear by the 1846 protests and their bloody repression, was that encounters between the Chinese and foreigners could be volatile, so openness needed to be controlled through policing, discipline and (strangely) walls. The immediate commentary on the riot did not mention sailors, maybe because sailors' manpower was integral in suppressing the riot and reports and officials chose their words carefully. However, there certainly was not fear of interactions between the merchant community of foreigners and the hong, who had worked together for mutual profit for years. Indeed, they formed a vibrant cross-cultural society within the Thirteen Factories, sharing meals, entertainment and some camaraderie. Presumably, they also believed that they could control their own interactions with the Chinese workers. They interacted on a daily basis with servants, shopkeepers and boat people. Their fear was the groups they did not believe they could control: the sailors and the Chinese working people. This, however, was the cost of openness. And while the problem of the sailors in foreign ports would never be resolved, the merchant communities in the treaty ports learned very quickly that their power needed to be institutionalized if it was to be effective.

The Image of the Sailor in Treaty Ports

Sailors played a crucial role in the expansion of European empires in the Pacific. Largely maritime and commercial in their early years, the European empires in the Pacific brought with them large numbers of working people. These sailors vastly outnumbered the merchants, missionaries and diplomats who populate our memory of the treaty ports. Yet, it was these workers who transported the tea, maintained the ships and ensured that the merchants and missionaries reached distant ports safely. They are the unsung heroes of European imperialism in the Pacific, although few of them saw their role as empire builders or conquerors. The realization of their importance contrasts with their image as a problem. Some of the bad reputation the sailors gained was not unearned. We do not need to be reminded that sailors did seek 'liberty on the waterfront',[16] often with unfortunate and even criminal consequences. Few sailors in Chinese ports appreciated the scandalous nature of parading the streets intoxicated or with prostitutes. Nevertheless, the images of the foreign sailor consumed in Western media centred on their most notorious activities.

Missionaries felt conflicted about sailors. On the one hand, they wanted to convince them to embrace a religious life. On the other hand, their literature on sailors emphasized sin. Organizations like the Seamen's Friend Society and their publications (e.g. *The Seamen's Friend*) celebrated reformed sailors alongside narratives of their fallen, drunken and sinful colleagues. In 1860, a medical missionary working in Shanghai, Dr Lockhart, reported on the medical missions in China and he reserved some of his harshest words for sailors.

> Before I close, I would allude for a moment to one thing, which has been found a great obstacle to the success of missions in all Eastern and heathen countries; and, in a sea-port like this, I would speak of it with all the power and emphasis that I can employ. I refer to the debauchery, licentiousness, and wickedness of our sailors, who go forth and sow the seeds of wickedness and sin in all heathen lands, and in none more than in China. It makes the heart of the missionary sad indeed, to see his work day by day undone by the wickedness and debauchery of these sailors. It is same in the ports of India, in the South Seas, in Africa and in the West Indies. When the Chinese see, for instance, our sailors on leave ashore on the Sabbath-day getting drunk, going into the various villages, and by their violence and wickedness setting the minds of the people against them, they naturally say to us – 'You teachers come to preach the Gospel of Jesus Christ; do you call these men Christians?'[17]

Missionaries believed that the best way to solve the problem of sailors was the creation of religious institutions in port areas. A proposal made by Robert Morrison in 1822 called for the creation of a 'Floating Chapel' and a 'Floating Hospital' to attend to the spiritual and physical needs of the 'two to three thousand' sailors that dwelled in Whampoa at any one time. The implication of the proposal was that sailors in Chinese ports were drunk, ill and in desperate need of religious guidance.[18] A published sermon delivered to sailors in 1822, again by Morrison, suggests the poor reputation of sailors involved in the China trade.

> Some people deem sailors an inferior tribe of human animals; degraded somehow or other (they know not how) to a state that is incapable of ratiocination; and therefore good feeding and hard flogging are the only means to be employed for inducing them to do their duty.[19]

The disobedient, drunken and cantankerous sailor also made an appearance in the Parliamentary discussions about the ending of the monopoly of the East India Company in the 1820s. During the hearings by the Select Committee on the Foreign Trade of the Country in 1821, Parliament heard testimony from Captain Daniel Ross, who argued that one of the reasons to continue the East India Company monopoly was that opening trade to more merchants would create a problem in the ports, as there would be fewer controls over sailors. When asked what 'would be the effect of opening the trade to British subjects, particularly with relation to the conduct of our seamen at the port of Canton', he answered that 'the seamen would create considerable disturbances'. He later clarified that this was a large problem already and led to many conflicts between British merchants and China, particularly when disturbances led to the loss of life of Chinese. When asked to explain why British sailors seemed more troublesome than American sailors, he pointed out that 'it arises from the generality of our seamen having served in the navy, and after having again served in a merchant ship, they do not conceive they ought to be under such control'.[20]

As we can see, sailors – including those participating in the Canton trade – had developed for themselves a reputation as causing problems through their drunkenness, violence and lack of religious perspective in life. Whether deserved or not, this reputation, combined with the troublesome Canton streets, convinced much of the merchant, diplomatic and missionary communities that the problem of the sailors required an institutional solution.

The Origins of the Treaty Port Prisons

During the Canton trade, a formal prison never emerged, although it was sometimes discussed as a possible solution to some of the social problems of drunkenness among cantankerous sailors in Whampoa. The main reason it was not required was that the merchant ship brought with it an entire apparatus of disciplinary mechanisms. Ship captains had the power to confine, fine and physically abuse sailors. Especially since most of the sailors, most of the time, were confined to the anchorage where those mechanisms could remain in force, there was no clear need for a separate institution. Nevertheless, it was not a new idea. A fort was used as a jail for sailors in Honolulu during the 1830s.[21] In Shanghai, the British decided to establish a prison as part of a series of regulations designed to limit the potential conflicts between the British subjects residing in Shanghai and the Chinese.

One of these regulations, developed by the British consuls in Shanghai, was a prohibition on the use of firearms. This policy developed in response to the critical injury of an eight-year-old Chinese boy in November 1843 by a 'foreigner who landed, from one of the ships', in other words, a sailor.

> As I consider the wounds above described as having been inflicted from the grossest carelessness in, and – ignorance of, the use of firearms (on the part of the perpetuators) and as such acts tend too much to create an unfavorable idea of the Foreign Community in the minds of the Chinese, I deem it incumbent for the protection of the Lives and Bodies of the inhabitants and for the Preservation of the Public Peace, to [forbid the use of firearms in the city].[22]

One month later, the Counsel, George Balfour, revised the order to allow the elite to continue to use firearms for 'sporting'. Shooting for sport could only be done more than 800 yards from the city walls and by residents registered and approved for the activity by the Consulate.[23]

Balfour created a similar balance between the recreational desires of the elite residents of Shanghai and the dangers of allowing too much freedom of mobility for the sailors. In 1844 he proclaimed the boundaries for both groups ('Her Majesty's Subjects permanently residing at, or occasionally resorting to, Shanghae').

That boundary was estimated at 'the distance to which a Person can travel, during the Day, so as to return to Shanghae in time not to be obliged to sleep out of the place'. This distance varied, of course, according to wealth because they could 'freely hire, purchase or make use of boats, Horses, and Chairs without any hindrance'. Balfour further restricted this policy by clarifying that it did not grant any such 'liberty' of movement to 'crews of ships anchored within the Port'.[24]

A regular court was also necessary to both protect the rights of British citizens and ensure control of the sailors. Balfour made this connection clear in an 1845 declaration on the establishment of the courts. Balfour foresaw that sentences of imprisonment might lead to sailors being left behind by their ships. When ships were responsible for the punishment of sailors without formal courts, the 'criminals' would always leave with the ship, liberating the local authorities and merchants from the burden of caring for prisoners. At first, before the establishment of a British prison, the solution was to house British criminals in 'the Chinese prison' with regular visits by officers of the Consulate to ensure proper treatment.

> [T]he greatest difficulty I experience, is disposing of seamen whose ships may have left the port before the men have undergone their sentences, it being obviously inconvenient and even dangerous to the peace for the place to allow such men to go about at liberty.[25]

Eventually, a British prison had to be established. Even if it did not solve the problem of what to do with sailors who had served their time, it did remove the odious situation of using Chinese jails when much of the justification for extraterritoriality rested on the poor conditions in those institutions. Balfour made the following request:

> I suggest that complete plans, sections, and estimates of the building may be supplied from the proper Department at Hong Kong for a prison with suitable out houses and offices for the prisoners, say ten in number; besides buildings for the jailer and police or prison attendants.[26]

Even this request makes clear that the primary use of the prison will be the punishment and confinement of 'chiefly sailors' whose presence created the need for a prison for 'the peace of this place, the respect to our character, urgently calls for the outlay of money whereby to restrain disorderly characters'.[27]

Another need was a police force to regulate the actions of the foreign community, which did not yet exist in Shanghai or other treaty ports. The British consul in Shanghai in 1847, Rutherford Alcock, wrote a letter to his colleague in Beijing stressing the need for professional police in the port.[28] As might be expected, his largest concern was the sailors.

> With a large number of vessels anchoring throughout the year at Shanghae, with crews among whom are very indifferent characters – British, Lascars and Manila men

... drunkenness and violence on shore are by no means uncommon, [and] require the strong arm of authority to be used upon men not in a state to remain in steady obedience to the law.[29]

Control of these people was not just good for the reputation of the European merchant community, but it also ensured the smooth workings of the trade. Sailors' mobility, Alcock pointed out, meant that ships were often put in a position of replacing deserting crew members. He recommended a 'steady-intelligent and able bodied European' to be the head policeman and a marine unit of one boat for patrolling the waterways.[30]

As early as 1855, growing trade in Shanghai proved that the ad hoc prison established in the 1840s was inadequate for the needs of the resident community. Daniel Brooke Robertson, then British consul in Shanghai, wrote to Hong Kong seeking funding for an expanded prison. '[T]he insubordinate state of British seamen generally have – at times – compelled me to fill the jail to an extent far exceeding its accommodations; and fever and dysentery, having broken out amongst the prisoners.' This required him to release most of the prisoners. This act upset the ship masters in port because this introduced a large number of disorderly sailors into the streets of Shanghai.[31] Brooke Robertson's primary suggestion was an expanded staff.

> It is all but impossible for one man to look after twenty prisoners and keep them in order ... I am sorry, too, to say that there being no means for punishing refractory sailors beyond locking them up for a period, tends much to the increase of their numbers, for seamen have no objection to a month's imprisonment and idleness. A treadmill, were it possible to establish such a thing, would do more towards keeping order in the port than any other means that could be devised.[32]

As with the poor laws in England, this proposal would unify punishment with a labour regimen, with the hopes of implementing moral reform among prisoners.

That same year (1855) the consuls reported on the total number of criminal cases that passed through the foreign consuls in Shanghai. Of course, as the consuls lacked a police force, most of these cases emerged from investigation and arrests by the Chinese police, who passed the criminals to the consuls for judicial treatment. It was true that criminal investigation was a daily affair. That year saw 534 cases, including 4 murders, 9 cases of 'house breaking', 13 kidnappings, 29 cases of drunkenness, 48 assaults, 191 misdemeanours, and 82 cases listed under the heading of 'suspicious character'. This final case is interesting as these individuals were likely arrested as vagabonds and were not necessarily engaged in any of the enumerated crimes.[33]

The Americans in Shanghai used, when possible, the British jail to house criminals convicted through their courts. This apparently was becoming an unsustainable situation by the later 1850s due to overcrowding in the British jail and the desire by Americans to maintain their own institutions of power. As R. C. Murphy, the American consul, reported in 1857: 'The want of a jail at this port has become a source of serious embarrassment.'[34] The Assistant Secretary of State, J. A. Thomas, amended Murphy's request with a clarification that between August and December of 1856, eighteen criminal cases were heard by the Shanghai consular court. Making matters worse, the British sent a notice to Murphy telling him that '[t]he insufficiency of room in her majesty's jail for the imprisonment of the large number of seamen and others convicted before me' required that the Americans find another place to house their criminal sailors.[35]

This request was supported broadly by the merchant community in Shanghai as well as by ship masters, who wrote a letter in support of the idea of an American jail in Shanghai to the US government. They focused on four major justifications. The primary justification was 'the necessity for erecting a prison and instituting the means of punishing [sailors] with hard labor or solitary confinement'. The second reason had to do with the large number of criminal cases in the consular courts, which often led to criminals going free at the end of trial for lack of a proper jail. Next, they cited the difficulty in managing relations between sailors and ship masters. Again, they emphasized the problem of regulating the lives of the common seamen in ports. Finally, the need for a jail in Shanghai was a point of national pride. Asking for the use of a British jail was not worthy of a 'great nation like the United States of America'. The letter was signed by sixteen ship masters in Shanghai who hailed from Boston, New York and other ports.[36]

One justification for the new jails, run by foreigners, was the continuing poor reputation of Chinese-style jails. Edward Cunningham of the office of the Shanghai consul wrote Humphrey Marshall, the US Commissioner for China, in July 1853, informing him that 'the only place of confinement available for refractory sailors being the Chinese jail, totally unfit for Europeans, from want to [*sic*] cleanliness and ventilation, and strength to hold them'.[37] He goes on to point out that Chinese prisoners spread disease and in any case, the Chinese jails failed to prevent escapes by Western sailors. But Cunningham is clear that it is not simple benevolence that urges him to create better jails. The streets, in his view, are awash in criminal behavior.

> [T]here are on shore upwards of sixty or seventy men from American vessels, mostly deserters – some from ships that have left, and some from those now in port. A vessel arrives from California, where they are shipping by the run to this place, to take port wages on arrival to a port of discharge in the United States. The crew uniformly ask for their discharge, which is of course refused, when they as uniformly desert; and there is no power in existence here to prevent this outrageous infraction of the law ... They roam about the suburbs of the Chinese city, getting into constant broils with the natives, in which both sides use weapons, and dangerous wounds and even death are the consequences.[38]

Cunningham was not unique in this view and reflected the desires of the entire merchant community, the ship masters and the diplomats. However, although Congress passed laws providing funding for jails in the treaty ports, precious few resources flowed to China.

The American prison was slow in arriving in Shanghai. In 1858, William R. Reed sent Secretary of State Lewis Cass a letter informing him that once again all American convicts in the British jail had to be discharged and left 'ready for new outrages and new shame to their country and its representatives'.[39] The case of Charles Jackson, a sailor convict in China, became the prime example used by the consulate to secure funds for a jail (which Robert Bennet Forbes estimated to be around $1,500 a year for Canton (Whampoa) and $1,500 a year for Shanghai). Jackson was an American sailor who decided to stay in Ningbo, but lacked any work to sustain himself. In the old Canton system, people like Jackson were limited in their mobility. In a place like Whampoa, deserting sailors could do little but wait for another ship to arrive and sign on to serve on a return voyage. In the treaty port era, freedom of mobility made people like Jackson a more common sight. How such men and women could earn money to survive was not clear. Jackson, for one, turned to crime. He served one year in a Shanghai jail (presumably the British jail) 'for having coolly shot a man through the head' at Ningbo. This victim survived. In 1858 Jackson again came before the consular courts for attempted murder, assault and robbery. After trying to get a British marine drunk in order to rob him, he assaulted the marine and threatened him with a gun, taking $14. And while the conviction was rather clear, there was no place to confine the man. No naval ships were in port – naval ships had jails and could serve in a pinch but the American navy did not sustain a large presence in the Pacific until later in the century – and the British jail was again full. A. L. Freeman of the Shanghai consulate sent a letter to Hong Kong requesting Jackson be allowed to stay in the fairly well-developed jails there. When that request failed, Jackson had to be handed over to a local American marshal for confinement in 'a common dwelling-house' and he escaped 'almost immediately'. As the Ningbo consul reported, Jackson was essentially free to commit any crimes he desired because of the lack of a jail.[40]

The conclusion drawn by the consulates was that the sailors in the treaty ports were a critical problem and the single biggest threat to peaceful commerce between China and Europe. Charles William Bardley, the consul at Ningbo, articulated this view best in his analysis of the Jackson case.

> And here I beg leave to call your excellency's attention to the notoriously low state of morals among transient foreigners at this port, who are, for the most part, deserters from European and American ships at Shanghai and Fuhchau [Fuzhou], adventurers who have fought at Chinkiang [Zhenjiang] and Nanking [Nanjing] either for or against the Imperialists [mercenaries serving on either side during the Taiping

Rebellion] ... or disappointed gold-seekers from California ... Runaway sailors and other lawless individuals have for some time past been in the habit of making this port their place of rendezvous – going about *masked*, and under the cover of night plundering the foreign flags (and in several instances under our own flag,) extorting *what is called* 'convoy money', but what is in reality *plunder*, from fishing boats of the Chinese; or, under the pretense of being damaged by collision with the native craft, demanding from the Chinese unreasonable and extortionate sums of money ... The criminal statistics drawn from the British and American consular courts at Ningpo [Ningbo] abound in evidence of the commission of piracy, assassination, highway robbery, assault and battery, theft, perjury, and other lesser crimes, among subjects of these two governments.[41]

In his view, the streets of the treaty ports were all but in the hands of criminal elements. Without a proper legal and judicial apparatus, including prisons, the streets could not be cleaned.

The lack of a prison remained a problem for Americans in treaty ports as revealed in an 1859 incident in Amoy. On 16 May 1859 a sailor William Soule (called Murphy) was killed in a brawl with other sailors. The trial was ad hoc, as was common in the early treaty port era, with four assessors, two missionaries, two ship masters and the consul in Amoy sitting in judgment. They determined that it was Antonio Bass, a Spanish sailor, who killed Murphy and they sentenced him to three years' hard labour. Two others were sentenced to three days' imprisonment and fined $30 each 'for insubordination and disorderly, mutinous conduct'. It is not clear in the report how Bass was imprisoned, three years being far too long for a consular jail, which did not have the mechanism for hard labour in any case. The two Americans charged with disorderly conduct were placed in the British jail as was common. Yet again, the report of this affair became an opportunity for the consul to point out the humiliation involved in lacking a jail.[42] The Americans in the treaty ports never quite resolved this problem and would remain dependent on luck and the British throughout the 1850s. The solution, reached in 1903, was the establishment of an international prison, the Tilanqiao prison.[43] But until then, corrections would remain disparate. Yet, the merchant and diplomatic community agreed on the need for formal institutions of power, courts, police and jails as the solution to the problem of sailors.

Sailors, Ship Masters and Port Regulations

In lieu of proper institutions to enforce the laws and prevent sailors from taking over the streets, consuls created regulations and codes of conduct to help prevent problems, which again worked in practice to restrict the mobility and autonomy of working people, especially sailors. At least from 1851, these regulations came from Washington, DC. That year, Peter Parker was charged with distributing a set of rules for conduct in the Chinese ports. All seven of the 'Rules and

Regulations for Masters, Officers, and Seamen of Vessels of the United States of America at the Free Ports of China' had as their goal the limiting of encounters between sailors and Chinese and preventing the mobility of those workers through the application of the existing disciplinary regimen of the ship.

1 While courts were to be used to maintain peace, masters were primarily responsible and they should 'use due vigilance to preserve the peace, and prevent difficulties between all seamen and subjects of China'.

2 Sailors were not to be allowed to visit port cities without the approval of their masters and never overnight, unless a master could vouch for his good character.

3 Sailors who were not on board ships 'within the time specified' were to be fined.

4 Chinese boatmen who worked near the ships providing necessary services needed to be registered.

5 Masters were to allow ships selling liquor near the boat only at times that they 'may deem proper'.

6 Masters were to oversee all financial exchanges between sailors and Chinese 'to prevent ... the Chinese from defrauding seamen'.

7 Sailors who committed violence against Chinese were to be immediately brought to the consul for justice.[44]

The United States consul in Shanghai expanded on these regulations the same year, requiring that all foreigners in China who wished to open a '[b]oarding or eating house' for sailors needed to secure the approval of the consuls and were required to accept responsibility for all the actions of the sailors who used their establishment. Furthermore, '[i]t is understood that no Chinese subject under any pretense whatever shall be permitted to open either Grog shop or Boarding house for foreign sailors to drink, debauch, and gamble in'. In addition, they issued a broad ban on the discharging of any sailors in Shanghai without the permission of the consul, which was only to be given when the sailor's good behaviour was proven and the master of the ship provided funds for his upkeep.[45] Although the 1850s would prove that such regulations had limited ability to contain the mobility of sailors in the rapidly changing and cosmopolitan Shanghai (as well as other treaty ports), they do show an attempt to use the power of the state and the power of merchant ship masters to create walls between the sailors and the recently 'opened' China.

The most problematic sailors were deserters and these regulations had the prevention of desertion in mind, by giving masters more incentive to prevent flight and making the lives of deserters in the treaty ports as uncomfortable as possible. From the days of Magellan, desertion was one of the most pressing and persistent problems facing Europeans in the Pacific. Long voyages, brutal discipline and more attractive surroundings in the islands and ports of the Pacific meant that few merchant, whaling or naval voyages to the Pacific in the age of sail avoided desertion. Herman Melville's popular early works *Typee* and *Omoo* both put desertion at the centre of the tale. Desertion created problems for the ship masters, who had to spend time and money securing replacements. Unlike the heavily manned naval ships, merchant shipping was highly economical and masters did not take on excess labour. Of course this also meant that deserting sailors had to be replaced. Since many desertions seemed to take place immediately before a ship was scheduled to depart a port (either to facilitate escape or maximize pay), they could prevent timely departures from port. Moreover, as we have seen, desertions placed a burden on masters because they were responsible for preventing unauthorized discharges. Those who did successfully desert would often find work on other ships, but until then they morphed into a problem for the local authorities, as we have already seen in the consular insistence on well-manned and well-constructed jails in the treaty ports.

Missionaries and Extraterritoriality: Fighting for Openness

One projection of extraterritoriality rights onto the lives of Chinese not under foreign jurisdiction in the treaty ports was the defence of Chinese Christians, which was an extension of the claimed foreign jurisdiction over missionaries. Some cases of such defence certainly evolved from lobbying of the consuls by missionaries. In an 1856 letter, the missionaries of Amoy identified a long list of abuses against Chinese Christians. In one case, 'Ong-In-Sia' was imprisoned for several months for selling a house to foreigners for the purpose of Christian preaching. But situations like this were a grey area in the treaty system. While the Treaty of Nanjing (and its American counterpart) provided the right to missionaries to profess their faith, the Chinese state could harass Chinese Christians by enforcing the letter of the law. It is notable that the missionaries targeted the British and American consuls together with a unified voice, assuming that the defence of Christianity was something that could be broadly supported. As was true with the regulation of sailors in the ports, collaboration was possible. Now, while the Qing state retained authority to enforce their laws over Chinese, the missionaries' strategy paid some dividends. In January 1857, after being informed of the arbitrary arrest of the Chinese Christian Wang Yuen-Shay, Peter Parker of the US delegation in Canton wrote a letter to the Chinese Governor of Canton urging him to release Wang.[46]

Another dispute that dragged on for seven years concerned the right of the missionary I. J. Roberts to distribute books in the interior of China. Peter Parker, always eager to push the limits of American treaty rights in China, drafted a letter to the Chinese authorities stressing Robert's right to access the countryside for the purposes of missionary work. When Robert's home was destroyed by Chinese looters, the issue exploded into a diplomatic crisis that was not resolved for years, but indeed involved a massive assertion by the US consuls of the right of missionaries to work in the interior of China. The United States legation summarized its position in 1853, as the case was winding down: not only did the Chinese surrender the right to restrict the movements of foreigners in the interior of China, they also inherited a duty to 'to defend and protect the citizens of the United States residing in the five open ports, and peaceably attending to their own affairs, from all insult or injury on the part of the Chinese'.[47] Of course, these claims were made at the same time that the consuls were constructing mechanisms and regulations to prevent sailors from fully enjoying even the streets of the treaty ports, and also from entering the interior, a right of mobility that was fiercely defended by the consuls for missionaries.

The Problem of Perspective in Maritime History

The argument of this chapter is that the formation of the major institutions of power in the treaty ports between 1842 and 1860 (particularly the institutions of extraterritoriality such as courts and prisons) were created to regularize the lives of sailors in the ports. The creation of the treaty port system made it more difficult to maintain control over the mobility and activities of a growing maritime working class. The merchant community looked on the broader maritime community with fear and trepidation. Sailors and their associates were seen as a source of difficulties between trading partners, a cause of a fragmented and unstable labour market, a population in need of moral reform or a threat to their own security. In the Canton system, these working people were regulated in large part by geography. The opening of the cities and the geographic expansion of trade to the five treaty ports required new means of control: courts, police and jails. I also argue that the application of extraterritoriality was heavily shaped by class prejudices, creating the seemingly bizarre situation where the merchant and diplomatic communities tried to expand mobility for themselves while restricting mobility for working people. One reason for this inequality was a deep suspicion of sailors by the merchant communities and their allies in the consuls.

Merchant communities had values that often differed from those of many other members of the maritime enclaves that their economic activities fostered. However, they also had the economic and political power to enforce their vision of openness on the working people surrounding them. This vision of well-regulated openness gave the merchant community the freedom to enjoy the city, profit from its trade and cultivate an urban enclave of elite culture, but provided little place for the broader residents of the maritime community.

I hope to suggest a broader point that can inform maritime history and world history, both of which tend to sideline or completely neglect the histories of working people. It is clear from this chapter that the international capitalist class in the treaty ports did not ignore working people. In many ways, they were almost obsessed with their activities and focused heavily on maintaining class discipline. When resources were not forthcoming from stingy governments, the elite communities in these ports expressed their concerns in letters and requests. When cases came before the consular courts, they again expressed their desire to control working people's movements and activities. Merchant communities did not exist in isolation from the working people who made global trade possible.

Maritime historians need to spend more time considering how the presence of labour shaped the institutional formation of merchant communities, trade networks and their values. Maritime historians rightfully focus on merchants; however, that focus inevitably distorts how we look at their actions, particularly when we attempt to understand how they applied power. As many of the other chapters in this book show, merchant communities regularly made alliances with various state institutions. We should ask why they accepted imperial or state authority. One of the clichés of globalization since the 1990s has been the growing weakness of states as compared to large corporations. However, there is little sign that the regulatory powers of the state, such as the police who defend meetings of trade organizations from protestors or who help regulate cities increasingly divided by class, are declining.[48] This chapter suggests that the same state authority that registered merchant mobility and profits ensured protection from a cantankerous and often hostile working class.

World history (the larger historiographical unit in which contemporary maritime history finds itself) often reads like a new version of elite history.[49] Whether it focuses on commodities, international institutions and corporations, empire builders, world religions or great explorers, world history returns us to the perspective from above that a generation of new social historians worked to displace in national history. The working-class community in the treaty ports, disciplined, imprisoned, engaged in criminal activities or simply performing their jobs, challenges us to unify the approaches of world and maritime history with those of new social history. In the same way, our study of empire needs to be complicated. In most cases, when we consider empire, we centre on the application of power by imperial powers on non-Western, or so-called 'native', populations. As this chapter reveals, those institutions of power targeted the working-class empire builders as well, even if they were just lowly sailors. Such workers are the often unseen actors in imperial studies. Even something as simple as a treaty port jail or court cannot be explained without their unwilling participation in those institutions. Criminals like Charles Jackson deserve a space in maritime history, world history and imperial history. They were the marginalized actors who formed the merchant communities.

NOTES

Preface

1. J. K. Fairbank, *Trade and Diplomacy on the China Coast, 1842–1854* (Stanford, CA: Stanford University Press, 1969), p. vii.

1 Trade, Public Affairs and the Formation of Merchant Associations in Taiwan in the Eighteenth Century

1. *Huiguan*, meaning literally 'clubhouse', was an association of persons of common geographical background in a place away from their hometown. K.-C. Liu, 'Chinese Merchant Guilds: An Historical Inquiry', *Pacific Historical Review*, 57 (1988), pp. 1–23, on p. 9.

2. As to the study and review of Chinese *huiguan* and *gongsuo*, see Chuan Han-sheng [Quan Hansheng], *Zhongguo Hanghui Zhidushi* [The History of the Chinese Guild System] (Taipei: Shihuo, 1986); Chiu Peng-sheng [Qiu Pengsheng], *Shiba, Shijiu Shiji Suzhou Cheng de Xinxing Gongshangyetuanti* [The New Associations of Merchants and Artisans in the City of Suzhou, 1700–1900] (Taipei: National Taiwan University Press, 1990), pp. 1–17; Feng Xiaocai, 'Zhongguo Dalu Zuijin zhi Huiguanshi Yanjiu', [Recent Studies in China of the History of Huiguan], *Jindai Zhongguoshi Yanjiu Tongxun*, 30 (November 2000), pp. 90–108; C. Moll-Murata, 'Chinese Guilds from the Seventeenth to the Twentieth Centuries: An Overview', in J. Lucassen, T. De Moor and J. L. van Zanden (eds), *The Return of the Guilds* (Utrecht: Utrecht University, 2006), pp. 213–48.

3. *Shinkoku Shokyo Shisatsu Fukumeisho* [Report of the Investigation on Commercial Affairs in Qing China]. Collected by the Diplomatic Record Office, Ministry of Foreign Affairs of Japan, No. 3-3-9, 1897.

4. For example, Zhuo Kehua stated that *jiao* was the same as *huiguan* and *gongsuo*. Zhuo Kehua, *Qingdai Taiwan Hangjiao Yanjiu* [Research on Taiwan Guilds during the Qing Dynasty] (Xiamen: Fujian People's Publishing House, 2005).

5. J. Lucassen, T. De Moor and J. L. van Zanden, 'The Return of the Guilds: Towards a Global History of the Guilds in Pre-Industrial Times', in J. Lucassen, T. De Moor and J. L. van Zanden (eds), *The Return of the Guilds* (Utrecht: Utrecht University, 2006), pp. 5–18.

6. Fu Yiling, *Ming Qing Shidai Shangren ji Shangye Ziben* [Businessmen and Commercial Capital in the Ming and Qing Dynasties] (Taipei: Kufeng, 1986), p. 244.

7. Chen Zhiping, *Minjian Wenshu yu Ming Qing Dongnan Zushang Yanjiu* [Private Documents and the Studies of Southeastern Family Businesses in the Ming-Qing Period] (Beijing: Chinese Publishing House, 2009), chs 2, 3.

8. Fang Hao could not obtain many historical documents, and did not understand clearly that *jiao* referred to merchant associations made up of many firms (*shanghao*); hence, many of his views should be modified. For example, he considered the term *jiao* 'neither refined nor presentable', so it was not included in official records (Fang Hao, *Fang Hao Liushi zhi Liushisi Zixuanshi Dinggao* [Works of Fang Hao, Selected by Himself from the Age of Sixty to Sixty-four] (Taipei: Self-published, 1974), p. 259). In fact, there were many records of *jiao* in the Danxin local government archives held at National Taiwan University in Taipei. Furthermore, Fang Hao adopted the views of Wu Yisheng, thinking that Mengjia did not have the Xiangxia Jiao, which was established during the early Japanese colonial period. The fact that *jiao* constantly underwent disintegration and reorganization was neglected.

9. In 1990, Zhuo Kehua published his master's thesis, *Qingdai Taiwan de Shangzhan Jituan* [Warring Commercial Groups in Qing-dynasty Taiwan] (Taipei: Taiyuan, 1990). In 2005, he again compiled all relevant studies into *Qingdai Taiwan Hangjiao Yanjiu* [Research on Taiwan Guilds during the Qing Dynasty] (Xiamen: Fujian People's Publishing House, 2005). Please consult these two works for relevant research by Zhuo.

10. According to the Danxin Archives, *jiao* remained involved in many public works until the 1890s. See Lin Yu-ju [Yuru], *Qingdai Zhuqian Diqu de Zaidi Shangren jiqi Huodong Wangluo* [Local Merchants and Their Networks of Association in the Zhuqian Area during the Qing Dynasty] (Taipei: Lianjing Books, 2000), ch. 5.

11. Cai Yuanqie, 'Qingdai Taiwan Jiceng Zhengzhi Tixi zhong Feizhengshi Jiegou zhi Fazhan [The Development of Informal Structures in Qing Taiwan's Local Political System], *Bulletin of Historical Research*, 11 (June 1983), pp. 97–111; 'Qingdai Taiwan Hangjiao de Fazhan yu Difang Quanli Jiegou zhi Bianqian' [The Development of Guilds and Changes in Local Power Structures in Qing Taiwan], *Tunghai Journal of Historical Research*, 7 (December 1985), pp. 189–207.

12. See Tu Zhaoyan, *Riben Diguo Zhuyi xia de Taiwan* [Taiwan under Japanese Imperialism], trans. Li Mingjun (Taipei: Renjian Press, 1992), pp. 374–5.

13. Lin Man-houng [Manhong], 'Taiwan Ziben yu Liang'an Jingmao Guanxi (1895–1945): Taishang Tuozhan Waimao Jingyan zhiyi Zhongyao Pianzhang' [Taiwan Capital and the Economic and Trade Relations between Taiwan and the Chinese Mainland (1895–1945): An Important Chapter in the Expansion of External Trade by Taiwan Merchants], in Song Guangyu (coll. and ed.), *Taiwan Jingyan 1: Lishi Jingji Pian* (Taipei: Dongda, 1993), pp. 67–139; 'Qingmo Dalu Lai Tai Jiaoshang de Xingshuai: Taiwanshi, Zhongguoshi, Shijieshi zhiyi Jiehe Sikao' [The Rise and Fall of Guild Merchants who Moved from the Chinese Mainland to Taiwan: Integrating World History, Chinese History, and Taiwan History], *Proceedings of the National Science Council: Humanities and Social Science*, 4:2 (1994), pp. 173–93.

14. C. Daniels, 'Shinmatsu Taiwan Nanbu Seitōgyō to Shōnin Sihon: Sen Happyaku Nanajū-sen Happyaku Kyūjū Go Nen' [The Sugar Industry and Capital in Southern Taiwan during the Late Qing Period: 1870–95], *Journal of the Research Department of the Toyo Bunko*, 64:3, 5 (March 1983), pp. 289–326; 'Shindai Taiwan Nanbu ni okeru Seitōgyō no Kōzō: Tokuni Sen Happyaku Rokujū Nen Izen o chūsin toshite' [The Structure of the Sugar Industry in Southern Taiwan: Before 1860], *Taiwan Kindaishi*

Kenkyū, 5 (December 1984), pp. 47–113.

15. Kurihara Jun, 'Shindai Taiwan ni okeru Beikoku Ishutsu to Kōshōnin' [Taiwan's Grain Export and Guild Merchants in the Qing Dynasty], *Taiwan Kindaishi Kenkyū*, 5 (December 1984), pp. 5–45.

16. Lin, *Qingdai Zhuqian Diqu de Zaidi Shangren jiqi Huodong Wangluo*, ch. 5; Lin Yu-ju, 'Shangye Wangluo yu Weituo Maoyi Zhidu de Xingcheng: Shijiu Shijimo Lugang Quanjiao Shangren yu Zhongguo Neidi de Fanchuan Maoyi' [Commercial Networks and the Formation of a Cooperative Commissioning System: The Traditional Junk Trade between Lugang Quan Guild Merchants and Mainland China during the Late Nineteenth Century], *New History*, 18:2 (June 2007), pp. 61–103.

17. Chiu Peng-sheng, 'Huiguan, Gongsuo yu Jiao de Bijiao: You Shangren Gongchan Jianshi Qingdai Zhongguo Shichang Zhidu de Duoyangxing' [A Comparison of *Huiguan, Gongsuo* and *Jiao*: The Diversity of Market Systems in China from the Aspect of the Public Property of Merchants], in Lin Yu-ju (ed.), *Bijiao Shiye Xia de Taiwan Shangye Chuantong* [Commercial Traditions in Taiwan: A Comparative Perspective] (Taipei: Institute of Taiwan History, Academia Sinica, 2012), pp. 267–313.

18. Lin, *Qingdai Zhuqian Diqu de Zaidi Shangren jiqi Huodong Wangluo*, pp. 179–84; various kinds of donation steles mention 'shops in Fucheng' for Taiwan capital and '*jiefen* (a share) of Quanzhou Street' for Lugang. These were informal organizations that would later become merchant associations.

19. Ding Shaoyi, *Dongying Shilüe* [Records of Dongying], fasc. 2, p. 32.

20. C. K. Ng, *Trade and Society: The Amoy Network on the China Coast, 1683–1735* (Singapore: Singapore University Press, 1983), pp. 95–111, 163–6; Lin Yu-ju, 'Congshu yu Fenli: Shijiu Shiji Zhongye Taiwan Gangkou Chengshi de Shuangchong Maoyi Jizhi' [Subordinate vs. Independent: Port Cities under the Dual Trade System in Mid-Nineteenth-Century Taiwan], *Studies on Taiwanese History*, 17:2 (June, 2010), pp. 4–7.

21. In steles and chronicles, firms (*shanghang*) were often collectively referred to as *jiaoshang chuanhu* (shipping firms) but might also be named directly, such as Quan Jiao *chuanhu* or Xia Jiao *chuanzhi*. (Huang Tien-ch'üan [Tianquan], *Nanbu Taiwan Beiwen Jicheng* [Collection of Epitaphs from Southern Taiwan], fasc. 218, p. 668; Zhou Xi, *Zhanghua Xianzhi* [Changhua County Gazetteer], fasc. 156, p. 23; *Gamalan Tingzhi* [Kavalan Subprefecture Gazetteer], fasc. 160, p. 7. In 1871, in the *Danshui Tingzhi* [Tamsui Subprefecture Gazetteer], Chen Peigui said even more plainly, 'There were *jiao* firms who rented or purchased ships. Those going to Fuzhou, Jiangsu and Zhejiang were the Northern Jiao. Those going to Quanzhou were the Quan Jiao, also [called] Upper Jiao. Those going to Xiamen were the Xia Jiao' (fasc. 172, p. 299). These firms might well be owned by the same proprietor; however, most of them were jointly built and owned by several partners. See K. T. Chen, 'Shipping and Trade of Chinese Junks in South-East Asia, 1730–1830: A Survey', in S. P. Ville and D. M. Williams (eds), *Management, Finance and Industrial Relations in Maritime Industries: Essays in International Maritime and Business History* (St John's, Newfoundland: International Maritime Economic History Association, 1994), pp. 203–4.

22. Lin, 'Shangye Wangluo yu Weituo Maoyi Zhidu de Xingcheng', pp. 76, 80–6.

23. Cai Maofeng, *Yuanli Zhi* [*Yuanli Gazetteer*], fasc. 48, p. 83.

24. See Lin, *Qingdai Zhuqian Diqu de Zaidi Shangren jiqi Huodong Wangluo*, ch. 5, sec. 1 for details on the transformation of *jiao* firms and water *jiao* into Quan Jiao. It is difficult to find texts from the eighteenth century about the formation of *jiao*, but in the Danxin Archives, for instance, Jihean *jiao* in Tongxiao was established in 1875 due to

the struggle with the local Superintendant (*zongli*) over the imposition of an export tax on ships.

25. Zhuo, *Qingdai Taiwan Hangjiao Yanjiu*, pp. 329–30.

26. For details on transaction costs of long-distance trade, see F. Chen and R. H. Myers, 'Coping with Transaction Costs: The Case of Merchant Associations in the Qing Period', in R. A. Brown (ed.), *Chinese Business Enterprise* (London and New York: Routledge, 1996), vol. 2, pp. 256–9.

27. Lin, 'Congshu yu Fenli', p. 6.

28. During the late years of the reign of the Emperor Kangxi, Huang Shujing noted in *Taihaishi Chalu* [Record of a Tour of Duty in the Taiwan Sea] that cane sugar, which was mainly exported to Jiangsu, had to go first to Xiamen for inspection (fasc. 4, p. 21). In 1835, Zhou Xi also made a similar comment in his *Zhanghua Xianzhi*: 'Quan Jiao and Xia Jiao in Lugang who wanted to go north, though they had their ships loaded in Lugang, still had to go inland for inspection and then go northward along the coasts' (pp. 23–4).

29. Zhang Guoqing, *Tianyige Mingzhou Beilin Jilu* [Collection of Mingzhou Epitaphs from the Tianyi Pavilion] (Shanghai: Shanghai Classics Publishing House, 2008), p. 243.

30. For instance, there was an inscription written in 1719 in Dongshan, Zhangzhou which mentioned the Taiwanese shipmen.

31. For example, it was inscribed on a stele dated 1790 that the Northern Jiao Suwanli had made donations to build the Taiping Bridge in 1728 (He Peifu, *Taiwan Diqu Xiancun Beiji Tuzhi* [Collection of Epitaphs Extant in Taiwan] (Taipei: National Taiwan Library, 1992), p. 59); also Chen Peigui recorded in *Danshui Tingzhi* that *jiao* firms built the Water God Temple in Mengjia during the early Qianlong reign (1736– 95) (fasc. 172, p. 153).

32. For example, when the foundation of the Medicine God Temple on Beishi Street in Fucheng was laid, donations came from merchants all over Taiwan. In 1764, they raised funds again to rebuild it. In 1824, it was renovated by *jiao* firms and local people. As for the Temple of the Empress of Heaven in Ben'gang, its construction in 1730, reconstruction in 1751 and restoration in 1775 were all initiated by Xue Zhaohuang, the assistant magistrate of Ben'gang County and Zhuluo County, who donated his salary, and financed by contributions from directors, supervisors, *zongyue* (village heads), *hanghu* (*jiao* firms) and monks. The names of *jiao* were not among the donors. Huang, *Nanbu Taiwan Beiwen Jicheng*, fasc. 218, pp. 96–7, 259–60.

33. In the Palace of the Water God, the Water God is worshipped. It was an important deity among *jiao*. *Jiao* from Tainan, Ben'gang (Beigang), Zhuqian (Hsinchu), Mengjia (Wanhua) and Penghu all worshipped it and even built temples to it.

34. Xie Jinluan, *Xuxiu Taiwan Xianzhi* [A Continued Revision of the *Taiwan County Gazetteer*], fasc. 140, p. 339.

35. Sanyitang was later turned into the council chamber of the Three Jiao in Tainan during the reign of Emperor Daoguang (1821–50).

36. Huang, *Nanbu Taiwan Beiwen Jicheng*, pp. 29–30.

37. Xie, *Xuxiu Taiwan Xianzhi*, p. 340.

38. Liu Liangbi, *Chongxiu Fujian Taiwanfu Zhi* [A Revision of Fujian's Taiwan Prefecture Gazetteer], fasc. 74, p. 88.

39. Xie, *Xuxiu Taiwan Xianzhi*, p. 14; Huang, *Nanbu Taiwan Beiwen Jicheng*, p. 92.

40. Huang, *Nanbu Taiwan Beiwen Jicheng*, pp. 69–71, 89–91.

41. The stele erected in commemoration of the reconstruction of South China Sea Putuo Temple in 1791 is currently a historical relic preserved at the temple site.

42. During the Qing dynasty, when means of communication were relatively undeveloped, travel between Taiwan and mainland China was a significant journey over a considerable distance. Without knowing of the existence of their counterparts across the strait, some merchant associations might choose the same names. For example, the Tobacco-Grocery Jiao in the prefectural capital of Taiwan, Ran (Dye) Jiao in Lugang, Quan Jiao in Ben'gang and Ben Jiao in Quanzhou were all called Jinheshun. Instances of the same names appearing in different port cities in mainland China and Taiwan included Jinyongshun (Southern Jiao in Fucheng, 1770; Fu Jiao in Xiamen, 1819), Jinjinshun (Quan Jiao in Mengjia, 1813; Dan Jiao in Quanzhou, 1861), Jin Wanli (Northern Jiao in Mengjia, 1868; Northern Jiao in Xiamen, 1878), Jinheshun (Quan Jiao in Ben'gang, 1831; Ben Jiao in Quanzhou, 1861), and Jinzhenshun (Lu Jiao in Xiamen, 1803; Xia Jiao in Lugang, 1814; Southern-Northern Jiao in Puzaijiao, 1896). The years listed above indicate the time these names first appear in the literature.

43. Yao Ying, *Dongming Zougao* [Reports of Dongming], fasc. 49, p. 37; Yao Ying, *Zhongfutang Xuanji* [Anthology of Zhongfutang], fasc. 83, p. 100.

44. 'Tong'an County', in Zheng Zhenman and Ding Hesheng (eds), *Fujian Zongjiao Bei ming Huibian: Quanzhoufu Fence* [Epigraphical Materials on the History of Religion in Fujian: Quanzhou Region] (Fuzhou: Fujian Renmin Chubanshe, 2003), p. 1121. The same can be seen among the donors listed on the stele erected in commemoration of the restoration of the City God Temple. See also 'Chongxiu Chenghuangmiao Juanyin Siyuan Yishang Xingmingbei', pp. 1122–3.

45. Wang Shih-ch'ing [Shiqing], *Qingdai Taiwan Shehui Jingji* [Taiwan Society and Economics in the Qing Dynasty] (Taipei:Lianjing Books, 1994), pp. 97–120.

46. For example, in 1775, the Quan Jiao and Xia Jiao in Lugang jointly donated resources to establish a charitable burial ground in Jingyiyuan; in 1779, shipping firms from Quanzhou and Xiamen, Xia Jiao *choufan* (tax agencies of the Xia Jiao), the Quan Jiao, Xia Jiao and local citizens, and Taiwanese merchants from Yongding County and Haideng County all contributed to the restoration of Ci You Temple in Xinzhuang; in 1780, the Xia Jiao donated funds to build the ferry pier in Mengjia; in 1785, the Quan Jiao and Xia Jiao jointly made sacrificial offerings to the gods of Ci You Temple in Xinzhuang. Liu Chih-wan [Zhiwan], *Taiwan Zhongbu Beiwen Jicheng* [Collection of Epitaphs from Central Taiwan], fasc. 151, pp. 7–8; He, *Taiwan Diqu Xiancun Beiji Tuzhi*, Taipei City, p. 8; Taipei County, pp. 11–12; addendum, p. 164.

47. Details on various construction and restoration projects of Fucheng in 1775 were included in a compilation put together by the Taiwan magistrate Jiang Yuanshun; see his *Chongxiu Taijun Ge Jianzhu Tushuo* [Pictures and Interpretations of Restoring Official Buildings in Taiwan Prefecture] (Nantou: Historical Records Committee of Taiwan Provincial Government, 1994).

48. He, *Taiwan Diqu Xiancun Beiji Tuzhi*, addendum, p. 7.

49. 'Inscription of Longshan Temple Restoration', at Anhai Longshan Temple.

50. Huang, *Nanbu Taiwan Beiwen Jicheng*, p. 155.

51. Lin Yu-ju, *Qingdai Taiwan Gangkou de Kongjian Jiegou* [The Spatial Structure of Taiwan Harbors in the Qing Dynasty] (Taipei: Zhi Shufang, 1996), chs 5, 6.

52. Murakami Tamakichi also gave the example that the Medicine Jiao purchased medicine from the Northern Jiao. See his *Nanbu Taiwan Shi* [Gazetteer of Southern Taiwan] (Tainan: Society for Co-prosperity in Tainan State, 1933), p. 381.

53. According to surveys conducted in 1896, the eleven firms were Taipu Zhen He, Pujie Xie Shun, Taipu Fu An, Mao Shun, Taipu Dong Baoxing, Taipu Jin Yuanhe, Taipu Yi Yuan, Benjie Shun Ji, Taipu Fu Qingchang, Taipu Zhen Li and Taipu Jin Fuchang. See *Taiwan Zongdufu Gongwenlei Zuan* [Taiwan Sotokufu Archives, vol. 9765, pp. 5-5-19, 1898, held at Taiwan Historica in Nantou.

54. However, as Hosea Ballou Morse observed, the Great Guild of Newchang also participated in a wide range of public works in the local society; it maintained streets, reservoirs and drains, as well as controlling the common land, helping the poor and supporting charitable groups. See H. B. Morse, *The Gilds of China: With an Account of the Gild Merchant of Co-hong of Canton* (London: Longmans, Green and Co., 1909), p. 49. William T. Rowe emphasized that the Hankow guilds engaged in philanthropy, fought fires and provided defense for the city in times of unrest. See his *Hankow: Commerce and Society in a Chinese City, 1796–1889* (Stanford, CA: Stanford University Press, 1984), pp. 317–19.

55. The Empress of Heaven, also called Mazu, is the protectress of seamen on the China coast.

56. Zheng Pengyun and Zeng Fengchen, *Xinzhu Xianzhi Chugao* [Drafts of *Hsinchu County Gazetteer*], fasc. 61, p. 177; Taiwan Kanshū Kenkyūkai, *Taiwan Guanxi Jishi* [Notes on Taiwan Etiquette and Customs], trans. by Liu Ningyan et al. (Taichung: Historical Records Committee of Taiwan Provincial Government, 1989), book 2, vol. 1, pp. 34–5.

57. The practical duties of the *Jushi* are still not very clear. In No. 14301-6 of *Danxin dang'an* [Danxin Archives], it is only recorded that he could take charge of levying export taxes on ships.

58. Rinji Taiwan kyūkan chōsakai (ed.), *Taiwan Shihō* [Taiwan Private Laws] (Taipei: Printed by the author, 1910), vol. 3, p. 162.

59. Zhuo, *Qingdai Taiwan de Shangzhan Jituan*, p. 64.

60. Zhuo, *Qingdai Taiwan de Shangzhan Jituan*, p. 58; Rinji Taiwan kyūkan chōsakai, *Taiwan Shihō*, vol. 3, p. 162; Dai Yanhui, *Qingdai Taiwan de Xiangzhi* (Taipei: Lianjing Books, 1979), p. 227.

61. Zhuo, *Qingdai Taiwan de Shangzhan Jituan*, p. 58.

62. Rinji Taiwan kyūkan chōsakai, *Taiwan Shihō*, vol. 3, pp. 162–3.

63. The monuments of guilds in mainland China would record their histories, the rituals they observed, and a list of donors. Appended was usually a list of properties owned by the *huiguan* or *gongsuo*. Liu, 'Chinese Merchant Guilds', pp. 16–18.

2 Seoul Merchant Communities in Late Chosŏn Korea

1. Literature on *shijŏn* in Kaesong is limited. See for example, Kim Byung-Ha, 'Tojung e Kwanhan Yŏn'gu' [A Study on Tojung], *Kyŏng'yŏng Sahak*, 8 (1993), pp. 47–67; Byun Kwang-Seok, '18–19 segi Kaesŏng ŭi Shijŏn kwa Sang'ŏp Kwanhaeng' [The Patronized Store and Commercial Practice in 18th and 19th-Century Gaesung], *Yŏksa wa Kyŏnggye*, 64 (2007), pp. 137–68.

2. One Japanese *koku* is approximately 180 litres.

3. Lee Hun-Chang, 'Kyŏngje T'onghap Ch'ejewa Kŭ Pyŏnhwa'e Kwanhan Yŏn'gu' [The System of Economic Integration and Its Transformation in the Chosŏn Dynasty], in Lee Hun-Chang (ed.), *Chosŏn Hugi Chaejŏnggwa Shijang* [State Finance and the Market in Late Chosŏn Korea] (Seoul: Seoul National University Press, 2010), pp. 439–72,

on pp. 442–4.

4. Lee Hun-Chang, 'Han'guksa esŏŭi Sudo Chipjung' [The Primacy of Capital Cities in Korean History], *Han'guksa Yŏn'gu*, 134 (2006), pp. 1–34.

5. H. C. Lee, 'When and How Did Japan Catch Up with Korea? A Comparative Study of the Pre-industrial Economies of Korea and Japan', *CEI Working Paper Series*, 2006–15 (Tokyo: Institute of Economic Research, Hitotsubashi University, 2006).

6. H. C. Lee and P. Temin, 'The Political Economy of Preindustrial Korean Trade', *Journal of Institutional and Theoretical Economics*, 166:3 (2009), pp. 548–71.

7. Tashiro Kazui, *Kinsei Nitchō Tsūkō Bōekishi no Kenkyū* (Tokyo: Sōbunsha, 1981).

8. Lee Hun-Chang, 'Han'guk Chŏn'gŭndae Muyŏgŭi Yuhyŏnggwa Kŭ Pyŏndong'e Kwanhan Yŏn'gu' [A Study on the Pattern of and Changes in the Pre-industrial Korean Trade], *Kyungje Sahak*, 36 (2004), pp. 83–122.

9. D. C. North, 'Markets and Other Allocation Systems in History: The Challenge of Karl Polanyi', *Journal of European Economic History*, 6:3 (1977), pp. 703–16. North accepted three major economic integrating forms formulated by Karl Polanyi. We agree with the premise of North that Polanyi did not provide an economic theory to explain the changes in the economic system.

10. Lee and Temin, 'The Political Economy of Preindustrial Korean Trade'.

11. Sukawa Hidenori, 'Chōsen Shoki ni okeru Keizai Kōsō' [Economic Policies in the Chosun Dynasty], *Tōyōshi Kenkyū*, 58:4 (2000), pp. 57–88.

12. Park Yi-Taek, 'Chosŏn Hugiŭi Kyŏngje Ch'eje [The Economic System in Late Chosŏn Korea], in Lee Dae-Keun (ed.), *Saeroun Hanguk Kyŏngje Paljŏnsa* [New Perspective on History of Korean Economic Development] (Seoul: Nanam Ch'ulp'an, 2005), pp. 53–5.

13. Lee Hun-Chang, 'Chosŏn Wangjoŭi Kyŏngje T'onghap Ch'ejewa Kŭ Pyŏnhwa'e Kwanhan Yŏn'gu'.

14. Cho Young-Jun, '19–20 segi Pobusang Chojig e Taehan Chaep'yŏngga' [Traditional Society of Peddlers in Early Modern Korea], *Kyunje Sahak*, 47 (2009), pp. 39–77.

15. Yang Jeong-Pil, 'Kŭndae Kaesŏng Sanginŭi Sangŏpchŏk Chŏnt'onggwa Chabon Ch'ukchŏk' [Commercial Traditions and Capital Accumulation of Modern Gaesung Merchants] (PhD dissertation, Yonsei University, 2012).

16. Park Byoung-Ho, *Kŭnseŭi Pŏpkwa Pŏpsasang* [Law and Legal Thought in Modern Times] (Seoul: Chinwŏn, 1996).

17. T. De Moor, 'The Silent Revolution: A New Perspective on the Emergence of Commons, Guilds and Other Forms of Corporate Collective Action in Western Europe', in J. Lucassen, T. De Moor and J. L. van Zanden (eds), *The Return of the Guilds* (New York: Cambridge University Press, 2008), pp. 179–212, on pp. 208–9.

18. Lee Hun-Chang, 'Chosŏn Wangjoŭi Kyŏngje T'onghap Ch'ejewa Kŭ Pyŏnhwa'e Kwanhan Yŏn'gu'.

19. R. Huang, 'The Ming Fiscal Administration', in D. C. Twitchett and F. W. Mote (eds), *The Ming Dynasty, 1368–1644, Part 2*, vol. 8 of D. C. Twitchett and J. K. Fairbank (eds), *The Cambridge History of China* (New York: Cambridge University Press, 1998), pp. 106–71, on p. 145.

20. Sukawa Hidenori, *Richō Shōgyō Seisakushi Kenkyū* [Economic Policy in the Later Chosŏn Period of Korea] (Tokyo: University of Tokyo Press, 1994).

21. *Pang* literally means 'room'.

22. Kokushō Iwao, 'Girudo toshiteno Keijō Yuku-i-chon' [The Six Major Merchant Communities in Seoul as Guilds], *Keizaishi Ronkō* [Essays on Economic History] (Tokyo:

Iwanami Shoten, 1923), p. 19.

23. *Pangse* literally means 'taxes' on each division, but it denotes shop 'fee' or shop 'dues' to community members.

24. Several studies suggest that the organization of *shijŏn* merchants had already emerged before the seventeenth century. See for example, Kim Dong-Chul, 'Koryŏmal ŭi Yut'ong Kujo wa Sang'in' [Distribution Structure and Merchants in the Late Koryo Dynasty], *Pudae Sahak*, 9 (1985), pp. 205–39; Baek Seung-Cheol, '16 segi Pusan Taego ŭi Sŏngjang kwa Sangŏp Hwaldong' [Growth of Wealthy Merchants and Business Magnates and Their Commercial Activities in the Sixteenth Century], *Yŏksa wa Hyŏnsil*, 13 (1994), pp. 242–74; Park Pyeong-Sik, *Chosŏn Chŏn'gi Sangŏpsa Yŏngu* [Studies on the Commercial History of the Early Chosŏn Dynasty] (Seoul: Chisik San'ŏpsa, 1999), pp. 119–20; Park Pyeong-Sik, *Chosŏn Chŏn'gi Kyowhan Kyŏngje wa Sang'in Yŏn'gu* [Studies on Commerce and Merchants in the Early Chosŏn Dynasty] (Seoul: Chisik San'ŏpsa, 2009), pp. 88–9; Seo Seong-Ho, '15 segi Sŏul Shijŏn ŭi Sangŏp' [Commerce of Shijŏn in Seoul in the Fifteenth Century], in Yi T'ae-jin (ed.), *Sŏul Sangŏpsa* [A Commercial History of Seoul] (Seoul: T'aehaksa, 2000), pp. 33–78.

25. *Shijŏn* guilds had benefits and burdens, which will be explained in the next section.

26. *Yugjubijŏn* is assumed to be more popular in speech, *yugŭijŏn* more common in writing.

27. Necessities such as rice and salt were excluded.

28. Kokushō, 'Girudo toshiteno Keijō Yuku-i-chon', pp. 1–35. Other scholars also performed extensive research on *shijŏn* before liberation (1945), but the 'organization' of *shijŏn* was spotlighted only by Kokushō. See, for example, Zenshō Eisuke, *Chōsenjin no Shōgyō* [Commerce of the Chosŏn People] (Keijō: Chōsen Sōtokufu, 1925); Ayukai Fusanoshin, 'Shitenkō' [A Study of *Shijŏn*], *Zakkō*, 8 (Keijō: Chōsen Insatsu, 1937), pp. 233–317; Ri Nōwa, 'Richō Jidai Keijō Shisei' [The Market System in Seoul in the Yi Dynasty], *Mansenshi Ronsō* (Tokyo: Inaba Hakashi Kanreki Kinenkai, 1938), pp. 695–728.

29. O. Miller, 'The Silk Merchants of the Myŏnjujŏn: Guild and Government in Late Chosŏn Korea' (PhD dissertation, University of London, 2007), pp. 93–5; Sukawa Hidenori, 'Shijŏn Sang'in kwa Kukka Chaejŏng' [The Licensed Guild and State Finance], in Lee Hun-Chang (ed.), *Chosŏn Hugi Chaejŏnggwa Shijang* (Seoul: Seoul National University Press, 2010), pp. 357–8.

30. Miller, 'Silk Merchants of the Myŏnjujŏn', p. 95.

31. Chung Seung-Mo, 'Chosŏn Shidae Sŏul ŭi Sangp'um Yut'ong Ch'egye wa Sangŏp P'ungsok' [Distribution Mechanism and Folklore of Commerce in Seoul in Chosŏn Korea], in Institute of Seoul Studies (ed.), *The History of Social Folklore in Seoul* (Seoul: Institute of Seoul Studies, 1995), pp. 89–91.

32. *To* literally means 'total' or 'aggregate'.

33. Kokushō, 'Girudo toshiteno Keijō Yuku-i-chon', p. 19. One *tsubo* is approximately 3.3 square metres.

34. Ch'oe Pyŏngmu, 'Rijo Sigi ŭi Shijŏn' [Shijŏn in the Yi Dynasty], *Ryŏksa Ronmunjip*, 2 (1958), pp. 386–7 already pointed out this aspect.

35. Kokushō, 'Girudo toshiteno Keijō Yuku-i-chon', p. 26. The word *yang* is a cognate of the Chinese tael (*liang*), so 1 yang was worth 100 copper coins.

36. The question of whether or not *shijŏn* is kin-based can be raised, because sons-in-law do not have any blood ties. Contrary to the situation among the *yangban* elite class, lineage succession by affines seems to have remained in practice among merchants in late Chosŏn Korea. In this chapter, kinship includes both paternal and maternal lines.

37. Several documents report the existence of *samjwa* between *sŏnsaeng* and *ojwa*.

38. In pre-modern Japan, the name of merchant guilds was *za*, which also literally meant 'seat'. See M. L. Nagata, 'Brotherhoods and Stock Societies: Guilds in Pre-modern Japan', in J. Lucassen, T. De Moor and J. L. van Zanden (eds), *The Return of the Guilds* (New York: Cambridge University Press, 2008), pp. 121–42.

39. Kokushō, 'Girudo toshiteno Keijō Yuku-i-chon', p. 31.

40. Ko, 'Chosŏn Hugi Shijŏn ŭi Kujo wa Kinŭng', p. 72; Ko, 'Shijŏn Sang'in ŭi Chojik kwa Tosŏng Munhwa', p. 136.

41. Miller, 'Silk Merchants of the Myŏnjujŏn', p. 102.

42. Sukawa, 'Shijŏn Sang'in kwa Kukka Chaejŏng', p. 353. Everyone in the guild was supposed to have his own share, but some members had only a half share. This arrangement means that in the merchant guild, a person who was not an actual merchant could have only a part share. In Korean, a share is called *kit* (literally, 'collar'); it has the same meaning as *kabu* (literally, 'tree stump') in Japanese. *Kabu* is the word used for shares in joint-stock companies. See Nagata, 'Brotherhoods and Stock Societies', p. 122.

43. Han Sang-Kwon, 'Yŏngjo-Chŏngjo ŭi Saeroun Sangŏpkwan kwa Sŏul Sangŏp Chŏngch'aek' [The New Viewpoint on Commerce of King Yŏngjo and King Chŏngjo and Their Commercial Policy in Seoul], in Yi T'ae-jin (ed.), *Sŏul Sangŏpsa* (Seoul: T'aehaksa, 2000), p. 286.

44. *Pibyŏnsa Tŭngnok*, 4 September 1788.

45. Ko Dong-Hwan, *Chosŏn Shidae Sŏul Toshisa* [Urban History of Seoul in Chosŏn Korea] (Seoul: T'aehaksa, 2007), pp. 139–40.

46. Miller, 'Silk Merchants of the Myŏnjujŏn', p. 65. Miller cites Ch'oe as well as Byun. See Ch'oe, 'Rijo Sigi ŭi Shijŏ'; Kwang-Seok Byun, *Chosŏn Hugi Shijŏn Sang'in Yŏn'gu* [A Study of Shijŏn Tradesmen in the Latter Half of the Chosŏn Dynasty] (Seoul: Hyean, 2001).

47. Ko Dong-Hwan, 'Chosŏn Hugi Wangsil kwa Shijŏn Sang'in' [The Royal Family and Merchants of Shijŏn (Licensed Shops) in the Latter Half of the Chosŏn Dynasty], *Sŏulhak Yŏn'gu*, 30 (2008), pp. 90–3.

48. Cho Young-Jun, '19 segi Huban Naesusa wa Shijŏn ŭi Kŏrae Shilt'ae' [Practice and Condition of Transactions between Naesusa and *Shijŏn* in the Late Nineteenth Century], *Sŏulhak Yŏn'gu*, 31 (2008), pp. 167–201; Cho Young-Jun, 'Chosŏn Hugi Wangsil ŭi Chodal Chŏlch'a wa Sot'ong Ch'egye' [The Procurement Process and Communication System of Royal Finance in Late Chosŏn Korea], *Komunsŏ Yŏn'gu*, 37 (2010), pp. 91–121.

49. Ko, 'Chosŏn Hugi Wangsil kwa Shijŏn Sang'in', pp. 75–82.

50. Sukawa, 'Shijŏn Sang'in kwa Kukka Chaejŏng', p. 357.

51. *Yŏnjo Sillok,* 18 December 1768.

52. Kokushō, 'Girudo toshiteno Keijō Yuku-i-chon', p. 20.

53. Rhee Young-Hoon, 'Chosŏn Hugi P'alkyŏl Chakpuje e taehan Yŏn'gu' [A Study on the System of P'alkyŏl Chakpu in Late Chosŏn Korea], *Han'guksa Yŏn'gu*, 29 (1980), pp. 75–137; Lee Sung-Im, '16 segi Chibang Kunhyŏn ŭi Kongmul Punjŏng gwa Such'ui' [Distribution of Special Items to be Submitted and the Collection of Such Items in the Sixteenth Century Local Gun and Hyeon Units], *Yŏksa wa Hyŏnsil*, 72 (2009), pp. 33–68. *Jubi* was also known as having the same meaning of 'share', which was *kabu* in Japanese. See Ayukai, 'Shitenkō', p. 254 and n. 42 in this chapter.

54. Research has recently grasped and emphasized the function of *kye* in a *shijŏn* guild; however, an uncertain aspect remains. Although several scholars have mentioned the

existence and function of *kye* (see especially Ko, 'Chosŏn Hugi Shijŏn ŭi Kujo wa Kinŭng', pp. 90–1; Sukawa, 'Shijŏn Sang'in kwa Kukka Chaejŏng', p. 359), the existence of *kye* in addition to the '*chŏn, pang, k'an*' system poses a major question to their explanations. A variety of documents report the existence of *so* under each *kye*; thus, we assume that a system of '*chon, kye, so*' existed in every *shijŏn* guild. The relationship between the '*chŏn, pang, k'an*' and '*chŏn, kye, so*' systems should be investigated.

55. S. R. Epstein, 'Craft Guilds in the Pre-Modern Economy: A Discussion', *Economic History Review*, 61:1 (2008), pp. 155–74.
56. S. Ogilvie, 'Rehabilitating the Guilds: A Reply', *Economic History Review*, 61:1 (2008), pp. 175–82, on p. 175.
57. S. Ogilvie, '"Whatever Is, Is Right"? Economic Institutions in Pre-industrial Europe', *Economic History Review*, 60:4 (2007), pp. 649–84, on p. 649.
58. A. Greif, *Institutions and the Path to the Modern Economy: Lessons from Medieval Trade* (New York, NY: Cambridge University Press, 2006).
59. Greif, *Institutions and the Path to the Modern Economy*.
60. Greif, *Institutions and the Path to the Modern Economy*.
61. Park Pyeong-Sik, *Chosŏn Chŏn'gi Sang'ŏpsa Yŏngu*, p. 100; Ko, *Chosŏn Shidae Shijŏn Sangŏp Yŏn'gu* (Seoul: Chisik San ŏpsa, 1999), p. 114.
62. Greif, *Institutions and the Path to the Modern Economy*, p. 122.
63. Ko, *Chosŏn Shidae Shijŏn Sangŏp Yŏn'gu*, pp. 246–9.
64. Tetsuji Okazaki, *Edōno Shijōkeizai* [The Market Economy of Edō] (Tokyo: Kōdansha, 1999).
65. Lee, 'When and How Did Japan Catch Up with Korea?'
66. W. T. Rowe, 'Ming-Qing Guilds', *Ming Qing Yanjiu*, 1 (1992), pp. 47–60. Chiu Peng-sheng, 'You Gongchan dao Faren – Qingdai Suzhou, Shanghai Shangren Tuanti de Zhidu Bianqian' [From "Common Property" to Corporation: The Institutional Changes of the Merchant Associations of Suzhou and Shanghai in Late Qing], *Fazhishi Yanjiu*, 10 (2006), pp. 117–54.
67. K. Pomeranz, *The Great Divergence: China, Europe and the Making of the Modern World Economy* (Princeton, NJ: Princeton University Press, 2000).
68. Lee Hun-Chang, 'Kŭndae Kyŏngje Sŏngjang ŭi Kiban Hyŏngsŏnggi Rosŏ 18 segi Chosŏn ŭi Sŏngch'wiwa kŭ Han'gye' [The Korean Economy in the Eighteenth Century as a Preparatory Stage for Modern Economic Growth], in Yŏksa Hakhoe (ed.), *Chŏngjowa 18 segi* [King Chŏngjo and the Eighteenth Century] (Seoul: P'urŭn Yŏksa, 2013), pp. 134–78.

3 Rice, Treaty Ports and the Chaozhou Chinese Lianhao Associate Companies: Construction of a South China–Hong Kong–Southeast Asia Commodity Network, 1850s–1930s

1. For example, see Chen Jinxi, 'Dejiao Haiwai Yangjiao yu "Xiang Le Xian Shan" Maoyi Tixi' [Mission of the De Jiao Overseas and the Trading System of "Hong Kong-Singapore-Bangkok-Shantou"], *Hai Jiao Shi Yanjiu* [Maritime History Studies], 53:1 (2008), pp. 106–22.
2. Akira Suehiro, *Capital Accumulation in Thailand, 1850–1985* (Tokyo: Centre for East Asian Cultural Studies, 1989), pp. 89ff.
3. Chen Shouzhi, 'Chaozhou Ren Zai Rukou Mishang' [Chaozhou Merchants as Rice

Importers], in Chaozhou Chamber of Commerce in Hong Kong, *Xianggang Chaozhou Shanghui Chengli Sishi Zhounian ji Chaoshang Xuexiao Xin Xiaoshe Luocheng Jinian Tekan* [A Special Volume Commemorating the Fortieth Anniversary of the Hong Kong Chaozhou Chamber of Commerce and the Completion of the New Building of the Chaozhou Merchant School] (Hong Kong: Chaozhou Chamber of Commerce, 1961), pp. 12–13. Chen was owner of Kin Tye Lung, one of the largest rice import-export firms in Hong Kong.

4. N. B. Dennys, W. F. Mayers and C. King, *The Treaty Ports of China and Japan: A Complete Guide to the Open Ports of Those Countries, Together with Peking, Yedo, Hong Kong and Macau* (London: Trubner and Co., 1867), p. 232.

5. *Xin Shantou* [New Shantou] (Shantou: Shantou Shi Shizhengting, 1928), p. 2; *Shantou Gaikuang* [General Survey of Shantou] (Shantou: Shantou Shi Difang Zhi Bianzuan Weiyuanhui Bangongshi, 1987), pp. 22–3, 46–57.

6. J. Davids (ed.), *American Diplomatic and Public Papers: The United States and China, Series 1: The Treaty System and the Taiping Rebellion, 1842–1860*, vol. 8 (Wilmington, DE: Scholarly Resources, 1973), p. 305; henceforth cited as *American Diplomatic and Public Papers*.

7. According to Rao Zongyi, Shantou had a population of 36,851 in 1914. The number increased to 163,423 in 1930 after the area under the jurisdiction of Shantou expanded. See 'Hukou Zhi' [Population] of *Chaozhou Zhi* [Gazetteer of Chaozhou], in Rao Zongyi (ed.), *Chaozhou Zhi Huibian* [A Compendium of Chaozhou Gazetteers] (Hong Kong: Longmen Shudian, 1965), pp. 930–1.

8. Imperial Maritime Customs, *Decennial Reports on the Trade, Navigation, Industries, etc., of the Ports Open to Foreign Commerce in China and Corea, and on the Condition and Development of the Treaty Port Provinces, 1882–1892* (Shanghai: Statistical Department of the Inspectorate General of Customs, 1893), p. 525; hereafter, *Decennial Reports, 1882–1892*.

9. J. Arnold (ed.), *Commercial Handbook of China, Vol. 1: United States: Bureau of Foreign and Domestic Commerce* (Washington: [s.n.], 1919–20), pp. 600–10.

10. Arnold (ed.), *Commercial Handbook of China*, vol. 1.

11. 'Report on the Trade of Swatow for the Year 1863', *British Parliamentary Papers, China* (hereafter, *BPP, China*) (Shannon: Irish University Press, 1971), vol. 6, p. 279.

12. 'Enclosure no. 1 in consul Haseuin no. 3 of 4 Feb. 1907', FO228/1671. These fourteen stations are: Pao Tai, Dong Long, Huang Gang, Shen Quan, Hou Xi, Wai Pu, Shuang Xi, Mei Xi, Hai Men, Jing Hai, Shui Jing, Da Hao and Zhe Lin.

13. Luo Yudong, *Zhongguo Lijin Shi* [A History of Domestic Transit Taxes in China] (Shanghai: Shangwu Yinshu Guan, 1936), pp. 343–58. See also 'Enclosure no. 1 in consul Haseuin no. 3 of 4 Feb. 1907', FO228/1671.

14. Dennys, Mayers and King, *The Treaty Ports of China and Japan*, p. 237.

15. Dennys, Mayers and King, *The Treaty Ports of China and Japan*, p. 235.

16. Report of G. W. Caine [Consul of Shantou], 20 June 1863, in *Commercial Reports from Her Majesty's Consuls in China*, in *BPP, China*, vol. 6, *Commercial Reports, 1854–66*, year 1863, p. 54.

17. Report of G. W. Caine [Consul of Shantou], 20 June 1863, p. 278.

18. About the *baoxiao* tax, see Swatow Consulate to Peking Ambassador Ernest Satow, 'Establishment of Pao Hsiao Office', in FO228/2467 (British Foreign Office); see also *Lingdong Ribao* [Lingdong Daily], 10 February 1903, p. 27 and 9 March 1903.

19. From the late nineteenth century to 1907, the dispute between the British and the

Chinese governments concerning levies on commodities was centred on two different taxing principles. The British government insisted that if the goods were for import or export purposes, the merchants, unless they were native Chinese, should pay duties at the Maritime Customs only. However, the Chinese Foreign Office claimed that the exemption from local taxes was only applicable to non-Chinese merchants depending on the nature of the goods they carried. In other words, the former emphasized the principle of commodities whereas the Chinese officials stressed the nature of human agency. This difference was solved only when the power of taxation shifted from the hands of Chinese officials to those of foreigners. In 1901, the Shantou Maritime Customs was given the power to regulate and control other coastal ports within fifty miles of the portport, hence securing provincial and national revenues. Swatow Consulate to Peking Ambassador Ernest Satow, 'Establishment of Pao Hsiao Office', in FO228/2467. See also reports published in *Lingdong Ribao*, 10 Feburary 1903, 27 February 1903 and 9 March 1903, as well as those published in the *North China Herald* (Shanghai: North China Herald, 1850–1940) in 1902, for example, 'Likin and Transit Passes', 68, 30 April, pp. 850–1; 'Swatow', 68, 28 May 1902, pp. 1047–8; and 'Swatow', 69, 2 July, p. 19.

20. For example, the national government successfully implemented legal tender in this year after nearly two decades of effort in reforming the financial sectors. See Rao, *Chaozhou Zhi Huibian*, section 4, 'Da Shi Ji' [Major Events], pp. 685–91.

21. Li Yuesheng, 'Jiefang Qian Shantou Shi Shangye Shulüe' [A Brief Account of Commerce in Pre-Liberation Shantou], *Shantou Fangzhi Tongxun*, 2 (1990), pp. 20–34, on p. 20.

22. *Decennial Reports, 1882–1891*, p. 538.

23. *Decennial Reports, 1882–1891*, pp. 537–40.

24. Chen Haizhong, *Jindai Shanghui yu Difang Jinrong* [Guilds and Local Finance in Modern China] (Guangzhou: Guangdong Renmin Chunbanshe, 2011), pp. 317ff. See also reports in *Nanyang Siang Pau* [South Sea Commercial Newspaper] from 1934: 3 March, p. 13; 16 November, p. 14; 17 November, p. 14; 29 November, p. 12; 8 December, p. 12; 10 December, p. 12; and in *Nanyang Siang Pau Sunday Edition*, 30 December 1934, p. 1.

25. For example, there were seventy-one agencies issuing paper notes in 1933. These included seventeen traditional Chinese banks and twenty-three business firms registered with the remittance guild; eighteen traditional Chinese banks; and thirteen business firms registered with the banking guild. See Xie Xueying, *Shantou Zhinan* [Handbook of Shantou] (1933; Shantou: Shantou Shishi Tongxun She, 1947), pp. 82–3; Rao, *Chaozhou Zhi Huibian*, section 4 'Da Shi Ji', pp. 685–91 has a detailed summary of the process of legislation surrounding local currency.

26. Zhongguo Haiguan Xuehui Shantou Haiguan Xiaozu and Shantou-Shi Difangzhi Bianzuan Weiyuanhui Bangongshi (eds), *Chao Haiguan Shiliao Huibian* [Collection of Historical Documents Relating to the Chaozhou Maritime Customs] (internal reference, 1988), pp. 23–7.

27. Xie Xueying, *Chaoshan Shangye Renming Lu* [Business Directory of Chaozhou and Shantou] (Shantou: Shantou Shishi Tongxunshe, 1934), pp. 1–66, 100–1.

28. These included (a) a feud among the Chaozhou- and Hakka-speaking students of the Tongwen School in 1904; (b) the dispute over *baoxiao* contributions from 1901 to 1907, specifically as to whether the tax, initially levied on Chaozhou merchants in Shantou, should be extended to include Hakka merchants; and (c) an intellectual de-

bate, begun in the late nineteenth century, over whether the Hakka was an ethnic group distinct from the Chaozhou. See Choi Chi-cheung [Cai Zhixiang], 'Shantou Kaibu yu Haiwai Chaoren Shenfen Renting de Jian'gou: Yi Yuenan Xigong Shi de Yi'an Huiguan wei Li' [The Opening of the Shantou Treaty Port and Construction of Identity: A Case Study of the Ngee Ann Guild in Saigong, Vietnam], in Lee Chee Hiang [Li Zhixian] (ed.), *Haiwai Chaoren de Yimin Jingyan* [Migration Experience of the Overseas Chaozhouese] (Singapore: Global Publishing, 2003), pp. 514–18.

29. Reports in *Lingdong Ribao*, 19 December 1902 and 24 March 1903.

30. Rao, *Chaozhou Zhi Huibian*, section 4, 'Shiye Zhi: Shangye' [Enterprises: Business], pp. 870ff.

31. Pan Xingnong, *Malaiya Chaoqiao Tongjian* [Gazetteer of the Chaozhou Chinese in Malaya] (Singapore: Nandao Chubanshe, 1950), p. 20; Xia Chenghua, *Jindai Guangdong Sheng Qiaohui Yanjiu (1862–1949)* [Study of Remittances of Guangdong Province in the Modern Period (1862–1949)] (Singapore: Xinjiapo Nanyang Xuehui, 1992), p. 27.

32. For instance, until the beginning of the twentieth century, Wei Tai Hou was the only Shanxi bank that survived in Shantou; from 1865 to 1938, HSBC operated their business only through an agency, Bradley and Company. King attributed this phenomenon to the following possible reasons: 'the great experience of the southerners as bankers, or to clannishness'. See F. H. H. King, *Money and Monetary Policy in China, 1845–1895* (Cambridge, MA: Harvard University Press, 1965), pp. 93, 262; F. H. H. King, *The History of the Hong Kong and Shanghai Banking Corporation*, vol. 1, *The Hong Kong Bank in Late Imperial China, 1864–1902* (Cambridge: Cambridge University Press, 1987), pp. 95, 501; F. H. H. King, *The History of the Hong Kong and Shanghai Banking Corporation*, vol. 3, *The Hong Kong Bank between the Wars and the Bank Interned, 1929–1945* (Cambridge: Cambridge University Press, 1988), pp. 455, 496–7.

33. Xie, *Shantou Zhinan*, pp. 82–3.

34. Xie, *Shantou Zhinan*, pp. 82–3.

35. Please refer to C. C. Choi, 'Competition among Brothers: The Kin Tye Lung Company and its Associate Companies', in R. A. Brown (ed.), *Chinese Business Enterprise in Asia* (London: Routledge, 1995), pp. 96–114; and C. C. Choi, 'Kinship and Business: Paternal and Maternal Kin in the Chaozhou Chinese Family Firms', *Business History*, 40:1 (1998), pp. 26–49.

36. Imperial Maritime Customs, *Decennial Reports, 1902–1911*, vol. 2, *Southern and Frontier Ports* (Shanghai: Statistical Department of the Inspectorate General of Customs, 1913), p. 118.

37. Inspectorate General of Chinese Customs, *Decennial Reports, 1912–1921* (Shanghai: Statistical Department of the Inspectorate General of Customs, 1924), p. 176.

38. For example, in 1874 the British Consul reported that 'rice... show[ed] a decreased importation last year in comparison with 1873, nearly the whole of which was due to a falling off in raw cotton and rice. The harvests were good, in consequence of which it was not necessary to bring rice into the market' (*BPP, China*, vol. 10, p. 316). In 1884, it was reported that 'the import of rice from northern ports has been very small, local crops having been very abundant; rate of freight was very low on what came forward' (*BPP, China*, vol. 15, p. 53).

39. This information is drawn from the 'Report on the Trade of Swatow' found in the British Parliamentary Papers; for 1864, see *BPP, China*, vol. 6, p. 416; for 1865, *BPP, China*, vol. 7, p. 97; for 1885, *BPP, China*, vol. 15, pp. 453–4; and for 1898, *BPP,*

China, vol. 21, p. 467.

40. 'Report on the Trade of Swatow for the year 1864', *BPP, China*, vol. 6, p. 416. See also the report of 1885: 'the import of rice was very small in the first ten months, but in the last two considerable supplies have been coming forward from Shanghae. This is owing to the damage caused to the second crop of the year by the heavy rainfalls in September. In the Hai Yang district embankments were carried away, and large tracts of rice-ground were under water. At one time it was feared that the embankments about Chao Chow-foo would give way, in which case ten times the damage would have been done, and the district would not have been cleared of water for years; fortunately the rain ceased before any serious break took place' (*BPP, China*, vol. 15, p. 453).

41. *BPP, China*, vol. 7, p. 97. See also the report of 1894: 'The total import of rice and paddy, foreign and native, during the year was 2,229,172 cwts, as against 2,047,005 cwts in 1893, an increase of 182,167 cwts ... there was undoubtedly a scarcity of rice in the district in the late spring and summer, and prices rose very seriously, but it seems probable that they were forced up partially by panic, owing to the closing of the Yang-tze ports to the export of rice by the Chinese authorities. Towards the end of the year the prohibition was removed in the case of Chinkiang, and the tension here was imme-diately relaxed. One or two small rice riots occurred in the district, but the impression is that these were caused rather by the idea that the dealers were holding back rice than actual scarcity' (vol. 19, p. 113).

42. 'Report on the Trade of Swatow for the Year 1882', *BPP, China*, vol. 14, pp. 340, 519.

43. 'Report on the Trade of Swatow for the Year 1886', *BPP, China*, vol. 15, p. 739; 'Report on the Trade of Swatow for the Year 1889', *BPP, China*, vol. 16, p. 555; 'Report on the Trade of Swatow for the Year 1890', *BPP, China*, vol. 17, p. 97.

44. 'Report on the Trade of Swatow for the Year 1891', *BPP, China*, vol. 17, p. 365.

45. 'Report on the Trade of Swatow for the Year 1882', *BPP, China*, vol. 14, p. 340.

46. 'Report on the Trade of Swatow for the Year 1887', *BPP, China*, vol. 16, p. 41.

47. 'Report on the Trade of Swatow for the Year 1897', *BPP, China*, vol. 21, p. 241.

48. 'Report on the Trade of Swatow for the Year 1898', *BPP, China*, vol. 21, p. 467.

49. Cheung Sui-wai argued that rice trade was not necessarily a result of price based on supply and demand, but rather one of consumer taste. S. W. Cheung, 'A Desire to Eat Well: Rice and the Market in Eighteenth-Century China', paper presented at the 'New Histories of Rice Workshop' under the sponsorship of the research programme on 'Concepts and Modalities: Practical Knowledge Transmission', held at Max Planck Institute for the History of Science, Berlin, 25–6 March 2011.

50. For the early trade in Chaozhou, see Zhang Yingqiu, 'Zhanglin Gangpu yu Hongtou Chuan' [Zhanglin Port and the Red-head Junks], *Shantou Wenshi* [Documents and History of Shantou], 8 (1990), pp. 205–15.

51. The Chens are natives of Qianxi village, Longdu district, which was under the jurisdic-tion of Raoping county before 1949. Since 1949, the district has been part of Chenghai county. The Gaos are natives of Yujiao [or Huajiao] village of Shanghua district, Cheng-hai county. For the history of the Longdu district see Choi Chi-cheung, 'Shequ he Zongzu' [Community and Lineage], in Choi Chi-cheung (ed.), *Xu Shu Boshi Suocang Tudi ji Shangye Qiyue Wenshu: di yi ji: Qiantailong Tudi Qiyue Wenshu* [Land Deeds and Business Documents Collected by Dr. James Hayes, volume 1: Land Deeds of the Kin Tye Lung Company] (Tokyo: Tōkyō Daigaku Tōyō Bunka Kenkyūjo Fuzoku Tōyōgaku Bunken Sentā, 1995), pp. 231–2. For a general description of the villages in Longdu and Shanghua districts, see Chenghai Xian Renmin Zhengfu Qiaowu Bangong

Shi [Overseas Chinese Affairs Office of the People's Government of the Chenghai County] (ed.), *Chenghai Xian Huaqiao Zhi* [Gazetteer of Overseas Chinese from Chenghai County] (Chenghai: Chenghai Xian Huaqiao Zhi Lingdaozu, 1986).

52. The Yuan Fa Sheng company was owned by the Gaos of Chenghai county. The company was sold to Gao Chuxiang in the beginning of the 1850s. Gao renamed the company Yuan Fat Hong. See Lin Xi, 'Cong Xianggang de Yuan Fa Hang Tanqi' [On Yuan Fat Hong of Hong Kong], *Da Cheng*, 117 (1983), pp. 47–52.

53. See Choi, 'Competition among Brothers', p. 98.

54. See Zhang Yingqiu, 'Taiguo Huaqiao Gao Chuxiang yu Hongli Jiazu di Yeji' [Achievements of the Thai Chinese Gao Chuxiang and Chen Hongli Families], *Shantou Wenshi*, 8 (1990), pp. 26–41.

55. See Choi Chi-cheung, 'Cong Tudi Qiyue Kan Xiangcun Shehui Guanxi' [Rural Social Relations as Seen from Land Deeds], in Choi, *Xu Shu Boshi Suocang Tudi ji Shangye Qiyue Wenshu*, p. 269.

56. For instance, Xuanming's son Cizong (or Ziyin as he was known in Hong Kong), was regarded as 'a well-known Chinese merchant ... in Bonham Strand [Hong Kong], as well as in the Strait'. See *South China Morning Post*, 9 October 1931.

57. Choi, 'Kinship and Business', pp. 26–49.

58. Ownership of the associate companies is interlocking. However, financially they are independent from each other. See Choi, 'Competition among Brothers'.

59. This criterion was emphasized repeatedly by Mr Chen Songrui during my interviews with him conducted from 1993 to 1996.

60. Chen Chengqu, also a member of the five families, was Cizong's brother's grandson. His generation order is 1-1-2-1-1-4-1-1-2-4-1, while Cizong's generation order is 1-1-2-1-1-4-1-1-3.

61. *BPP, China*, vol. 12, p. 79.

62. P. Y. S. Chung, 'Surviving Economic Crisis in Southeast Asia and Southern China: The History of Eu Yan Sang Business Conglomerates in Penang, Singapore and Hong Kong', *Modern Asian Studies*, 36:3 (2002), pp. 579–618.

4 The Rise of Chinese Commercial Dominance in Early Modern Southeast Asia

1. P. L. Berger and H. H. Hsiao, *In Search of an East Asian Development Model* (New Brunswick, NJ: Transaction Books, 1988); W. M. Tu, 'Cultural China: The Periphery as the Center', *Daedalus*, 120:2 (1991), pp. 1–32; R. McVey (ed.), *Southeast Asian Capitalists* (Ithaca, NY: Southeast Asia Program, Cornell University, 1992); K. S. Jomo and B. C. Folk (eds), *Ethnic Business: Chinese Capitalism in Southeast Asia* (London: RoutledgeCurzon, 2003).

2. C. Trocki, 'The Rise and Fall of the Ngee Heng Kongsi in Singapore', in D. Ownby and M. Heidhues (eds), *Secret Societies Reconsidered* (Armonk, NY: M. E. Sharpe, 1993), pp. 89–119; B. Yuan, *Chinese Democracies: A Study of the Kongsis of West Borneo (1776–1884)* (Leiden: CNWS, 2000); H. K. Kwee, 'Money and Credit in Chinese Mercantile Operations in Colonial and Precolonial Southeast Asia', in D. Henley and P. Boomgaard (eds), *Credit and Debt in Indonesia, 860–1930: From Peonage to Pawnshop, from Kongsi to Cooperative* (Singapore: Institute of Southeast Asian Studies Press, 2009), pp. 126–44.

3. D. Rudner, *Caste and Capitalism in Colonial India: The Nattukottai Chettiars* (Berkeley, CA: University of California Press, 1994); J. Israel, *Diasporas within a Diaspora: Jews, Crypto-Jews and the World Maritime Empires (1540–1740)* (Leiden: Brill, 2002); I. B. McCabe, G. Harlaftis and I. P. Minoglou (eds), *Diaspora Entrepreneurial Networks: Four Centuries of History* (Oxford: Berg, 2005); A. Greif, *Institutions and the Path to the Modern Economy* (New York: Cambridge University Press, 2006); S. D. Aslanian, *From the Indian Ocean to the Mediterranean: The Global Trade Networks of Armenian Merchants from New Julfa* (Berkeley, CA: University of California Press, 2011).

4. D. North, 'Institutions', *Journal of Economic Perspectives*, 5:1 (1991), pp. 97–112.

5. N. Steensgaard, *The Asian Trade Revolution of the Seventeenth Century* (Chicago, IL: University of Chicago Press, 1974); K. Pomeranz, *The Great Divergence: Europe, China and the Making of the Modern World Economy* (Princeton, NJ: Princeton University Press, 2000).

6. J. Israel, 'Diasporas Jewish and Non-Jewish and the World Maritime Empires', in I. McCabe, G. Harlaftis and I. P. Minoglou (eds), *Diaspora Entrepreneurial Networks* (Oxford: Berg, 2005), pp. 3–26, on p. 7.

7. A. Reid, *Southeast Asia in the Age of Commerce 1450–1680*, 2 vols (New Haven, CT, and London: Yale University Press, 1993).

8. S. Arasaratnam, *Merchants, Companies, and Commerce on the Coromandel Coast, 1650–1740* (Delhi and New York: Oxford University Press, 1986); A. Wink, *Al-Hind, the Making of the Indo-Islamic World*, 3 vols (Leiden: Brill, 1990); J. Christie, 'Javanese Markets and the Asian Sea Trade Boom of the Tenth to Thirteenth Centuries A.D.', *Journal of the Economic and Social History of the Orient [JESHO]*, 41:3 (1998), pp. 344–81.

9. M. A. P. Meilink-Roelofsz, *Asian Trade and European Influence in the Indonesian Archipelago between 1500 and about 1630* (The Hague: Martinus Nijhoff, 1962); Arasaratnam, *Merchants, Companies and Commerce*; B. Andaya, *To Live as Brothers: Southeast Sumatra in the Seventeenth and Eighteenth Centuries* (Honolulu, HI: University of Hawaii Press, 1993); Reid, *Southeast Asia in the Age of Commerce 1450–1680*, vol. 2.

10. The most fateful episode would be the bloody Dutch East India Company conquest of the nutmeg-producing Banda Islands in the 1620s. This event not only enabled the Dutch monopoly of nutmeg and mace but also resulted in the demise of one of the most entrepreneurial trading groups in the region. See W. A. Hanna, *Indonesian Banda: Colonialism and its Aftermath in the Nutmeg Islands* (Philadelphia, PA: Institute for the Study of Human Issues, 1978).

11. A. Das Gupta, *Indian Merchants and the Decline of Surat, 1700–1750* (Wiesbaden: Steiner, 1979); S. Subrahmanyam, *The Political Economy of Commerce: Southern India 1500–1650* (Cambridge: Cambridge University Press, 1990).

12. Reid, *Southeast Asia in the Age of Commerce*; L. Andaya, 'The Bugis-Makassar Diasporas', *Journal of the Malaysian Branch of the Royal Asiatic Society*, 68 (1995), pp. 119–38.

13. J. Cushman, *Fields from the Sea: Chinese Junk Trade with Siam during the Late Eighteenth and Early Nineteenth Centuries* (Ithaca, NY: Southeast Asia Program, Cornell University, 1993); A. Reid, 'A New Phase of Commercial Expansion in Southeast Asia, 1760–1850', in A. Reid (ed.), *The Last Stand of Asian Autonomies* (London: Macmillan Press; New York: St Martin's Press, 1997), pp. 57–81.

14. G. J. Knaap and H. Sutherland, *Monsoon Traders: Ships, Skippers and Commodities in Eighteenth-Century Makassar* (Leiden: KITLV, 2004), p. 61.

15. L. Andaya, 'Local Trade Networks in Maluku in the 16th, 17th and 18th Centuries', *Cakalele: Maluku Research Journal*, 2:2 (1991), pp. 71–96; Cushman, *Fields from the*

Sea; N. Cooke and T. Li (eds), *Water Frontier: Commerce and the Chinese in the Lower Mekong Region, 1750–1880* (Singapore: University Press; Oxford: Rowman and Littlefield, 2004).

16. G. J. Knaap, *Shallow Waters, Rising Tide: Shipping and Trade in Java around 1775* (Leiden: KITLV, 1996).

17. E. Wickberg, *The Chinese in Philippine Life, 1850–1898* (New Haven, CT, and London: Yale University Press, 1965); see also Tina Clemente's essay, 'Spanish Colonial Policy toward Chinese Merchants in Eighteenth-Century Philippines', in this book.

18. Knaap and Sutherland, *Monsoon Traders*; A. Ota, *Changes of Regime and Social Dynamics in West Java: Society, State, and the Outer World of Banten, 1750–1830* (Leiden: Brill, 2006); N. Hussin, *Trade and Society in the Straits of Melaka* (Singapore: NUS Press, 2007).

19. D. na Pombejra, 'Ayutthaya at the End of the Seventeenth Century: Was There a Shift to Isolation?' in A. Reid (ed.), *Southeast Asia in the Early Modern Era* (Ithaca, NY: Cornell University Press, 1993), pp. 250–72.

20. Reid, *Southeast Asia in the Age of Commerce*, vol. 2, pp. 308–9.

21. C. Chen, 'Mac Thien Tu and Phraya Taksin: A Survey on their Political Stand, Conflicts, and Background', in *Proceedings of the Seventh IAHA Conference* (Bangkok: Chulalongkorn University, 1977), pp. 1534–75; L. Nagtegaal, *Riding the Dutch Tiger: The Dutch East Indies Company and the Northeast Coast of Java, 1680–1743* (Leiden: KITLV, 1996); Cooke and Li, *Water Frontier*.

22. G. J. Knaap and L. Nagtegaal, 'A Forgotten Trade: Salt in Southeast Asia, 1670–1813', in R. Ptak and D. Rothermund (eds), *Emporia, Commodities, and Entrepreneurs in Asian Maritime Trade, c. 1400–1750* (Stuttgart: Steiner Verlag, 1991), pp. 127–58; Knaap, *Shallow Waters, Rising Tide*; H. K. Kwee, *The Political Economy of Java's Northeast Coast, c. 1740–1800* (Leiden: Brill, 2006).

23. H. Sutherland, 'Trepang and Wangkang: The China Trade of Eighteenth-Century Makassar, *c.* 1720s–1840s', in R. Tol et al. (eds), *Authority and Enterprise among the Peoples of South Sulawesi* (Leiden: KITLV, 2000), pp. 73–94; H. Sutherland, 'A Sino-Indonesian Commodity Chain: The Trade in Tortoiseshell in the Late Seventeenth and Eighteenth Centuries', in E. Tagliacozzo and W. C. Chang (eds), *Chinese Circulations: Capital, Commodities and Networks in Southeast Asia* (Durham, NC: Duke University Press, 2011), pp. 172–99.

24. L. Blusse, 'In Praise of Commodities: An Essay on the Crosscultural Trade in Edible Bird's-Nests', in R. Ptak and D. Rothermund (eds), *Emporia, Commodities, and Entrepreneurs* (Stuttgart: Steiner Verlag, 1991), pp. 317–35; H. Hagerdal, *Lords of the Land, Lords of the Sea: Conflict and Adaptation in Early Colonial Timor, 1600–1800* (Leiden: KITLV, 2012).

25. Pombejra, 'Ayutthaya at the End of the Seventeenth Century'; S. Ariyasajsiskul, 'The So-Called Tin Monopoly in Ligor: The Limits of VOC Power vis à vis a Southern Thai Trading Polity', *Itinerario*, 28:3 (2004), pp. 89–106; A. Reid, 'Chinese on Mining Frontier in Southeast Asia', in E. Tagliacozzo and W. C. Chang (eds), *Chinese Circulations: Capital, Commodities and Networks in Southeast Asia* (Durham, NC: Duke University Press, 2011), pp. 21–36.

26. Chen, 'Mac Thien Tu and Phraya Taksin'; Reid, 'A New Phase of Commercial Expansion'; L. Blusse, 'Chinese Century: The Eighteenth Century in the China Sea Region', *Archipel*, 58 (1999), pp. 107–29.

27. Blusse, 'Chinese Century'.

28. Andaya, *To Live as Brothers*.
29. Nagtegaal, *Riding the Dutch Tiger*; Knaap and Sutherland, *Monsoon Traders*.
30. Kwee, 'Money and Credit'; H. K. Kwee, 'Chinese Economic Dominance in Southeast Asia: A Longue Duree Perspective', *Comparative Studies in Society and History*, 55:1 (2013), pp. 5–34.
31. Meilink-Roelofsz, *Asian Trade and European Influence*; Pombejra, 'Ayutthaya at the End of the Seventeenth Century'; E. Ho, *The Graves of Tarim: Genealogy and Mobility across the Indian Ocean* (Berkeley, CA: University of California Press, 2006).
32. B. Andaya, *Perak, the Abode of Grace: A Study of an Eighteenth-Century Malay State* (Kuala Lumpur: Oxford University Press, 1979).
33. C. Dobbin, *Islamic Revivalism in a Changing Peasant Economy* (London: Curzon Press, 1983); Knaap and Sutherland, *Monsoon Traders*.
34. Nagtegaal, *Riding the Dutch Tiger*.
35. Andaya, *Perak, the Abode of Grace*.
36. S. Arasaratnam, *Maritime Commerce and English Power: Southeast India, 1750–1800* (Aldershot: Variorum, 1996), p. 266.
37. Arasaratnam, *Merchants, Companies, and Commerce*, ch. 7.
38. K. A. Wellen, 'Credit among the Early Modern To Wajoq', in D. Henley and P. Boomgaard (eds), *Credit and Debt in Indonesia, 860–1930: From Peonage to Pawnshop, from Kongsi to Cooperative* (Singapore: Institute of Southeast Asian Studies Press, 2009), pp. 80–101.
39. C. R. Boxer, *The Portuguese Seaborne Empire, 1415–1825* (London: Hutchinson, 1969); Steensgaard, *The Asian Trade Revolution*; Das Gupta, *Indian Merchants and the Decline of Surat*.
40. Nagtegaal, *Riding the Dutch Tiger*; B. Andaya and L. Andaya, *A History of Malaysia* (Basingstoke: Palgrave, 2001); Knaap and Sutherland, *Monsoon Traders*.
41. F. Gaastra, *The Dutch East India Company: Expansion and Decline* (Zutphen: Walburg, 2003).
42. J. Villiers, 'Trade and Society in the Banda Islands in the Sixteenth Century', *Modern Asian Studies*, 15:4 (1981), pp. 723–50; G. J. Knaap, *Kruidnagelen en Christenen: de Verenigde Oost-Indische Compagnie en de bevolking van Ambon 1656–1696* (Leiden: KITLV, 2004).
43. Knaap, *Shallow Waters, Rising Tide*; Knaap and Sutherland, *Monsoon Traders*.
44. Y. Ishii, *The Junk Trade from Southeast Asia* (Singapore: ISEAS; Canberra: Research School of Pacific and Asian Studies, 1998). P. van Dyke, *The Canton Trade, 1700–1845* (Hong Kong: Hong Kong University Press, 2005).
45. L. Blusse, 'No Boats to China: The Dutch East India Company and the Changing Patterns of the China Sea Trade, 1635–1690', *Modern Asian Studies*, 30:1 (1996), pp. 51–76.
46. R. Laarhoven, 'The Power of Cloth: The Textile Trade of the Dutch East India Company (VOC), 1600–1780' (PhD thesis, Australian National University, 1994); Andaya, *To Live as Brothers*; Cooke and Li, *Water Frontier*.
47. Laarhoven, 'The Power of Cloth'; D. Lewis, *Jan Compagnie in the Straits of Malacca, 1641–1795* (Athens, OH: Ohio University Center for International Studies, 1995); J. Warren, *The Sulu Zone 1768–1898: The Dynamics of External Trade, Slavery and Ethnicity in the Transformation of a Southeast Asian Maritime State* (Singapore: NUS Press, 2007).
48. R. Vos, *Gentle Janus, Merchant Prince: The VOC and the Tightrope of Diplomacy in*

the Malay World, 1740–1800, trans. B. Jackson (Leiden: KITLV, 1993); Andaya and Andaya, *A History of Malaysia*.

49. Nagtegaal, *Riding the Dutch Tiger*; Kwee, *Political Economy of Java's Northeast Coast*.
50. Cushman, *Fields from the Sea*; Cooke and Li, *Water Frontier*.
51. Dobbin, *Islamic Revivalism*; H. Knapen, *Forests of Fortune? The Environmental History of Southeast Borneo, 1600–1880* (Leiden: KITLV, 2001); Ota, *Changes of Regime and Social Dynamics*.
52. Knaap and Sutherland, *Monsoon Traders*; H. K. Kwee, 'The End of the "Age of Commerce"? Javanese Cotton Trade Industry from the Seventeenth to the Eighteenth Centuries', in E. Tagliacozzo and W. C. Chang (eds), *Chinese Circulations: Capital, Commodities and Networks in Southeast Asia* (Durham, NC: Duke University Press, 2011), pp. 283–302.

5 The Merchants of the Korea–China Ginseng Trade in the Late Nineteenth Century

1. Original texts of the main treaties regarding Korea of this period can be seen in Gaimusho, *Kyū jōyaku isan* [Consolidated Expired Treaties of Japan], vol. 3: Korea and Ryūkyū (Tokyo: Gaimushō, 1930).
2. In China, foreigners were not exempted from domestic taxation (like *lijin,* a kind of transit duty) unless they paid an additional duty to get a transit pass at the Imperial Maritime Customs. In the case of Japan, the right of foreigners to engage in domestic commerce was not admitted until Japan succeeded in reclaiming jurisdiction over foreigners in 1899.
3. On the land tax system of Chosŏn Korea, see Miyajima Hiroshi, *Chōsen Tochi Chōsa Jigyō no Kenkyū* [Study on Land Investigation in Korea] (Tokyo: Institute of Advanced Studies on Asia, University of Tokyo, 1991). After the eighteenth century, the government ceased to inspect the real acreage of cultivated land and trusted local officials and clerks to collect fixed amounts of land tax (pp. 177–94). On commercial taxes, see Sukawa Hidenori, *Richō Shōgyō Seisakushi Kenkyū* [Study on the Commercial Policy of Chosŏn Korea] (Tokyo: Tokyo University Press, 1994).
4. Sukawa, *Richō Shōgyō Seisakushi Kenkyū*, pp. 139–44.
5. See for example *T'ongsŏ Ilgi* [Journal of the Foreign Office] (Seoul: Asiatic Research Institute, Korea University, 1972). See also Yi Pyŏngch'ŏn, 'Kaehanggi Oeguk Sang'in ŭi Naeji Sangkwŏn Ch'imip' [Intrusion of Foreign Merchants into the Interior Market after the Opening of the Ports]', *Kyŏngje Sahak*, 9 (1985), pp. 295–331; Na Aeja, 'Kaehanghu Oeguk Sang'in ŭi Ch'imt'u wa Chosŏn Sang'in ŭi Taeŭng' [Intrusion of Foreign Merchants and Domestic Merchants' Reaction after the Opening of the Ports], in Han'guk Yŏksa Yŏn'guhoe (ed.), *1894 nyŏn Nongmin Chŏnjaeng Yŏn'gu* [Study on the Peasants' War of 1894], vol. 1 (Seoul: Yŏksapip'yŏngsa, 1991), pp. 173–212.
6. K. W. Larsen, *Tradition, Treaties, and Trade: Qing Imperialism and Chosŏn Korea, 1850–1910* (Cambridge, MA: Harvard University Press, 2008), p. 17.
7. Details of the traditional overland trade will be mentioned in the next section.
8. *Zhongguo Chaoxian Shuilu Maoyi Zhangcheng* [Regulations for Maritime and Overland Trade between Chinese and Korean Subjects]. There is a great deal of research on the diplomatic aspects of this regulation. See for example Akizuki Nozomi, 'Chōchūkan no San Bōeki Shōtei no Teiketsu Keii' [The Process of Concluding Three Trade Regulations be-

tween China and Korea], *Chosen Gakuhō,* 115 (April 1985), pp. 103–37; Kwŏn Hyŏksu, *19 Sekimal Hanchung Kwan'gyesa Yŏn'gu* [Study on the China–Korean Relationship in the Late Nineteenth Century] (Seoul: Paeksancharyowŏn, 2000).

9. For example, the maritime customs in Inch'ŏn reported that there were 2,504 Japanese, 678 Chinese and 31 other foreigners in the port in 1893. See Imperial Maritime Customs, *Returns of Trade and Trade Reports, 1893,* Appendix 2: Corea (Shanghai: Imperial Maritime Customs Press, 1893).

10. Larsen, *Tradition, Treaties, and Trade*; Furuta Kazuko, *Shanghai Network to Kindai Higashi Ajia* [Shanghai Network: The Economic Order in Late Nineteenth-century East Asia] (Tokyo: University of Tokyo Press, 2000).

11. In the trade regulations governing Japanese people in Korea (1883), only Koreans were permitted to export ginseng (Clause 18). The Korea–China regulations in 1882 included a similar article (Clause 6). Treaties with Western countries categorized red ginseng as an embargoed good. For example, see Clause 6 of the Korea-America treaty of 1882 and the tax table of the Korea–Britain treaty of 1883.

12. The documents of Tongshuntai consist of about 3,000 items of commercial correspondence and invoices, ranging from the late 1880s to the mid-1900s. These documents are now housed at Seoul National University, South Korea. About the details and characteristics of these documents, see R. Ishikawa, 'Commercial Activities of Chinese Merchants in the Late Nineteenth Century Korea: With a Focus on the Documents of Tong Shun Tai Archived at Seoul National University, South Korea', *International Journal of Korean History,* 13 (2009), pp. 75–97; Kang Jin'a, *Tongsunt'aeho: Tong'asia Hwagyo Chabon kwa Geundae Chosŏn* [Tongshuntai: A Chinese Merchant Network in East Asia and Modern Korea] (Taegu: Kyŏngbuk University Press, 2011).

13. The archive of the documents of the Chinese delegation in Seoul from the 1880s, the Zhu Han Shiguan Dang'an, is housed at the Institute of Modern History, Academia Sinica, in Taiwan. It includes a number of items about commercial disputes because China had had so-called consular jurisdiction in Korea before the latter's annexation to Japan. On this collection, see Ishikawa Ryota, 'Kaikōki Kanjō ni okeru Chōsen-jin, Chūgoku-jin kan no Shōtorihiki to Funsō' [Commercial Disputes between Korean and Chinese in Seoul after the Opening of the Ports], *Nenpō Chōsengaku,* 10 (2007), pp. 93–127.

14. Furthermore, there were three periodic markets on the border (*gaeshi*), which opened once or twice a year. In respect to the red ginseng trade, we can omit the role of these markets, although they had a large influence on the local economy.

15. For an outline of tributary missions and their trade, see Chŏn Haejong, 'Ch'ŏngdae Hanjung Chogong Kwangye Ko' [Study on the Korea–China Tribute Relationship in the Qing Era], in Chŏn, *Hanjung Kwangyesa Yŏn'gu* [History of the Korea–China Relationship] (Seoul: Iljogak, 1970), pp. 59–112; Zhang Cunwu, *Qing-Han Zongban Maoyi, 1637–1984* [Sino-Korean Tributary Trade, 1637–1984] (Taipei: Jindaishi Yanjiusuo, Zhongyang Yanjiuyuan, 1978); Terauchi Itaro, 'Sakumon Kōshi to Wanshō' [Ch'akmun Hushi and Ŭiju Merchants], in Kanda Nobuo Sensei Koki Kinen Ronbunshū Hensan Iinkai (ed.), *Shinchō to Higashi Ajia* [The Qing Dynasty and East Asia] (Tokyo: Yamakawa Shuppansha, 1992), pp. 381–401.

16. Imamura Tomo, *Ninjinshi* [The History of Ginseng], 7 vols (Keijo: Chōsen Sōtokufu Senbai-kyoku, 1934–40; Kyoto: Shibunkaku, 1971). As for the success of growing ginseng especially, see Kang Mangil, *Chosŏn Hugi Sang' ŏp Chabon ŭi Palt'al* [Development of Commercial Capital in the Late Chosŏn Era] (Seoul: Koryo Daehakkyo Ch'ulp'anbu, 1973).

17. For example, the affairs of the agency responsible for border tax, the Kwanse-ch'ŏng, which was established in Ŭiju in 1813 to collect tax on export goods, were in the charge of Ŭiju merchants.

18. The institutional history of ginseng trade in this paragraph and the next is based on the following studies: Kim Chŏnmi, 'Chosŏn Hugi Daech'ŏng Muyŏk ŭi Chŏn'gae wa Muyŏk Suseje ŭi Sihaen' [Korea–China Trade and its Taxation System in the Late Chosŏn Period], *Han'guk Salon*, 36 (1996), pp. 153–217; Yi Ch'ŏlsŏng, *Chosŏn Hugi Daech'ŏng Muyŏksa Yŏngu* [Study on Korea–China Trade in the Late Chosŏn Period] (Seoul: Kukhak Charyowŏn, 2000); Yu Sŭngju and Yi Ch'ŏlsŏng, *Chosŏn Hugi Jungguk Gwaŭi Muyŏksa* [The History of Trade with China in the Late Chosŏn Period] (Seoul: Gyŏng'in Munhwasa, 2001).

19. One *nyang* is equivalent to one hundred pieces of copper cash (100 *mun*).

20. Yi, *Chosŏn Hugi Daech'ŏng Muyŏksa Yŏngu*, p. 227. In 1867, out of the total amount of 210,000 *nyang* collected in tax, 150,000 *nyang* was sent to the Hojo. Yu and Yi, *Chosŏn Hugi Jungguk Gwaŭi Muyŏksa*, pp. 191–210.

21. For the reign of Hŭngsŏng Taewŏn'gung, see J. B. Palais, *Politics and Policy in Traditional Korea* (Cambridge, MA: Harvard University Press, 1975).

22. Yi, *Chosŏn Hugi Daech'ŏng Muyŏksa Yŏngu*, pp. 241–3.

23. Ŭn Chŏnt'ae, 'Kojong Ch'injŏng Ihu Chŏngch'i Ch'eje Kaehyŏk kwa Chŏngch'i Seryŏk ŭi Tonghyang' [Political Reform and Elite Groups under the Personal Rule of Kojong], *Han'guk Saron*, 40 (1998), pp. 159–214, on p. 169. For another example, Kojong dispatched sixty-nine students to Tianjin in 1881 to learn modern military technology, and made them bring red ginseng to pay the cost. M. Deuchler, *Confucian Gentlemen and Barbarian Envoys* (Seattle, WA: University of Washington Press, 1977), pp. 99–101.

24. Kim T'aegyŏng, 'Insamji' [Memo on Ginseng], *Sohodangjip*, vol. 8, reprinted in *Kim T'aegyŏng Chŏnjip* [The Complete Works of Kim T'aegyŏng], vol. 2 (Seoul: Aseamunhwasa, 1978), p. 158; Ch'oe T'aeho, 'Hongsam Chŏnmae Chedo ŭi Sŏngnip Kwajŏng e Kwanhan Yŏn'gu' [The Formation of the Monopoly System of Red Ginseng], *Kyŏngje Nonch'ong* [Kukmin University], 5 (1983), pp. 47–67; Yang Sanghyŏn, 'Daehan Chegukki Naejangwŏn ŭi Insam Gwalli wa Samse Chingsu' [Control and Taxation System of Red Ginseng by Naejangwŏn], *Kyujanggak*, 19 (1996), pp. 123–77. According to the records of the Tongshuntai in 1890, which will be discussed below, the king's ginseng [*byŏlbu*] was about 15,000 *gŭn*, the government's 10,000 and bootlegged 10,000 or 15,000. Tan Jiesheng to Liang Lunqing, 1890/9/9, *Tongsunt'ae Wangbok Munsŏ*, vol. 33. *Tongsunt'ae Wangbok Munsŏ* is one of the folder titles of Tongshuntai documents housed at the Central Library, Seoul National University (call number 6100–61). The title will be abbreviated as *Wangbok Munsŏ* hereafter.

25. Traditional Korean merchants left very few records about their own management, generally. Additionally, the government records rarely refer to this trade, perhaps because it was related to the king's private property.

26. For an outline of Tongshuntai documents, see n. 12. Correspondence from the Inch'ŏn branch which will be cited in this section are included in the folders named *Tongtailaixin* (vol. 1, 2, 3, 15, 16, call number Kyu 27584), housed in the Kyujanggak Institute for Korean Studies, Seoul National University.

27. Tongshuntai's branch in Inch'ŏn to Tongshuntai's branch in Seoul (henceforth Inch'ŏn to Seoul), Letter no. 6, 9/Jan/1889, *Tongtailaixin*, vol. 1; Letter no. 7, 9/Jan/1889, *Tongtailaixin*, vol. 1. Months and dates given here are in the lunar calendar. For exam-

ple, '9 January' refers to the ninth day of the first lunar month. The same goes for dates in the body of the text.

28. Inch'ŏn to Seoul, Letter no. 60, 3/Mar/1889, *Tongtailaixin*, vol. 15.
29. Inch'ŏn to Seoul, Letter no. 3, 7/Jan/1889, *Tongtailaixin*, vol. 1.
30. Inch'ŏn to Seoul, Letter no. 8, 11/Jan/1889, *Tongtailaixin*, vol. 1.
31. Inch'ŏn to Seoul, Letter no. 12, 15/Jan/1889, *Tongtailaixin*, vol. 1.
32. Inch'ŏn to Seoul, Letter no. 21, 26/Jan/1889, *Tongtailaixin*, vol. 1.
33. Inch'ŏn to Seoul, Letter no. 23, 27/Jan/1889, *Tongtailaixin*, vol. 2.
34. Inch'ŏn to Seoul, Letter no. 31, 2/Feb/1889, *Tongtailaixin*, vol. 2. The reason is not clear in the letter, but the government's record notes that Hyŏn retired from his official post on 18 January due to illness (*Sŭngjŏngwŏn Ilgi*, the same day; on this source, see n. 45, below).
35. Inch'ŏn to Seoul, Letter no. 36, 8/Feb/1889, *Tongtailaixin*, vol. 2.
36. Inch'ŏn to Seoul, Letter no. 42, 13/Feb/1889, *Tongtailaixin*, vol. 2.
37. Inch'ŏn to Seoul, Letter no. 43, 14/Feb/1889, *Tongtailaixin*, vol. 15. Tongshuntai may have decided to withdraw from the transaction, because no further mention is found in the letters after this.
38. That is, the ninth lunar month of 1889. See n. 27, above, for an explanation of the handling of dates.
39. *Liang* is a Chinese ounce of silver, also known as a *tael*.
40. Sun Zhaoji to Tang Shaoyi, 15/Jan/1890, *Zhu Han Shiguan Dang'an*, 141–40-24. For an outline of *Zhu Han Shiguan Dang'an*, see n. 13. This will be abbreviated as *Shiguan Dang'an* hereafter.
41. According to the Korea–China regulation of 1882, lawsuits brought by Chinese against Koreans were to be judged by a joint court presided over by officials from both sides.
42. The summary of the conjoint court, 25/Jan/1890, *Shiguan Dang'an*, 141–40-24.
43. Sheng Xuanhuai to Yuan Shikai, 24/Jul/1890, *Shiguan Dang'an*, 141–30-39.
44. Yuzengxiang to Tang Shaoyi, ?/Jul/1891, *Shiguan Dang'an*, 141–40-24.
45. For more information on O Kyŏngsŏk's family, see 'Han'guk Yŏktae Inmul Chonghap Chŏngbo Sisŭt'em' [General Database of Korean Historical Figures], provided by the Academy of Korean Studies, South Korea, at http://people.aks.ac.kr/index.aks [accessed 14 December 2013].
46. In the Chosŏn period, official interpreters were selected through the civil examination. But in actual practice, most of the posts were occupied by several specific families. The family of O Kyŏngsŏk of the Haeju O clan is a typical example.
47. Kim Yunsik, *Ŭmch'eongsa*, the article of 18/Nov/1881, reprinted edition of *Han'guk Saryo Ch'ongsŏ*, vol. 1, p. 22; *Sŭngjŏngwŏn Ilgi*, the article of 10/Sep/1882. The *Sŭngjŏngwŏn Ilgi* is the diary of the Sŭngjŏngwŏn, a government office. In consulting this source, the author used the database of the National Institute of Korean History, South Korea, at http://sjw.history.go.kr/main/main.jsp [accessed 14 December 2013].
48. Sin Yongha, 'O Kyŏngsŏk ŭi Kaehwa Sasang kwa Kaehwa Hwaldong' [O Kyŏngsŏk's Ideas and Activities regarding Civilization], *Yŏksa Hakpo*, 107 (1985), pp. 107–35.
49. Chen Shutang to Min Yŏngmuk, 22/Jan/1884, *Kuhan'guk Oegyo Munsŏ* (Seoul: Aseamunhwa Yŏngugo, Korea University, 1973), Ch'ŏng'an 1, p. 29.
50. Kim Yunsik to Yuan Shikai, 8/Mar/1887, *Kuhan'guk Oegyo Munsŏ*, p. 342. This ginseng may be the same as that entrusted to Yuzengxiang in 1887, although there is no direct evidence.

51. *Sŭngjŏngwon Ilgi*, the article of 21/Feb/1888.

52. *Sŭngjŏngwon Ilgi*, the article of 24/Aug/1888.

53. His political position seems not to have been very stable. He was banished in May 1889, just after the case of Tongshuntai, on the charge of excessive minting of copper cash. His career path after that is not clear. *Sŭngjŏngwon Ilgi*, the article of 9/May/1888; 8/Jun/1889.

54. Kim Wŏnmo, 'Kyŏnmi Chosŏn Bobyŏngsa Suwŏn Pyŏn Su, Ko Yŏngch'ŏl, Hyŏn Hŭngt'aek Yŏn'gu' [Study of Accompanying Personnel of the Mission to the United States in 1883: Pyŏn Su, Ko Yŏngch'ŏl and Hyŏn Hŭngt'aek], *Sangmyŏng Sahak*, 3:4 (1995), pp. 574–88.

55. Min Yŏng'ik passed the civil examination in 1877. He successively filled high-ranking positions as one of the core figures among Queen Min's relatives. He was eager to learn about Western civilization and had intimate relationships with reform-oriented officials, especially in his youth. On the political position of Min's family, including Min Yŏng'ik, see M. Finch, *Min Yŏng-hwan: A Political Biography* (Honolulu, HI: University of Hawaii Press, 2002), pp. 22–6.

56. Kim, 'Kyŏnmi Chosŏn Bobyŏngsa Suwŏn Pyŏn Su, Ko Yŏngch'ŏl, Hyŏn Hŭngt'aek Yŏn'gu', pp. 575–6.

57. *Ilsŏngnok*, the article of 11/May/1887. The data from *Ilsŏngnok*, the diary of the king, were searched on the database provided by the Kyujanggak Institute of Korea Studies, Seoul National University, at http://kyujanggak.snu.ac.kr/sub_index.jsp?ID=ILS [accessed 27 October 2014]. On Kwangmuguk, see Yi Paeyong, *Han'guk Kŭndae Kwang'ŏp Ch'imt'alsa Yŏn'gu* [History of Foreign Usurpations of Mining] (Seoul: Iljogak, 1989), pp. 17–19.

58. *Ilsŏngnok*, the article of 27/May/1887.

59. Yang Chŏnp'il, '19 Segi–20 Segich'o Kaesong Sang'in ŭi Samŏp Chabon Yŏn'gu' [The Capital of the Ginseng Industry in the Nineteenth and Early Twentieth Century] (MA thesis, Yonsei University, 2001), pp. 20–1. The list, called *Kup'o Kŏnsam Torokch'aek*, is housed at Seoul National University (call number Kyu 9862). The list notes that 15,000 *gŭn* of the amount to which he held export rights was aimed at procuring silver. This implies that he contracted to export ginseng for the specific objective of securing a supply of silver, which was needed to buy machines or arms abroad.

60. Yang, '19 Segi–20 Segich'o Kaesong Sang'in ŭi Samŏp Chabon Yŏn'gu', pp. 26–8.

61. Kim Wŏnmo, 'Kyŏnmi Chosŏn Bobyŏngsa Suwŏn Pyŏn Su, Ko Yŏngch'ŏl, Hyŏn Hŭngt'aek Yŏn'gu', pp. 574–88; Yang, '19 Segi–20 Segich'o Kaesong Sang'in ŭi Samŏp Chabon Yŏn'gu', pp. 26–8.

62. Sheng Xuanhuai to Yuan Shikai, 19/Sep/1890, *Shiguan Dang'an*, 141–30-39.

63. Ishida Kohei, *Manshu ni okeru Shokuminchi Keizai no Shiteki Kenkyu* [Development Process of the Colonial Economy in Manchuria] (Kyoto: Mineruba shobo, 1964).

64. Zhang, *Qing-Han Zongban Maoyi, 1637–1984*, pp. 103–6.

65. Zhang, *Qing-Han Zongban Maoyi, 1637–1984*, p. 106; Imperial Maritime Customs, *Trade Reports: Newchwang, 1874* (Shanghai: Imperial Maritime Customs Press, 1875), p. 5.

66. Li Hongzhang to Yuan Shikai, 4/Aug/1890, *Shiguan Dang'an*, 141–30-39; Li Hongzhang to Yuan Shikai, 19/Aug/1890, *Shiguan Dang'an*, 141–30-39.

67. See n. 17.

68. Donglaifu to Tang Shaoyi, 19/Dec/1887, *Shiguan Dang'an*, 141–47-17. Donglaifu was a Chinese merchant in Fenghuang-cheng, an area which traded red ginseng with Ŭiju

merchants.

69. Libu to Zongli Yamen, 16/Oct/1882, *Qingji Zhong-Ri-Han Guanxi Shiliao* (Taipei: Zhongyang yanjiuyuan jindaishi yanjiusuo, 1972), p. 1052.

70. Sun Zhaoji to Tang Shaoyi, August 1890, *Shiguan Dang'an*, 141–40-24.

71. Sim Sunt'aek to Yuan Shikai, 4/Aug/1891, *Shiguan Dang'an*, 141–30-39; Tang Shaoyi, Memorandum of the conjoint court on the case of Yuzengxiang, 13/Jun/1892, *Shiguan Dang'an*, 141–40-24.

72. Unknown, List of debtors of Yuzengxiang, Sep/1890, *Shiguan Dang'an*, 141–30-39; Sim Sunt'aek to Yuan Shikai, 17/Mar/1891, *Shiguan Dang'an*, 141–30-39.

73. Inspector General of Customs, *Trade Reports for 1880: Newchwang* (Shanghai: Imperial Maritime Customs Press, 1881), p. 3.

74. Inspector General of Customs, *Trade Reports for 1881: Newchwang* (Shanghai: Imperial Maritime Customs Press, 1882), p. 13.

75. Ishikawa, 'Kaikoki Kanjo ni okeru Chosen-jin, Chugoku-jin Kan no Shotorihiki to Funso', p. 15. Yuan Shikai, who was in Seoul from 1885 to 1894, requested the Korean government to recruit Korean interpreters from Ŭiju. Yuan Shikai to Min Chongmuk, 6/Feb/1891, *Kuhan'guk Oegyo Munsŏ* (Seoul: Aseamunhwa Yŏngugo, Korea University, 1973), Ch'ŏng'an 2, p. 10.

76. Tang Shaoyi, Memorandum of the Conjoint Court on the Case of Yuzengxiang (Statements of Chong Sŭngjo and Hong Ulak), 13/Jun/1892, *Shiguan Dang'an*, 141–40-24.

77. Just after the opening of Inch'ŏn in 1883, some of the Korean merchants working there were those who had accumulated experience in traditional trade in Pusan and Ŭiju. O Miil, 'Kaehang (chang) kwa Ijusang'in' [Immigrant Merchants in Treaty Ports], *Han'guk Kŭnhyŏndaesa Yŏn'gu*, 47 (2008), pp. 40–79.

78. For the history of Tongshuntai, see the studies cited in n. 12, above.

79. Tongshuntai to Ma Tingliang, June 1906, *Shiguan Dang'an*, 235–62-7; Tongshuntai to Ma Tingliang, 13/Apr (intercalary) /1906, *Shiguan Dang'an*, 235–62-7.

80. Copy of Son Kyŏngmun's pledge to Tongshuntai, 15/Jan/1888 (original document), *Shiguan Dang'an*, 235–62-7.

81. Pak Wŏngsŏn, *Kaekchu* (Seoul: Yŏnse Taehakkyo Chu'lpanbu, 1968); Yi, 'Kaehanggi Oeguk Sang'in ŭi Naeji Sangkwŏn Ch'imip'; Na, 'Kaehanghu Oeguk Sang'in ŭi Ch'imt'u wa Chosŏn Sang'in ŭi Taeŭng'. As for the actual transaction customs between Chinese merchants and Korean *kaekchu*, see Ishikawa, 'Kaikōki Kanjō ni okeru Chōsen-jin, Chūgoku-jin kan no Shōtorihiki to Fūnso'.

82. See the preceding note.

83. Tan Jiesheng to Liang Lunqing, Letter no. 1, 3/Jan/1890, *Wangbok Munsŏ*, vol. 33.

84. In March 1889, Tongshuntai was allowed by the administrator of Seoul to deliver 2,000 *gŭn* of imported copper metal and lend money to a mint managed by Li Doe. Inch'ŏn to Seoul, Letter no. 64 (cont.), 7/Mar/1889, *Tongtailaixin*, vol. 15.

85. When Son Yunp'il's business failed at the end of 1889, a manager of the mint supported Tongshuntai to settle accounts with Son. Tan Jiesheng to Ma Tingliang, Jun/1906, *Shiguan Dang'an*, 235–62-7.

86. Tan Jiesheng to Liang Lunqing, Letter no. 37, 9/Sep/1890, *Wangbok Munsŏ*, vol. 33.

87. Tan Jiesheng to Zhao Songzhi, Letter no. 13, 9/Sep/1890, *Wangbok Munsŏ*, vol. 33.

88. For a discussion of the trading networks of Tongshuntai in the 1890s, please see Ishikawa Ryota, 'Chōsen Kaikō-go ni okeru Kashō no Tai Shanhai Bōeki – Tongshuntai Shiryō o Tsūjite' [Trade with Shanghai by Chinese Merchants after the Opening of Korean Ports– Viewed through the Historical Records of Tongshuntai], *Tōyōshi Kenkyū*,

63:4 (2005), pp. 21–62.

89. Inch'ŏn to Seoul, Letter no. 28, 30/Jan/1889, *Tongtailaixin*, vol. 2.

90. Ishikawa Ryota, 'Kaehanggi Chunggugin Sang'in ŭi Hwaldong kwa Chŏngbo Maech'e' [Commercial Activity of Chinese Merchants after the Opening of the Treaty Ports and their Information Media], *Kyujanggak*, 33 (2008), pp. 183–234, on p. 221.

91. Tan Peinan to Zhao Lanpu, Letter no. 25, 11/Aug/1891, *Wangbok Munsŏ*, vol. 34.

92. Tan Jiesheng to Zhao Lanpu, Letter no. 9, 6/Jun/1892, *Wangbok Munsŏ*, vol. 34.

93. Tan Jiesheng to Zhao Lanpu, Letter no. 38, 15/Jul/1892, *Wangbok Munsŏ*, vol. 34.

94. Tan Jiesheng to Zhao Lanpu, Letter no. 42, 24/Jul/1892, *Wangbok Munsŏ*, vol. 35.

6 Transcending Borders: The Story of the Arab Community in Singapore, 1820–1980s

1. For examples of this scholarship, see A. Reid, *Southeast Asia in the Age of Commerce, 1450–1680*, vol. 2, *Expansion and Crisis* (New Haven, CT: Yale University Press, 1993); T. Day, *Fluid Iron: State Formation in Southeast Asia* (Honolulu, HI: University of Hawaii Press, 2002); H. Sutherland, 'Southeast Asian History and the Mediterranean Analogy', *Journal of Southeast Asian Studies*, 34 (2003), pp. 1–20; H. Sutherland, 'Contingent Devices', in P. H. Kratoska, R. Raben and H. Schulte Nordholt (eds), *Locating Southeast Asia: Geographies of Knowledge and Politics of Space* (Leiden: KITLV Press, 2005), pp. 20–60; H. Sutherland, 'Geography as Destiny: The Role of Water in Southeast Asian History', in P. Boomgaard (ed.), *A World of Water: Rain, Rivers and Seas in Southeast Asian Histories* (Leiden: KITLV Press, 2007), pp. 27–70.

2. H. Sutherland, 'Southeast Asian History and the Mediterranean Analogy'; C. Reynolds, 'A New Look at Old Southeast Asia', *Journal of Asian Studies*, 54:2 (1995), pp. 419–46.

3. U. Freitag, 'Hadhramaut: A Religious Centre for the Indian Ocean in the Late 19th and Early 20th Centuries?', *Studia Islamica*, 89 (1999), pp. 165–83. See also J. Miran, 'Red Sea Translocals: Hadhrami Migration, Entrepreneurship, and Strategies of Integration in Eritrea, 1840s–1970s', *Northeast African Studies*, 12:1 (2012), pp. 129–68.

4. U. Freitag, 'Reflections on the Longevity of the Hadhrami Diaspora in the Indian Ocean', in A. I. Abushouk and H. A. Ibrahim (eds), *The Hadhrami Diaspora in Southeast Asia: Identity Maintenance or Assimilitation?* (Leiden: Brill, 2009), pp. 17–32; S. Sait and H. Lim, *Land, Law and Islam: Property and Human Rights in the Muslim World* (London: Zed Press, 2006); M. Yegar, *Islam and Islamic Institutions in British Malaya* (Jerusalem: The Hebrew University, 1979).

5. On the origin of the idea of 'Malay', please see Encyclopedia Britannica, *Britannica Guide to the Islamic World Guide to the Islamic World: Religion, History and the Future* (London: Constable & Robinson Ltd, 2009), pp. 378–82; see also E. Ho, *The Graves of Tarim: Genealogy and Mobility across the Indian Ocean* (Berkeley, CA: University of California Press, 2006); U. Freitag and W. Clarence-Smith (eds), *Hadhrami Traders, Scholars and Statesmen in the Indian Ocean, 1750s–1960s* (Leiden: Brill, 1997).

6. See, for example, W. H. Ingrams, *A Report on the Social, Economic and Political Conditions of the Hadhramaut* (London: HMSO, 1937); P. G. Riddell, 'Religious Links between Hadhramaut and the Malay-Indonesia World, *c.* 1850–1950', in U. Freitag and W. Clarence-Smith (eds), *Hadhrami Traders, Scholars, and Statesmen in the Indian Ocean, 1750s–1960s* (Leiden: Brill, 1997), pp. 217–30.

7. M. Abaza and M. A. Shahab, 'A Portrait of an Indonesian Hadhrami Who Bridged the Two Worlds', in E. Tagliacozzo (ed.), *Southeast Asia and the Middle East: Islam, Movement, and the Longue Durée* (Singapore: National University of Singapore Press, 2009), pp. 250–74. See also W. G. Clarence-Smith, 'Hadhrami Entrepreneurs in the Malay World, *c.* 1750 to *c.* 1940', in U. Freitag and W. Clarence-Smith (eds), *Hadhrami Traders, Scholars and Statesmen in the Indian Ocean, 1750s–1960s* (Leiden: Brill, 1997), pp. 297–314.

8. Cited in J. A. E. Morley, 'The Arabs and the Eastern Trade', *Journal of the Malayan Branch of the Royal Asiatic Society*, 22:1 (1949), pp. 143–75, on p. 165. See also C. B. Buckley, *An Anecdotal History of Old Times in Singapore* (Singapore: Fraser and Neave Limited, 1902), p. 85.

9. See, for example, N. Mobini-Kesheh, *The Hadrami Awakening: Community and Identity in the Netherlands East Indies, 1900–1942* (Ithaca, NY: Southeast Asia Press, 1999); Clarence-Smith, 'Hadhrami Entrepreneurs in the Malay World', p. 303.

10. See, for example, N. Steensgaard, *The Asian Trade Revolution of the Seventeenth Century: The East India Companies and the Decline of the Caravan Trade* (Chicago, IL: University of Chicago Press, 1973); J. Kostiner, 'The Impact of the Hadhrami Emigrants in the East Indies on Islamic Modernism and Social Change in the Hadhramawt during the 20th Century', in R. Israeli and A. H. Johns (eds), *Islam in Asia*, vol. 2, *Southeast and East Asia* (Boulder, CO: Westview Press, 1984), p. 210; U. Freitag, 'Arab Merchants in Singapore: Attempt at a Collective Biography', in H. de Jonge and N. Kaptein (eds), *Transcending Borders: Arabs, Politics, Trade and Islam in Southeast Asia* (Leiden: KITLV Press, 2002), pp. 107–42.

11. Y. Mattar, 'Arab Ethnic Enterprises in Colonial Singapore: Market Entry and Exit Mechanisms, 1819–1965', *Asia Pacific Viewpoint*, 45:2 (August 2004), pp. 165–179, on p. 174; Clarence-Smith, 'Hadhrami Entrepreneurs in the Malay World', pp. 297–314; A. Talib, 'Hadhramis in Singapore', *Journal of Muslim Minority Affairs*, 17:1 (April 1997), pp. 89–97.

12. Fatimah & Ors vs Logan & Ors (1871), in J. W. N. Kyshe, *Cases Heard and Determined in Her Majesty's Supreme Court of the Straits Settlements 1808–1884*, vol. 1, *Civil Cases* (undated) (Somerset: Legal Library Publishing Services, 1885), p. 269; A. Qadir, 'Institution of Wakf in Southeast Asia', in his *Wakf: Islamic Law of Charitable Trust* (Delhi: Global Vision Publishing House, 2004), pp. 151–8; W. Heffening, 'Wakf', *Encyclopedia of Islam*, 1st edn (Leiden: E. J. Brill, 1931), vol. 7, pp. 1096–102; G. C. Kozlowski, *Muslim Endowments and Society in British India* (Cambridge: Cambridge University Press, 1985), pp. 1–2; S. M. Mahamood, *Waqf in Malaysia: Legal and Administrative Perspectives* (Kuala Lumpur: University of Malaya Press, 2006), pp. 27–38.

13. Freitag, 'Arab Merchants in Singapore', p. 119; R. Brown, 'Islamic Endowments and the Land Economy in Singapore: The Genesis of an Ethical Capitalism, 1830–2007', *South East Asia Research*, 16:3 (2008), pp. 343–403. See also M. Cizakca, *Islamic Capitalism and Finance: Origins, Evolution and the Future* (Cheltenham: Edward Elgar, 2011); M. Cizakca, *A History of Philanthropic Foundations: The Islamic World From the Seventh Century to the Present* (Istanbul: Bogazici University Press, 2000); M. Cizakca, *Comparative Evolution of Business Partnerships* (Leiden: E. J. Brill, 1996); T. Kuran, 'The Provision of Public Goods under Islamic Law: Origins, Impact and Limitations of the Waqf System', *Law and Society Review*, 35:4 (2001), pp. 841–98.

14. A. Milner, *The Malays* (Chichester: John Wiley & Sons, 2008), p. 57. See also A. Milner, 'The Malay Raja: A Study of Malay Political Culture in East Sumatra and the

Malay Peninsula in the Early Nineteenth Century' (PhD thesis, Cornell University, 1977).

15. B. L. Chua, 'Land Registration in Singapore and the Federation of Malaya', *Malaya Law Review*, 1 (1959), pp. 318–30, on p. 318; L. S. Lim, 'The Arabs of Singapore: A Sociographic Study of their Place in the Muslim and Malaya World' (BA Thesis, Department of Sociology, National University of Singapore, 1987), p. 23; S. O. Alhabshi, 'Waqf Management in Malaysia', in M. Ariff (ed.), *The Muslim Private Sector in Southeast Asia* (Singapore: Institute of Southeast Asian Studies, 1991), pp. 188–216. On colonial law in British Malaya, see also I. R. Hussin, 'The Politics of Islamic Law: Elites and Authority in Colonial Malaya, India and Egypt' (PhD dissertation, University of Washington, 2008). For a discussion on land and economy, please refer to D. North, 'Institutions', *Journal of Economic Perspectives*, 5:1 (Winter, 1991), pp. 97–112.

16. Another significant Arab family was the Aljuned. See for example Freitag, 'Arab Merchants in Singapore', p. 119. See also 'The Enterprising Alsagoffs of Singapore: Men of Property', in *Singapore: Days of Old, A Special Commemorative History of Singapore Published on the 10th Anniversary of Singapore Tatler* (Hong Kong: Illustrated Magazine Pub., 1992), p. 15; S. M. Alsagoff, *The Alsagoff Family in Malaysia A. H. 1240 (A.D. 1824) to A.H. 1382 (A.D. 1962)* (Singapore: Mun Seong Press 1963), pp. 28–30. See also the transcript of an interview with Prof. Syed Mohsen Alsagoff, Pioneers of Singapore series, Oral History Centre, the National Archives of Singapore [hereafter, Alsagoff Transcript, NAS].

17. U. Freitag, *Indian Ocean Migrants and State Formation in Hadramaut: Reforming the Homeland* (Leiden: Brill, 2003), pp. 333–4.

18. NAS, Oral History Centre, transcript of Interview with Alwee Alkaff, A000124, 1.

19. NAS, Oral History Centre, transcript of Interview with Alwee Alkaff, A000124, 18.

20. Re Syed Shaik Alkaff, Deceased; Alkaff & Anor vs Attorney-General [1923] MC 1.

21. S. M. Alsagoff, *The Alsagoff Family in Malaysia A. H. 1240 (A. D. 1824) to A. H. 1382 (A. D. 1963)*, (Singapore: Mun Seong Press, 1963), p. 9.

22. Alsagoff, *The Alsagoff Family in Malaysia*, pp. 9–10.

23. On the discussion of matriarchy on the Malay archipelago and Java, see B. W. Andaya, 'Gender, Islam and the Bugis Diaspora in Nineteenth- and Twentieth-Century Riau', *Sari*, 21 (July 2003), pp. 77–108; J. Hadler, *Muslims and Matriarchs: Cultural Resilience in Indonesia through Jihad and Colonialism* (Ithaca, NY: Cornell University Press, 2008). See also 'Alsagoff & Co.', in A. Wright (ed.), *Twentieth Century Impressions of British Malaya* (London: Lloyd's Greater Britain Publication Company, 1908), pp. 705–6. See also C. B. Buckley, *An Anecdotal History of Old Times in Singapore: 1819–1867* (Singapore: Oxford University Press, 1984), pp. 564–5.

24. Alsagoff, *The Alsagoff Family in Malaysia*, pp. 21–38. See also Alsagoff Transcript, NAS.

25. Kukup is a small fishing village located about forty kilometres south-west of Johor Bahru, on the Strait of Malacca in Malaysia. It is particularly popular with tourists from Singapore. N. M. Tachimoto, 'Coping with the Currents of Change: A Frontier Bugis Settlement in Johir, Malaysia', *Southeast Asia Studies*, 32:2 (September 1994), pp. 197–230.

26. A British colonial officer wrote of Mohamed that 'he is now a very wealthy man, and although much younger than many rich Arabs in this place, is looked up to by all. He has the character of being open-handed, and ever since his father's death, he and his family have given public feasts in the mosque every Friday ... My experience of Syed Mohamed

Alsagoff is that, although a strict Mohamedan, he is liberal in his views and is certainly not fanatical, mixes freely with Europeans, and amongst them is probably the best known Arab in the place. He was during the year 1883, a member of the Municipal Board of Commissioners.' Cited from E. Lee, *The British as Rulers Governing Multiracial Singapore* (Singapore: National University of Singapore Press, 1991), p. 165. See also Freitag, 'Arab Merchants in Singapore', pp. 115–6; 'The Municipality', *Strait Times*, 13 January 1883, p. 2; 'Municipal Election', *Strait Times Weekly Issue*, 24 November 1883, p. 12.

27. On this practice of sending descendants to the Middle East for education, please see U. Freitag, 'From Golden Youth in Arabia to Business Leaders in Singapore: Instructions of a Hadhrami Patriarch', in E. Tagliacozzo (ed.), *Southeast Asia and the Middle East: Islam, Movement, and the Longue Durée* (Singapore: NUS Press, 2009), pp. 235–49.

28. On Omar's interaction with the local leaders in Singapore and Johor, see 'Sultan of Johore's Birthday', *Eastern Daily Mail and Straits Morning Advertiser*, 19 September 1907, p. 3; 'Sultan of Johore', *Straits Times*, 18 September 1908, p. 7; 'Johore Celebrations', *Singapore Free Press and Mercantile Advertiser*, 21 September 1908, p. 5.

29. From the late 1860s, with the opening of the Suez Canal, a number of Europeans shippers were attracted to the Haj business. In 1879, uncertainties generated by competition between shipping companies led to the rise of a monopoly of exclusion by European shippers. See M. B. Miller, 'Pilgrims' Progress: The Business of the Hajj', *Past and Present*, 191 (May 2006), pp. 189–228.

30. In 1919, for instance, pilgrim brokers in Singapore agreed to purchase Mansfield shipping tickets exclusively through Alsagoff & Co. Miller, 'Pilgrim's Progress'; see also 'Notice: The Singapore Steamship Company Limited', *Straits Times*, 19 April 1886, p. 2.

31. Alsagoff, *The Alsagoff Family in Malaysia*, p. 15; 'Syed Omar Alsagoff – Sudden Death While Visiting Java', *Straits Times*, 18 May 1927, p. 9.

32. Alsagoff, *The Alsagoff Family in Malaysia*, p. 19. See also Alsagoff Transcript, NAS; 'Loss to Singapore Arab Community', *Straits Times*, 2 January 1931, p. 11; 'Tragedy of the Alsagoff Cousins', *Singapore Free Press and Mercantile Advertiser*, 6 January 1931, p. 10.

33. Alsagoff, *The Alsagoff Family in Malaysia*, pp. 28–30. See also Alsagoff Transcript, NAS. On Syed Ibrahim as a community leader, please see 'Arabic Social Club', *Straits Times*, 14 August 1933, p. 12; 'Local Arab Leader's Tribute to Britain', *Straits Times*, 17 August 1936, p. 13; 'Leaders of Business in Malaya', *Straits Times*, 2 April 1953, p. 10.

34. 'Estate of Syed Ahmed bin Adbulrahman Alsagoff, Deceased: Auction Sale of Valuable Singapore Properties', *Straits Times*, 6 July 1961, p. 12.

35. 'Notice by H. M. Alsagoff', *Singapore Free Press and Mercantile Advertiser*, 11 July 1916, p. 10.

36. Freitag, 'Arab Merchants in Singapore', p. 11; R. D. Pepler, Unpublished Reports from Royal Tropical Research Unit, Singapore, to Med. Res. Co.'s R. N. Personnel Research Committee, 1951; W. G. Clarence-Smith, 'Hadhrami Arab Entrepreneurs in Indonesia and Malaysia: Facing the Challenge of the 1930s Recessions', in P. Boomgard and I. Brown (eds), *Weathering the Storm: The Economies of Southeast Asia in the 1930s Depression* (Singapore: Institute of Southeast Asian Studies, 2000), pp. 229–303; Y. Mattar, 'Arab Ethnic Enterprises in Colonial Singapore: Market Entry and Exit Mechanisms, 1819–1965', *Asia Pacific Viewpoint*, 45:2 (August 2004), pp. 165–79.

37. For details, please see 'Alsagoff and Company', *Straits Times*, 15 February 1917, p. 8.

38. From 1931 onwards, his company even took care of the Kathiri sultan's properties and family trust in Singapore. See Freitag, 'Arab Merchants in Singapore', pp. 109–42; A. Talib, 'Hadhramis in Singapore', *Journal of Muslim Minority Affairs*, 17:1 (April 1997),

pp. 89–97.

39. The Straits Settlements (Penang, Singapore, Malacca) were the first areas to be settled by the British East India Company (EIC) in peninsular Malaysia. The British settlement at Penang was founded in 1786, at Singapore in 1819. In 1824 the Dutch ceded Malacca to the British Crown. In the following year, Malacca and Singapore were transferred to the administration of the East India Company, and became, with Penang, the Straits Settlements. On EIC's changing land policy in the Straits Settlements, please see V. Dharmalingan, 'The British and the Muslim Religious Endowment in Colonial Malaya' (MA thesis, National University of Singapore, 1995); R. St John Braddell, *The Law of the Straits Settlements: A Commentary* (Kuala Lumpur: Oxford University Press, 1982); see also B. W. Andaya and L. Y. Andaya, *A History of Malaysia* (London: Palgrave Macmillan, 1984).

40. See, for example, B. S. A. Yeoh, *Contesting Space in Colonial Singapore: Power Relations in the Urban Built Environment* (Singapore: Singapore University Press, 2003), pp. 28–84; Y. C. Liu and K. C. Chen, 'The Characteristics of Agricultural Land-Use in Prewar Singapore', *Journal of Geographical Research*, 49 (November 2008), pp. 93–6. See also A. Farrington, *Trading Places: The East India Company and Asia, 1600–1834* (London: British Library, 2002); P. Lawson, *The East India Company: A History* (London: Longman, 1993); S. Sen, *Empire of Free Trade: The East India Company and the Making of the Colonial Marketplace* (Philadelphia, PA: University of Pennsylvania Press, 1998). On land and governance, see J. de Vere Allen, 'Malayan Civil Service, 1874–1941: Colonial Bureaucracy/Malayan Elite', *Comparative Studies in Society and History*, 12 (1970), pp. 149–78. Allen commented that 'when the British first became involved officially in the Malay States in 1874 they were represented there by a very small and oddly assorted group of men quite separate and different from, and only loosely controlled by, the official colonial establishment in the Straits Settlements. By the time of the Japanese occupation this had grown to a group which was very large by normal British colonial standards and had become much more homogeneous, [and] conformed much more closely to general Colonial Office type'.

41. S. Siddique, 'Administration of Islam in Singapore', in T. Abdullah and S. Siddique (eds), *Islam in Society in Southeast Asia* (Singapore: Institute of Southeast Asian Studies, 1986), pp. 315–31; V. Sinha, 'The Mohammedan and Hindu Endowments Board, 1905–1968: The Singapore Experience', in *Religion-State Encounters in Hindu Domains, from the Straits Settlements to Singapore* (Singapore: ARI-Springer Series, 2011), pp. 125–84. See also 'Moslem Loyalty', *Straits Times*, 16 December 1915, p. 10; 'Muhammedan Advisory Boards', *Singapore Free Press and Mercantile Advertiser*, 25 January 1930, p. 13.

42. Yeoh, *Contesting Space in Colonial Singapore*, pp. 28–84; O. G. Ling, S. Siddique and S. K. Cheng (eds), *The Management of Ethnic Relations in Public Housing Estates* (Singapore: Institute of Policy Studies/Times Academic Press, 1993).

43. S. P. Chung, 'At the Crossroads of East and West – Arab Merchants in Singapore, 1819–1980s', Paper Presented at the *Eighth International Convention of Asia Scholars* (*ICAS* 8), Macao, 24–7 June 2013.

44. J. A. Nagata, *The Reflowering of Malaysian Islam: Modern Religious Radicals and their Roots* (Vancouver: University of British Columbia Press, 1984); W. R. Roff, 'The Malay-Muslim World of Singapore at the Close of the 19th century', *Journal of Asiatic Studies*, 24:1 (1964), pp. 15–90; M. T. Osman, 'Islamization of the Malays: A Transformation of Culture', in A. Ibrahim, S. Siddique and Y. Hussain (eds), *Readings on Islam*

in Southeast Asia (Singapore: Institute of Southeast Asian Studies, 1985), pp. 44–7.

45. 'The Singapore Landlord on his Critics', *Straits Times*, 30 July 1947, p. 4.

46. Untitled, *Singapore Free Press*, 20 July 1946, p. 4. For a general background, please also see 'Huge Interests of the Local Arab Community', *Singapore Free Press and Mercantile Advertiser*, 17 August 1936, p. 3.

47. R. A. Brown, 'Capitalism and Islam: Arab Business Groups and Capital Flows in Southeast Asia', in C. Smith, B. McSweeney and R. Fitzgerald (eds), *Remaking Management: Between Global and Local* (Cambridge: Cambridge University Press, 2008), pp. 217–50.

48. 'The Landlords' Petition', *Straits Times*, 24 March 1947, p. 4.

49. 'The Landlords' Petition', *Straits Times*, 24 March 1947, p. 4; this 'firm' is referred to as an entity founded by a wealthy Arab family in Singapore.

50. 'Landlord Attacks Rent Bill', *Straits Times*, 1 July 1947, p. 3.

51. 'Exploiting the Landlord', *Straits Times*, 4 August 1950, p. 6.

52. 'Mr. Alsagoff Backs Up the Sub-tenants', *Straits Times*, 12 August 1950, p. 9.

53. 'Twenty Percent on Rents', *Straits Times*, 25 June 1947, p. 4; see also 'The Singapore Landlord on his Critics', p. 4; Yeoh, *Contesting Space*; N. H. Chua, *The Golden Shoe: Building Singapore's Financial District* (Singapore: Urban Redevelopment Authority, 1989); R. Goh and B. Yeoh, *International Conference on the City, Theorizing The Southeast Asian City as Text: Urban Landscapes, Cultural Documents, and Interpretative Experiences* (Singapore: World Scientific Pub. Co., Inc., 2003); H. Y. Lee, 'The Singapore Shophouse: An Anglo-Chinese Urban Vernacular', in R. G. Knapp (ed.), *Asia's Old Dwellings: Tradition, Resilience, and Change* (New York: Oxford University Press, 2003), pp. 115–34.

54. Brown, 'Capitalism and Islam'. See also her 'Islamic Endowments and the Land Economy in Singapore: The Genesis of an Ethical Capitalism, 1830–2007', *South East Asia Research*, 16:3 (2008), pp. 343–403.

55. K. Y. L. Tan, 'Singapore: A Statist Legal Laboratory', in E. A. Black and G. F. Bell (eds), *Law and Legal Institutions of Asia: Traditions, Adaptations and Innovations* (Cambridge: Cambridge University Press, 2011), pp. 330–70.

56. Y. M. Yeung, *National Development Policy and Urban Transformation in Singapore: A Study of Public Housing and the Marketing System*, Research Paper No 149 (Department of Geography, University of Chicago, 1973); Yegar, *Islam and Islamic Institutions in British Malaya*.

57. Siddique, 'Administration of Islam in Singapore', pp. 315–31; T. A. Alias, 'Unleashing the Potential of the Waqf as an Economic Institution: Policy, Legal and Economic Reforms' (DPhil thesis, INCEIF [International Centre for Education in Islamic Finance], 2011), pp. 449–61.

58. Qadir, 'Institution of Wakf in Southeast Asia', pp. 151–8; Yeung, *National Development Policy and Urban Transformation in Singapore*.

59. Ling, Siddique and Cheng (eds), *The Management of Ethnic Relations in Public Housing Estates*; see also Yeoh, *Contesting Space in Colonial Singapore*.

60. 'S. O. Alsagoff, 1947–1972', Registry of Businesses, ROB 149, National Archive of Singapore. See also 'More Colony Trade with Middle East Sought', *Straits Times*, 2 November 1956, p. 14.

61. S. Carapico, *Civil Society in Yemen: The Political Economy of Activism in Modern Arabia* (London: Cambridge University Press, 1998), p. 101.

7 Spanish Colonial Policy toward Chinese Merchants in Eighteenth-Century Philippines

1. Chinese merchants in the Philippines were referred to colloquially as 'Sangleys'. They were described as 'infidels' or 'heathen', reflecting the low regard of the Spanish. This chapter focuses on Chinese merchants who were not of mixed race and who were not baptized into Catholicism. Furthermore, 'merchant' and 'trader' are used synonymously.

2. Chinese merchant community simply refers to the Chinese traders in the Philippines. More formal trader organizations were formed in the nineteenth century.

3. R. Bernal, 'The Chinese Colony in Manila, 1570–1770', in A. Felix, Jr (ed.), *The Chinese in the Philippines, 1570–1770, Vol. I* (Manila: The Historical Conservation Society, 1966), pp. 40–66, on pp. 53–6; V. Purcell, *The Chinese in Southeast Asia*, 2nd edn (Oxford: Oxford University Press, 1965), pp. 513–14; L. Diaz-Trechuelo, 'The Role of the Chinese in the Philippine Domestic Economy', in Felix, Jr (ed.), *The Chinese in the Philippines, 1570–1770, Vol. I*, pp. 175–210, on p. 183; M. Guerrero, 'The Chinese in the Philippines, 1570–1770', in Felix, Jr (ed.), *The Chinese in the Philippines, 1570–1770, Vol. I*, pp. 15–39, on pp. 33–4.

4. For varied perspectives in the literature regarding transnational merchant communities, see W. C. Chang and E. Tagliacozzo, 'Introduction: The Arc of Historical Commercial Relations between China and Southeast Asia', in E. Tagliacozzo and W. C. Chang (eds), *Chinese Circulations: Capital, Commodities, and Networks in Southeast Asia* (Durham, NC: Duke University Press, 2011), pp. 1–17.

5. L. Alonso, 'Financing the Empire: The Nature of the Tax System in the Philippines, 1565–1804', *Philippine Studies*, 51:1 (2003), pp. 63–95.

6. D. O. Flynn and A. Giráldez, 'Born with a "Silver Spoon": The Origin of World Trade in 1571', *Journal of World History*, 6:2 (1995), pp. 201–21, on pp. 202, 205. The authors also contend that from 1500 to 1800, Latin America's silver output may have gone beyond 80 per cent of global output. See also Bernal, 'The Chinese Colony in Manila, 1570–1770'.

7. B. J. Legarda, Jr, *After the Galleons: Foreign Trade, Economic Change & Entrepreneur-ship in the Nineteenth-Century Philippines* (Quezon City: Ateneo de Manila Univesity Press), p. 33.

8. R. K. Skowronek, 'The Spanish Philippines: Archaeological Perspectives on Colonial Economics and Society', *International Journal of Historical Archaeology*, 2:1 (1998), pp. 45–71.

9. See T. S. Clemente, 'Guanxi in Chinese Commerce: Informal Enforcement in Spanish Philippines', *Seoul Journal of Economics*, 26:2 (2013), pp. 203–38.

10. E. Wickberg, *The Chinese in Philippine Life, 1850–1898* (Manila: Ateneo de Manila University Press, 2000), p. 6.

11. S. S. C. Liao, 'How the Chinese Lived in the Philippines from 1570 to 1898', in S. S. C. Liao (ed.), *Chinese Participation in Philippine Culture and Economy* (Manila: Book-man, Inc., 1964), pp. 19–33, on p. 24; M. Guerrero, 'The Chinese in the Philippines, 1570–1770', pp. 31–2; Bernal, 'The Chinese Colony in Manila, 1570–1770', p. 56.

12. Felipe II, 'Royal Decree Regarding Commerce, August 9, 1589', in E. H. Blair and J. A. Robertson (eds), *The Philippine Islands, 1493–1898*, 55 vols (Cleveland, OH: The Arthur H. Clark, Co., 1903–9), vol. 7, pp. 138–9; Felipe II, 'Instructions for Gov. Tello, May 25, 1596', in Blair and Robertson (eds), *The Philippine Islands, 1493–1898*, vol. 9, pp. 234–5.

13. D. de Salazar, 'Affairs in the Philipinas Islands', in Blair and Robertson (eds), *The Philippine Islands, 1493–1898*, vol. 5, pp. 236–40.
14. W. L. Schurz, *Manila Galleon* (New York: E. P. Dutton, 1959), p. 78.
15. Anon., 'Events in Manila, 1662–63', in Blair and Robertson (eds), *The Philippine Islands, 1493–1898*, vol. 36, pp. 218–53.
16. C. Diaz, 'The Augustinians of the Philippines, 1670–1694', in Blair and Robertson (eds), *The Philippine Islands, 1493–1898*, vol. 42, pp. 248–51.
17. B. Vela, 'Letter from Vela to Gonzalez, July 24, 1764', in Blair and Robertson (eds), *The Philippine Islands, 1493–1898*, vol. 49, pp. 291–3.
18. Anon., 'Events in the Filipinas Islands from August 1639 to August 1640', in Blair and Robertson (eds), *The Philippine Islands, 1493–1898*, vol. 29, p. 202–5; Anon., 'Relation of the Insurrection of the Chinese', in Blair and Robertson (eds), *The Philippine Islands, 1493–1898*, vol. 29, pp. 212–27, 248–9.
19. A. Santamaria, 'The Chinese Parian (*El Parian De Los Sangleyes*)', in Felix, Jr (ed.), *The Chinese in the Philippines, 1570–1770, Vol. I*, pp. 78–9.
20. See P. de Acuña et al., 'The Sangley Insurrection', in Blair and Robertson (eds), *The Philippine Islands, 1493–1898*, vol. 12, pp. 142–67; the diplomatic letter from China, officially endorsed by three officials – the Inspector-General, Viceroy and Eunuch of Chincheo – reveals three salient points. First, the letter communicated that China would not wage war on account of the massacre because of friendly relations between China and the Spanish. Second, victory was uncertain. Third, those who were killed were 'a base people, ungrateful to China, their native country, to their parents, and to their relatives, since so many years had passed during which they had not returned to China'. The king 'did not consider these people of any value'. Nevertheless, peace was contingent on sending back surviving Sangleys and monetary payment for the goods seized from them. Otherwise, merchant ships would not be allowed to sail to the Philippines and war would be imminent with the help of tributary states. When the Philippines was captured, it would be awarded to the tributary states. While the letter appears contradictory on the point of 'maintaining peace' and instituting punitive action if peace conditions were not met, China nevertheless demonstrated both economic strength and military might, both of which the Spanish in Manila considered in dealing with the Sangleys. See the entire letter in Inspector-General of Chincheo, 'Letter from a Chinese Official to Acuña', in Blair and Robertson (eds), *The Philippine Islands, 1493–1898*, vol. 13, pp. 287–91.
21. G. Wang, *China and the Chinese Overseas* (Singapore: Eastern Universities Press, 2003), pp. 87–102.
22. Bernal, 'The Chinese Colony in Manila, 1570–1770', pp. 48–9, 58–9; Wickberg, *The Chinese in Philippine Life, 1850–1898*, pp. 8–10.
23. Diaz-Trechuelo, 'The Role of the Chinese in the Philippine Domestic Economy', pp. 187–90.
24. Diaz-Trechuelo, 'The Role of the Chinese in the Philippine Domestic Economy', pp. 187–90.
25. In the Spanish Philippines, Governor-Generals were under the administrative jurisdiction of the Viceroyalty of New Spain from 1564–1821; after that, Governor-Generals reported directly to Spain following Spain's loss of the Mexican colony.
26. Married Sangleys are necessarily male Chinese who married indigenous women. Only male Chinese travelled to the archipelago to become traders during the Spanish colonial period.

27. J. Villa, F. de Santa Ynes, J. Lopez, L. de Morales and S. de la Bartolome, 'Conditions of the Islands, October 7, 1701' in Blair and Robertson (eds), *The Philippine Islands, 1493–1898*, vol. 44, pp. 135–6.

28. Wickberg, *The Chinese in Philippine Life, 1850–1898*, p. 15.

29. For a good discussion on how Catholic conversions and marriage practices among Chinese merchants were adaptive strategies in the colonial setting of the late nineteenth and early twentieth centuries, see R. T. Chu, *Chinese and Chinese Mestizos of Manila: Family, Identity, and Culture, 1860s–1930s* (Mandaluyong City: Anvil, 2012), ch. 4.

30. J. de la Concepcion, 'Events of 1701–1715', in Blair and Robertson (eds), *The Philippine Islands, 1493–1898*, vol. 44, pp. 142–7.

31. Royal Order addressed to the Audiencia de Manila. Another order bearing the same date was sent to the Archbishop, *Archivo General de Indias Filipinas*, 202; as cited in Diaz-Trechuelo, 'The Role of the Chinese in the Philippine Domestic Economy', p. 195.

32. Guerrero, 'The Chinese in the Philippines, 1570–1770', p. 195.

33. *Archivo General de Indias Filipinas*, 202 and 568; as cited in Diaz-Trechuelo, 'The Role of the Chinese in the Philippine Domestic Economy', p. 197, see nn. 63–6.

34. M. de Zuñiga, *An Historical View of the Philippine Islands: Exhibiting their Discovery, Population, Language, Government, Manners, Customs, Productions and Commerce*, Vol. II , trans. J. Maver (London: J. Asperne, Nonaville and Fell, 1814); M. de Zuñiga, 'Events in Filipinas, 1739–1762', in Blair and Robertson (eds), *The Philippine Islands, 1493–1898*, vol. 48, pp. 137–93, on p. 146; Purcell, *The Chinese in Southeast Asia*, p. 526

35. De Zuñiga, *An Historical View of the Philippine Islands*; De Zuñiga, 'Events in Filipinas, 1739–1762', pp. 153–4.

36. J. L. Phelan, 'Authority and Flexibility in the Spanish Imperial Bureaucracy', *Special Issue on Comparative Public Administration, Administrative Science Quarterly*, 5:1 (1960), pp. 47–65; N. P. Cushner, *Spain in the Philippines: From Conquest to Revolution* (Quezon City: Ateneo de Manila University, 1971), p. 157.

37. De Zuñiga, 'Events in Filipinas, 1739–1762', pp. 180–3; Diaz-Trechuelo, 'The Role of the Chinese in the Philippine Domestic Economy', p. 207; De Zuñiga, *An Historical View of the Philippine Islands*.

38. De Zuñiga, *An Historical View of the Philippine Islands*.

39. This English translation of the decree is from S. de Anda y Salazar, 'March 3, 1763 Decree', in *Manila Consultations, Records of Fort St. George, 1763* (Madras: Superintendent, Government Press, 1940), vol. 5, p. 131.

40. S. P. Escoto, 'Expulsion of the Chinese and Readmission to the Philippines: 1764–1779', *Philippine Studies*, 47:1 (1999), pp. 48–76, on p. 48; Purcell, *The Chinese in Southeast Asia*, pp. 526–7; Bernal, 'The Chinese Colony in Manila, 1570–1770', pp. 57–8.

41. See de Anda y Salazar, 'March 3, 1763 Decree'.

42. P. de Tavera, 'Memorial de Anda y Salazar', in Blair and Robertson (eds), *The Philippine Islands, 1493–1898*, vol. 50, pp. 161–2, n. 90.

43. See F. L. de Viana, 'Viana's Memorial of 1765', in Blair and Robertson (eds), *The Philippine Islands, 1493–1898*, vol. 50, pp. 197–338, on pp. 197, 287, 272.

44. W. L. Schurz, 'The Royal Philippine Company', *Hispanic American Historical Review*, 3:4 (1920), pp. 491–508, on p. 494.

45. F. L. de Viana, 'Financial Affairs of the Islands, 1766', in Blair and Robertson (eds), *The Philippine Islands, 1493–1898* (Cleveland, OH: The Arthur H. Clark, Co., 1903–9),

vol. 50, pp. 77–117.

46. F. L. de Viana, 'Letter from Viana to Carlos III, May 1, 1767', in Blair and Robertson (eds), *The Philippine Islands, 1493–1898*, vol. 50, pp. 118–36.

47. M. R. de Borja, *Basques in the Philippines* (Reno, NV: University of Nevada Press, 2005), pp. 63–6.

48. J. Raon, 'The So-Called Ordinances of Raon', in Blair and Robertson (eds), *The Philippine Islands, 1493–1898*, vol. 50, p. 253.

49. Carlos III, 'Royal Decree of April 17, 1766', in *Expechente del Gobernador y Fiscal de la Audiencia de Filipinas sobre la expulsion de los sangleyes, 1769–1770. Archivo General de India, Filipinas, Leg. 621*; trans. in Escoto, 'Expulsion of the Chinese and Readmission to the Philippines: 1764–1779', p. 53; Carlos III invokes law 8, title 18, and book 6 of the Code of the Indies for stipulations regarding Chinese who are allowed to stay under the second exception.

50. De Anda y Salazar, 'Anda's Memorial to the Spanish Government on April 12, 1768, Madrid', in Blair and Robertson (eds), *The Philippine Islands, 1493–1898*, vol. 50, pp. 157–63, on pp. 157–9.

51. De Viana, 'Letter from Viana to Carlos III, May 1, 1767', pp. 121–3.

52. De Anda y Salazar, 'Anda's Memorial to the Spanish Government on April 12, 1768, Madrid', pp. 159–60; P. B. Villella, '"Pure and Noble Indians, Untainted by Inferior Idolatrous Races": Native Elites and the Discourse of Blood Purity in Late Colonial Mexico', *Hispanic American Historical Review*, 91:4 (2011), pp. 633–63; L. A. Newson, *Conquest and Pestilence in the Early Spanish Philippines* (Manila: Ateneo de Manila University Press, 2011), pp. 48–9.

53. De Anda y Salazar, 'Anda's Memorial to the Spanish Government on April 12, 1768, Madrid', p. 159.

54. Villella, '"Pure and Noble Indians, Untainted by Inferior Idolatrous Races"'; Newson, *Conquest and Pestilence in the Early Spanish Philippines*, pp. 48–9.

55. De Anda y Salazar, 'Anda's Memorial to the Spanish Government on April 12, 1768, Madrid', pp. 168–9.

56. J. Montero y Vidal, 'Events in Filipinas, 1764–1800', in Blair and Robertson (eds), *The Philippine Islands, 1493–1898*, vol. 50, pp. 23–76, on p. 28.

57. Montero y Vidal, 'Events in Filipinas, 1764–1800', pp. 28, 50, 57.

58. Cushner, *Spain in the Philippines*, pp. 186–7.

59. J. Basco y Vargas, 'Agriculture in Filipinas', in Blair and Robertson (eds), *The Philippine Islands, 1493–1898*, 55, vol. 52, pp. 291–308; Montero y Vidal, 'Events in Filipinas, 1764–1800', pp. 47–58. Useful secondary materials are O. D. Corpuz, *An Economic History of the Philippines* (Quezon City: University of the Philippines Press, 1997), pp. 87–91; Cushner, *Spain in the Philippines*, pp. 188–9; de Borja, *Basques in the Philippines*.

60. S. P. Escoto, 'Expulsion of the Chinese and Readmission to the Philippines: 1764–1779', *Philippine Studies*, 47:1 (1999), pp. 48–76, on pp. 67, 69.

61. Cushner, *Spain in the Philippines*, pp. 160–1.

62. G. Bankoff, 'Redefining Criminality: Gambling and Financial Expediency in the Colonial Philippines, 1764–1898', *Journal of Southeast Asian Studies*, 22:2 (1991), pp. 267–81.

63. Phelan, 'Authority and Flexibility in the Spanish Imperial Bureaucracy', p. 50; J. A. Barbier, 'Peninsular Finance and Colonial Trade: The Dilemma of Charles IV's Spain', *Journal of Latin American Studies*, 12:1 (1980), pp. 21–37, on p. 21.

64. Barbier, 'Peninsular Finance and Colonial Trade', pp. 21–37.
65. Barbier, 'Peninsular Finance and Colonial Trade', pp. 21–37.
66. Clemente, 'Guanxi in Chinese Commerce: Informal Enforcement in Spanish Philippines'.
67. See Choi Chi-cheung's essay, 'Rice, Treaty Ports and the Chaozhou Chinese Lianhao Associate Companies: Construction of a South China–Hong Kong–Southeast Asia Commodity Network, 1850s–1930s', in this volume.
68. K. C. Wong, *The Chinese in the Philippine Economy, 1898–1941* (Manila: Ateneo de Manila University Press), pp. 174–7.
69. See Kwee Hui Kian's essay, 'The Rise of Chinese Commercial Dominance in Early Modern Southeast Asia', in this volume.
70. J. D. Blanco, *Frontier Constitutions: Christianity and Colonial Empire in the Nineteenth-Century Philippines* (Quezon City: The University of the Philippines Press, 2009), p. 31.
71. Blanco, *Frontier Constitutions*, p. 31.
72. Wickberg, *The Chinese in Philippine Life, 1850–1898*; Wong, *The Chinese in the Philippine Economy, 1898–1941*.
73. See the section in this chapter entitled 'The Colonial Policy of Containment in the Eighteenth Century' and n. 20, above, for the reaction of China to the 1603 'massacre', and see also 'The Colonial Policy of Containment in the Eighteenth Century' for the appeal from the Chinese to the expulsion order of the late 1680s.

8 Merchant Communities in a Qasba (Market Town) of Western India in the Late Maratha and the Early British Period (1760s–1840s)

1. P. J. Marshall (ed.), *The Eighteenth Century in Indian History: Evolution or Revolution?* (New Delhi: Oxford University Press, 2005): S. Alavi (ed.), *The Eighteenth Century in India* (New Delhi: Oxford University Press, 2002).
2. F. Perlin, 'The Problem of the Eighteenth Century', in Marshall (ed.), *The Eighteenth Century in Indian History*, pp. 53–61, on pp. 54–5.
3. P. J. Marshall, 'Introduction', in Marshall (ed.), *The Eighteenth Century in Indian History: Evolution or Revolution?*, pp. 1–49, on p. 15.
4. S. Alavi, 'Introduction', in Alavi (ed.), *The Eighteenth Century in India*, pp. 1–56, on p. 12.
5. S. Subrahmanyam and C. A. Bayly, 'Portfolio Capitalists and the Political Economy of Early Modern India', in S. Subrahmanyam (ed.), *Merchants, Markets and the State in Early Modern India* (New Delhi: Oxford University Press, 1990), pp. 242–65, on p. 256.
6. Sumitra Kulkarni studied several *qasbas* in Western Deccan and pointed out that agriculture was very important in these *qasbas*. S. Kulkarni, '*Qasbas* (Small Towns) in the Maratha Country', unpublished BCUD Project, University of Pune.
7. Kulkarni, '*Qasbas* (Small Towns) in the Maratha Country', unpublished BCUD project, University of Pune, p. 46.
8. J. T. Molesworth, *Marathi and English Dictionary* (1831; repr. New Delhi and Madras: Asian Educational Services, 2005), p. 567.
9. *Bara* means 'twelve', and *balutedar* means 'a servant' in Marathi.
10. *Mahar* and *mang* were untouchables. *Mahar* carried out various low-status jobs. *Mang*, who were chiefly tanners, were similarly employed. A. R. Kulkarni, 'The Maratha

Balute System', in A. R. Kulkarni, *Maharashtra: Society and Culture* (Pune: Diamond Publications, 2008), pp. 1–51, pp. 14, 17.

11. J. G. Duff, *A History of the Mahrattas*, vol. 3 (London: Longman, 1826/1864), p. 23.

12. Peshwa was the prime minister of the Maratha Confederacy. Peshwa replaced the Maratha King in the 1730s.

13. H. H. Wilson, *A Glossary of Judicial and Revenue Terms, and of Useful Words Occurring in Official Documents Relating to the Administration of the Government of British India* (1855; repr., New Delhi: Munshiram Manoharlal Publishers, 1997), p. 350.

14. Akar Kasbe Indapur Fusli 1219 etc., Pune Jamav, Rumal nos. 707–10 and 713, Maharashtra State Archives, Pune (hereafter MSAP).

15. R. E. Enthoven, *The Tribes and Castes of Bombay*, 3 vols (1922; repr., Delhi: Low Price Publications, 1997), vol. 2, p. 310; vol. 3, p. 374.

16. Akar Kasba Indapur (Shuhur 1186), Pune Jamav, Rumal no. 708, MSAP.

17. The names of the shepherd and goldsmith working as shopkeepers are not found under the heads of each profession. Probably the Dhanagars and Sonars who owned their shops did not work as artisans. These shopkeepers and the artisans belonging to the same community had their own territories.

18. A. R. Kulkarni, 'The Maratha Balute System', in A. R. Kulkarni, *Maharashtra: Society and Culture* (Pune: Diamond Publications, 2008), pp. 1–51, on pp. 11–12.

19. 'The *balute* is generally looked upon as a portion of the *pandhur puttee* [another name for *mohtarfa*] signifying a "tax" on the "respectable" classes and I have comprised the respects from it in the general returns, but they are so placed, as to give a distinct view of them, if required. I have separated the payers of *mohtarfa* into four classes – Shopkeepers, craftsmen (not being village servants), village artificers and servants (*balloote*) and miscellaneous payers. The persons who are classified under these four heads respectively, will be seen from the tables of each class appended to Number which I hope may be of some use in a statistical point of view although from the little attention paid hitherto to the details of the *mohtarfa* I apprehend the numbers of payers may not be quite accurate.' H. Borradaile to L. R. Reid, 5 October 1838, Revenue Department Vol. 73/1056 of 1839, Maharashtra State Archives, Mumbai.

20. Enthoven, *Tribes and Castes of Bombay*, vol. 3, pp. 412–13, and J. Campbell (ed.), *Gazetteer of the Bombay Presidency* (hereafter, *GBP*), vol. 18: Poona District, part 1 (Bombay: Government Central Press, 1885), p. 273. The community called *gujar* is found in Rajasthan. *GBP* pointed out that they were originally Rajputs, who were landlords and soldiers of Kshatriya, from Rajasthan. Campbell (ed.), *GBP*, vol. 9, part 1, Gujarat Population: Hindu (Bombay: Government Central Press, 1901), p. 71.

21. *GBP*, vol. 9, part 1, p. 96.

22. S. Kulkarni, '*Qasbas* (Small Towns) in the Maratha Country', p. 39.

23. Sumitra Kulkarni distinguished *gujars* from the Gujarati merchants who came to the Pune area in the 1760s in her work. Kulkarni, '*Qasbas* (Small Towns) in the Maratha Country', p. 39.

24. A. Kaur, 'Indians in Southeast Asia: Migrant Labour, Knowledge Workers and the New India', in R. Rai and P. Reeves (eds), *The South Asian Diaspora: Traditional Networks and Changing Identities* (London: Routledge, 2009), pp. 71–88, on p. 83.

25. N. Charlesworth, *Peasant and Imperial Rule: Agricultural and Agrarian Society in the Bombay Presidency, 1850–1935* (London: Orient Longman, 1985), pp. 107, 113.

26. Jhada Mauj Shaha (Shuhur 1218), Pune Jamav, Rumal no. 781, MSAP.

27. One *rumal* or bundle (Rumal no. 59) in the section 'Jakatikadil Hisebi Kagad' deals

with the collection of transit duties at the custom house in Qasba Indapur only. The analysis by use of the records on transit duties is based on this rumal. Another *rumal* (Rumal no. 58) deals with the collection in other villages. Jakatkadil Hisebi Kagad, Rumal no. 59, MSAP.

28. Though the rural area of Qasba Indapur was the largest producer of sorghum, it is believed that much sorghum was brought to Peth Indapur for redistribution in Indapur Pargana.

29. Jakatkadil Hisebi Kagad, Rumal no. 58, MSAP.

30. The title of a caste was used often as surname. In this chapter, a surname begins with a capital letter.

31. Though the standard *bigha* is equal to 5/8 acre, the actual ratio varied from region to region. Wilson, *Glossary of Judicial and Revenue Terms*, p. 85.

32. Akar Kasbe Indapur (Shuhur 1182), Pune Jamav, Rumal no. 707, MSAP.

33. For example, Akar Kasbe Indapur (Shuhur 1182), Pune Jamav, Rumal no. 707; Jama Mukund Seth Gujar (Shuhur 1188), Pune Jamav, Rumal no. 708; Jama Mukund Seth Gujar (Shuhur 1195), Pune Jamav, Rumal no. 710, MSAP.

34. Jama Mukund Seth Gujar (Shuhur 1191 and 1195), Pune Jamav, Rumal no. 710, MSAP.

35. For example, Jama Sakharam Gujar (Shuhur 1193), Pune Jamav, Rumal no. 710, MSAP.

36. J. T. Molesworth, *Marathi and English Dictionary* (1831; repr. New Delhi and Madras: Asian Educational Services, 2005), p. 88.

37. Telyacha Kharch Gavkikade (Shuhur 1182), Qasba Indapur, Pune Jamav, Rumal no. 705, MSAP.

38. Wasul Kularag Peth Indapur (Shuhur 1180), Pune Jamav, Rumal no. 716, MSAP.

39. Kharch Kasbe Indapur (Shuhur 1177), Pune Jamav, Rumal no. 706, MSAP.

40. Yadi Teli yakadil Tel Nandadip (Fusli 1194) etc., Pune Jamav, Rumal no. 707, MSAP.

41. Nemnukbad Kasbe Indapur (Shuhur 1186) Pune Jamav, Rumal no. 710, and Akar Kasbe Indapur (Shuhur 1216), Pune Jamav, Rumal no. 712, MSAP.

42. Kharch Kasbe Indapur (Shuhur 1177), Pune Jamav, Rumal no. 706, MSAP.

43. Nemnukbad Kasba Indapur (Shuhur 1195), Pune Jamav, Rumal no. 710, MSAP.

44. Borrowed money is written down as *karj jama*, which means the revenue by debt, in the accounts of Qasba Indapur. Yadi Wasul Peth Indapur (Shuhur 1214), Pune Jamav, Rumal no. 716, MSAP.

45. 20 Sawal Shuhur 1183 (AD 1783), Prant Ajmas Pune, Rumal no. 547, MSAP.

46. Names of Joti Teli and Apa Sonar are not found in a list of taxpayers of *balute* and *mohtarfa* in the accounts of Peth Indapur. They worked not as artisans but as money-lenders.

47. Tahshil Kasbe Indapur (Shuhur 1191–5), Pune Jamav, Rumal no. 710, MSAP.

48. Molesworth, *Marathi and English Dictionary*, p. 759.

49. Hisebi Pargana Indapur (Shuhur 1189), Prant Ajmas, Pune, Rumal no. 62, MSAP.

50. Ranu Teli Jama Kharch (Shuhur 1161), Pune Jamav, Rumal no. 703, MSAP.

51. For example, Kharch Sadashiv Gujar Uchapati (Shuhur 1779), Pune Jamav, Rumal no. 704, MSAP.

52. Radkarj Qasba Indapur (Shuhur 1187), Pune Jamav, Rumal no. 708, MSAP.

53. Dasara is a popular festival for Durga, who is a warrior goddess. This festival starts on 10 Ashwin (the seventh month of the Hindu year), which overlaps September and October. Wilson, *Glossary of Judicial and Revenue Terms*, p. 127.

54. For example, Tahsil Kasba Indapur, Dasara Patti (Shuhur 1191), Pune Jamav, Rumal no. 710, and Chiti Baji Set Gujar, Peth Indapur, Fusli 1213, Pune Jamav, Rumal no. 716, MSAP.

55. Jama Kala Gujar, Qasba Indapur (Shuhur 1186), and Jama Motiram Gujar, Qasba Indapur (Shuhur 1187), Pune Jamav, Rumal no. 708, MSAP.

56. In northern China in the early twentieth century, the conditions that qualified an outsider to become a villager differed from village to village. In the case of Qasba Indapur, different conditions were required within one village. Although *gujars* were allowed to join festivals as members, they were not allowed to be regular members. On China, see P. Duara, *Culture, Power, and the State: Rural North China, 1900–1942* (Stanford, CA: Stanford University Press, 1988), pp. 208–11.

57. In 1796, the last Peshwa or Bajirao II took office as Peshwa, but some chiefs in the Maratha Confederacy opposed his assumption. Holkar, one of these chiefs, occupied Pune and attacked Pune Subha.

58. *GBP*, vol. 18, part 2, pp. 282, 284.

59. *Istawa* means the practice of gradually increasing the reduced revenue up to the full assessment. Molesworth, *Marathi and English Dictionary*, p. 83.

60. Tembhrni was a *qasba* in the *pargana* next to Indapur Pargana.

61. Kaulnama, Peth Indapur (Shuhur 1214), Pune Jamav, Rumai no. 716, MSAP.

62. For example, Jhadti Qasba Indapur (Shuhur 1216), Pune Jamav, Rumal no. 713, MSAP.

63. Botkhat Qasba Indapur Sarkar Bharna (Shuhur 1214), Pune Jamav, Rumal no. 712, MSAP.

64. Wasul Jama, Qasba Indapur (Shuhur 1214), Pune Jamav, Rumal no. 712, MSAP.

65. Jama Baji Seth Gujar, Qasba Indapur (Shuhur 1213), Pune Jamav, Rumal no. 712, MSAP.

66. Jama Panse Samaste, Qasba Indapur (Shuhur 1215), Pune Jamav, Rumal no. 711, MSAP.

67. Chitti Baji Seth Gujar, Peth Indapur (Shuhur 1213), Pune Jamav, Rumal no. 716, MSAP.

68. After the disasters, the revenue and the military systems under the Marathas in the late eighteenth century came to an end in Indapur Pargana. Military soldiers stationed there and the hereditary local officers lost their power between 1804 and 1818, and the government officer sent by the Peshwa government gained power. In this context, administrative centralization in Indapur Pargana started even before British rule began in 1818. This is the great change that Indapur Pargana saw in the last phase of the Peshwa government. M. Ogawa, 'Socio-Economic Study of Indapur Pargana (1761–1828)' (PhD thesis, University of Pune, 2013).

69. This was not uncommon in India under colonization. Dilbagh Singh studied the increase in the importance of the moneylender in a village called *mahajan* in eighteenth-century Rajasthan. D. Singh, 'The Role of the Mahajan in the Rural Economy in Eastern Rajasthan during the 18th Century', *Social Scientist*, 2:22 (1974), pp. 20–31, on p. 26.

70. Botkhat Kasba Indapur (Shuhur 1225), Pune Jamav, Rumal no. 713, MSAP.

71. Yadi Kulwar Chitta Peth Indapur (Shuhur 1225), Pune Jamav, Rumal no. 715, MSAP.

72. For example, Jama Bandi Chitta Kasbe Indapur (Shuhur 1236), Pune Jamav, Rumal no. 715, MSAP.

73. R. Clarke, *The Regulations of the Government of India in Force at that Presidency* (London: J. & H. Cox, 1851), Act 19 of 1844, p. 557.

74. P/349/27 & 41, Proceedings of General Department, Bombay Presidency, India Office Records, BL.
75. S. Subrahmanyam and C. A. Bayly, 'Portfolio Capitalists and the Political Economy of Early Modern India', in S. Subrahmanyam (ed.), *Merchants, Markets and the State in Early Modern India* (New Delhi: Oxford University Press, 1990), pp. 261–4.

9 Mid-Nineteenth-Century Nagasaki: Western and Japanese Merchant Communities within Commercial and Political Transitions

1. W. McOmie, *The Opening of Japan, 1853–1855: A Comparative Study of the American, British, Dutch and Russian Naval Expeditions to Compel the Tokugawa Shogunate to Conclude Treaties and Open Ports to their Ships* (Folkestone: Global Oriental, 2006).
2. It was estimated that on the eve of Nagasaki's designation as a treaty port on 1 July 1859, thirty British merchants were operating there. P. Montague Paske-Smith, *Western Barbarians in Japan and Formosa in Tokugawa Days, 1603–1868* (Kobe: J. L. Thompson & Co. (retail) Ltd., 1930), p. 256.
3. Although beyond the scope of this chapter, the Western traders depended upon a fourth merchant community to facilitate trade: Chinese employees. Experienced Chinese merchants provided knowledge of existing trade routes and goods that proved indispensable for the newcomers at Nagasaki.
4. J. K. Fairbank, *Trade and Diplomacy on the China Coast* (Stanford, CA: Stanford University Press, 1969), pp. 286–7.
5. M. H. Lin, *China Upside Down: Currency, Society, and Ideologies, 1808–1856* (Cambridge, MA: Harvard University Asia Center, 2006), pp. 72–114.
6. R. Ishikawa, 'The Merchants of the Korea–China Ginseng Trade in the Late Nineteenth Century', this volume.
7. Ishii Ryōsuke and Harafuji Hiroshi (eds), *Bakumatsu Ofuregaki Shūsei* [A Compilation of Official Proclamations from the Final Years of the Edo Period], vol. 5 (Tokyo: Iwanami Shoten, 1992), p. 569.
8. R. Hellyer, *Defining Engagement: Japan and Global Contexts, 1640–1868* (Cambridge, MA: Harvard University Asia Center, 2009), pp. 116–49.
9. Yamawaki Teijirō, *Nagasaki no Tōjin Bōeki* [The Trade of Chinese Merchants at Nagasaki] (Tokyo: Yoshikawa Kōbunkan, 1964), pp. 95, 280–8; R. Innes, 'The Door Ajar: Japan's Foreign Trade in the Seventeenth Century' (PhD dissertation, University of Michigan, 1980), vol. 1, pp. 341–6.
10. The Dutch bazaar was so named because of its proximity to Dejima, and the Russian market was said to have been established as a concession after Russian appeals. S. Osborne, *A Cruise in Japanese Waters*, 2nd edn (London: William Blackwood, 1859), pp. 41–2.
11. Osborne, *A Cruise in Japanese Waters*, pp. 41–6.
12. C. Pemberton Hodgson, *A Residence at Nagasaki and Hakodate in 1858–1859, With an Account of Japan Generally* (London: Richard Bentley, 1861), pp. 13–14.
13. 'Report on British Trade at Nagasaki for 1859', Inclosure 1 in No. 2 in *Correspondence Respecting Trade with Japan, Presented in Both Houses of Parliament by Command of Her Majesty 1860* (London: Harrison and Sons, 1860), pp. 5–6.
14. Jardine, Matheson, and Company (hereafter JM) Archives, Cambridge University. Mackenzie to JM Shanghai, 11 October 1859 (letter 30). JM In-correspondence

(unbound) Japan, Nagasaki 1859–64, letters 1–310. 'Business Letters: Nagasaki, 1859–1886', B10-4. I thank Matheson & Company for permission to research the archive and cite this and other documents in this chapter.

15. JM In-correspondence Japan, Nagasaki 1859–64, Mackenzie to JM Shanghai, 27 October 1859 (letter 32).

16. JM In-correspondence Japan, Nagasaki 1859–64, Mackenzie to JM Shanghai, 31 October 1859 (letter 33).

17. JM In-correspondence Japan, Nagasaki 1859–64, Mackenzie to JM Shanghai, 2 November 1859 (letter 33 [2]).

18. JM In-correspondence Japan, Nagasaki 1859–64, Mackenzie to JM Hong Kong, 9 May 1860 (letter 54).

19. B. Burke-Gaffney, *Holme, Ringer and Company: The Rise and Fall of a British Enterprise in Japan, 1868–1940* (Boston, MA: Global Oriental, 2013), pp. 13–14.

20. 'Kenneth R. Mackenzie', entry in 'Oura Biographies', in L. R. Earns and B. Burke-Gaffney, *Nagasaki: People, Places, and Scenes of the Nagasaki Foreign Settlement, 1859–1941*, at http://www.nfs.nias.ac.jp/index.html [accessed 5 June 2013].

21. E. Ward, *The Journal of Edward Ward, 1850–1851: Being his Account of the Voyage to New Zealand in the Charlotte Jane and the First Six Months of the Canterbury Settlement* (Christchurch: Pegasus Press, 1951), p. 11.

22. William Alt to Mother, 30 May 1854, Port Adelaide; Alt to Mother, Barbados (date unknown, probably 1854–5). Personal correspondence of William John Alt (hereafter WA), 1854–65. I thank Tessa Montgomery, a direct descendant of William Alt, for generously allowing me access to the letters and to publish excerpts from them in this chapter.

23. WA to Mother, 6 November 1857, Shanghai.

24. *North China Herald*, Shanghai, 3 March 1860, p. 1.

25. WA to Mother, 3 February 1860, Nagasaki.

26. *North-China Herald*, Shanghai, 14 January 1860, p. 6.

27. Hirao Michio, *Tosa-han Shōgyō Keizai-shi* [An Economic History of Commerce in the Tosa Domain] (Kōchi: Kōchi Shiritsu Shimin Toshokan, 1960), p. 223.

28. B. Burke-Gaffney, *Nagasaki: The British Experience, 1854–1945* (Folkestone: Global Oriental, 2009), pp. 23–4.

29. M. B. Jansen, *Sakamoto Ryōma and the Meiji Restoration* (New York: Columbia University Press, 1994), pp. 111, 118–21.

30. Hirao, *Tosa-han Shōgyō Keizai-shi*, p. 223.

31. WA to Mother, 3 February 1860, Nagasaki.

32. M. Paske-Smith, *Western Barbarians in Japan and Formosa in Tokugawa Days, 1603–1868* (Kobe: J. L. Thompson & Co. (retail) Ltd., 1930), p. 340.

33. *Sir Charles Forbes* was previously employed in Indian Ocean routes, for example in 1851 the steamer is listed as arriving in Bombay from Bushire (Būshehr), a Persian Gulf port in what is today Iran. *Allen's Indian Mail and Register of Intelligence for British and Foreign India, China and All Parts of the East*, vol. 9, January–December 1851 (London: William H. Allen and Company, 1851), p. 108.

34. WA to Mother, 2 March 1863, Nagasaki. The ship was a steamer built in London in 1856.

35. Acting Consul Gower to Sir R. Alcock, Inclosure 1 in No. 5, Nagasaki January 3, 1865. *Commercial Reports from Her Majesty's Consuls in Japan, 1863–64* (London: Harrison and Sons, 1865), p. 16.

36. *Nagasaki Shipping and Advertiser*, 7:7, 20 July 1861, p. 21.
37. Nagasaki Kenshi Henshū Iinkai, *Nagasaki Kenshi, Taigai Kōshōhen* [The History of Nagasaki Prefecture: Interactions with the Outside World] (Tokyo: Yoshikawa Kōbunkan, 1985), pp. 849–50.
38. *Nagasaki Shipping and Advertiser*, 1:4, 10 July 1861, pp. 12–13.
39. Earns and Burke-Gaffney, 'Life and Work in the Nagasaki Foreign Settlement, 1859–1899', *Nagasaki: People, Places, and Scenes of the Nagasaki Foreign Settlement, 1859–1941*, at http://www.nfs.nias.ac.jp/page003.html#2ō [accessed 22 January 2014].
40. Paske-Smith, *Western Barbarians*, pp. 255–62.
41. Nagasaki Kenshi Henshū Iinkai, *Nagasaki Kenshi, Taigai Kōshōhen*, pp. 849–50.
42. T. S. Clemente, 'Spanish Colonial Policy towards Chinese Merchants in Eighteenth-Century Philippines', this volume.
43. 'Rōjū tashi', 1862/07/05 [1862/07/31 on Gregorian calendar] BU045–0088 [record number], Dai Nihon Ishin Shiryō Kōhon [Manuscript of Historical Records Related to the Meiji Restoration of Japan] (hereafter DNISK), Unpublished document collection, Historiographical Institute, University of Tokyo.
44. W. G. Beasley, *The Meiji Restoration* (Stanford, CA: Stanford University Press, 1972), pp. 195–200.
45. Burke-Gaffney, *Nagasaki*, p. 41.
46. WA to Mother, 15 October 1863, Hong Kong.
47. Beasley, *The Meiji Restoration*, pp. 205–32.
48. Sugiyama Shinya, *Meiji Ishin to Igirusu Shōnin: Tomasu Guraba no Shōgai* [English Merchants and the Meiji Restoration: The Life of Thomas Glover] (Tokyo: Iwanami Shoten, 1993), p. 85.
49. S. Sugiyama, 'Thomas B. Glover: A British Merchant in Japan, 1861–1870', *Business History*, 26 (July 1984), pp. 115–38, on pp. 120–1.
50. For example, Tsushima would obtain sappanwood at Nagasaki for use in trade with Korea. Tashiro Kazui, 'Kinsei Kōki Nitchō Bōekishi Kenkyū Josetsu' [An Introduction to the History of Japanese–Korean Trade in the Latter Half of the Early Modern Period], *Mita Gakki Zasshi*, 79:3 (August 1986), pp. 14–29, on pp. 22–3.
51. The *bakufu*'s move to limit Chōshū marked a departure from a policy of previous decades of placing minimal restrictions on the purchase of arms by domains. Arima Narisuke, 'Bakumatsu ni okeru Seiyō Kaki no Yunyu' [Imports of Western Firearms during the Bakumatsu Period], *Nihon Rekishi*, 120 (June 1958), pp. 2–13, on pp. 2–3.
52. Burke-Gaffney, *Nagasaki: The British Experience*, p. 41.
53. S. D. Brown, 'Nagasaki in the Meiji Restoration: Choshu Loyalists and British Arms Merchants', *Crossroads: A Journal of Nagasaki History and Culture*, 1 (Summer 1993), pp. 1–18, on pp. 10–15.
54. Hellyer, *Defining Engagement*, p. 183.
55. Nagasaki Kenshi Henshū Iinkai, *Nagasaki Kenshi, Taigai Kōshōhen*, pp. 889–92.
56. M. B. Jansen, *Sakamoto Ryōma and the Meiji Restoration* (New York: Columbia University Press, 1994), pp. 241–8.
57. Iwasaki Yatarō, *Iwasaki Yatarō Nikki* [The Diaries of Iwasaki Yatarō] (Tokyo: Iwasaki Yatarō Denki Hensan-kai, 1975), p. 120. Iwasaki kept several diaries recording his time in Nagasaki, including an official diary, with entries from 14 June 1867 to 2 February 1868. He also kept a private diary from 21 May 1867 to 11 October 1867. This and subsequent references, except where indicated, are to the aforementioned official diary.

58. Iwasaki, *Iwasaki Yatarō Nikki*, p. 128.
59. Iwasaki, *Iwasaki Yatarō Nikki*, pp. 130, 132. Yūgao and Otome are characters in the novel, *Tale of Genji*, written in the Heian period (794–1185). Morita Toshihiko provides a detailed list of Tosa's acquisitions in Nagasaki from 1866 to 1867 in 'Kaiseikan Shihō no Tenkai to Sono Genkai' [The Development and Limits of Procedures at the Kaiseikan], in Ishii Takashi (ed.), *Bakumatsu Ishinki no Kenkyū* [Research on the Bakumatsu and Meiji Restoration Periods] (Tokyo: Yoshikawa Kōbunkan, 1978), pp. 271–321, on pp. 290–1.
60. Iwasaki, *Iwasaki Yatarō Nikki*, pp. 133–4.
61. Ike Michinosuke, *Ike Michinosuke Nikki, Gendaigo Yaku* [The Diary of Ike Michinosuke, A Translation into Modern Japanese], trans. Suzuki Noriko (Kōchi-shi: Riburu shuppan, 2011), p. 195.
62. Ike, *Ike Michinosuke Nikki*, pp. 136, 146.
63. Hirao Michio, *Tosa-han Shōgyō Keizai-shi* [An Economic History of Commerce in the Tosa Domain] (Kochi: Kochi Shiritsu Shimin Toshokan, 1960), p. 224.
64. Iwasaki, *Iwasaki Yatarō Nikki*, p. 121.
65. Iwasaki, *Iwasaki Yatarō Nikki*, pp. 170–2 (private diary). Iwasaki had travelled to Karatsu to discuss coal several months earlier. Ibid., p. 121.
66. Ike also reported an additional meeting with Karatsu officials on 28 February 1867. *Ike Michinosuke Nikki*, p. 136.
67. Jansen, *Sakamoto Ryōma*, pp. 262–4.
68. Iwasaki, *Iwasaki Yatarō Nikki*, p. 136.
69. Iwasaki, *Iwasaki Yatarō Nikki*, p. 137
70. Jansen, *Sakamoto Ryōma*, pp. 307–8.
71. W. G. Beasley (trans. and ed.), *Select Documents on Japanese Foreign Policy, 1853–1868* (London: Oxford University Press, 1955), p. 319.
72. S. Sugiyama, *Japan's Industrialization in the World Economy, 1859–1899: Export Trade and Overseas Competition* (London: Athlone Press, 1988), p. 154.
73. H. Bolitho, 'The Echigo War, 1868', *Monumenta Nipponica*, 34:3 (Autumn 1979), pp. 259–77, on pp. 261, 266.
74. Hirao Michio, *Tosa-han Shōgyō Keizai-shi* [An Economic History of Commerce in the Tosa Domain] (Kochi: Kochi Shiritsu Shimin Toshokan, 1960), pp. 225–30.
75. K. Yamamura, 'The Founding of Mitsubishi: A Case Study in Japanese Business History', *Business History Review*, 41:2 (Summer 1967), pp. 141–60, on pp. 146–51.
76. P. Alt, 'An Abridged Biographical Sketch of her Parents', unpublished manuscript, presented by Viscountess Montgomery of Alamein, née Tessa Browning, Great-Grand-Daughter of William and Elisabeth Alt, on the occasion of her visit to Nagasaki in October 1985, pp. 3–4; Earns and Burke-Gaffney, 'William J. Alt', entry in 'Oura Biographies', at http://www.nfs.nias.ac.jp/page019.html [accessed 22 January 2014].
77. JM In-correspondence, Unbound Letters Japan, Kobe, 1877–81.
78. Both are presented as prominent firms in a chapter on Japan's tea trade in W. H. Morton Cameron and W. Feldwick, *Present Day Impressions of Japan: The History, People, Commerce, Industries and Resources of Japan and Japan's Colonial Empire, Kwantung, Chosen, Taiwan, Karafuto* (Chicago, IL: The Globe Encyclopedia Company, 1919), pp. 335–40.
79. J. A. Fogel, *Articulating the Sinosphere: Sino-Japanese Relations in Space and Time* (Cambridge, MA: Harvard University Press, 2009), p. 84.
80. Sugiyama, 'Thomas B. Glover', pp. 126–30.
81. Iwasaki, *Iwasaki Nikki*, pp. 486–7 (volume 2 of diary kept in Osaka from 1 February

1870 to 22 November 1870); Hirao Michio, *Tosa Han* [The Domain of Tosa] (Tokyo: Yoshikawa Kōbunkan, 1965), p. 210.

82. Tōyō Keizai Shinpōsha (ed.), *Nihon Bōeki Seiran: Sōritsu 80-shūnen Kinen Fukkoku* [A Complete Index of Japanese Trade: A Reprint Commemorating Eighty Years of Publication] (Tokyo: Tōyō Keizai Shinpōsha, 1975), pp. 2–151.

10 The Problem of the Sailors: Power, Law and the Formation of the Merchant Community in Treaty Port China, 1842–60

1. J. L. Scott, *Narrative of a Recent Imprisonment in China after the Wreck of the Kite*, in E. H. Chang (ed.), *British Travel Writing*, vol. 2, *Mid-Century Explorations, 1841–1863* (London: Pickering & Chatto, 2010), p. 8.

2. Scott, *Narrative of a Recent Imprisonment*, p. 20.

3. P. Linebaugh, *The London Hanged: Crime and Civil Society in Eighteenth-Century London*, 2nd edn (New York: Verso Press, 2006); D. McNally, *Monsters of the Market: Zombies, Vampires and Global Capitalism* (Chicago, IL: Haymarket Books, 2012).

4. E. Hayot, *The Hypothetical Mandarin: Sympathy, Modernity and Chinese Pain* (Oxford and New York: Oxford University Press, 2009).

5. Scott, *Narrative of a Recent Imprisonment*, p. 33.

6. For Scott's story, see his *Narrative of a Recent Imprisonment*, from which the above narrative is drawn. For more on the international perspective of sailors see P. Linebaugh and M. Rediker, *The Many-Headed Hydra: Sailors, Slaves, Commoners, and the Hidden History of the Revolutionary Atlantic* (Boston, MA: Beacon Press, 2001). For a similar analysis looking at the China trade, see E. Lampe, *Work, Class, and Power on the Borderlands of the Early American Pacific: The Labors of Empire* (Lanham, MD: Lexington Press, 2013).

7. On the regulation of working people in Chinese cities in the twentieth century, see Z. Lipkin, *Useless to the State: 'Social Problems' and Social Engineering in Nationalist Nanjing, 1927–1937* (Cambridge, MA: Harvard East Asia Monographs, 2006).

8. The newest history of the Chinese merchant class in Canton is P. A. Van Dyke, *Merchants of Canton and Macao: Politics and Strategies in Eighteenth-Century Chinese Trade* (Hong Kong: Hong Kong University Press, 2011).

9. For a labour history of Whampoa during the China trade, see E. Lampe, '"The Most Miserable Hole in the Whole World": Western Sailors and the Whampoa Anchorage, 1770–1850', *International Journal of Maritime History*, 22:1 (2010), pp. 15–40. The account of Whampoa here is drawn from this study.

10. S. Reynolds, *The Voyage of the New Hazard: To the Northwest Coast, Hawaii, and China, 1810–1813*, ed. F. W. Howay (Fairfield, WA: Ye Galleon Press, 1970), pp. 116–40. For more on Reynolds and the *New Hazard*, see Lampe, *Work, Class and Power*, ch. 2.

11. My concept of liquidity is borrowed from Zygmunt Bauman's analysis of late capitalism as 'liquid modernity', characterized by openness and mobility for all, but also violent and brutal inequalities. Z. Bauman, *Wasted Lives: Modernity and Its Outcasts* (London: Polity, 2003).

12. 'Communication. Governor General Ke-Ying to Forbes', in *The Canton City Question and US Relations with the European Powers*, Vol. 3 of *American Diplomatic and Public Papers: The United States and China: Series 1: The Treaty System and the Taiping Rebellion, 1842–1860* (Wilmington, DE: Scholarly Resources, 1973), p. 4.

13. 'Riot in Canton on the Evening of July 8th, 1846, from the *Chinese Repository* for July 1846', in *The Canton City Question and US Relations with the European Powers*, p. 9.

14. 'Riot in Canton on the Evening of July 8th, 1846, from the *Chinese Repository* for July 1846', p. 9.

15. 'Riot in Canton on the Evening of July 8th, 1846, from the *Chinese Repository* for July 1846', pp. 10–11.

16. P. Gilje, *Liberty on the Waterfront: American Maritime Culture in the Age of Revolution* (Philadelphia, PA: University of Pennsylvania Press, 2007).

17. *Conference on Missions Held at Liverpool* (London: James Nisbet & Co, 1860), pp. 106–7.

18. R. Morrison, *Memoirs of the Life and Labours of Robert Morrison* (London: Longman, Orme, Brown, Green, and Longmans, 1839), pp. 43–5.

19. *A Sermon to Sailors, at Whampoa, in China, on the Deck of the American Ship Pacific* (Malacca: Mission Press, 1822).

20. *Foreign Trade: Minutes of Evidence Taken before the Select Committee Appointed to Consider the Means of Maintaining and Improving the Foreign Trade of the Country* (London, 1821), pp. 245, 253.

21. See S. Reynolds, *Journal of Stephen Reynolds, Vol. 1, 1823–1829*, ed. P. N. King (Honolulu, HI: Ku Pa'a Incorporated, 1989), pp. 76–7.

22. *Shanghai: Political and Economic Reports, 1842–1943: British Government Records from the International City, Vol.1, Introduction and Reports for 1839–1846*, ed. R. L. Jarman (Slough: Archive Editions, 2008), pp. 561–2.

23. *Shanghai: Political and Economic Reports, 1842–1943*, pp. 564–6.

24. *Shanghai: Political and Economic Reports, 1842–1943*, pp. 641–3.

25. *Shanghai: Political and Economic Reports, 1842–1943*, pp. 653–5.

26. *Shanghai: Political and Economic Reports, 1842–1943*, p. 711.

27. *Shanghai: Political and Economic Reports, 1842–1943*, p. 710.

28. In the context of the British Asian Empire, the question of police is interesting. The Malaysian Straits Settlements, with a large number of convict workers from India and massive populations of Chinese immigrants in the 1840s and 1850s, created quite elaborate prisons and policing procedures. A. Pieris, *Hidden Hands and Divided Landscapes: A Penal History of Singapore's Plural Society* (Honolulu, HI: University of Hawaii Press, 2009).

29. *Shanghai: Political and Economic Reports, 1842–1943*, p. 152.

30. *Shanghai: Political and Economic Reports, 1842–1943*, pp. 156–8.

31. *Shanghai: Political and Economic Reports, 1842–1943*, p. 607.

32. *Shanghai: Political and Economic Reports, 1842–1943*, pp. 608–9.

33. *Shanghai: Political and Economic Reports, 1842–1943*, pp. 693–4.

34. *Executive Documents Printed by Order of the House of Representatives, 1858–59, Vol. 13, Commerce and Navigation* (Washington, DC: James B. Steedman, 1859), p. 77.

35. *Executive Documents Printed by Order of the House of Representatives, 1858–59*, p. 78.

36. *Executive Documents Printed by Order of the House of Representatives, 1858–59*, pp. 79–81.

37. 'Letter, Cunningham to Marshall', in *Extraterritoriality, American Diplomatic and Public Papers: The United States and China: Series 1: The Treaty System and the Taiping Rebellion, 1842–1860* (Wilmington, DE: Scholarly Resources, 1973), vol. 8, p. 217.

38. 'Letter, Cunningham to Marshall', p. 217.

39. 'Letter, Cunningham to Marshall', p. 82.

40. This story is extracted from three letters submitted to the US House of Representatives. 'Letter, Cunningham to Marshall', pp. 83–6.
41. 'Letter, Cunningham to Marshall', pp. 87–8.
42. 'Letter, Hyatt to Ward, China Dispatches, Vol. 18', in *Extraterritoriality*, vol. 8, pp. 287–8.
43. The idea of one central prison was suggested by John Elliot Ward, consul for Amoy in the late 1850s. He correctly predicted that local prisons would be more efficient if supported by merchants, and worried that the transportation costs would make a central prison impractical for any short disciplinary confinements.
44. 'Official Notification by Peter Parker', in *Extraterritoriality, American Diplomatic and Public Papers: The United States and China: Series 1: The Treaty System and the Taiping Rebellion, 1842–1860* (Wilmington, DE: Scholarly Resources, 1973), vol. 9, pp. 3–5.
45. 'Circular, Port of Shanghai regulations', in *Extraterritoriality*, vol. 9, pp. 12–15.
46. 'Letter, Peter Parker to Governor General Wang', in *Extraterritoriality, American Diplomatic and Public Papers: The United States and China: Series 1: The Treaty System and the Taiping Rebellion, 1842–1860* (Wilmington, DE: Scholarly Resources, 1973), vol. 8, pp. 432–4.
47. 'Dispatch #33: Marshall to Marcy', in *Extraterritoriality*, vol. 9, pp. 234–5.
48. On urban inequality see M. Davis, *Planet of Slums* (New York: Verso, 2007).
49. This critique of world history has yet to be written but it is implied in works such as Linebaugh and Rediker's *The Many-Headed Hydra*. Some historians boldly state that world history is essentially maritime history, but are less conscious of the relationship between maritime history and elite, capitalist history. See for instance, D. Finamore, *Maritime History as World History* (Gainesville, FL: University Press of Florida, 2008). Finamore sees the sea as a conduit for virtually all of the major cross-cultural encounters, but fails to mention working people.

Index

For Product Safety Concerns and Information please contact our EU
representative GPSR@taylorandfrancis.com Taylor & Francis Verlag GmbH,
Kaufingerstraße 24, 80331 München, Germany

Printed and bound by CPI Group (UK) Ltd, Croydon, CR0 4YY
01/05/2025
01858422-0009